A World History of Higher Education Exchange

Teresa Brawner Bevis

A World History of Higher Education Exchange

The Legacy of American Scholarship

Teresa Brawner Bevis
Fayetteville, AR, USA

ISBN 978-3-030-12433-5 ISBN 978-3-030-12434-2 (eBook)
https://doi.org/10.1007/978-3-030-12434-2

Library of Congress Control Number: 2019934151

© The Editor(s) (if applicable) and The Author(s) 2019
This work is subject to copyright. All rights are solely and exclusively licensed by the Publisher, whether the whole or part of the material is concerned, specifically the rights of translation, reprinting, reuse of illustrations, recitation, broadcasting, reproduction on microfilms or in any other physical way, and transmission or information storage and retrieval, electronic adaptation, computer software, or by similar or dissimilar methodology now known or hereafter developed.
The use of general descriptive names, registered names, trademarks, service marks, etc. in this publication does not imply, even in the absence of a specific statement, that such names are exempt from the relevant protective laws and regulations and therefore free for general use.
The publisher, the authors and the editors are safe to assume that the advice and information in this book are believed to be true and accurate at the date of publication. Neither the publisher nor the authors or the editors give a warranty, express or implied, with respect to the material contained herein or for any errors or omissions that may have been made. The publisher remains neutral with regard to jurisdictional claims in published maps and institutional affiliations.

This Palgrave Macmillan imprint is published by the registered company Springer Nature Switzerland AG.
The registered company address is: Gewerbestrasse 11, 6330 Cham, Switzerland

Preface

Writing from the perspective of the nineteenth century, Horace Mann believed that education, beyond any other device of human origin, was the great equalizer of the conditions of men—the balance-wheel, as he put it, of the social machinery. Mann, the newly appointed secretary of America's first board of education, was thinking locally but also globally. He would visit every American state to observe its education systems first-hand, and, in 1843, he traveled to Europe with a similar mission. Even then, visionary educators were looking to the future, and the future was international. Two centuries have passed, but his broadly held conviction remains steadfast. Knowledge is a great equalizer, and the migration of education is indeed a balance-wheel of international social machinery. Around this idea has grown a philosophy and a worldwide industry, designed to endorse and advance global scholarship, with the United States its undisputed leader. This book tells that story.

To clarify terms and definitions for the reader, a few explanations are due. The terms "foreign student" and "international student" are used interchangeably throughout this text. Until the late twentieth century, the term "foreign" was most-often employed, but later it came to be regarded by some as politically incorrect. More recently, the term has come back into fashion. By definition, "foreign student" is more precise, as it simply means a student from another country. Rather than attempting to weigh the legitimacy of either term, both are used interchangeably.

Terms for the Middle East also require some explanation. Alternative terms such as Arab World or Islamic World, which are generally less accurate with regard to ethnicity or religious make-up, do correctly emphasize the preeminence of Arabic and Islam in the historical development of the Middle East's culture and identity. Early uses of the term "Middle East" were most often references to the area between Mesopotamia and Burma, somewhere between what Westerners termed the "Near East" and the "Far East"—terms that have now fallen into disuse.

One of the first uses of the term Middle East can be found in a 1902 article penned by naval strategist Alfred Thayer Mahan, published in a British journal called the *National Review*. In it, Mahan used the term Middle East to designate the territory between Arabia and India. The article was reprinted in *The Times*, followed by 20 more articles by another author, Sir Ignatius Valentine Chirol, who employed the term for the same region. The modern definition took shape after World War II, when the region was partitioned into various nations. In 1957, the Eisenhower Doctrine described the Middle East as the area between and including Libya on the west and Pakistan on the east, with Syria and Iraq on the north and the Arabian Peninsula to the south, plus Sudan and Ethiopia. In 1958, the US State Department further defined the region as including only Egypt, Syria, Israel, Lebanon, Jordan, Iraq, Saudi Arabia, Kuwait, Bahrain, and Qatar. Today the definition has expanded to include much of North Africa, and also Iran, thus the acronym MENA (Middle East and North Africa).

Regarding the use of language, the author's limited understanding of Chinese and its many variations will be evident. Where possible and appropriate, Chinese translations or equivalents of names and terms are included. In the Romanization of Chinese personal names and place names, the simplified spelling is generally used; however, when relying on older sources that utilize Wade-Giles or some other Romanization system, the original spelling has sometimes been retained. In cases where an older form has become an accepted standard, such as Hong Kong, the popular term is applied.

Regarding Arabic, the author respectfully borrows Colonel H.R.P. Dickson's disclaimer from his 1959 book *The Arab of the Desert, A Glimpse into Badawin Life in Kuwait and Saudi Arabia*. "I wrote what I heard," Dickson said, however far removed from literary forms. "I lay no claim to a profound knowledge of classical or literary Arabic, and I therefore crave the indulgence of those learned in these matters."

The purpose of this book is to combine 20 years of research and several previous publications into a single updated volume that provides an overview of the history of international higher education exchange. It is mostly intended for those involved with or interested in the fields of international higher education exchange or comparative education—faculty, university administrators, policymakers, support service personnel, exchange program personnel, researchers, admissions officers, advisers, graduate students in international degree programs, foreign student alumni—as they propel this worldwide enterprise. It is designed to serve as a brief, but foundational, historical reference, a sequential chronicle of knowledge migration, and America's unprecedented legacy of scholarly exchange.

Fayetteville, AR, USA   Teresa Brawner Bevis

Acknowledgments

Because this text is a compilation of my earlier works on the topic, which include five books and a number of journal articles, I wish to acknowledge and thank those who have provided help, friendship, criticism, and support, with this new volume and also with the previous projects.

I owe my initial thanks to the late Dr. Christopher J. Lucas, with whom I co-authored my first book, and without whose wise guidance I may not have found a publisher; and Dr. John Murry, Dean of Graduate Education at the University of Arkansas, who encouraged my writing and research pursuits, and who sent some good publicity my way. Appreciation is extended to Dr. Kent Farnsworth, former president of Crowder College, with whom I co-authored a guidebook on college instruction; and Dr. James Hammons, who, though I failed to fully appreciate it at the time, made me push myself harder during my doctoral studies. I am grateful to Dr. Allan E. Goodman, President of the Institute of International Education, for providing his comments for the back cover of this new book. I also thank the late Doris Sharp of Prairie Grove, Arkansas, who believed in me.

Appreciation is due Michael Freeman, Director of International Services at the University of Arkansas, who enabled my first journal article, many years ago. I am grateful to my Iranian friend and colleague Dr. Yassaman Mirdamadi, who kindly provided a peer review for my Middle Eastern book; and Hoyt Purvis, former Professor of Asian Studies and Director of the Fulbright Program at the University of Arkansas, who volunteered as a reviewer for my book on China. My thanks go to Dr. Lyle Gohn, who graciously invited me to contribute a chapter on international education exchange to his excellent book on student populations. Dr. Robert

Pederson of Washington DC, who reminded me about the significance of smaller colleges and community colleges in the history of international student exchange, was a welcome voice. I thank Steve Courtney, Connecticut historian and author, for taking time to write thoughtful and much-appreciated reviews for my publishers, and for lending me some rare Chinese Educational Mission (CEM) information, which he was kind enough to trust me to return. The Connecticut Historical Society was likewise gracious to help me find old photographs of Yale and the CEM boys. I also thank the staff at the Library of Congress in Washington DC, for devoting late hours to assist me in finding dozens of obscure sources. I thank the City of New York. The many years spent working in the fashion and garment districts, blissful requirements of my first career, served to imbed my appreciation of human energy and capacity, and of the value of diversity, insights that have served me well.

Appreciation is due HRH Princess Areej Ghazi of Jordan, my longtime colleague and friend, who provided conversations, resources, and a deeper understanding of Islam and its application to international education exchange. I still owe Her Highness a cup of Starbucks, which I hope to have an opportunity someday to repay. The two beautiful Qurans she gave me after our writing collaboration occupy a special place in my library. I am equally grateful to her husband, HRH Prince Ghazi bin Muhammad of Jordan, a true Arab scholar who generously took the time to read my manuscript draft on the Middle East and provide his edits—almost all of which I applied. He helped me better understand the centuries-old hierarchy of Arabs, the Hashemite family, and Islam's contributions to higher learning. He also corrected a few misspellings, a reflection of my limited knowledge of Arabic.

I continue to appreciate and miss the many foreign students and scholars I had the privilege of working with and befriending at the University of Arkansas during my years as coordinator of international student programs. Their insights and personal accounts of experiences as exchange students provided an intimate understanding of the blessings and traumas involved with the earnest pursuit of higher learning. These students were my original inspiration for researching and writing about global knowledge migration and comparative education.

Thanks are due the Walker Heart Institute in Fayetteville, Arkansas, whose kind staff and able cardiologists, Drs. Soliman A. Soliman, Charles Cole and Shaun Senter and their fine assistants Brian and Taylor, took care of my husband as I wrote the final pages of this book from the hospital.

Without their skills and the blessing of his recovery, completing this project would not have been possible.

My greatest appreciation and thanks are reserved for my family, especially my parents, the late Thomas Albert and Louise King Brawner, who took a chance in the early 1960s and moved their young family from California to the Middle East to work with Kuwait's fledgling oil industry. The childhood years I spent there forever internationalized my view of the world. I thank my husband David, who has been my loving partner and support for almost 40 years, our amazing and accomplished offspring, Thomas and Elizabeth, and my wonderful stepson David. I love you all.

Contents

1 **Introduction/Learning Migration in Antiquity** — 1
   Middle Eastern Origins of Language and Scholarship — 2
   Foundations of Scholarship in Ancient Asia — 7
   Greco-Roman Scholarship — 16
   Mesoamerica — 21
   Knowledge Migration in Early Europe — 27
   References — 32

2 **The Notion of Universities** — 35
   Guilds and Nations — 41
   Town and Gown — 46
   Medieval Universities in Britain — 48
   The Grand Tour — 50
   References — 52

3 **The Rise of American Scholarship** — 55
   The Birth and Growth of American Science — 58
   College-Building and the College Movement in America — 64
   References — 68

4 **Education Exchange in America in the 1800s** — 69
   From Europe's Perspective — 69
   The First Foreign Students in America — 72
   Anson Burlingame — 79

A Plea to the Imperial Court 81
The Chinese Educational Mission 83
What Became of the CEM Boys? 89
America's First Immigration Policies 93
America's First Students from Japan 95
References 100

5 **The Early Twentieth Century** 103
Governmental Policies and Immigration Laws 103
Students from the Philippines: The Pensionados 106
The Barbour Scholarships and Gender Issues 108
Cosmopolitan Clubs 110
The Committee on Friendly Relations Among Foreign Students 113
Foreign Student Enrollments 115
The International Houses 118
The Institute of International Education 120
Teachers College 122
A Second Wave of Chinese Students 123
Tsinghua College and the Indemnity Scholarships 125
Notable Boxer Indemnity Students 127
The Critics 129
References 133

6 **The Student Exchange Boom Following World War II** 135
Foreign Student Enrollments 136
UNESCO 139
Swords into Plowshares: The Fulbright Program 140
Postwar Middle Eastern Exchanges 143
AMIDEAST 145
The Institute of International Education in the Postwar Years 147
NAFSA 149
Fields of Study 151
Evaluating International Student Credentials 152
Postwar Chinese Enrollments 153
McCarthyism, the Cold War, and the McCarran Act 156
The 1955–1956 Foreign Student Census 159
The 1960s and 1970s 161
The 1969–1970 Foreign Student Census 164
References 168

7	**The Late Twentieth Century (1979–1999)**	171
	Rebuilding Middle Eastern Enrollments	174
	Middle East Studies	177
	A New Wave of Chinese Students	179
	Jimmy Carter and Deng Xiaoping	181
	Hong Kong and Taiwanese Enrollments	182
	The World Competes for International Students	184
	Research on Foreign Students	186
	Late-Century Enrollments, Events, and Immigration Issues	190
	The 1999–2000 Census	195
	References	199
8	**September 11 and Student Mobility**	201
	SEVIS	204
	Post-9/11 Enrollments	209
	References	212
9	**Escalation of Exchange with Asia**	215
	China	215
	Enrollments 2000–2010	217
	The Allure of China	218
	An Ivy League in China	221
	Little Emperors and Migrant Children	223
	China's Ten-Year Plan	226
	President Obama's 100,000 Strong Initiative	227
	American Higher Education in China	229
	Critics	232
	Confucius Institutes and Soft Power	235
	References	242
10	**US-Middle East Exchange in the Early Twenty-First Century**	245
	American Outposts	246
	Competition for Middle Eastern Enrollments	251
	Initiatives	253
	Middle Eastern Enrollments 2000–2010	257
	Middle Eastern Studies in American Universities	258

	Intercultural and Recruitment Programs in High Schools	261
	American Study Abroad in the Middle East: "The 9/11 Kids"	261
	Online Learning	265
	References	269

11 World Leaders with American Degrees — 271
Royals, Diplomats, and Dignitaries — 272
A Penchant for the Ivy League — 274
The Rankings — 285
Wealthy Foreign Alumni = Generous Gifts — 288
References — 293

12 Approaching Midcentury — 295
Are Foreign Students Diverting from America? — 295
The Present and Coming "Youth Bulge" — 297
Optional Practical Training and the Migration of Intellectual Capital — 299
If It Sounds like Theft: America's Intellectual Property — 302
Facing Extinction? The Fulbright Program — 304
Naysayers Be Silent: The Threat of Political Correctness — 306
Education Exchange and Online Degrees: Caveat Emptor — 308
Foreign Propaganda and Academic Freedom — 312
Exchange Enrollments and Projections — 314
Oracles and Prognostications — 317
A New Golden Age? — 322
References — 327

Index — 329

About the Author

Teresa Brawner Bevis earned an EdD in Higher Education Administration from the University of Arkansas, where she was program coordinator for its international students. She later served as an adjunct professor at Crowder College in Missouri. Her previous books on the topic include *International Students in American Colleges and Universities* (2006), *A History of Higher Education Exchange: China and America* (2014), *Higher Education Exchange between America and the Middle East through the Twentieth Century* (2016), and *Higher Education Exchange between America and the Middle East in the Twenty-First Century* (2016).

List of Tables

Table 6.1	Foreign student enrollments for 1948–1949: top countries of origin	138
Table 6.2	Foreign student enrollments for 1948–1949: top ten institutions	138
Table 6.3	Foreign student enrollments for 1955–1956: top countries of origin	159
Table 6.4	Foreign student enrollments for 1959–1960: top countries of origin	161
Table 6.5	Foreign student enrollments for 1969–1970: top countries of origin	164
Table 7.1	Foreign students in the United States from OPEC for selected years	172
Table 7.2	Foreign student enrollments for 1999–2000: top places of origin	196
Table 9.1	Foreign student enrollments in the United States 2009–2010 and 2010–2011: Asia	216
Table 9.2	Chinese students in the United States and Americans studying in China 2000–2010	217
Table 10.1	Foreign student enrollments: MENA region (2005–2010)	259
Table 12.1	Chinese students in the United States and Americans studying in China 2010–2018	315
Table 12.2	Foreign student enrollments: MENA region (2016–2017 and 2017–2018)	316

CHAPTER 1

Introduction/Learning Migration in Antiquity

In its broadest sense, education is an informal means by which the observed actions and habits of people continue from one generation to the next. In its narrow sense, education is a formalized process by which a society purposely and systematically communicates its skills and traditions, usually to the young, for preservation and posterity. Through informal and formal means, civilizations since ancient times succeeded in passing down wisdom inherent to their own environments. As centers of learning developed, at the core of each was a belief system that gave purpose and direction to educational pursuits.

The educational character of every civilization was also shaped by the acquisition of imported information—knowledge brought in from foreign lands. These transfers of knowledge sometimes took place when the curious, drawn by tales of advanced scholarship in distant places, ventured across borders to acquire it for themselves. As centers of learning arose in the ancient world, and their reputations for enlightenment spread, the gathering of knowledge-seekers they drew invariably included "foreigners"—students not native to the immediate local area. Then as now, inquisitive people were compelled to explore, leaving behind the familiarity of home to seek fresh abilities, and then returning to their native lands to apply them. Few societies have been so remote or removed that they could not be affected by student migration. Other transfers of knowledge were not so peaceful. They could be by-products of conquering armies who sought to impose their own traditions onto occupied territories, either through extended human contact or by mandate.

Knowledge exchange, in its many forms, has deep roots in antiquity. This history will therefore first examine the origins of higher learning, and the earliest examples of academic migration. A brief review of the ancient and scholarly contributions of several world regions—the Middle East, Asia, Europe, and the Americas—begins the narrative.

Middle Eastern Origins of Language and Scholarship

Citizens of ancient Phoenicia were called "purple people." From about 800 to 1200 BCE, when the civilization was at its prime, Phoenicia comprised a series of city-states along the coast of the Mediterranean Sea in what is now Syria, Lebanon, and northern Israel. The island city of Tyre and the city of Sidon were its most powerful centers. A great maritime populace, Phoenicia was known for its fine ships, decorated with elegant carvings of horses' heads that paid tribute to Yamm, their god of the sea. The region was also renowned for the magnificent purple dyes that had been manufactured in Tyre for centuries, prized for their exceptionally rich and deep colors. Initially used for the robes of Mesopotamian royalty, the dyes had given Phoenicia its name, derived from the Greek word *Phoinikes*, or Tyranian purple. For generations, the industry would render the hands and arms of its workers a vibrant hue.[1]

Phoenician innovation went much further than dyes and decorative arts. It was no less than the birthplace of the alphabet, proclaimed the Greek chronicler Herodotus, and a basis for all Western languages. Evidence of ancient Phoenician words can still be found throughout the English language. The city of Gebal (called Byblos by the Greeks), for example, gave the Christian Bible its name.

The ancient Near East witnessed the origins of civilization in an area known as the Fertile Crescent, a region between and surrounding the Tigris and Euphrates Rivers. Referred to as Mesopotamia, which means "between rivers" in Greek, its territory extended into what is now eastern Syria, southeastern Turkey, and Iraq. Among the first to flourish there were the Sumerians and Akkadians (later known as Babylonians and Assyrians), who by the fourth millennium BCE had developed city-states in the region, adorned with massive ziggurats built for the worship of patron deities. The most prominent of these city-states was Sumer, which gave its language to the area and invented the world's first known formal cuneiform system of written communication, a predecessor of the Phoenician alphabet. Later the Assyrian Empire (1250–612 BCE) and the Neo-Assyrian Empire (911–605 BCE) dominated, governing all of what is now Iraq, Syria, Lebanon, Israel, Palestine, Kuwait, Jordan, Egypt, Cyprus, and Bahrain, along with areas of Iran, Turkey, Armenia, Georgia, Sudan, and Saudi Arabia. Assyrian imperial expansion brought into their sphere many nomadic and barbaric communities.

In ancient Mesopotamia and the immediately surrounding regions, the chief languages were Semitic, subdivided into several different families. The Akkadian family, to which both Assyrians and Babylonians belonged, was the oldest and most used of the languages in Mesopotamia. The Canaanite family included Biblical Hebrew, Phoenician, with its North African offshoot Carthaginian, as well as a few other closely related tongues. By the beginning of the Christian era, many of these languages had for the most part disappeared, replaced by a group belonging to another Semitic family, called Aramaic. Of the Canaanitic languages, Phoenician was still spoken in the Levant seaports and the North African colonies and Hebrew survived in Jewish regions as a language of religion, literature, and scholarship.[2]

The Arabic language, historically the last of the Semitic types to enter the region, was for the most part confined to the central and northern parts of the Arabian Peninsula. At the dawn of the Christian era, the more advanced communities of the southwest, present-day Yemen, spoke another Semitic language known as Southern Arabian, similar to Ethiopic. Arabic speakers entered and settled in the Syrian and Iraqi borderlands in the north, even before the great Arab conquests of the seventh century, leading to the triumph of Arabic throughout the region. In the Fertile Crescent, Arabic eventually replaced Aramaic, although the latter still survives in the rituals of some of the Eastern Churches and in some remote villages.[3]

It may be helpful to note here that the world's language systems can be classified into several types, including pictographic, ideographic, logographic, syllabic, and alphabetic. Pictographic writing systems are designed to represent words, ideas, or groups of words by means of a visual portrayal of their associated meanings—a box image to portray a house, for example. This method was inconvenient for conveying ideas other than simple nouns, however, so it gradually yielded to a more abstract system of marks called cuneiform, which could function both phonetically (representing a sound) and semantically (representing a meaning or concept). Ideographic systems represent words or ideas by less obvious means. Logographic writing systems represent whole morphemes or words. Syllabic writing combines syllables with signs, and alphabetic systems represent the individual and distinctive sounds, or phonemes, of language.[4] English is an alphabetic writing system based upon phonetic signs. Many subcategories of languages exist, some combinations of different writing systems.

Most historians agree that the alphabet was a product of the Middle East, largely an invention of the Phoenicians, and a vast improvement on the earlier methods of hieroglyphs or cuneiform. Latin, Greek, Hebrew, and Arabic would be derived from the first alphabet conceived by these mercantile people of the Levant coast.

The proximity to coastal ports and the geographical position of the Middle East had made it the center of trade routes. It also put it in the path of invading armies, a circumstance that exposed the region to many outside cultures. Routes converged upon these territories from the east through the Iranian plateau and from the north through the Caucasus, the Hellespont, and Asia Minor. Ancient trails penetrated the Middle East from the west through the Mediterranean Sea; and from the south through Arabia, Egypt, the Persian Gulf, and the Red Sea. Along these same routes also came migrations of peoples, who brought with them unfamiliar languages, beliefs, and traditions—influences that continuously re-shaped the cultural environments and educational capabilities of the various territories.

By the first century CE, the expanding Eastern Roman (Byzantine) Empire had come to govern the entire Eastern Mediterranean, a region that extended from the Balkans to the Euphrates. Defined by Christianity, the Byzantines would rule for the next 500 years, but in the seventh century a new religion, Islam, was gaining momentum. Like Christians, those of the Islamic faith sought to convert non-believers. And just as Christianity had done, Islam quickly developed into more than one sect. Most Muslims came to identify themselves as either Shia—those who believe Muhammad's successor to be a descendent of the Prophet's daughter Fatima—or Sunni, who hold to the philosophy that Muhammads's successor should be the most promising, chosen individual. It is a division of ideals that has since developed a duality in the Muslim world.

For about four centuries, it seemed likely that Shia Islam would prevail, and it reached a height of power around 1000 CE, but then the Seljuk Turks came to dominate, followed by their Ottoman successors, all fiercely

Sunni. Shi-ism continued to survive in Persia and other areas, but over time constituted a declining minority of Islam. In fact, the basic beliefs and rituals of Sunni and Shia Islam are quite similar. The original divisions were to some degree political and had to do with disagreements regarding the succession of power after Muhammad's death.

Muhammad had upheld the importance of learning and literacy, and information important to Islam and its traditions was routinely recorded and archived by hand. It was the introduction of paper from China in the eighth century, aided by the development of printing, that enabled its dissemination to the broader population.

Printing was not entirely unknown in the early Middle East, as there is evidence of woodblock stamps from ancient times. When movable type and other more advanced printing techniques reached the Middle East, centuries after their invention, it was not via China but from the West, with Christians and Jews serving as the first typesetters.[5] By the seventeenth century, printing presses were operating in the Ottoman Empire. Ottoman chroniclers, who rarely wrote about anything related to the West or Western progress, enthusiastically reported the invention, devoting an unusual amount of coverage to Gutenberg's first press. Convincing the skeptical Turks of the value of printed materials took time, however. Many rejected the idea of books produced by printing houses, preferring handwritten ones. Published books lacked the grace and beauty of the traditional texts, claimed Ottoman intellectuals, who were keen on aesthetics, favoring the shining ink and the elegance of golden gilt. Besides, they argued, there were many well-established calligraphers with fine reputations working in the region, and they could all write very quickly.

The practicality of the printed product eventually won out, to the world's academic benefit. Before printing, much of what was known about the ancient Middle East came from individual handwritten documents that were painstakingly translated from Greek or other ancient languages into Arabic, then later from Arabic into European languages. Only a few could access these earliest historical and scholarly documents. Representing a different sort of higher learning migration, the subsequent dissemination of printed materials provided educational sources far beyond the previous scope.

The dissemination of Islamic writings brought with it fresh inclinations toward education and scholarship, with a special interest in the heavens. Islamic tradition mandates daily prayers and other rituals take place in accordance with specific positions of the sun; therefore, astronomical timekeeping was a central focus for early Muslim scientific scholars. The Quran, the source of many traditions in Islamic teaching, refers to astronomical patterns in the writings. In addition to providing a means for knowing when to pray or perform religious rituals, the study of astronomy served to determine the latitude and longitude of important places in the Islamic world, helping the faithful pray in the correct direction—facing toward Mecca. Muslim scholars offered a model of the solar system with the Earth as one of several planets orbiting the sun, centuries before Copernicus, and even today at least half of the charted stars bear Arabic names—Aldebaran and Algol, for example. Many currently used terms in astronomy are of Arabic origin, such as *zenith*, *nadir*, and *azimuth*. Islamic scholars also created the astrolabe, an invention that enabled astronomers to accurately measure the position of the stars.

The word Quran is itself derived from a term meaning "read" and the first verse is in part a call for the faithful to be literate. Under the Abbasid dynasty especially, during the caliphate of Harun al Rashid and his son al-Mamun, the Middle East was considered the intellectual capital of the world.[6] In the ninth century, Baghdad's *Bayt al-Hikma* (House of Wisdom) was a library and research facility where scholars translated the great writings of Greek thinkers. Muslim scholars during this Golden Age made important contributions to the world's understanding of mathematics. Mathematicians such as Habash al-Hasib ("he who calculates"), Abu'l Waa al-Buzjani, Abu Nasr al-Iraq, and Ibn Yunus would develop all six functions of trigonometry—*sin*, *cosec*, *cos*, *sec*, *tan*, and *cot*—to a level far above that introduced by Hipparchus in the second century BCE. Persian mathematician al-Khwarizmi's writings became core mathematics and astronomy textbooks in Europe and in the Muslim world. In Cordoba, experiments by Armen Firman ibn Faris and Ahmed Celebi were forerunners of modern-day flight.

Medicine was likewise advanced during this Golden Age of education. Arab physicians translated most of the Hippocratic Corpus into Arabic by the ninth century, and important scholars made fundamental contributions to science and medical practice. A case in point is Al Rhazes (865–925), who wrote more than 180 books and articles on philosophy and medicine, which, once translated into Latin, helped encourage and influence the rebirth of arts and sciences at the outset of the European Renaissance. Arabic medical practitioners provided an integrated ventricular theory drawn from the tenets of Aristotle, Hippocrates, and Galen.[7] Muslim physicians were first to diagnose smallpox, measles, and hemophilia, and were known to use pharmacology and advanced surgical techniques to treat eye ailments.

Arab education was appreciative of the arts in the region, styles which had uniquely evolved under the influences of various conquering powers. Arabic arts and crafts were affected early on by Sassanian, Chaldean, and Persian works. In Syrian artworks, Byzantine and Egyptian influences are especially evident, and in North Africa the Neo-Latin arts of the Spanish, Byzantines, Greeks, and Romans left stylistic footprints along with their scholarly contributions.

Arab scholarship may have first presented the concept of the university. Some historians suggest that the first colleges were outgrowths of the Arabic *madrasa*, or hall of learning, which sometimes provided rooms where students could live during their studies. The degree or diploma may be a descendent of *ajaza*, a document authorizing a student to teach what he had learned at the madrasa. What is undisputed is that Islamic institutions promoted learning on a high level well before the rise of the European universities in the Middle Ages. Islamic educational institutions such as Al-Azhar in Cairo were in operation in advance of institutionalized higher learning in Europe, delivering the linguistic and literary traditions of Arabic, not just to Egyptians but also to students from far-distant regions.[8]

Foundations of Scholarship in Ancient Asia

Like the Middle East, Asia advanced knowledge and began formalizing procedures for learning in ancient times. In China, schools were implemented at least as early as the Xia dynasty (2017–1600 BCE). As in most ancient civilizations, they were for the most part reserved for the male elite, thereby establishing and empowering its intelligentsia. Scholar-officials, the predecessors of the intelligentsia of later centuries, constituted a group of leaders in various fields and occupied a superior position over the other classes of Chinese society. Historian Y.C. Wang believed that studying the changing intelligentsia was the key to understanding China.[9] With rare exception, the dynasties sponsored the collecting of books, and from ancient times knowledge was considered a virtue, with society a hierarchy of intellect over ignorance. Higher learning reflected the Confucian principles that had profoundly influenced the actions of the scholar class, and thus society at large.

Confucianism may be explained as a system of social and ethical philosophy rather than a religion. It was built upon ancient foundations to establish social values, institutions, and ideals of traditional Chinese culture. Its institutions were not a separate church, but those of society, family, school, or state. Priests were not separate liturgical experts, but parents, officials, and teachers. The arena of religion, to Confucians, was everyday life, and a commitment to the building and strengthening of one's character, while continuously learning. As Confucius (551–479) himself explained: "At fifteen, I set my heart on learning. At thirty, I was firmly established. At forty, I had no more doubts. At fifty, I knew the will of heaven. At sixty, I was ready to listen to it. At seventy, I could follow my heart's desire without transgressing what was right."[10]

As Wang put it, Chinese thought was devoted to the realization of true good for all mankind. "True good" referred to the attainment of happiness in one's current life. There was little concern about such questions as the origins of human existence, man's position in the universe, or the relation between the natural and supernatural.[11] Man was what he was, and the only significant question was how he should live. For most, a good life meant maintaining harmony and peace with others through the fulfillment of one's role in the perpetuation of Chinese social life. Confucianism concerned itself with a sort of mundane happiness, which defined a good life as incorporating a minimum of material wants with a maximum of moral cultivation, recognizing the uneven intellectual capacities of men. The Chinese sociopolitical structure could be viewed as an application of the concept of *jen* (benevolence), which holds that man is by nature good, and that because he has sympathy for others shares joys and sufferings as part of his own experience.[12] Within this context, the family became the basic unit in the system, and the state an extended form of family.

In his 1922 book *The Problem with China*, Bertrand Russell wrote that apart from filial piety, Confucianism was in practice a code of civilized behavior. It taught self-restraint, moderation, and, above all, courtesy. Confucianism upheld a moral code that was different from that of Buddhism or Christianity, which only a few saints could hope to live up to, contended Russell.[13]

Buddhism developed from the teachings of the Buddha ("Awakened One" in Sanskrit), who was a teacher in northern India. Spreading from India to Central and Southeast Asia, China, Korea, and Japan, Buddhism played a central role in the spiritual, cultural, and social life of Asia. Ancient Buddhist scripture and doctrine developed in several closely related literary languages of ancient India, especially Pali and Sanskrit. Imported from India in the middle of the first century, Buddhism coexisted alongside

Confucianism from the time of the Tang dynasty and was similar in that it emphasized moral behavior. Education also formalized during the "Buddhist Age" (500–850), a period that witnessed the implementation of clerical examinations for both Buddhist and Confucian classical scholars. It was a system that would regulate education and occupational promotion, and determine intellectual boundaries, for several centuries.

The imperial examination system had taken form around 400 CE and reached its full institutional development in the Tang dynasty (618–907). During the Song dynasty (960–1279) it settled into patterns that were to last right up to the opening years of the twentieth century, according to historian Ruth Hayhoe. While the medieval universities of Europe had faculties of law, medicine, and arts, the imperial examination system of the Song standardized (for evaluation purposes) an integrated canon of texts, the Four Books and Five Classics, arranged and annotated by the Neo-Confucius intellectual Zhu Xi. It was only in the late nineteenth century that it was challenged by additional examinations introduced in the fields of mathematics and foreign languages. The system was abolished in favor of a modern curriculum in 1905.[14]

While the terms "intellectual" and "literati" could take on different definitions when applied to the general population of China, among the elite the meaning was simple. Either of these terms simply meant one was educated, and both implied the separation between the learned few and the uneducated masses.[15] Because "intellectual" is a more modern term, "literati" may be best used when referring to China's educated elite prior to the twentieth century.

Comprising about 10 percent of the population, China's pre-twentieth-century elite was made up of scholars, charged with the responsibility of preserving traditional ethical values while also attending to the business of governing. Positioned at the top of the hierarchy was the emperor, followed by the elite, then below them were the imperial clansmen, comprising a small number of officials who had inherited titles. Next were the civil bureaucrats, also known as scholar-officials or mandarins, who had passed civil-service examinations and earned official positions, and beneath them were men of means who had passed the exams but held no official position. At the next descending level were farmers and peasants, who made up about 80 percent of China's population, followed by the lowest rung of the societal ladder, which was reserved for beggars, actors, butchers, and prostitutes, all assumedly uneducated.

The Chinese valued knowledge, but the attainability of education in China was largely dependent on one's place in society, and for the overwhelming majority, higher learning remained unavailable until recent times. Even as late as the 1800s, only about half of the male population in China had acquired any level of literacy, despite the numerous instances of special imperial support for the education of poor boys. Neither schools nor imperial support existed for the formal education of Chinese girls.

In early China, boys and girls were attended to similarly for the first few years of life. After the age of seven, however, boys began school, while girls were barred from pursuing anything but domestic affairs and prepared exclusively for the roles of wife and mother. At every level of Chinese society, girls were groomed under the Confucian ideal of the "Three Obediences"—to the father before marriage, to the husband after marriage, and to the sons in widowhood.[16] The notion that illiterate and untalented women were desirable had been perpetuated for centuries. Ample evidence exists, however, that within their domestic environments women were often supremely in charge. Hu Shi (Hu Shih), a well-known scholar writing in the mid-twentieth century, described Chinese men as the most "henpecked" in the world, and traditional Chinese humor abounds with stories of men intimidated by women in comical situations. Even so, outside the home females were afforded few advantages, and little education. Some nevertheless managed to achieve varying levels of literacy, usually with the help of an educated family member. This comparatively small population of female literati succeeded in making significant contributions to a broad field of education, particularly the arts and poetry.

Opportunities for female education were not constant from dynasty to dynasty. For example, when Confucian ideology strengthened at the close of the Song dynasty (960–1279), the repression of Chinese women likewise increased. A publication from that period titled "Wen's Book of Mother Indoctrination" stated that a virtuous woman was one who had no talent. Ideally, females should only be taught a few hundred fundamental words, such as *fuel*, *rice*, *fish*, or terms necessary for daily use. For women to know more than simple terms could do society more harm than good.[17]

The levels of female literacy in China before the nineteenth century are difficult to approximate, as the evidence is largely unrecorded. What is known is that a girl's access to education was typically dependent on external factors such as the family's wealth, academic background, or geographical location. It was not uncommon for families with a literary tradition to provide some rudimentary education for their daughters or nieces. The place of residence was also a factor, as evidence indicates that women residing in certain regions, such as the lower Yangtze delta, enjoyed a considerably higher incidence of literacy than females born in other provinces. An important influence in the advancement of female literacy was China's invention of printing in the ninth century and the subsequent distribution of written materials. Public attitudes tended to shift in favor of women's education as a result of a widespread readership of popular novels, which often portrayed *ts' ai nu* (literary-talented women) as an acceptable ideal for females.[18] Opportunities for advanced education for Chinese women would remain scarce, however, until the final decades of the twentieth century, when Deng Xiaoping ended China's isolation, revitalized its universities, and reinstated higher education exchange with the United States.

Nearby Japan followed a somewhat different path toward literature and the arts, and scholarly exchange. Among the earliest examples of art in Japan are the intricate rope designs found on the pottery of the Jomon people (10,000–400 BCE), who occupied the islands.[19] More advanced wheel-turned pottery and metals were implemented by 300 BCE in the Yayoi culture. During the Tomb Period, from about 300 CE, great earthen grave mounds containing funerary objects, such as terra cotta figurines or models of buildings, offer evidence of Japan's rising level of sophistication in the arts and architecture. The Heian and Late Heian (Fujiwara) Period witnessed a blooming of classical Japanese culture in the capital at Heian-kyo (Kyoto) especially, where the aristocracy, including many women, produced a vast amount of literature.

Teachings from nearby China had flowed into Japan from the sixth to the ninth centuries, along with an introduction to Buddhist ideals. From Buddhism emerged the Chinese system of writing along with its literary tradition, and Confucianism influenced advanced scholarship. The city of Heian-kyo was host to five institutions of higher learning by the ninth century, and during the remainder of the Heian period, additional schools were established. Zen Buddhist monasteries were especially important centers of learning during the medieval period, from 1185 to 1600, and the Ashikaga School, Ashikaga Gakko, flourished in the fifteenth century as a center of education.[20]

The Tokugawa (or Edo) regime, which extended from 1603 to 1867, was the final era of traditional Japanese government, culture, and society, before the Meiji Restoration of 1868 toppled the shoguns and moved

Japan into the modern era. It was also the period when Japan first had extended contact with the peoples of Europe. Along with Portuguese traders came Jesuit missionaries, who preached Christianity and began religious schools where Japanese students could study Latin and Western classical music in addition to their own language. At the time, the Yushima Seido in Edo (Tokyo) was the main educational institution of the state and served as a training school for shogunate bureaucrats. Few ordinary citizens in Japan could read or write at the beginning of the Tokugawa period, but by its end, education had become widespread. An increasingly literate populace and a meritocratic ideology, with emphasis on discipline and competence, would be its legacies. The last half of the Tokugawa period was a time of dynamic intellectual activity. Although Neo-Confucianism was the orthodox learning sanctioned by the government and retained its paradigmatic hold on Japanese intellect, politics, and society, the presence of other ideologies was increasingly visible as nativism (kokugaku), Mito loyalty (mitogaku), new religion, and Western studies gained followers.[21]

Japan's feudal society modernized under the subsequent Meiji Period (1868–1912), a time when the roles of many of the *bushi*, or *samuri*, changed from warriors to government bureaucrats. Consequently, their expectations for formal education increased. The Samurai curriculum stressed morality, and included both military and literary studies, the memorization of Confucian classics, arithmetic, and calligraphy. Samurai were typically sponsored by their *Han* (domains), and by the time of the Meiji Restoration of 1868, more than 200 of the 276 Han had schools in Japan. There were also private academies, attended sometimes by Samurai and also commoners. These taught specialized Japanese subjects, such as Western medicine, modern military science, gunnery, and *Rangaku*, or "Dutch studies," as European studies were called.

Commoners were most often provided instruction in practical and general education, such as reading, writing, arithmetic, calligraphy, and the use of the abacus, with instruction taking place in *terakoya* or "temple schools," which had evolved from the earlier Buddhist halls of learning. By the latter part of the nineteenth century, they were no longer religious institutions, nor were they always located in temples. More than 11,000 schools existed at the end of the Tokugawa period, attended by an estimated 750,000 students.

The new Meiji leadership put Japan on a rapid course of modernization, with an emphasis on establishing a public education system that could help Japan catch up with the advances of the West. A traditionally isolated culture, attitudes toward crossing borders were modified during the Meiji period, sometimes through the arts, and some Japanese embarked on journeys designed for learning and enlightenment. Few poems inspired Meiji youth as much as one by the monk Cessho, which was an early commentary on student migration. It offers evidence of study abroad, similar to Chaucer's writings about England's wandering scholars, emphasizing both the importance and the dangers of seeking knowledge in foreign lands, as in these selected lines:

> A young man sets a goal before himself
> And leaves his ancestral home.
> Should he fail in his studies
> He will never again return, even though he dies.
> How can the village graveyard be the only resting place?
> There are green hills for men everywhere.[22]

The sentiment called for a revolution of consciousness, not only for the former samurai and the intelligentsia but also for ordinary people. Students were sent abroad to study the educational systems of those advanced regions, returning with such ideas as decentralization, teacher autonomy, and school boards, many of which were implemented. By the late 1800s, textbooks on Confucian ethics had for the most part been replaced by modern, westernized books. However, some of the former Confucian and Shinto precepts, especially those relating to the hierarchical nature of society, service to the state, and morality, gradually returned to the forefront. The 1890 Imperial Rescript on Education, along with renewed centralized control over education, guided Japanese education until their revocation in 1945. This coincided with a resurgence of education exchange with the West, in tandem with similar efforts from other Asian countries seeking to modernize. India especially would begin to send large numbers of students to the United States after World War II.

In ancient times, education in India centered on the Gurukula system, where *shishya*, those wishing to study, went to the home of the Guru (teacher), to request instruction. Those accepted then took up residence at the teacher's home and were expected to help with the daily chores along with their studies. The Gurus taught a variety of subjects, ranging from Sanskrit to mathematics, with an instruction method that focused on three distinct processes: Sravana was the process of listening to the truths as taught by the teacher; the second, Manana, referred to the students' thinking through the spoken messages, in order to assimilate them fully; the third process was known as Nidhyasana, where students reached complete comprehension, and the ability to live by the truths, rather than simply explain them. The Gurukula system involved a study of nature and was not confined to rote learning. Any sort of professional or technical training was typically left to the families, as sons usually followed the occupations of their fathers.[23]

Excavation sites in the Indus Valley have revealed India's rich tradition of learning in ancient times, but after Aryans settled in the Gangetic valley (around 1500 BCE) there is evidence of more elaborate systems. It was also around this time that the Vedas, a large body of knowledge that had passed orally from generation to generation, were compiled and recorded. Two systems developed: the Vedic and the Buddhist.

In the first system, the four Vedas, six Vedangas (phonetics, ritualistic knowledge, grammar, exegetics, metrics, and astronomy), and Upanishads were the primary subjects, with Sanskrit the medium of instruction. Education typically commenced at the age of five with a ceremony called *Vidyarambha*, marked by the child's first learning of the alphabet. Another ceremony was held when the child was old enough to leave home to reside and study at the house of the teacher. At this point, the students were referred to as *Brahmacharin*. Upon completing his education, he was deemed eligible to be a house-holder, or *Grihasta*.

The other system taught the schools of Buddhist thought, using Pali as the medium of instruction. In the Buddhist system, education for boys began at age eight, marked by a ceremony, or *abbajja*, which was open to all castes. The Upanayana ceremony in the Vedic system allowed participation only by boys in the Brahman, Kshatriya, or Vaishya castes. Both systems offered vocational training as part of the curriculum, where master craftsmen or artisans taught specific skills to the students, who also served as their apprentices. Similar to the Vedic, in the Buddhist system a child left home to live in a monastery under the tutelage of a preceptor. The boy was now referred to as *Sramana*, and was to wear a yellow robe. When education was complete under the Buddhist system, a *Sramana* was given full status of monkhood or *Bhikshu*.

Women fell into two classes regarding education during the Vedic age—either *Sadyodwahas*, who pursued studies until their marriages, or *Bramhavadinis*, who did not marry and pursued education throughout their lifetimes. Within the system, women were taught the Vedas and Vedangas, but study was restricted to hymns necessary to perform the

Yajna (sacrifice) or other rituals. Scholarly women in early India, such as Maitreyi and Gargi, took part in public debates and were a part of important philosophical discussions. Women sages were referred to as *Rishikas*.[24]

Different types of teachers worked within the Vedic system. One who taught Vedas without charging a fee was known as an *Acharya*, while an *Upadhyaya* was one who earned his living by teaching. Wandering scholars, while not regarded as teachers, served as sources for knowledge for many. *Sikshaka* was an instructor for studio or performing arts and *Yaujanasatika* were instructors known for advanced scholarship, sought out by students from both local and foreign regions.

In early India, *Ghathikas* referred to an institution of the highest learning, where the top levels of scholarship could be found, especially knowledge of religious literature. Among the most famous of India's educational institutions in antiquity was Takshashila, a center of scholarship in the sixth century BCE, where 16 branches of learning were taught by masters. Salotgi, in Karnataka, was another important center, with 27 hostels to house its students, many of whom were from foreign lands. It was richly endowed by Narayana, the minister of Krishna II, in 945 CE. Other important early institutions included the Universities of Vikramashila, which was founded by Pala king Dharmapala in the late eighth or perhaps early ninth century. Prospering for about 400 years, it was among the largest Buddhist universities, with more than 100 teachers and an estimated 1000 students. The curriculum included the subjects of philosophy, grammar, metaphysics, logic, and others, and it would produce eminent scholars who were often invited by foreign countries to instruct Buddhist learning. Among its most distinguished graduates was Atisa Dipankara, a founder of the Sarma traditions of Tibetan Buddhism. Perhaps the largest of India's medieval universities was Nalanda, a university and Buddhist monastic center that taught the subjects of art, architecture, literature, logic, grammar, philosophy, economics, law, medicine, as well as Buddhism and Hinduism. At one time as many as 10,000 students were reported to have been enrolled at Nalanda. Vallabhi and Somapura were other important universities of the period.[25]

There were times in its antiquity when India enjoyed a high standard of education, drawing students from far-away places. Sufi writer Amir Khusrau (1252–1325 CE) mentions that scholars came from different parts of the world to study in India, but that no Indian scholar had found it necessary to go abroad to acquire knowledge. Indian scholars at times were in high demand and their reputation for knowledge widespread.

Arab caliphs like Al Mansur and the previously mentioned Harun al Rashid, for example, were reported to have sent embassies to India in the ninth century to procure Indian scholars. One result of those efforts was the translation of the medical books of Charaka, Susruta, and Vagbhatta into Arabic.

Later contacts with the Arabs would not be so peaceful. As the spread of Islam found its way into the country, Muslim invasions brought with them a steep decline in Indian education, as learning institutions and their archives were looted and plundered. Indian universities were destroyed, including Vikramashila, devastated by Muslim armies fighting the Sena dynasty around 1200. Its remains at the village Anticha in the Bhadalpur district, Bihar state, India, are still being excavated. Another university lost in the name of Islam was Nalanda, which was burned to the ground in 1197 CE, each of the scholarly monks mercilessly slaughtered. Kanauj and Kashi were likewise devastated, replaced by mosques. Hindu scholarship, or what was left of it, escaped to remote parts of the country, where some of its elements survived.[26] The Buddhist system of education was virtually extinguished, as the Vedic system found sanctuary in the southern peninsula, in Hampi, Sringeri, and Kanchi and a few other places.

The integration of Indian traditions and Muslim influence would bring about new universities, such as Delhi, Lucknow, and Allahabad. These taught similar subjects as India's medieval universities, but they replaced Buddhist and Hindu studies with Islamic topics and gave greater importance to the study of astronomy.

Greco-Roman Scholarship

Greece is about the size of England, or of Alabama in the United States. The landscape is very rugged, with mountains covering around 75 percent of its territory. Its soil and climate support the "Mediterranean triad" of grain, grapes, and olives.[27]

In Classical Athens, education was two-fold. The physical component, or *gumnastike*, emphasized strength, stamina, and preparation for battle, a rigorous process that started for boys as early as their elementary years. They first learned from private instructors known as *paidotribes*, then later moved on to the schools, or *gymnasiums*. The term for intellectual education was *mousike*, and it involved training in the arts, including music, dance, and poetry. Instruction focused on recitation and memorization, with writing perhaps done with a stylus on a waxed board.

Classical Sparta likewise valued physical training, as it was considered the duty of able young men to be conditioned to protect their polis. Spartan educational centers, or *agoge*, were run like military boot camps, with the common goal of producing an indestructible Spartan *phalanx*. Things like reading and writing were kept to a minimum, as quests for knowledge were regarded with little importance. As in Athens, schooling in Sparta usually began early, around age seven, when a boy was separated from his parents and placed in a barracks with others his age. They would become his new home and family. Instruction was provided by adult males who had completed military training and had gained experience on the battlefield, and discipline was stressed. To enhance their ability to endure hardship, the boys were provided little sustenance, leaving them no choice but to manage with meager means and to find creative ways to forage and steal, all important survival skills for war. Upon completing their instruction at the *agoge*, at about the age of 18, trainees were obliged to hunt down and kill a Greek slave, or *helot*, without being apprehended. If successful, they were awarded the title of *ephebes* as they pledged their formal allegiance to Sparta.[28]

Spartan women, unlike their Athenian counterparts, received a formal education that was conducted and controlled by the state, and, as with males, the focus was physical education. Girls and young women were taught to run, wrestle, throw a discus, and accurately project javelins, and there were competitions such as the footraces held each year at the Heraea in Elis, a prestigious event equivalent for women as the Olympic competitions were for men. Girls were also instructed in music, dance, and the playing of musical instruments.

Higher forms of education began developing around 420 BCE in Athens, alongside the advance of many now-famous philosophers. As with any rise in higher learning, it was a period that encouraged education migration, as many students traveled from distant lands to study at the feet of the masters. Socrates (470–399 BCE), for example, and the Sophist movement welcomed the inclusion of not just foreign students but also foreign teachers, a preference that helped shift the focus from physical training to an emphasis on academics. Studies increasingly turned to mathematics, astronomy, harmonics, and dialect, with an awareness of developing each student's philosophical awareness and insight. Ideally, individuals should gain an ability to take their knowledge and apply it to their understanding of reason and logic.

As in societies past and present, a family's wealth and status played a major role in the level of education a young person received, as the amount of scholarship received was most-often related directly to how much they could afford. Education at the highest levels was usually taught by sophists who charged, sometimes substantially, for their instruction. Influential educators included Isocrates, an Athenian orator, who had learned from Socrates and Gorgias, training that helped him develop an exceptional rhetoric for which he was well known. Isocrates believed rhetoric to be the key to virtue, disregarding the importance of the arts or of sciences. The ability to speak well and persuade was the foundation of his educational theory, and he founded a school of rhetoric around 393 BCE, far different from Plato's Academy, which emphasized science, philosophy, and dialect. Both schools drew notable numbers of foreign students.

While earlier civilizations are known to have attracted students from foreign lands, the ancient Greeks were among the first to capitalize on the opportunity. A distinguishing feature of Classical and Hellenistic Greek education was the mobility afforded to all parties. Because instruction was usually conducted without the benefit of actual brick-and-mortar facilities, "classes" could move from place to place as circumstances dictated and meet wherever it was convenient. A city's open marketplace or agora, or perhaps the shade of a nearby temple, could be a fine setting for a classroom. Whether convened in a building or outdoors, these so-called rhetorical schools turned out to be remarkably durable, numbering in the hundreds well into the Hellenistic era. The famous ones attracted students from far beyond the host cities, lending a global presence to the local communities, and adding revenue to the economy.

One of the earliest references to the participation of foreign students and scholars in Greek higher learning is from the writings of Socrates, who noted the arrival in Athens of the Sophists (*sophisai*, or teachers of wisdom). These teachers, he observed, were often accompanied by numerous protégés—youths from distant regions who traveled and studied with their masters. "Most of Protagoras' followers seem to be foreigners," Socrates wrote. "The Sophist drew them with his eloquent and learned speeches, and they followed where he led."[29]

Plato, a student of Socrates, may have instituted the first physical "school" devoted expressly to higher learning in Greece. Founded around 387 BCE, the Platonic Academy derived its name from the hero Academos. Hippias built a circuit wall to enclose the area to be used for classes and the Athenian Cimon landscaped the grounds, providing trees for beauty and shade. The compound was also furnished with an elaborate enclosed area for lectures. Over an extended period, the complex developed into a major classical center of learning, appealing to foreign students from across the Mediterranean world. In Hellenistic Greece, Athens especially attracted students from various countries to its higher learning institutions.[30]

More great philosophical centers were founded in Athens and they, like Plato's Academy, drew foreign students and scholars. Aristotle's *Lykeion*, or Lyceum, was established in 335 BCE; the Porch, or *Poecile* of the Stoics, was operating by 310 BCE; and the *Kepos*, or Garden, was founded by the Epicureans just four years later.[31] Other smaller scholarly centers were created in subsequent years, in sufficient numbers to further mark Athens as the premier center of intellectual learning and activity. For wayfarers and youths whose primary intent was to learn with the masters, the favored destination was Athens. Cicero, the great orator and rhetorician, reportedly spent six months in Athens studying under Demetrius the Syrian. The scholarly facilities marked Athens as an intellectual center, a reputation that the city enjoyed through the final years of the Hellenistic era, when internationally mobile scholars began turning their attention to Rome.

The migration of knowledge through scholarship was supremely evident regarding Greek and Roman civilizations, in part due to the mobility of students to the Athenian and Spartan schools. Greek influence on Rome dated from the beginning of the city's history and had become an integral part of Roman culture. Not surprisingly, Greek literature and art were familiar to many upper-class Romans, who had opportunities to study in foreign centers of learning. Senators such as Fabius Pictor (c. 220 BCE), referred to as the father of Roman history, was sufficiently fluent in Greek to write books in the language.[32]

Rome had become an important academic destination because of its commitment to learning and its investment in literature and the arts. From the outset of the Roman Empire, it was customary for its brightest youths to first attend one of the private primary or elementary schools, common throughout the imperium. Grammarians and rhetors could be found in practically any place of cultural importance, offering adolescents more advanced instruction. Aspiring scholars could then elect to attend a rhetor's school. These systems existed in the East, at Cos, Ephesus, Smyrna, Pergamon, Antioch, Constantinople, and Athens. The Romans hosted sufficient numbers of foreign students to prompt education authorities to create official policies pertaining to their actions and needs, such as admissions, housing, and immigration requirements. Many of these exchange policies bear a striking resemblance to those employed by universities today. The issues of foreign students presenting false documents or overstaying their welcome are nothing new, according to Roman archives.

In the fourth century CE, the Roman Empire was tottering, a situation that led to a large rise in taxation. This placed a particularly heavy burden on the wealthy, the *decuriones*, who ran the local government, as it was their responsibility not only to collect local taxes but also to make up any shortfall. The Roman leaders had provided a few tax exemptions, however, one of which was for students. There was a sudden enthusiasm for education, encouraging many applicants, from both local and remote regions. To help manage this new rise of students, in 370 CE Rome put procedures in place to authenticate credentials. Those coming to Rome with the desire to learn first had to present letters to the Chief Tax Officer, from the provincial judges who gave them permission to travel there. The letters were required to contain the student's town and birth certificate, along with reports of achievements. Upon arrival in Rome, students were expected to declare which branch of study they proposed to follow, after which a tax officer would investigate to verify that they were devoting their efforts to the stated subject. Students were warned that they should behave in a manner befitting those who wanted to avoid a bad reputation. Students should not frequent shows or seek out inappropriate company or parties. If a student did not behave with the dignity a liberal education requires, stated Rome's foreign student policy, he should be publicly flogged, immediately placed on a boat, expelled from the city, and sent home.

Reminiscent of today's Optional Practical Training, industrious students who traveled to Rome for their education, who graduated and had jobs, were given leave for a period of time. They were then expected to return home voluntarily, or face being sent back forcibly in disgrace. A precursor of the current student-tracking system known as SEVIS (Student and Exchange Visitor Information System), the Roman tax office kept records of foreign students, where they came from and when they should return, "whether Africa or any other province."[33]

Another type of educational institution that drew foreign scholars in Greco-Roman times was the *Mouseion*, or Museum (dwelling of the muses), which served as a scholarly research center for higher learning. The most famous among these was the great Museum at Alexandria, founded around 280 BCE under the royal patronage of Ptolemy Soter I. The institution attracted poets, geometers, astronomers, physicians, dramatists, critics, and grammarians—many of the most eminent scholars of the day.

The Museum was more a center for scholarly inquiry and research than a place for advanced instruction. Its scholars-in-residence usually sought seclusion to pursue their studies; and they were under no obligation to deliver lectures or teach. Nevertheless, many did. Museum pensioners and temporary residents alike lived in community near Ptolemy's palace, drawn by the promise of enlightenment. While they paid no taxes and apparently were not obliged to perform duties, most of them resided in luxurious facilities at royal expense, spending most of their time engaged in educational pursuits, after the fashion of scholars on sabbatical. In his *Satirical Poems*, Timon poked fun at their pretensions, comparing the Museum to a bird cage, where "pen pushers and readers of musty tomes ... are never tired of squabbling with each other."[34]

The Museum at Alexandria boasted several magnificent botanical and zoological gardens as well as a world-famous library. The Museum and its annex, the *Serapeum*, are said to have contained no less than 120,000 volumes, according to records drafted by its third librarian, Callimachus, between 260 and 240 BCE. Many details about the facility's whereabouts, layout, holdings, organizations, administration, and physical structure, however, are still debated.[35] What can be said with some confidence is that the Alexandrian edifice, along with other rival institutions at Rhodes, Antioch, Ephesus, Smyrna, and Pergamon, was intended to sustain a community of scholars, more or less imitating the spirit of the Athenian school of the early Pythagoreans, and the later Academy, Lyceum, and the Garden of the Epicureans. The Museum, perhaps in concert with two or three other centers of knowledge, attracted students from many places, from as far away as Cappadocia.[36] The facility and its irreplaceable holdings were devastated by a massive fire during a time when Julius Caesar and his army occupied the area, leading some to suspect he may have borne some responsibility.

Mesoamerica

The Americas were settled during the Upper Paleolithic period, between 50,000 and 10,000 BCE, when humans are believed to have migrated to Alaska via the Bering land bridge. Research indicates that the indigenous peoples of the Americas descended from a common ancestral group who, except for Arctic peoples such as Eskimo and Aleut, emerged from a subsequent wave of migrants. The Archaic Period in Mesoamerica saw the hunter-gatherer tradition move toward agriculture and community living, and there is evidence of corn being cultivated as early as 2700 BCE.

The Olmec civilization would rise around 1200 BCE, giving birth to stonework and the first urban communities.[37] Much about the Olmecs is still a mystery. While their origin and demise are debated, it is generally agreed that they helped set in place the foundations of Mesoamerican civilization. It is unclear what the Olmecs called themselves, but there is evidence that the Aztecs referred to them as Olmecs, a term meaning "rubber people" in the Aztec tongue. It is known that the Olmecs codified and recorded their gods and their religious practices with the use of symbols, and the construction of colossal stone sculptures. Also called the Pre-Classic or Formative Period, the Olmec civilization existed along the Gulf of Mexico in the area that is now Veracruz and Tobasco. Ball games, chocolate, and animal gods frequently appeared in the personality of their culture.

There is evidence of engineering and other educational advancements among the Olmecs. Mound structures in the capital of San Lorenzo reveal carved basalt drains, and there are painted floors at structures such as the Red Palace. The city of La Venta, with a population of 18,000, had a bilateral symmetry in its planning design, and religious buildings suggest a pre-meditated architectural layout. Buildings were placed symmetrically along a north-south axis with four enormous heads that faced outwards at key points, and there were pyramids constructed along a sunken plaza with basalt columns—architectural features that were copied in the cities of later Mesoamerican cultures. There is evidence of medical advances among the Olmecs as well, such as the surgical procedure of trephination. Animals played important roles in Olmec culture. Jaguars, eagles, caimans, snakes, sharks, and others were each identified with a divine being.[38] Art embellished the Olmec civilization. Carvings and paintings were often found around the entrances to caves, such as the carved figures at Oxtotitlan or at Chalcatzingo. Most striking perhaps are the colossal stone heads the Olmecs left behind, each weighing several tons. The civilization ended sometime between 300 and 400 BCE.

Indigenous to Mexico and Central America, the Maya inhabited what are now the Yucatan, Quintana Roo, Campeche, Tobasco, Chiapas, and southward through Guatemala, Belize, El Salvador, and Honduras. The ancient Yucatan city of Mayapan, the last capital during the Post-Classic Period, gave the Maya the name by which they are now known. A consolidation of power in the great cities of the Yucatec Maya came about during the Classical Maya Period (250–900 CE). During this time new traditions in art and architecture were occurring, including education advances in mathematics and astronomy, and a calendar was perfected.

At its zenith, the Mayans of the Classical Period were making important cultural advances, centered on their deep belief in the cyclical nature of life. According to the Mayans, one did not go to a heaven or hell, but rather embarked on a journey toward paradise, or *Tamoanchan*, a trek involving several levels, that began with the treacherous underworld of Xibalba. There were only a few ways one could be exempted from this difficult journey. If someone died in childbirth, during warfare, on the ball court, by suicide, or as a sacrificial victim, he or she could then avoid the transitional levels and ascend directly to heaven. Some think this may explain the acceptance of human sacrifice, and why people may have volunteered for the death ritual. The Mayan calendar provides another clue into the cyclical nature of Mayan philosophy.

Much of Mayan architecture was decorated with various markings. The principal subject matter on public buildings, tombs, and stelae seems to be historical and sociopolitical propaganda regarding the rulers, state histories, conquests, and genealogies. Also listed were dates, place names, and captives that had been conquered and then sacrificed. Some codices were astronomical or astrological in nature.[39] The Popal-Vuh, the great religious book of the Mayas, tells of this view of life through the tale of hero twins Hunahpu and Xbalanque, and their victory over chaos and darkness, symbolized by the lords of Xibalba. The twins played a game called Poc-a-Toc, which symbolized human struggle. Opposing teams of seven players each faced each other on a court, the objective to send the small rubber ball through a vertical hoop that was affixed to a wall, usually several feet higher than an average man was. Only hips, shoulders, head, and knees could be used to maneuver the ball—the use of hands or feet was not allowed. And the game was exceedingly fast. Spanish bishop Diego de Landa wrote in his journal that viewing a Poc-a-Toc game was like watching lightening.[40]

A great deal remains unknown about the civilization, in part because of the scarcity of Mayan records. Few exist, as many were destroyed at the hands of Diego de Landa. He traveled from Spain to the Yucatan in 1549, assigned to the task of routing out heathens from the Mayan groups who had converted to Christianity. Believing that subversive activities were growing among the Maya, on July 12, 1562, Landa and his men burned most of the holdings at the church at Mani, a collection including the Mayan Codices and over 20,000 images. Only three volumes escaped the conflagration. These would later be named for the cities where they were discovered, long after they were taken from the Yucatan—the Madrid Codex, the Dresden Codex, and the Paris Codex. Created by scribes, they included thousands of historical documentations and careful observations in astronomy. The Dresden Codex alone devotes six pages to accurately calculating the rising and positions of Venus.

Unsatisfied with the destruction of most of the codices, Landa then authorized the torture of anyone considered to be subversive, correctly determining that brute force was the most expedient and efficient means of returning them to Christianity. He would defend all of these actions in his 1566 work *Relacion de las Cosas de Yucatan*, where he documented the events in great detail. Ironically, it is within Landa's own writings that much of the information about the culture was preserved. The Mayan Post-Classical Period, 950–1524 CE, would see the abandonment of their great cities. The defeat of the Quiche Maya at the Battle of Utatlan in 1524 is the traditional ending date of the civilization.

The Toltecs had migrated in the ninth century CE from the deserts of the northwest to Colhuacan in the Valley of Mexico. First settling at Colhuacan, they later established a capital at Tollan (or Tula), a term meaning "place of reeds." The term also referred to any large settlement. Tollan, with a population of perhaps 30,000, was laid out in a grid pattern very similar to the Mayan city of Chichen Itza. Mythology describes it as ornate and sumptuous, with palaces made from gold, jade, turquoise, and quetzal feathers, all crafted by gifted artisans. Toltecs were masterful farmers of maize and traded in obsidian, which was used for blades and arrowheads and mined in nearby Pachuca. Their monuments, which included two large pyramids, a colonnaded walkway, a palace, and two ball courts, surrounded by an area of housing, attest to the accuracy of the legends. Like the Mayans, the demise of the Toltec civilization remains a mystery, although there were signs of violence in Tollan. The remaining Toltec people are believed to have fled to Chapultepec, on the banks of Lake Texcoco, around 1156 CE.[41]

The Aztec Empire flourished between 1345 and 1521 CE. Despite its popular use, the term "Aztec," when used to refer to the empire that ruled ancient Mexico during that time, may not be accurate. None of the writings from the Spanish Conquest refer to Aztecs, nor can the name be found in the recordings of Franciscan friar Bernardino Sahagun, an important chronicler for the region. Early Spanish reports referred the conquered subjects as "Mexica," although the term Aztec can be found in a handful of sixteenth-century documents. According to mythology, the people who founded the capital city of Tenochtitlan originally called themselves Aztlaneca or Azteca, meaning citizens of Aztlan. When the Toltec empire crumbled, the Azteca left Aztlan, combined with other wandering tribes, and settled in what is now Mexico.

At its height, the Aztecs ruled an estimated 11,000,000 people and dominated most of northern Mesoamerica. It was a civilization accomplished in agriculture and trade and noted for its advances in art and architecture. Tenochtitlan, the capitol on Lake Texcoco, is estimated to have had a population of around 200,000 in the early sixteenth century. The largest city in the Pre-Columbian Americas, it was a bustling center of trade, with goods such as gold, greenstone, turquoise, cotton, cacao beans, tobacco, pottery, tools, weapons, and slaves. Technology and infrastructure had been advanced. There were dykes to avert floods, artificial reservoirs to provide fresh water, and public gardens. From 1430, the empire expanded, with the help of the Aztec military, which had grown large through the conscription of males, and the capture of men from conquered territories. Warriors wore padded cotton armor, and carried wooden shields covered in hide, alongside sharp obsidian sword-clubs and dart-throwers or bows and arrows. Elaborate feathered costumes and headdresses brightly denoted the various ranks.[42]

Unlike previous Mesoamerican civilizations, the history of the Aztecs is relatively well documented, with sources that include codices, archeology, and detailed accounts from Spanish conquerors, both military and Christian. An array of deities presided over almost every aspect of an Aztec's life, and ceremonies were dictated by a variety of calendars. Aztecs appreciated the fine arts, often favoring monumental sculptures such as the statue of the goddess Coatlique, which measures almost nine feet in height. Artisans specialized in metal work and wood carving, and bright colors and mosaics were frequently employed, an example being the turquoise mask of Xuihtecuhtli. With the Aztecs came steps toward a formalized education system. Children were taught rudimentary life skills by their parents until the age of 15, at which point boys went to schools called *telpochcalli* (house of youth). Here they learned about the history and religion of the Aztecs, the art of war, and the duties of citizenship.[43]

This culture would likewise decline at the hands of the Spanish. When Hernan Cortes arrived with his entourage from the Old World, gifts were exchanged with Aztec leader Motechuzoma II, and the relationship at first appeared to be cordial.[44] Things abruptly changed when several Spanish soldiers were killed at Tenochtitlan. Cortes, who had clearly underestimated the Aztecs, was forced to withdraw, only to return ten months later, in 1521, this time laying siege to the city. Starved and ravaged by disease, the Aztecs ultimately succumbed as the great monuments of Tenochtitlan were ransacked. From the ashes rose the colony of New Spain. The age of colonialism, which had technically begun with the appearance of Christopher Columbus in 1492, had fully arrived. Traditional languages and religious beliefs were prohibited, and knowledge that supported European values and interests became the only educational option for most of the population—an example of involuntary and enforced learning migration.

The Incas, another of the late Mesoamerican civilizations, fell to Spanish forces fighting under the command of Francisco Pizarro, in 1530. The term "Late Horizon" sometimes denotes the age of the Inca Empire, when it was the dominant power of the Andes. Lacking a writing system, the Inca developed an intricate method of recording numbers with color-coded knotted cords. The Incas were also known for maintaining a network of running messengers, who carried news along the empires thousands of miles of roads.

Mesoamerican writing systems varied in the degree to which a phonetic component was incorporated. The advantage of a phonetic system is that it is a more precise recording method for a particular spoken language. The advantage of a non-phonetic pictorial system is that it can be "read" by speakers of different languages. This may explain why in the Mixtec, Zapotec, and Aztec areas the writing appears to be more of a system of pictorial conventions.[45]

The course of language and education in Latin America, and the spirit of the colonial period, became closely interwoven with the Church. Learning would be heavily affected by the relationship between Church and State, as educational institutions were to serve both simultaneously, often functioning by the authority of papal bulls or royal charters. First to receive a papal bull was the Dominican Republic's University of Santo Domingo, in 1538. Then the royal authorization was granted to Peru's University of San Marcos in 1551. Considered to be the first of such institutions founded in North America is the Royal and Pontifical University of Mexico (1551). In each case, Spain was successful in embedding much of its European culture into the educational curriculum.

Knowledge Migration in Early Europe

The first humans to inhabit Europe probably traveled there from Africa via the Middle East, settling much of the continent by 10,000 BCE. Proto-Indo Europeans appeared around 5000 BCE in the Caucus region of Russia and are thought to be the first to domesticate the horse, significant because the resulting ability to travel great distances succeeded in spreading their languages and learning traditions throughout the continent. Basque and Iberian populations were in place before 5000 BCE.

Genetic and archeological evidence indicates that the British Isles were first settled by people from the territory that is now Spain, and that Celtic language and culture arrived sometime between 800 and 400 BCE. Genetically, the initial Iberian composition was retained in modern Irish and Scottish descendants, and to a lesser extent English, due to exposure to Scandinavian and Germanic invaders in the post-Roman period. Meanwhile Proto-Uralic peoples inhabited areas around the Ural Mountains, spreading their traditions west to influence Finnish and Estonian cultures. Finnic and later Proto-Baltic-Slav populations established language and culture in the Scandinavian and Baltic areas.[46] Migrating to the mainland, Germans would form a separate ethnogroup from their kin to the north. Greek culture and language would branch off from the Proto-Indo-Europeans on the southern Balkan Peninsula. Due to its proximity to the more advanced civilizations to the east (the Hittites in what is now Turkey, the Phoenicians in what is now Syria, and the Egyptians), Greece would become Europe's most sophisticated civilization.

Peoples of central Europe slowly banded together around 1300–1000 BCE under a generally unified culture and language known as Celtic, and by 400 BCE the Celt nation covered much of Europe. Proto-Baltic-Slav culture and language spread south into what is now Ukraine, giving birth to the Slav peoples, who were the primary ancestors to Russians, Belarusians, Poles, Yugoslavians, and others.

The earliest inhabitants of the Italian Peninsula came from the region now occupied by Turkey. Concentrating in the central region, the people living there would be known as Etruscans. Intermixing with the Celts from the north and the Greeks to the south, they formed a culture that led to the establishment of the Roman Republic, in 753 BCE, which came to govern a vast empire. Between 133 BCE and 27 BCE, the Romans conquered much of Europe, including the area basically corresponding to modern England. The Scottish and Irish, however, managed to resist

Roman rule, enabling them to maintain their Celtic languages and cultures. This would result in a subdivision of Britain peoples, as those that fell under Roman rule later became English, while those that resisted became Scots and Irish. Although Celtic-based Scottish and Irish languages still exist, over time English would become the predominant language throughout England, Scotland, and Ireland. Christianity also proliferated during Roman rule, dominating the Empire by the fourth century, and all of Europe by the time of the Dark Ages.[47]

There were fundamental and practical reasons why the Roman Empire came to dominate Europe. First, they successfully developed a professional army, with full-time, well-paid, well-trained soldiers, whose impressive ranks could take full advantage of the extensive network of Roman roads. Their naval dominance also prevailed, exhibiting technological advances unknown to the rest of the world. The Romans were the world's first great engineers. Still-standing aqueducts and a strong infrastructure attest to their advanced abilities in both planning and construction. Additionally, to help unify the many Roman regions, a standardized currency was created to facilitate trade throughout the empire, along with a coded legal system that improved justice and equality. The Roman government and military established unprecedented sophistication. Nevertheless, when Roman soldiers invaded and absorbed territories, there was a general policy of respect for the indigenous culture, which had the effect of pacifying conquered populations. Roman ways most often prevailed however, as many of those conquered viewed citizenship in the Roman Empire a superior alternative to what had come before.

Factors leading to the fall of the Roman Empire included the spread of Christianity. This monotheistic religion at first ran counter to traditional polytheistic beliefs, resulting in widespread maltreatment of Christians, but in 313 CE the Emperor Constantine, a converted Christian, ended the persecution with the Edict of Milan, in which he declared that there should be toleration, not just for Christianity but for other religions as well. The edict was welcomed by Christian evangelists, who considered it an answer to their prayers, as they could now spread their belief to every corner of the empire in relative safety.

In 330 CE, Constantine enacted another change that would, in the clarity of hindsight, also lead to the empire's eventual fall. He split the realm into two halves. The western half remained centered in Rome, but in the east, Constantine instated another capital at Byzantium, a city that had been reconstructed during the time of Septimius Severus, modeled after the city of Rome. He renamed it Constantinople (now Istanbul) and it would be the headquarters for the Eastern Roman (Byzantine) Empire. The emperor Justinian (483–565 CE) had the Pagan temples of Byzantium removed entirely from what was now a Greek Orthodox Christian city, replacing them with the splendid Church of the Holy Wisdom, Sancta Sophia. The centerpiece of the capital, it would be known as Hagia Sophia.[48]

The division of the empire was now complete. While the western part spoke Latin and was chiefly Roman Catholic, the eastern half spoke mostly Greek and was Eastern Orthodox. Over time, the east thrived as the west declined. The Western Roman Empire would fall in 476 CE, an event commonly referred to as the "fall of the Roman Empire" even though the Eastern Roman Empire continued to survive for some time.

The fall marked the outset of a period referred to as the Dark Ages in Europe. As the security of Roman governance waned, barbaric invaders set about destroying civilization and scholarship across the region as a new and "unruly" ruling class emerged, largely tribal and decentralized. The result was a proliferation of small kingdoms whose varying interests brought on battles for control and supremacy. Within these enclaves, feudal lords were in the practice of bonding people to small plots of land in exchange for protection, a system that had the effect of condemning much of the population to lives of subjugation and poverty. During these "dark ages," any sort of formal education was a luxury reserved only for those who were wealthy, and much of the higher learning that was available was substantially stifled by the Church. The oppressed population was, not surprisingly, drawn to the Christian ideals of love, hope, and charity. In real terms, few had hope of transcending their class status, so the Christian doctrine was at once hopeful and promising, as it taught that, for the faithful, peace and plenty would be theirs in the next life.

The Bubonic Plague further served to terminate the Empire's advance. Emperor Justinian saw the disease destroy an estimated 25–50 percent of the Byzantine population, as the numbers and strength of his once-invincible army diminished. The rise of the Muslim Caliphate was to follow, a response to what Muslims professed to be God's call for Jihad against the Roman Empire. A brutal campaign, its quest for power, territory, and religious authority finally overpowered the Byzantines.[49]

Still deeply entrenched in feudalism, many areas of Europe were left with little protection from foreign encroachment. It was around 1299 when the Ottoman Turks began capturing territories in western Anatolia, and by the sixteenth century the Ottoman Empire controlled most of

Southeast Europe, the Middle East, and North Africa. When the Muslim armies conquered Constantinople in 1453, what was left of the Byzantine Empire disappeared. Hagia Sophia was now a mosque.

The so-called Age of Enlightenment in Europe was simultaneously underway. Driven by advancements in western philosophy and scientific and academic understanding, the Humanist movement existed in tandem with the Protestant Reformation, an effort famously championed by Martin Luther. The emerging Renaissance would become an extended period of learning and a proliferation of the arts, characterized by a re-birth of interest in Classical scholarship and scientific discovery. The era would witness the substitution of Copernican for the Ptolemaic system of astronomy, the decline of feudalism, and the implementation of literacy-spurring innovations such as the printing press. Europe had endured an extended and dark period of academic and cultural decline. Now, it was transforming its fledgling and mobile learning academies into Europe's first grand brick-and-mortar universities, institutions that would draw legions of bright students from every region of the civilized world and set standards for the coming rise of American scholarship.

Notes

1. Gerhard Herm, *The Phoenicians: The Purple Empire of the Ancient World* (Morrow, 1975).
2. Lewis, 24.
3. Bernard Lewis, *The Middle East: A Brief History of the Last 2000 Years* (New York: Scribner, 1995): 24–25.
4. M.A.K. Halliday, *Spoken and Written Language* (Oxford University Press, 1989): 9–10.
5. Ibid.
6. Mahmoud Abdullah Saleh, "Development of Higher Education in Saudi Arabia," *Higher Education*, Vol. 15, nos. 1–2 (1986): 17–23.
7. Anthony Graton, Glenn W. Most and Salvatore Settis, *The Classical Tradition* (Cambridge, MA: Harvard University Press, 2013).
8. H.A. Gibb, "The University in the Arab-Moslem World," in *The University Outside Europe*, ed. Edward Bradley (New York: Oxford University Press, 1939): 281–297.
9. Y.C. Wang, *Chinese Intellectuals and the West, 1872–1949* (Chapel Hill, NC: University of North Carolina Press, 1966): vii.
10. Many of the details of the moral and social ideals of Confucius appear in his Analects, or "Collection," which consists of twenty "books". This reference is extracted from Analect 2.4.

11. Wang, 3.
12. Ibid., 4–6.
13. Bertrand Russell, *The Problem of China* (Rockville, MD: Arc Manor, 2007): 18.
14. Ruth Hayhoe, *China's Universities 1895–1995* (New York: Routledge Publishing, 1996).
15. Ibid., 12–16.
16. Itty Chan, "Women of China: From the Three Obediences to Half-the-Sky," *Journal of Research and Development in Education*, Vol. 10, no. 4 (1977): 38–52.
17. Rosanne Lin, "Talents Oppressed," *China Daily* (April 18, 2002).
18. Li Yu-ning, ed., *Chinese Women through Chinese Eyes* (Armonk, NY and London: M.E. Sharpe, Inc., 1992), in Chapter 1, "Women's Place in History" by Hu Shi.
19. Junko Habu, *Ancient Jomon of Japan* (Cambridge University Press, 2004): 201–214.
20. John W. Hall, Marius B. Jansen, Madoka Kanai and Denis Twitchett, eds. *The Cambridge History of Japan, Vol. 3* (Cambridge University Press, 1990): 177–189.
21. Terrence Jackson, *Network of Knowledge* (Hawaii: University of Hawaii Press, 2016): 1.
22. Irokawa Daikichi, *The Culture of the Meiji Period* (Princeton University Press, 1985): 31.
23. Sahana Singh, *The Educational Heritage of Ancient India* (Chetpet, Chennai: Notion Press, 2017): 1–6.
24. Suresh Chandra Ghosh, *Civilisation, Education and School in Ancient and Medieval India* (New York: P. Lang, 2002).
25. Ibid.
26. B.N. Luniya, *Life and Culture in Medieval India* (Indore, India: Kamal Prakashan, 1978): 271.
27. Stanley Burstein and Walter Donlan, *Ancient Greece: A Political, Social and Cultural History* (Oxford University Press, 1999): 1–2.
28. John W. Walden, *The Universities of Ancient Greece* (New York: Charles Scribner, 1909): 68–97.
29. Quoted from Plato's Protagoras in John W. H. Walden, *The Universities of Ancient Greece* (New York: Charles Scribner's Sons, 1909): 16–17.
30. Ibid., 16.
31. W. W. Capes, *University Life in Ancient Athens* (New York: G.E. Stechert and Company, 1922): 8.
32. Burstein, 473.
33. Peter Jones, "Ancient Rome's Fraudulent Foreign Students," *The Spectator* (February 15, 2014). Available at: https://www.spectator.com.au/2014/02/ancient-romes-fraudulent-foreign-students/.

34. H.I. Marrou, *A History of Education in Antiquity* (New York: Mentor, 1964): 260.
35. Preston Chesser, "The Burning of the Library of Alexandria." Available at: https://ehistory.osu.edu/articles/burning-library-alexandria. Accessed December 2018.
36. Marrou, 261.
37. Jeffrey P. Blomster and David Cheetham, *The Early Olmec and Mesoamerica* (Cambridge University Press, 2017).
38. Richard Diehl, *Olmecs: America's First Civilization* (Thames and Hudson, 2004): 10.
39. Maya Civilization, Ancient History Encyclopedia. Available at: https://www.ancient.eu/Maya_Civilization/.
40. Diego de Landa, *Yucatan Before and After the Conquest*, Limited edition (The Maya Society, 1937).
41. William T. Sanders and Barbara J. Price, "Mesoamerica: The Evolution of a Civilization," 1968. Available at: https://www.questia.com/library/7763947/mesoamerica-the-evolution-of-a-civilization.
42. Michael E. Smith, *The Aztecs* (New York: Wiley-Blackwell, 2011): 3–28.
43. Ibid.
44. Michael E. Smith, "Motecuhzoma II, Emperor of Pre-Spanish Mexico," *The Berkshire Encyclopedia of World History*, Second edition (Berkshire Publishing Group, 2010).
45. Geoffrey Sampson, *Writing Systems: A Linguistic Introduction* (London: Hutchinson, 1985).
46. J.P. Mallory and D.Q. Adams, *The Oxford Introduction to Proto-Indo-European and the Proto-Indo-European World* (Oxford University Press, 2006): 12–36.
47. Ibid.
48. Polybius, *The Rise of the Roman Empire* (Penguin Classics, 1980): 302–353.
49. Ibid.

References

Blomster, Jeffrey P. 2017. *The Early Olmec and Mesoamerica*. Cambridge University Press.

Burstein, Stanley, and Walter Donlan. 1999. *Ancient Greece: A Political, Social and Cultural History*. Oxford University Press.

Capes, W.W. 1922. *University Life in Ancient Athens*. New York: G.E. Stechert and Company.

Chan, Itty. 1977. Women of China: From the Three Obediences to Half-the-Sky. *Journal of Research and Development in Education* 10 (4): 38–52.

Chesser, Preston. n.d. The Burning of the Library of Alexandria. The Ohio State University. https://ehistory.osu.edu/articles/burning-library-alexandria. Accessed December 2018.
Daikichi, Irokawa. 1985. *The Culture of the Meiji Period*. Princeton University Press.
Ghosh, Suresh Chandra. 2002. *Civilisation, Education and School in Ancient and Medieval India*, 1500–1757. New York: P. Lang.
Gibb, H.A. 1939. The University in the Arab-Moslem World. In *The University Outside Europe*, ed. Edward Bradley. New York: Oxford University Press.
Graton, Anthony, Glenn W. Most, and Salvatore Settis. 2013. *The Classical Tradition*. Cambridge, MA: Harvard University Press.
Habu, Junko. 2004. *Ancient Jomon of Japan*. Cambridge University Press.
Hall, John W., Marius B. Jansen, Madoka Kanai, and Denis Twitchett, eds. 1990. *The Cambridge History of Japan, Vol. 3*. Cambridge University Press.
Halliday, M.A.K. 1989. *Spoken and Written Language*. Oxford University Press.
Hayhoe, Ruth. 1996. *China's Universities 1895–1995*. New York: Routledge.
Herm, Gerhard. 1975. *The Phoenicians: The Purple Empire of the Ancient World*. Morrow.
Jackson, Terrence. 2016. *Network of Knowledge*. University of Hawaii Press.
de Landa, Diego. 1937. *Yucatan Before and After the Conquest*. Baltimore, MD: The Maya Society.
Lewis, Bernard. 1995. *The Middle East: A Brief History of the Last 2000 Years*. New York: Scribner.
Lin, Rosanne. 2002. Talents Oppressed. *China Daily*, April 18.
Luniya, B.N. 1978. *Life and Culture in Medieval India*. Indore, India: Kamal Prakashan.
Mallory, J.P., and D.Q. Adams. 2006. *The Oxford Introduction to Proto-Indo-European and the Proto-Indo-European World*. Oxford University Press.
Marrou, H.I. 1964. *A History of Education in Antiquity*. New York: Mentor.
Russell, Bertrand. 2007. *The Problem of China*. Rockville, MD: Arc Manor.
Saleh, Mahmoud Abdullah. 1998. Development of Higher Education in Saudi Arabia. *Higher Education* 15 (1–2): 17–23.
Sampson, Geoffrey. 1985. *Writing Systems: A Linguistic Introduction*. London: Hutchinson.
Sanders, William T., and Barbara J. Price. 1968. Mesoamerica: The Evolution of a Civilization. https://www.questia.com/library/7763947/mesoamerica-the-evolution-of-a-civilization.
Singh, Sahana. 2017. *The Educational Heritage of Ancient India*. Notion Press.
Smith, Michael E. 2010. Motecuhzoma II, Emperor of Pre-Spanish Mexico. In *The Berkshire Encyclopedia of World History*, 2nd ed. Great Barrington, MA: Berkshire Publishing Group.
———. 2011. *The Aztecs*. Wiley and Blackwell.

Walden, John W. 1909. *The Universities of Ancient Greece*. New York: Charles Scribner.

Wang, Y.C. 1996. *Chinese Intellectuals and the West, 1872–1949*. Chapel Hill, NC: University of North Carolina Press.

Yu-ning, Li, ed. 1992. *Chinese Women through Chinese Eyes*. Armonk, NY and London: M.E. Sharpe.

CHAPTER 2

The Notion of Universities

In the Muslim community, the mosque was a center of learning, in addition to its basic purpose as a place for worshiping and congregating. The eleventh century witnessed the rise of another institution of learning, the madrasa, dedicated mainly to the study of Islamic jurisprudence. The madrasa was intended to guarantee the perpetuation of judicial study and meet the needs of the expanding state system. Men educated there became religious functionaries, judges, notaries, and ministers. The madrasa emerged as an important vehicle for social mobility, becoming one of the pillars of sociopolitical order in the urban Muslim world.

The best-known madrasa in the Muslim world is Cairo's Al-Azhar University, established in 972 CE. For centuries, it has occupied a prominent religious status as the bastion of Islamic learning in Egypt and throughout the Muslim World. The Mamluk and Ottoman military elite sought political legitimation from it, while the common people looked to it for protection and representatives during periods of upheaval. Al-Azhar paid special attention, as it does today, to the Quranic sciences and traditions, while at the same time teaching modern fields of science and technology.

Less well-known, the University of Karaouine is considered the oldest institute of higher learning in the Middle East. The Karaouine mosque at Fez, Morocco, was founded in 859 by Fatima bint Muhammad al Fihry, daughter of a wealthy citizen from Kairouan in Tunisia, a hundred years before the founding of Al-Azhar. The original building was of modest

© The Author(s) 2019
T. B. Bevis, *A World History of Higher Education Exchange*,
https://doi.org/10.1007/978-3-030-12434-2_2

dimensions, but it was greatly enlarged the following century. After becoming the official mosque in 918, where the sultan attended Friday prayers, the Karaouine was taken over by the state. From the Idrisi to the Alaouites, the Karaouine was enlarged and embellished by successive dynasties. The library of the Karaouine today is a pale shadow of what it must have been at the time when Merinid Sultan Abu Inan stocked it with thousands of manuscripts, to form part of the booty won from the Christian King of Seville. The golden era of the Karaouine was in the twelfth, thirteenth, fourteenth, and fifteenth centuries, under the Almohades and throughout the reign of the Merinds. In those days, the university attracted students not only from Africa and the Muslim world beyond, but also from Europe.[1] Another of the earliest universities was Nizamiyya, a series of universities established by Khwaja Nizam al-Mulk in the eleventh century, in what is now Iran. The most celebrated is Al-Nizamiyya of Baghdad, established in 1065 in Dhu'l Qa'da, and it remains operational in Isfahan. Others existed in Nishapur, Amul, Mosul, Herat, Damascus, and Basra.[2]

On the heels of these early Middle Eastern schools would emerge the first medieval universities of Europe—the University of Bologna, the University of Paris, the University of Oxford, the University of Montpelier in France, the University of Cambridge, the University of Padua, the University of Salamanca in Spain, and others. They would evolve from congregations of students who followed a teaching master, without the benefit of brick and mortar structures, into impressive centers with buildings and landscaped grounds.

Arguably, more than any other indicator, the arrival of foreign students and scholars determined whether a gathering of learned academics had risen to the status of "university." The presence and actions of students who came from afar to learn from masters in the first academic centers of medieval Europe, by and large, shaped the character and function of the first Western universities. Until a center of learning gained reputation sufficient to attract significant numbers of students from foreign lands, it was not regarded as such.

The word "medieval," with its roots *medi*, meaning "middle," and *ev*, meaning "age," literally means "of the Middle Ages." In this case, it more specifically refers to the period between the Roman Empire and the Renaissance, which lasted from the fall of the Roman state until the "rebirth" of classical culture.

Before the birth of European universities in the medieval period, among the earliest teaching venues in Europe were grammar schools, usually positioned near a cathedral or large church. The main course of study was reading and writing in Latin, with the addition of public speaking and some mathematics, depending on the expertise of the educator. Similar to grammar schools, monastic schools were founded and run by religious orders such as the Benedictine monks, and as part of the monastery, they accepted only members of the cloth. Run by monks under the oversight of the Vatican, monastic schools slowly became havens of art and the sciences. Many of the monks focused on studying and copying ancient Greek and Roman books, and explored the theories of Plato, Eratosthenes, Aristotle, and Hippocrates. Their solitary studies and document-recording would contribute immeasurably in the effort to retain and revive long-slumbering classical knowledge.

To understand the path followed by Europe's first universities, it is necessary to observe the Greek and Roman schools from which they descended. Gregory of Nazianzus, in his Panegyric on his friend St. Basil, delivered about 382, described their life together as foreign students in Athens as he defended a culture that many Christians regarded with suspicion. An elaborate defense would hardly have been needed if there had been schools of the church itself. But, with scarce exception, the early Fathers who made their mark in Christian literature and apologetics are known to have been educated in the ordinary pagan grammar and rhetoric schools. These influences would serve to guide public education in much of Europe along a similar path as the classical schools of Greece and Rome.

The University of Bologna in Italy was established in 1088, the first institute of higher learning in the Western world. The second oldest university in Italy was the University of Padua, founded in 1222, when a group of students and professors left the University of Bologna in search of academic freedom. The University of Paris in France was operating at least as early as 1096, although there is some debate about its actual opening date. The University of Montpelier in France lists its founding date as 1150, although, like Paris, evidence suggests that classes began a few years earlier. In Spain, the University of Salamanca began its operation in 1218, officially obtaining the title "university" after Alexander IV's papal bull in 1225. It had been originally established by Leonese King Alfonso IX to allow the Leonese people to study at home rather than leave to study in Castile. Christopher Columbus, prior to his historic journey to the

Americas, is known to have traveled to Salamanca to consult scholars about seeking a western route to the Indies.[3]

Bologna and Paris are typically regarded as the two first great archetypal universities in Europe. Their reputation does not depend upon mere priority of date, but upon the impetus given to thought and education in Europe by their teachers or their methods. Bologna and Paris were two *studium generalia* but they were two different and irreconcilable types of *Universitas*. The Universitas of the Studium of Bologna were guilds of students. The Universitas of the Studium of Paris was a guild of masters. The great seats of learning in medieval Europe to follow would become either universities of students or universities of masters, modeled after the functions of Bologna or of Paris. Other universities would be founded using modifications of one or the other, or a combination of both systems.[4]

The dynamic between students and teachers in a medieval university was significantly different from today. At the University of Bologna, students hired and fired teachers by consensus. The students bargained as a collective, regarding fees and other matters, and could threaten teachers with strikes if their demands were not met. The "Denouncers of Professors" was a special committee that judged the quality of a professor's work and fined them if they hadn't completed a course on time, or if they failed to achieve the educational standard expected. Professors themselves were not entirely powerless. By forming a College of Teachers, they secured the rights to set their own examination fees and degree requirements. Eventually the city of Bologna ended this arrangement, paying professors from tax revenues and making the university a chartered, public institution.

New students typically entered the institution around the age of 14 or 15, following the successful completion of grammar school. Only the most capable were accepted at Bologna. Admission was not for the faint of heart, as studies often started before sunrise. A master of arts degree would have taken about six years, with a bachelor of arts degree awarded after completing the third or fourth year. "Arts" referred to the seven liberal arts, which consisted of arithmetic, geometry, astronomy, music theory, grammar, logic, and rhetoric. All were taught in Latin, which students were expected to write and speak fluently. The trivium comprised the three subjects which were taught first—grammar, logic, and rhetoric—as they were considered the most important of the seven liberal arts. The curriculum would evolve to include the three Aristotelian philosophies—physics, metaphysics, and moral philosophy. Subjects were separated into courses and each was essentially the study of a book or other key text, such as a book from the Bible or one of Aristotle's works. Once a student attained the level of Master, he was able to pursue studies in one of the higher faculties of law, medicine or theology, the latter being the most prestigious. Studies in the higher faculties could take up to 12 years for a master's degree or doctorate, which were initially considered the same. Upon completion, students were awarded a *licentiate* (license in Latin) which meant that the graduate had the right to exercise this discipline.

The draw of foreign students to these medieval institutions most often depended on the celebrity of the faculty. At Bologna, there was a great teacher of civil law in the first quarter of the 1100s, and a great writer on canon law who lived there in the middle of the same century. To Bologna, therefore, flocked students of law, though not of law alone. In the schools of Paris, there were renowned masters of philosophy and theology, to whom students crowded from all parts of Europe. Many of the foreign students at Paris were Englishmen, but at the time of Becket's quarrel with Henry II, the disputes between the sovereigns of England and France escalated, leading to the recall of English students from the domain of their King's enemy. The result was the birth of Oxford, which would become a great school, or *studium*, that soon rose to the fame of Paris and Bologna.

That rivalries should break out among the schools was almost inevitable. Rivalries were accentuated as the smaller and less notable *studia* came to claim equality of status with their older and greater contemporaries. There arose a necessity for a definition and a restriction of the term *studium generale*. The need for such a definition was spurred by the practice of granting ecclesiastics dispensations from their residences for purposes of study. In order to prevent abuses, it was said that such permission should be limited to a number of recognized institutions. The difficulty of enforcing such a definition throughout almost the whole of Europe was considerable. In the first half of the thirteenth century, the term was assuming recognized significance, and had certain requirements.[5]

According to the prescribed definition, one was the requirements was to enroll foreign students. Any school aspiring to be a university must not be restricted to natives of its own country. It should also have established a number of masters and must teach not only the seven liberal arts but also one or more of the higher studies of theology, law, or medicine.[6] However, the coveted title could still be adopted at will by ambitious schools, so the intervention of the great potentates of Europe was required to provide a mechanism for the differentiation of general from particular studia.

In the twelfth century, an emperor and a pope had already given special privileges to students at Bologna and other Lombard towns, and a King of France had conferred privileges upon the scholars of Paris. In 1224, the Studium Generale of Naples was founded by Emperor Frederick II, and in 1231 he gave a great privilege to the School of Medicine at Salerno, a studium that existed solely for the study of that field. Pope Gregory IX founded the Studium at Toulouse some 15 years before Innocent IV established the Studium of the Roman Court. In 1254 Alfonso the Wise of Castile founded the Studium Generale of Salamanca. Therefore, it became commonplace for a school claiming the status of studium generale to have the authority of a pope or monarch.

Long before the gifts of popes or monarchs, the *jus ubiqaue docendi*, which defined the studium generale, is the occurrence of the more familiar term *universitas*, which referred to a learning association that corresponded to a guild in the world of commerce, often a union among men living in a stadium, with common interests to protect and advance. In time the importance of these guilds increased to a point that the word *universitas* was coming to be equivalent to studium generale. Before the end of the fourteenth century, the two terms were synonymous.[7]

The fourteenth century was a great period in the growth of universities and colleges. Across Europe, privileges and endowments were granted by popes, emperors, kings, princes, bishops, and municipalities. Institutional forms had become definite, terminology fixed, and materials for study were abundant. The century witnessed the advent of Germany's universities, which to this point had no important institutions of higher learning. An institution at Prague was founded in 1347 or 1348; then others were established in Vienna, Erfurt, Heidelberg, and Cologne. While the provincial universities of France had tended to follow Bologna rather than Paris as their model, the German universities approximated more to the Parisian type of master's institutions. The first Scottish universities appeared a bit later, dating from the early part of the fifteenth century.

With the rise of Europe's universities, as historian Charles Haskins noted, students and scholars became increasingly mobile in their quest for education, moving from place to place in search of eminent masters, careless of curriculum or fixed periods of study.[8] They were singularly mobile, and singularly international in their determination to learn. Paris had its clerks (students) from Sweden, Hungary, Germany, Italy, and England, and Bologna had its English archdeacon and German civilians.

The decision to go to a distant location for study was not one to be taken lightly. In the medieval era a journey of any appreciable length was unlikely to be without some amount of difficulty and danger, and those who traveled did so at their own risk. Law and order could be tenuous at best, once the precincts of a town or city were left behind, and it was sometimes necessary to guard against bandits and brigands who could be waiting along the route for unwary travelers. There was the occasional threat of wild animals, or natural disasters, or damaged infrastructures such as bridges, creating circumstances that could leave sojourners injured or stranded. On many routes, places to secure food or lodging were few. Sometimes students traveling to a medieval university would band together for protection, as depicted in *Canterbury Tales*, where Chaucer describes travelers as religious mendicants, merchants, artisans, barristers, adventurers, soldiers of fortune, and would-be students who were seeking knowledge in a distant place.

Guilds and Nations

Foreign students and scholars, in a very real sense, determined a facility's legitimacy as a true center of higher learning. It was the growing presence of foreign students at universities that led to the development of guilds, or student nations. The first were formed at the University of Bologna.

Even as the institution's reputation had drawn them to study, the earliest foreign students had neither civil nor political rights, and the government under which they lived made little provision. The foreign students' strength was in their numbers, and the economic effect they had on the prosperity of the town, and they recognized early on the fortifying effect of organized groups. Many non-nationals who came to study in Italy were not schoolboys. Some were beneficed ecclesiastics, or lawyers, with an adequate means of earning a living. Provisions of Roman law favored the creation of protective guilds, as the privileges and immunities of the clergy advocated that foreign students should possess laws of their own, particularly in light of the potential secession of a large community of foreigners.

The growth of guilds was held together by common interests and safeguarded by oaths, a feature of the twelfth and thirteenth centuries, and the students of Bologna took no unusual step when organizing their own. No citizen of Bologna was permitted to be a member of a guild, as they required no such protection. The division and distinction of these student nations that started in Bologna is still preserved in some of today's Scottish universities, and the concept has evolved differently in others, but in most Western-type universities, the influence of the guilds remain evident.

Bologna had to struggle with both the guilds of the masters and the authorities of the city and state. Precedents had already been set. A guild of masters, doctors, or professors existed there before the rise of the university and had survived with limited but clearly defined powers. The words "doctor," "professor," and magister" or "dominus," were at first used indifferently, and a master of arts of a Scottish or German university is still described on the diploma as a doctor of philosophy. The term "master" was little used at Bologna, but it is convenient here to employ "master" and "student" as the general terms for teacher and taught. The masters were teachers of the studium who protected their own interests by forming a guild, and only its members had the right to teach. Graduation was originally an admission into the guild of masters, who had exclusive rights to instruction.[9]

At Bologna, the power of its students evolved from the circumstances under which the university developed. It started as a collection of teachers, who practiced as independent entrepreneurs. The teachers, most of whom were Bolognese, formed guilds early on, but they were informal and without power. Students would themselves form guilds, as most of them were foreign, but with a different motivation. Among other things, they hoped by organizing and empowering "student nations," they could better protect themselves from injustices by the city. Students began cooperating in the early part of the thirteenth century to form such societies, each based on their countries or regions of origin.[10] Patterned after the trade guilds that had come into vogue, each of the nations elected councilors who, as a group, elected the university rector. Both councilors and rectors were students. The rector was required to be at least 24 years of age; he should be unmarried, a secular clerk, and must have completed at least five years study of law.

The Guild or College of Masters who taught law at Bologna resented the rise of the universities of students. The students, they claimed, followed no trade and were merely the pupils of those who do practice a profession, and should therefore have no right to choose rulers for themselves. But the threat of migration turned the scales in favor of the students. Mass exits did sometimes happen, as there were few buildings and no endowments to render such a migration difficult. The masters themselves were dependent on student fees for their livelihood. It would not be until the founding of residential colleges, and the erection of buildings by the universities themselves, that the students were finally denied the weapon of a threatened migration.

Guilds or student nations were decided according to nationality, which produced some measure of unification. Some later evolved into groups that centered on particular fields of study. The law students at Bologna, for example, would cease to have more than two great guilds, distinguished on geographical principles as the *universitas citramontanorum* and the *universitas ultramontanorum*. Each was subdivided into nations, the cis-Alpine University consisting of Lombards, Tuscans, and Romans; and the trans-Alpine University of a varying number, including a Spanish, a Gascon, a Provencal, a Norman, and an English nation. The students of arts and medicine, who at first possessed no organization of their own, succeeded in the fourteenth century in establishing a new universitas within the studium. The influence of medicine predominated, for the arts course was, at Bologna, regarded as merely a preparation for the study of law or medicine. The third universitas provided status and rights to the students of arts.

Students comprising all of the nations constituted the congregation of the university at Bologna, which in turn established rules and regulations that applied not only to themselves but also to professors, and even to servants, landlords, and others with whom the students did business. Professors, who were not permitted to be members of the congregation and had no vote, opposed the growth of student power, but were unable to check it. In time, the faculty came to be dominated almost completely by students—for the most part, foreign students.

Student power prevailed at all medieval universities in varying degrees, but nowhere had students influenced the curriculum, course content, and the professors' behavior as in Bologna. This power was in part based on the fee-paying system. Each student negotiated directly with his professor concerning fees, and any professor who failed to comply with the rules and regulations passed by the congregation could be boycotted, thereby terminating his income. Professors were required to take an oath of obedience to the rector and to abide by all regulations that might be imposed on them. Professors were forbidden to be absent from classes, even for a single day, without good excuse, and then only by approval from the class, the councilor, and the rector. Students were pledged by oath to report any professor who was absent without permission. If the professor failed to attract at least five students to a given lecture, he was considered absent himself and fined. Student statutes also required that the professor start his lecture at the beginning of the book, cover each section sequentially, and complete the book by the end of the term. He was not permitted to skip a difficult portion with a view of returning to it later, lest it be overlooked entirely. Later in the period the professor was required to complete each section of the book according to a predetermined schedule. If he failed to achieve the schedule, he was fined from a sum which he had deposited at the beginning of the term with a local banker. To assure compliance, a committee of students was appointed to observe each professor and to report any violations.

At Paris, which was a masters-led rather than a student-led institution, things were quite different. The teachers tended to be young, some no older than the students at Bologna, and at Paris both teachers and students were for the most part non-Parisian. Thus, the masters also had need for a guild to protect them from the citizens. The students at Paris were much younger than those in Bologna, usually between 13 and 16 when they began. Most students at Bologna were past 20 when they entered, and, due to a longer period of study, were frequently around 30 years of age when the completed their course of studies. Therefore, in Paris, it was the masters' guilds that constituted the congregation and the governing body of the university.

The university at Montpellier was organized much like the one at Paris, but the role of students tended to more closely resemble the one at Bologna. Initially, the university government included two proctors selected by the masters, and one chosen by the students. Later there were two councilors, one a student and the other a bachelor, by today's definition a graduate student. The masters at Montpellier initially had almost complete control, but students increasingly demanded the same sort of privileges upheld by students at Bologna. By 1340 any statute affecting students would require their consent, and students were also given a say in selecting the courses to be offered.

At Toulouse, the rector was a master, but he was elected by the students. While students also enacted university rules, they had little influence upon their administration, which led to student rioting at Angers and Orleans during the last half of the fourteenth century. The incidents resulted in increased student representation in university government. At Avignon, riots and rebellion at first had little effect, in part because church influence was especially strong, but in 1459 students prevailed on Pope Pius II to support them, leading to a gain of two student seats on the university's ruling council. At Prague, students who were elected proctors of their nations sat with the faculty on the university council. At Salamanca, the Bologna pattern was adopted.[11]

In the first German universities, students never commanded quite the same power found in universities of other countries. Early in the development of the German university the power of the nations was transferred to a university council, which was composed of teachers. Later, about the only semblance of student power left was the student right to elect the rector. The limited student power in German universities was due in large measure to the fact that from the beginning professors were endowed, rather than having to rely on fees. Unlike Paris or Bologna, where professors were identified with a college or nation, German professors were university teachers.

No single picture of the medieval university emerges, as conditions of academic life varied by country and climate. While every student body had issues pertaining to academic and social protection and adjustment, or monetary concerns, the day-to-day life of students, especially those foreign to the local area, could also be problematic. There exist many stories of foreign matriculants who were destitute, unable to secure housing, or beleaguered by townspeople who sometimes tended to view young scholars, especially foreign ones, as arrogant drunkards, beggars, and troublemakers.

What was it like for a foreigner to attend school during this period? In A.F. Leach's book *The Schools of Medieval England*, he describes an Englishman who arrives at Bologna early in the fifteenth century to study law. He finds himself at once a member of the English nation of the Trans-Montane University, pays his fee, and takes the oath of obedience to the rector. His name is then placed upon the matricula or roll of members. He does not look about for a lodging facility but instead joins with some companions, probably of his own nation, to rent a communal house.[12] During his stay he was expected to participate in his student nation's activities, such as benefit societies.

Benefit societies, groups that had emerged from the guilds, cared for the sick and the poor, buried the dead, and provided for common religious services and feasts. Through these societies, representatives of the guilds were sent to cheer up and sometimes attend to the sick, or to reconcile guild members who had quarreled. Sometimes a guild would pay for the release of one of its members who was in prison for offences such as theft, but they also insisted upon the repayment of the debts, as it was paramount that the credit of the guild with the citizens of Bologna should be maintained. Harmony between student nations and the towns was essential if students, especially foreign ones, were to manage their daily existence.

TOWN AND GOWN

In medieval times, as today, relationships between university students and the local towns were sometimes precarious, as instigating factors presented themselves. Both students and faculty enjoyed certain privileges from the state in the Middle Ages. Teachers and students were for the most part free from taxation, free from military service, and, in many places, they were free from arrest and trial by civil authorities.[13] Students had gained many concessions from the city, some of which infringed on the local citizens. An example was the granting of authority over law violations (committed by students) to the university rector, who was also a student. In 1432, students in Bologna could be arrested only with permission of the rector.[14]

In time student control permeated Bologna, to the chagrin of many of its citizens. University officials inspected houses for rental to students and had the authority to set the rental rate. If a landlord exceeded the recommended rate, his property was boycotted by students for five years. Also mandated were the rates and services of tradesmen, and again, transgressions were punished by withholding student business. Local moneylenders had to be examined and approved by a university-appointed committee of students, who regulated the rates they could charge. A result of the many demands led to frequent conflicts between students and the citizens of Bologna.

In Paris, most reported incidents of "town and gown" trouble during the Middle Ages began in taverns. In 1200 a battle in a tavern at Paris resulted in several students being slain by police. Fearing the students would migrate, the king condemned the police and ordered that the homes of the citizens who had fought the students should be burned to the ground. In the future police must hand students over to the church for punishment, he decreed, and he required Parisians to take an oath not to harm students in the future. Parisians were also expected to act as informants and report any incidents of harm to students.

Among the best documented incidents between clerks and townspeople in medieval Paris occurred in 1229, when a group of intoxicated students at a suburban tavern assaulted the innkeeper. With the help of neighbors, the tavern keeper retaliated by beating one of the students severely. A group of angry clerks returned the following day with reinforcements, intending to destroy the tavern, and when the authorities arrived, a few of the students were killed. The incident created sufficient unrest to prompt several migrations of students and teachers to Oxford, Orleans, Toulouse, and other locations, as a retaliation against Paris.

Students, especially foreign ones, were sometimes regarded unfavorably, as most were young, nearly penniless, with languages and habits different from the local population. Often poorly dressed and dependent on handouts, wandering scholars were frequently referred to as blightsome, ragged, and begging. The unbeneficed clerks led very unclerical lives, wrote historian J.A. Symonds, and were often careless and pleasure-seeking. A monk in the twelfth century described the students as wanting to roam about the world, seeking liberal arts in Paris, classics in Orleans, or medicine at Salerno, but nowhere manners and morals. So-called Goliardic poetry, which was penned by the wandering clerks, illustrates their characteristic preoccupation with wine, women, and song. One poem affirms that they would "Eat to satiety, drink to propriety ... laugh till our sides we split, rags on our hides we fit; jesting eternally, quaffing infernally."[15] This sort of rebellious student lifestyle was celebrated in Goliardic-like poetry for centuries and was commonplace by the time of the great universities at the height of the Middle Ages.

When not in taverns or causing mischief, students lived fairly regimented lives. A fourteenth-century code of statutes from the College of Dainville, which was part of the old University of Paris, offers a snapshot of a university student's day. The time to rise in the morning, it says, was five o'clock, except on Sundays and Feast days when an hour's grace was allowed. At 5:30 chapel service began, which included prayers, a period of meditation, and a New Testament lesson, immediately followed by the mass of the college, which began about six, mandatory for all students. After mass, the day's academic work began, with attendance at the schools and the completion of exercises for their masters. At twelve o'clock a meal was served, during which a bursar or an external student would first read Holy Scripture, then a book appointed by the master, followed by a passage from a martyrology, or record of saints. An hour was then permitted for recreation, perhaps a walk within the precincts of the college, and then everyone retired to his own chamber. The evening meal was at seven, also accompanied by a reading, then the interval remaining until 8:30 was again flexible. The gates of the college would close at 8:30, as evening chapel began.[16]

Medieval Universities in Britain

The models for the schools of England arose not from the teachings of the Church but from the schools of heathendom—Athens, Alexandria—and of Rome, Lyon, and Vienne. These were the very pagan schools in which Horace and Juvenal, Jerome, and St. Augustine had studied the scansion of hexameters and the methods of speech-making and argument. The twelfth century was producing in Europe a renewal of interest and a revival of learning, brought about partly by the resurgence of the philosophies of great thinkers such as St. Anselm and Abelard.

The University of Oxford in England officially opened around the same time as the University of Paris, but there is evidence of teaching from the Oxford location considerably earlier than 1096. This institute would develop rapidly after 1167, when Henry II banned English students from attending the University of Paris. Today, this oldest English-speaking university comprises 38 colleges, each with its own internal structure.

The establishment of the second-oldest university in the English-speaking world, the University of Cambridge, was reportedly put in motion by a group of disgruntled scholars who had exited the University of Oxford over a dispute in 1209. It was a struggle between the clerks who studied at Oxford and the people of the town, at the time of John's defiance of the Papacy, when the king outlawed the clergy of England. The conflict led to the idea of a separate institution, which in turn led to the school at Cambridge. The schools at Oxford and Cambridge have been rivals ever since.

Both were endowed homes for the education of secular clerks. On entrance, all of them were required to have the tonsure (a portion of the head shaved bare), and provision was often made for the cutting of their hair and beard. At Christ's College, there was a regular barber. Students wore ordinary clerical dress, as any unnecessary expenditure on clothes or ornamentation was discouraged. Residence was continuous throughout the year, even during the vacation, which extended from early July to October, but sometimes leaves of absence were granted on reasonable grounds, especially during the vacation months.

The scheme of study at Cambridge was fashioned after the pattern that had become common in Italy and France, and the many students who flocked there would have found it very similar to the curriculum encountered at Oxford. Students first took a foundation of courses centered on grammar, logic, and rhetoric, followed by arithmetic, music, geometry, and astronomy, all leading to degrees of bachelor or master. No professors taught at this point. Instead, instruction was carried out by masters who had completed the course of study and had been approved or licensed by their colleagues. The teaching method took the form of reading and explaining written materials, followed by examinations and oral disputations. Some masters went on to advanced studies in divinity, canon and civil law, and sometimes medicine, courses that were taught and examined in the same way, but by those who had already passed through the program to become doctors. The doctors would in time group themselves into specific faculties.

It soon became necessary to identify and authenticate the persons to whom degrees were being granted. The first step was enrollment with a licensed master. This was called matriculation because of the condition that the scholar's name must be on the master's matricula or roll, although the university itself later assumed this duty. It became an accepted practice to mark the stage of a scholar's progress by a ceremony of graduation to the different grades, or degrees. These were conferred by the whole body of masters, with the chancellor exercising the power on their behalf, along with his deputy, the vice chancellor. The scholar's grades became differentiated by variations of color or design on the gown, hood, and cap, much like graduations today.

Among other developments, the regent masters, who were the teaching body, found that in addition to a ceremonial head they needed other representatives to speak and act for them. The first of these were the two proctors, whom they elected annually to negotiate on their behalf with the town and other lay authorities. Their duties were to keep the accounts, safeguard their books, moderate in examinations, and to supervise all other ceremonies, responsibilities soon to be shared by other elected officers. Bedels, at first attached to the faculties, presided over ceremonies; and a chaplain took charge of treasures and books. By the sixteenth century a registry recorded matriculations, degrees, and mandates from the regent masters; ceremonial letters and addresses were written by an orator. Today many of these positions are still in operation, although in some cases for ceremonial purposes only.[17]

By the sixteenth century, the patterns of student and faculty life now firmly embedded at Oxford and Cambridge would serve as models for the colleges that were soon to be founded in the American colonies. Unlike the Bologna model, it was inevitable that the English pattern, combined with a strong Puritan ethic, would foster a high degree of faculty control.

The English model would set academic precedents for American colleges. And like their predecessors, American colleges would become true universities only when they began attracting foreign students.

The Grand Tour

Historic accounts of international exchange most often limit themselves to stories of students making their way to distant locales to attend a celebrated establishment of higher learning. An interesting variation on the theme, the so-called grand tour, is less frequently covered. A grand tour was designed for young men who had already completed their formal education at home but who wished to acquire a veneer of cosmopolitanism. The grand tour was a distinctly English invention, that entailed educational student travel, an independent, not university-sponsored, component of study abroad.[18]

It is believed that the term "grand tour" was introduced in a 1670 book by Richard Lessels written about his voyage to Italy. It was an educational tradition that produced a cottage industry, complete with guidebooks, ready to meet the needs of the twenty-something male and female travelers and their tutors as they crossed the European continent. Queen Elizabeth I (1533–1603) herself judged that a grand tour of Europe's cultural centers seemed to provide a fitting culmination of an adolescent's liberal education.[19] Such a tour was a useful rite of passage, she claimed, a means of testing the ingenuity and initiative of a young man undergoing the rigors of travel abroad, prior to his posting to some appropriate position back home. As Francis Bacon (1561–1626) explained the monarch's view, the queen's injunction was to send abroad England's bright young men to be trained up and made fit for public employment. He hastened to add that the young men who embarked on a European tour did so as private gentlemen, without any royal stipend or other support. Their comportment during the travels, it was thought, served to reveal their character and suitability for public employment.[20]

A typical itinerary for a grand tour did not vary much between the sixteenth and early nineteenth centuries, and almost always included extended sojourns to France, Switzerland, Italy, Germany, and the Low Countries. When taking such a tour, often with help from a manservant, the traveler was expected to prepare himself to fully appreciate each region. He should carry with him a book describing the country where he was visiting, Bacon advised.[21] A tourist in the seventeenth or eighteenth century typically made his way by coach, sometimes traveling through the night in order to avoid the cost of renting a room at a tavern or way station. Commonplace were extended "courtesy visits" at British consular offices located in most of Europe's larger cities.

Sometimes the presence of so many young English visitors proved to be a burden on their hosts. For example, the envoy in Florence, Frances Colman, complained in 1772 that he hardly had an hour to himself, by reason of the concourse of English gentlemen. Due to the risk of highway robbers, tourists often carried little money, so letters of credit from their London banks were presented at the major cities. The travel expenditures of these English tourists contributed significant amounts of money to businesses abroad, a situation that caused some English politicians, in the interest of the local economy, to be publicly against the tradition of the grand tour.[22]

The great majority of youths who went abroad were serious-minded individuals anxious to benefit as much as possible from their travels. Writing of his own grand tour, one commentator reflected favorably on his experience, saying that he had "essentially profited from this my first entrance to the world."[23] Interest in the grand tour waned toward the end of the eighteenth century, but the precedent for including foreign travel as an integral part of higher learning was by now well established.

Notes

1. Rom Landau, "The Karaouine at Fez," *Muslim World*, Vol. 48, no. 2 (1958): 104–112.
2. "Top Ten Oldest Universities in the World," Ancient Colleges, College Stats. Available at: https://collegestats.org/2009/12/top-10-oldest-universities-in-the-world-ancient-colleges/.
3. Hilde de Ridder-Symoens, *A History of the University in Europe: Volume 1, Universities in the Middle Ages* (Cambridge University Press, 1991): 35.
4. Ibid.
5. Ibid., 4–30.
6. Hastings Rashdell, *The Universities of Europe in the Middle Ages, Vol. 1* (Salerno: Bologna Press, 1936, Forgotten Books, Reprint Series, 2018): 9.
7. Ibid.
8. Charles Homer Haskins, *The Renaissance of the Twelfth Century* (Cambridge, MA: Harvard University Press, 1928).
9. Charles Franklyn, "Academical Dress-a Brief Sketch from the Twelfth to the Twentieth Century, with Especial Reference to Doctors" (Oxford 78, Vol. 9, no. 2, 1946–1947).

10. Pearl Kibre, *Nations in the Mediaeval Universities* (Mediaeval Academy of America, 1948).
11. Ibid.
12. A.F. Leach, *The Schools of Medieval England* (New York: Macmillan, 1915).
13. Norton, 1909.
14. V.R. Cardozier, "Student Power in Medieval Universities," *Journal of Counseling and Development*, Vol. 46, no. 10 (June 1968): 944–948.
15. John Herman Randall, *The Making of the Modern Mind* (Cambridge: Riverside Press, 1940): 116.
16. Ibid.
17. Cardozier, 944–948.
18. Richard S. Lambert, *Grand Tour: A Journey in the Tracks of Aristocracy* (New York: E.P. Dutton & Company, 1937) and Jeremy Black, *The British and the Grand Tour* (Worcester, UK: Billing and Sons, 1985).
19. Lambert, 18; also see Joan Simon, *Education and Society in Tudor England* (Cambridge: Cambridge University Press, 1966).
20. Lambert, 18.
21. Lambert, 19.
22. Christopher Hibbert, *The Grand Tour* (New York: G.P. Putnam, 1969): 10.
23. William E. Mead, *The Grand Tour in the Eighteenth Century* (New York: Benjamin Bloom, 1972): 231.

References

Black, Jeremy. 1985. *The British and the Grand Tour*. Worcester, UK: Billing and Sons.
Cardozier, V.R. 1968. Student Power in Medieval Universities. *Journal of Counseling and Development* 46 (10, June): 944–948.
Cieslak, Edward Charnwood. 1955. *The Foreign Student in American Colleges*. Detroit, MI: Wayne University Press.
Haskins, Charles Homer. 1928. *The Renaissance of the Twelfth Century*. Cambridge, MA: Harvard University Press.
Hibbert, Christopher. 1969. *The Grand Tour*. New York: G.P. Putnam.
Kibre, Pearl. 1948. *Nations in the Mediaeval Universities*. Mediaeval Academy of America.
Lambert, Richard S. 1937. *Grand Tour: A Journey in the Tracks of Aristocracy*. New York: E.P. Dutton & Company.
Landau, Rom. 1958. The Karaouine at Fez. *Muslim World* 48 (2): 104–112.
Leach, A.F. 1915. *The Schools of Medieval England*. New York: Macmillan.
Mead, William E. 1972. *The Grand Tour in the Eighteenth Century*. New York: Benjamin Bloom.

Randall, John Herman. 1940. *The Making of the Modern Mind*. Cambridge, MA: Riverside Press.
Rashdall, Hastings. 2018. *The Universities of Europe in the Middle Ages, Vol. 1*. Salerno: Bologna Press. Forgotten Books, Reprint Series, 2018.
de Ridder-Symoens, Hilde. 1991. *A History of the University in Europe: Volume 1, Universities in the Middle Ages*. Cambridge University Press.
Simon, Joan. 1966. *Education and Society in Tudor England*. Cambridge University Press.

CHAPTER 3

The Rise of American Scholarship

After God had carried them safely to the New World, and they built the necessary houses and churches and towns and civil government, the next thing the colonists longed for was to advance higher learning, wrote the author of *New England's First Fruits* in 1640. Around a hundred Cambridge men had emigrated to New England before 1646, according to American historian Frederick Rudolph, and about a third as many had come from Oxford. Among them would be the founders of America's first colleges. Goals were varied but they had in common the desire to recreate some of "old England" in the colonies, colleges such as the ones they had known at Oxford, but particularly Cambridge, where Puritanism had been especially nurtured.

On the morning of October 28, 1636, the local newspaper was circulating through the town. One story reported that the Massachusetts General Court had granted five pounds for the loss of colonist George Munning's eye. Another said that the court had ordered towns in the region to fix wages, and had ceded an island to Charlestown, provided it would be used for fishing. But the most exciting news was the announcement of a legislative act that had just been passed—the colony's initial step toward the founding of America's first college. Puritan divine Increase Mather remarked in retrospect, "Twas therefore a brave and happy thought that first pitched upon this Colledge."[1]

The news was greeted with considerable enthusiasm. The prospect of having a center of higher learning in the colonies was a critical component in the

© The Author(s) 2019
T. B. Bevis, *A World History of Higher Education Exchange*,
https://doi.org/10.1007/978-3-030-12434-2_3

development of America's independence and autonomy. Young Americans would now have a means of earning a college degree without traveling to one of the faraway universities of Europe.[2] According to Rudolph, America's first college was not a luxury but a necessity. Puritan politics could not have done without it. Failing to set the world right in England, it was imperative they would do so as Englishmen in the New World.

The first college in America would take the name of the Reverend John Harvard, who had generously bequeathed to the institution half of his sizable estate, a gift that included more than 400 books. Harvard was officially chartered in 1636, a mere 16 years after the Mayflower landed at Plymouth Rock, in what is now Massachusetts. It would begin instruction in 1638, but after a few months of operation its doors closed over concern about reports of alleged misconduct by its first administrator, Nathaniel Eaton. Harvard reopened on August 27, 1640, with Henry Dunster, an alumnus of Magdalene College at Cambridge, as the new president, and the institution has been in continuous operation ever since. Eight more colleges would be founded between Harvard's opening and the eve of the Revolutionary War.[3]

For more than a half century, Harvard was the only degree-granting institution of higher learning in the colonies, until the chartering of the College of William and Mary in Williamsburg, Virginia, in 1693. Following William and Mary was the Collegiate School at New Haven, later named Yale College, in 1701. The College of Philadelphia, which would become the University of Pennsylvania, was founded in 1740, then the College of New Jersey (Princeton) in 1744. King's College, the predecessor of Columbia University in New York, opened ten years later, followed in 1764 by the College of Rhode Island, which would become Brown University. Queen's College, renamed Rutgers, opened its doors in 1766. The last to be founded before the Revolutionary War was Dartmouth College, which began instruction in 1769.[4] It is remarkable that, in the course of a century and a half, America had nine colleges in operation while England, vastly wealthier and more populated, had only two.

Modeled after their English predecessors, but without financing from England, the high cost of operating America's first colonial colleges made the price of an education prohibitive for most citizens. They did, however, provide an array of options for well-to-do white males, most of whom intending to become members of the clergy. In many cases the first colleges had religious affiliations. Puritan, Presbyterian, and Baptist sects exercised controls over some schools while William and Mary and King's College were primarily under the auspices of the Church of England. The mission and administration of these colleges directed their students toward religious studies that were in line with the tradition that accompanied colonial America's early years.

The course of study offered in a typical colonial college prior to the American Revolution was, not surprisingly, almost identical to that of English institutions such as Queen's College in Cambridge. For a young man seeking to become a learned clergyman and scholar, the generally accepted curricular mix included medieval learning, combined with devotional studies that upheld the preservation of confessionalism and Renaissance arts.[5] The fundamental disciplines required the study of Greek and Latin, and some level of proficiency in classical languages was required for admission. The first year of study typically included Greek, Latin, Hebrew, logic, and rhetoric, all of which usually continued into the second year with the addition of natural philosophy. The study of moral philosophy (ethics) and Aristotelian metaphysics was introduced in the third. Mathematics and advanced philological studies in classical languages were added the fourth year, sometimes supplemented by Syriac and Aramaic. Similar to Oxford or Cambridge, America's colonial colleges embraced a curriculum that served as a body of absolute truths rather than an induction to critical thinking or inquiry, a repository of facts to be committed to memory.[6] Classical learning was essential for success in the professions of law, medicine, or theology, a conviction that was, at the time, shared by almost everyone involved with the colonial colleges.

According to historian John Thelin, a peculiar character of the colonial college in their first decades was that there was little emphasis on completing degrees. Many students matriculated and then left their studies after a year or two, with little of the stigma now attached to "dropouts." Any time spent in college was considered special, as enrollments were only around 1 percent of the population. When the College of Rhode Island opened in 1765, only one student enrolled. Two years later the number of was only ten. In 1707, Yale College had conferred degrees upon just 18 students. At William and Mary, so few undergraduates petitioned for graduation that Lord Botetourt called for both prize money and medallion awards for commencement week oratory contests. Botetourt added the stipulation that all participants must be degree candidates. The plan proved to be appealing. It has been argued that the ascent of commencement ceremonies as solemn, prestigious events coincided with the increased recognition by colonial leaders that a college degree signaled a young man's eligibility to enter a position of responsibility.[7]

As the pursuit of higher education was being advanced in the American colonies, less frequently recognized was the status and condition of childhood academics. As colleges arose, less-than-higher education had remained remarkably undeveloped. At the start of the American Revolution, there were no public provisions for elementary education in the colonies, with the exception of New England, where a selection of "charity schools" run by an assortment of religious denominations existed. A few grammar schools also existed in coastal cities such as Philadelphia and New York. But for much of colonial America it was the parents' responsibility to see that children were taught to read, to write, and to do basic mathematics. These first grammar schools would be the forerunners of the modern high school. Among them was the Boston Latin School, created by the Town of Boston a year before the founding of Harvard. It remains in operation today, as a public high school.[8]

For many colonists, preparing their children to meet the academic requirements for entering the early colleges was a special challenge, particularly for those families residing in areas distant from New England or the larger cities. Those who did qualify for admission were nevertheless substantial enough in number to continuously expand colonial college enrollments until the eve of the American Revolutionary War, which was a period of dramatic enrollment setbacks. Before the outbreak of fighting in 1771, Harvard had graduated a class of 63 students, its largest ever. With aspiring new students put on hold during the conflict, it would take Harvard another 40 years to achieve that number again.[9]

THE BIRTH AND GROWTH OF AMERICAN SCIENCE

The colonial colleges had embraced Christian teaching and classical learning but the sciences that emerged after the revolution were not at all incompatible with the existing dogma. As Rudolph put it, science gained entry into the American college not as a course of vocational study, but as a handmaiden of religion. For the most part America's early scientists were men of religious principle who, in the tradition of the evangelical, saw science not just as empirical study but as an instrument for explaining the ways of God.[10]

Before America received its independence from England, the colonial colleges had for the most part been a means of educating political leaders and preparing a learned ministry. Soon the United States would turn to higher education as a means of providing fresh and progressive paths toward a bright future. New concepts for learning were emerging everywhere, including George Washington's proposal for a national or "federal" university. While his idea was not realized, this and other innovative notions had in common a focus on independence, progress, prosperity, and the building of a strong national identity.[11]

No seventeenth-century American approached the heights occupied by the Italian Galileo Galilei, the Frenchman Rene Descartes, or the Englishman Isaac Newton. Not until Benjamin Franklin in the mid-eighteenth century was an American recognized as part of the scientific elite—a sort of novelty—a scientist from Philadelphia, at the edge of the civilized world. From Europe's perspective American scientific progress was slow, but to colonial Americans it was fast. In colonial times settlers went from small agricultural enclaves, where nearly everyone worked as part of a farm household, to large cities with a varied economy and a variety of technologies. Over the same period, the sciences went from a body of knowledge based on the writings of the ancient Greeks, to a highly experimental and mathematical discipline marked by the work of Newton.[12]

The term "science" did not, at the time, have the same meaning as today. Science could refer to any or all of the different branches of knowledge, including theology and the humanities. The most common term for theoretical science in the early modern period was "natural philosophy." The term "scientist" was not coined until the nineteenth century, so a scientist such as Franklin would have been referred to as a natural philosopher, or simply a philosopher. Technology in the modern sense was called "the arts" or the "useful arts."

Even before the American Revolution, a few efforts to advance scientific discovery were enforced, such as Harvard's 1727 appointment of the first professor of mathematics and natural philosophy. Substantial changes in the college curriculum would not take place until after the fighting subsided, however, as postwar America turned its attention to the sciences, advancing this new knowledge to the forefront of scholarship. An early postwar champion of the sciences was Columbia, which added botany to its curriculum in 1792. In 1795 Princeton would add its first professor of chemistry, John MacLean, to the faculty.[13]

Another early professor of science was Benjamin Silliman, who had received his degree from Yale. With the endorsement of Yale's president Timothy Dwight, Silliman was appointed its first professor of chemistry and natural history, in 1802, even before he had witnessed a single chemical experiment. Nonetheless, his preparatory study at the University of Pennsylvania in Philadelphia and at John McLean's laboratory at Princeton qualified Silliman to offer his first course of lectures at Yale, which he followed with a brilliant career of experiments and scientific contributions. After amassing a distinguished collection of minerals for use with America's first illustrated course in mineralogy and geology (1818), he was instrumental in founding of *The American Journal of Science and Arts*, which for the first time provided scientists with a platform and an audience for their research.[14] He would be heralded as the "Father of American Scientific Education." Silliman helped found Yale's Sheffield Scientific School and is credited for being among the first to make other institutions aware, through his visiting lectures and writings, of the importance of instituting a scientific curriculum in America's colleges. Today Silliman College at Yale University bears his name. A noted chemist in his own right, Silliman's son continued the family legacy at Yale alongside son-in-law James Dwight Dana, another forerunner in the study of mineralogy. These and others would make Yale an undisputed center for scientific study, a reputation that would soon attract young scholars from around the world.

Amos Eaton, one of Benjamin's former students and an offshoot of the Silliman legacy, published a pioneering manual on botany which, along with his other writings, helped to stir nationwide interest in the sciences. Young Edward Hitchcock, who would become a professor of chemistry and natural history at Amherst, had been inspired by Eaton's lectures. Hitchcock would conduct the first state geological survey in America, a project conducted for the Commonwealth of Massachusetts. Eminent botanist Asa Gray was another. As Harvard's first Fisher Professor on Natural History, Gray was one of only three scientists to receive an advance copy of Charles Darwin's *Origin of Species*.[15] At Princeton Joseph Henry experimented with uses for electricity and was exploring physics; and at the College of William and Mary, William Barton Rogers was gaining worldwide acclaim for his work in physics and geology. America's first permanent astronomical observatory was completed. The United States was by now a center of invention, feeding on the ambition of American youth and strengthening by a deepening mood of nationalism—the language of manifest destiny.

Yet even as the sciences established acceptance, corresponding change in the American college curriculum was slow to take place. George Ticknor was among the first to lobby for widespread curricular change. Ticknor had attended a German university in 1815, an experience that left him with an abiding appreciation and admiration of its higher learning approach—particularly the flexibility of course offerings and the opportunities for scientific inquiry.[16] Ticknor thereafter promoted the German model as he worked to advance changes in the American college curriculum. Benjamin Franklin and Thomas Jefferson likewise supported comprehensive curricular change. Franklin had a long-time association with the German "gymnasium" and, like Ticknor, campaigned to incorporate some German components into the American system. The University of Virginia was experimenting with an innovative curriculum that allowed students to choose from a variety of courses offered within eight specialized schools—ancient languages, modern languages, mathematics, natural philosophy, history, anatomy and medicine, moral philosophy, and law.[17]

Jefferson was among the earliest proponents of state education in the United States based on scientific exploration as a pursuit distinct from religious teachings. Some of his ideas would not be implemented until after the Civil War, but alongside the movement toward the development of a state university system formed a foundation for secularism.[18] Jefferson also championed the lecture method, and the elective system. Jefferson's belief that education should reinforce republican politics by teaching citizens and leaders their rights and responsibilities was at the center of his policy. Jefferson advocated for a centralized university at the top of a pyramid-shaped educational system that he believed would promote a more natural aristocracy. This idea took shape in his Bill for the More General Diffusion of Knowledge in 1779 and would appear again in later incarnations. The chartering of his University of Virginia in 1819 and its eventual opening in 1825 realized some of Jefferson's ideas, but at the time Virginia was hardly an ideal space for the vision to reach many demographics, as sectionalism and religious opposition still dominated the political arena. Jeffersonian ideals would reemerge during Reconstruction.

Also envisioning new educational ideals was Yale's president Jeremiah Day, who in 1827 appointed a committee to put together a persuasive position paper on the topic of curricular change. The resulting Report of the Course of Instruction in Yale College, otherwise known as the Yale Report, was published in 1829 in *The American Journal of Science and Arts* and it would become the most widely circulated and the most influential proclamation on higher education of its time. The report was an affirmation of the classical curriculum in American college teaching, a definitive expression of nineteenth-century liberal arts education, as recognized by American scholars. Mental discipline, said the report, was a prime objective. Often interpreted as conservative, and in defense of tradition, the report in fact left ample room for the modernization of the curriculum, to best serve the advancing industrial age.[19] The Yale Report addressed public criticism of higher education's failure to adapt to nineteenth-century needs, making a case for change in the American college program. New studies in chemistry, mineralogy, geology, political economy, and other subjects had already been added to older courses at Yale, the report pointed out, and the new curriculum now balanced both classical learning and scientific studies. The arguments put forth by the Yale Report would not squelch the curriculum dispute any time soon, however, and deliberation between those holding to academic tradition and the proponents of curricular change would keep the debate going into the middle years of the century.

The push for a new direction was unrelenting, as new and influential voices joined the campaign for change. These included popular figures such as Ralph Waldo Emerson, who endorsed curricular change in his 1837 American Scholar address at Harvard. Adding to Emerson's convictions were those of president Eliot of Harvard, Brown's president Francis Wayland, and A.P. Barnard of Columbia, all of whom openly rejected the Oxford-Cambridge tradition as unsuited to America's future needs and purposes. They agreed that the sciences offered a utilitarian orientation that was lacking in ancient, classical studies. Before the end of the 1800s, the so-called new subjects—mathematics, natural philosophy, botany, chemistry, zoology, geology, and mineralogy—were being offered at some level in colleges and universities nationwide.

The idea of a scientific basis for knowledge independent of theological arguments substantially impacted American education in the latter half of the nineteenth century. In Europe, Social Darwinism had become acceptable ideology, in part because it was congenial to leaders in industry and higher education. For followers of early European sociologists, especially Herbert Spences, who coined the phrase "survival of the fittest," science became the rationale behind progress.[20]

Under the leadership of Louis Agassiz, the Swiss naturalist who emigrated to the United States in 1845, Harvard started the Lawrence School. Originally intended to focus on chemistry, it ended up emphasizing the natural sciences. In 1851 it offered a bachelor's degree in science. Yale began offering a degree in science about the same time. In 1847 Yale had created the School of Applied Chemistry and a department of civil engineering; then five years later the two came together as Yale Scientific School (1854) later renamed the Sheffield Scientific School.

Charles W. Eliot, president of Harvard for 40 years (beginning in 1869), was a liberal humanist who followed in Jefferson's footsteps by helping foster an elective system in education, as well as grounding the aristocracy. Democracy, in other words, should foster an aristocracy based on talent and quality—the so-called Jeffersonian meritocracy. Following that idea, Eliot pushed for college entrance examinations as a basis for admissions. High school would now become a prerequisite for advanced education, and, in turn, possessing a college degree was increasingly sought after by employers.

American colleges were also shaped by other influences. One was the flow of immigrants from Europe in the mid-nineteenth century. Two waves of German immigrants—one early in the century and another in the 1840s—brought with them fresh support for the gymnasium movement and the component of physical training.[21] Universities in Germany not only offered flexibility and choice in academic offerings, but they differed from American institutions in that they encouraged undergraduates to take part in organized physical activities alongside their studies. In their efforts to mimic the German approach to extracurricular opportunities, American colleges began sponsoring all sorts of physical activities along with class offerings—bowling, boxing, dancing, hunting, swimming, walking, skating, wrestling, and foot races. Some of these grew to be team activities, such as an early adaption of English rugby which would evolve into American football.

Originally played with a skull, an inflated cow's bladder, or some other home-fashioned projectile, the earliest "football" games were free-for-alls between teams, events that might be played on the college yard, a vacant lot, or perhaps in a nearby field. The impromptu games became so popular with the students that colleges began adopting them as regular activities, complete with organized competitions. The Princeton-Rutgers game of 1869 was the contest that officially inaugurated American football. This was significant not only because it incorporated the sport into the mainstream college experience, but also because it marked the first time American colleges engaged in any sort of ongoing intercollegiate relations.[22]

In time these intercollegiate collaborations relating to sports would lead to the establishment of America's "Ivy League." Officially coined after the formation of the National Collegiate Athletic Association (NCAA) Division One conference, the term Ivy League came to refer to an elite group of colleges that included Harvard, Yale, Columbia, Princeton, Dartmouth, Brown, Cornell, and the University of Pennsylvania. The Ivy League schools would be among the preferred destinations of international students.

COLLEGE-BUILDING AND THE COLLEGE MOVEMENT IN AMERICA

Forces supporting the emergence of the American university and the expansion of the American national state would spawn the Morrill Land Act of 1862, also known as the Land-Grant College Act. The act provided grants of land to states to finance the establishment of colleges that specialized in agriculture and the mechanical arts. Named for its sponsor, Justin Smith Morrill, the act offered each state 30,000 acres for each of its congressional seats; then upon selling the land, it could use the funds to establish schools. Or it could provide the money to existing state or private colleges to create schools of agriculture and mechanical arts—thus the term "A&M" colleges. Because the Morrill Land Act also required military training in the curriculum of land-grant colleges, the Reserve Officers' Training Corps (ROTC) developed a program for future armed forces officers.

It had been the vision of Senator Morrill to establish agricultural colleges, but he needed the secession of the southern states and the help of Ohio Senator Benjamin F. Wade to finally get it passed and signed into law by President Lincoln. Eventually 69 colleges were established, although a couple were built with private support, and many were not focused strictly on agriculture. But the Morrill Act did incite the coordination and entrepreneurship that would be essential for the formation of research universities, laying the foundations for the rapid growth of American higher education.[23] Existing institutions expanded their programs, often into areas of science and technology, building new colleges and disciplines into already preeminent universities. Beyond agricultural colleges and expansions, some revenue generated by the land grants combined with existing federal revenue and private endowments, such as that of philanthropist Ezra Cornell, to establish state flagship public universities and to support private universities. The second Morrill Act (1890) initiated regular appropriations to support land-grant colleges, which came to include 17 predominantly African American colleges, and 30 American Indian colleges.

The country's passion for progress would spawn dozens of new colleges and universities in the nineteenth century, even in sparsely populated regions. The state of Ohio, for example, with a population of only about three million, at one time was hosting 37 institutes of higher education. On the eve of the Revolutionary War, America had founded nine colleges, but on the eve of the American Civil War, there were around 250. All appealed for money from every possible source.[24] By far the most active financial supporters of colleges throughout the first half of the nineteenth century were the various religious denominations. Churches across America were eagerly establishing their own monuments to progress and posterity. Denominations sometimes joined forces, such as the Presbyterians and Eastern Congregationalists, who in 1843 formed the very successful Society for the Promotion of Collegiate and Theological Education in the West. Baptists and Methodists built colleges too. By the onset of the American Civil War, denominationalism had founded dozens of colleges across many states, including 11 in Kentucky, 21 in Illinois, and 13 in Iowa.[25] Most college-building discontinued during the war years, but as soon as fighting subsided, interest in founding new institutions resurfaced. American business and industry were now increasingly reliant on the development of the sciences to support a growing nation, and there was an expectation of innovation. There was at the same time an emergence of a more secular society. The amalgam of conditions served to make institutions that were still preoccupied with the training of clergymen seem obsolete.

Critically important was the growth in American surplus capital, enabling higher education's further promotion through generous donations from the fortunes of industrial entrepreneurs, railroad tycoons, and business magnates. With the advantage of increasingly available funds, most of America's colleges and universities were soon fully invested in a new curriculum that placed a much greater emphasis on science and technology.

Alongside curricular change was the appearance of greater numbers of women in American college classrooms. Women's names were appearing on the rosters in Iowa's colleges as early as 1855, and by the mid-1870s most collegiate institutions in the West were accepting female applicants into their programs. Enrollments were slow to increase, however. It is estimated that less than 1 percent of the nation's young women were attending college in 1870 and 20 years later the total was still no more than about 2.5 percent. Family obligations and a lack of independent funds were among the obstacles that bright young women faced when contemplating college at the time. Nonetheless, while few in number, women staked their claims in the institutions they began to occupy, quickly allaying any concerns about their academic abilities. The first female ever to enroll at Colby College, Mary Low Carver, graduated with honors in 1875 and was class valedictorian.[26]

Female enrollments in America's colleges would change the character and culture of the campus and classroom, as would the appearance of foreign students. A handful of international students, most from Latin America, had studied in the United States as early as the 1760s, but it would be another century before a significant number of the world's internationally mobile students would be drawn to the rising quality of American higher education. From that point the United States would host ever-greater numbers of international students and scholars from around the world.

The turn of the twentieth century through World War I saw a weakening of the American economy, which was financially crippling for some colleges and universities, and the period witnessed a decline in the number of higher education institutions. Nonetheless the modern research university took its shape during this period. Postwar prosperity and a fresh perspective on higher education caused college attendance to almost double between 1920 and 1930, while degrees conferred increased at a higher rate from 53,000 to nearly 140,000.[27] The next great leap in college enrollment and degrees came when members of the armed forces returned home from World War II. Following closely behind would be thousands of foreign students, from every region of the world.

Notes

1. Frederick Rudolph, *The American College and University, A History* (Athens, GA and London: The University of Georgia Press, 1990): 3–5.
2. Ibid., 5.
3. Ibid., 4–6.
4. Ibid., 4–22.
5. Christopher J. Lucas, *American Higher Education* (New York: St. Martin's Press, 1995).
6. Rudolph, 23–43.
7. John Thelin, *A History of American Higher Education* (Johns Hopkins University Press, 2004): 1–9.

8. Rudolph, 21.
9. Thelin, 21.
10. Rudolph, 68–85.
11. Richard Hofstadter and Wilson Smith, eds. *American Higher Education: A Documentary History* (Chicago: Chicago University Press, 1961).
12. William E. Burns, *Science and Technology in Colonial America* (Westport, CT: Greenwood Press, 2005).
13. Barbara L. Narendra, "Benjamin Silliman and the Peabody Museum," *Discovery*, Vol. 14 (1979): 13–29; also see Rudolph, *The American College and University*, 222.
14. Rudolph, 223.
15. A. Hunter Dupree, *Asa Gray, 1810–1888* (Cambridge: Belknap Press of Harvard University, 1959).
16. Samuel Elliot Morrison, *There Centuries of Harvard 1636–1936* (Cambridge: Harvard University Press, 1936): 230–231; also see Teresa Brawner Bevis and Christopher J. Lucas, *International Students in American Colleges and Universities: A History* (New York: Palgrave Macmillan, 2007): 31–40.
17. Rudolph, 125–127.
18. William M. Brickman, "Historical Development of Governmental Interest in International Higher Education," in *Governmental Policy and International Education*, Stewart Fraser, ed. (New York: John Wiley & Sons, Inc., 1965): 29.
19. Jurgen Herbst, "The 1828 Yale Report," *The Journal of the Classical Tradition*, Vol. 11, no. 2 (2004): 213.
20. Jonathan R. Cole, *The Great American University* (Public Affairs Publishers, 2002): 22–24.
21. Anna Galicich, *The German Americans* (New York: Chelsea House, 1989); also see Theodore Huebener, *The Germans in America* (Philadelphia, PA: Chilton Book Co., 1962).
22. Rudolph, 373–393; also see John S. Brubacher and Willis Rudy, *Higher Education in Transition: A History of American Colleges and Universities, 1636–1976*, 3rd edition (New York: Harper & Row, 1976): 131–136.
23. Nathan M. Sorber, *Land-Grant Colleges and Popular Revolt: The Origins of the Morrill Act and the Reform of Higher Education* (Cornell University Press, 2018).
24. Paul H. Mattingly, "The Political Culture of America's Antebellum Colleges," *History of Higher Education Annual*, Vol. 17 (1997): 73–95.
25. Rudolph, 44–67.
26. Rudolph, 307–328.
27. NCES, 2008.

REFERENCES

Bevis, Teresa Brawner, and Christopher J. Lucas. 2007. *International Students in American Colleges and Universities: A History*. New York: Palgrave Macmillan.

Brickman, William M. 1965. Historical Development of Governmental Interest in International Higher Education. In *Governmental Policy and International Education*, ed. Stewart Fraser. New York: John Wiley & Sons, Inc.

Brubacher, John S., and Willis Rudy. 1976. *Higher Education in Transition: A History of American Colleges and Universities 1636–1976*. New York: Harper & Row.

Burns, William E. 2005. *Science and Technology in Colonial America*. Westport, CT: Greenwood Press.

Cole, Jonathan R. 2002. *The Great American University*. Public Affairs Publishers.

Dupree, A. Hunter. 1959. *Asa Gray, 1810–1888*. Cambridge, MA: Belknap Press of Harvard University.

Galicich, Anna. 1989. *The German Americans*. New York: Chelsea House.

Herbst, Jurgen. 2004. The 1828 Yale Report. *Journal of the Classical Tradition* 11 (2): 227.

Hofstadter, Richard, and Wilson Smith, eds. 1961. *American Higher Education: A Documentary History*. Chicago University Press.

Huebener, Theodore. 1962. *The Germans in America*. Philadelphia, PA: Chilton Book Co.

Lucas, Christopher J. 1995. *American Higher Education*. New York: St. Martin's Press.

Mattingly, Paul H. 1997. The Political Culture of America's Antebellum Colleges. *History of Higher Education Annual* 17: 73–96.

Morrison, Samuel Elliot. 1936. *Three Centuries of Harvard 1636–1936*. Cambridge MA: Harvard University Press.

Narendra, Barbara L. 1979. Benjamin Silliman and the Peabody Museum. *Discovery* 14: 13–29.

Rudolph, Frederick. 1990. *The American College and University, A History*. Athens, GA and London: The University of Georgia Press.

Sorber, Nathan M. 2018. *Land-Grant Colleges and Popular Revolt: The Origins of the Morrill Act and the Reform of Higher Education*. Cornell University Press.

Thelin, John R. 2004. *A History of American Higher Education*. Baltimore, MD: Johns Hopkins University Press.

CHAPTER 4

Education Exchange in America in the 1800s

The appeal of universities in the United States was rising, a trend that did not escape European educators, who were at first critical of America's academic credentials. The attraction was abetted through exchange efforts sponsored by foreign governments that now viewed the United States as their best means of acquiring long-overdue knowledge about science, technology, and the military. Simon Bolivar of Venezuela would send his adopted son to learn at West Point around 1830, concluding that America was his best choice for such an acquisition. China, making the same determination, sent 120 students to the United States in the 1870s. The first Japanese students were admitted to Amherst College about the same time. This was also the period when America initiated its immigration policies.

From Europe's Perspective

In 1800, the United States was still a fledgling nation, but by the close of the century the country would stake its claim as a major power in the Western Hemisphere, transform the economy from agriculture to manufacturing, and suffer the schism of a civil war. Among the many important nineteenth-century events and developments in America would be the Louisiana Purchase, the War of 1812, the Monroe Doctrine, Jacksonian democracy, abolition, the war with Mexico, the Civil War, the Industrial Revolution, and the closing of the western frontier. The century also witnessed the continuous rise of American scholarship.

Early nineteenth-century assessments of higher education in America were fraught with criticisms. An illustration of that was the testimony of Thomas Hamilton, a Scottish novelist who chronicled the story of his tour of American colleges in 1831, in a publication titled "Education and National Characteristics." In it he describes his tour of Harvard College, saying that the buildings were not extensive but commodious. The library, the largest one in the United States, was not terribly impressive, said Hamilton, as it contained only about 30,000 volumes. The course of academics was designed to be completed in four years, and at its termination candidates were granted the degree of bachelor of arts, following the ordeal of examination. In three more years, one could earn the degree of master. Enrollments at the time were under 250, and students were housed either on campus or in the neighboring houses. Religious tenets were not taught, reported Hamilton, but the spirit was unquestionably Unitarian. "In extent, in opulence, and in number of students, the establishment is not equal even to the smallest of our Scottish universities."[1]

Hamilton further concluded that American colleges were not yet prepared to educate foreigners, citing the story of a young and wealthy Haitian who had come to Harvard with great hopes, but, in spite of his family's riches, was unable to secure decent accommodations because of his color. In Hamilton's view, the young Haitian, or for that matter any student of color, would be better off choosing a European school. In England such a student would have felt quite secure. Theaters, operas, concerts, coaches, chariots, cabs, wagons, steamboats, railway carriages, and air balloons would be at the student's disposal.[2]

English clergyman Isaac Fidler took an even dimmer view of American higher education. A classical scholar and linguist, Fidler came to America in 1831 with his family to explore teaching opportunities. He penned an article about his experience, titled "An Immigrant's Anecdotal View of the State of Learning in America," in which he described his overall disappointment, first with his reception and also with the lack of teaching opportunities, which he apparently encountered everywhere. Even Harvard, he wrote, had no appointment for a Sanskrit or Persian scholar. Having toured most of the prominent institutions, Fidler was embittered and disillusioned with US higher education. He asserted that Americans lacked refinement and took pleasure in humbling and scorning those whose manners differed from their own. He warned parents that if they allowed their children to mix with Americans, their conduct would be contaminated with republican principles, causing them to be "a source of hourly vexation."[3]

Criticisms from the Europeans began to shift in the latter part of the century. In an 1876 article titled "French Views of American Schools," Ferdinand Eduard Buisson described how American higher learning was improving. A French educator and politician, Buisson was well known as the editor (1882–1893) of the *Dictionaire de pedagogie et d'instruction primaire*. The French government had appointed Buisson and his assistant to examine and report on American scholarship, mainly focusing on public schools, but also reviewing education in general. Buisson's report would reflect a new European appreciation of American education. If any people ever used the power of education or made public instruction a supreme guarantee of its liberties and the condition of prosperity, he declared, that is most assuredly the people of the United States.[4]

Near the end of the century, Emil Hausknecht offered similar words of praise in his 1893 article, "German Criticism on American Education." A German educator and professor at the University of Japan in Tokyo and later the director of the second *Realschule* in Berlin, Hausknecht traveled around America, visiting places of interest and institutions of higher learning as he took copious notes. He found open expressions of exciting ideas on the part of leading persons in science and promoters of popular education. "He who has seen with his own eyes," wrote Hausknecht, "will know that in that country, though it is partly still in primitive development [is] everywhere progressing with gigantic strides, and disregarding Old World prejudices."[5] Hausknecht's report described the American college as a kind of intermediate institution between Germany's gymnasium and university, representing the upper grades of the former and the first two years at the latter. American institutions typically have dormitories, he said, remote from the noisy din of the cities and surrounded by park-like grounds. He described physical exercises, America's homage to the German gymnasium, to be very popular on the various campuses. With few exceptions he witnessed no beer drinking or smoking but described a student's life as gay and full of fun.[6] A passion for learning had seized the American population, he claimed, but there was still room for improvement.

English professor Michael E. Sadler, who worked with both Trinity and Oxford Universities, recorded his comments in "Impressions of American Education" in 1902. At rare intervals in the history of a nation, he wrote, there comes a great outburst of physical and intellectual energy which, with overmastering power, is carried forward by the masses of the people. Sadler believed that the United States was undergoing such a movement. In his view, American higher education had profoundly changed the organization of universities through the development of what were called "elective studies," which he believed was a direct outgrowth of America's appreciation of individuality.[7]

The First Foreign Students in America

Francisco de Miranda of Venezuela may have enrolled at Yale in or around 1784, although records are unclear. If he was indeed America's first foreign student, he set a colorful precedent. A revolutionary who sought to unite Hispanic America from the Mississippi to Cape Horn, Miranda was an international adventurer, friend of George Washington and Alexander Hamilton, and was rumored to be one of Catherine the Great's favorite paramours.

Another of the first foreign students was Fernando Bolivar of Caracas, nephew of Simon Bolivar, who came to the United States in 1822 at age 12. He would attend Germantown Academy in Pennsylvania, while his revolutionary uncle was fighting to create independent nations in South America. Having no children of his own, Simon Bolivar legally adopted Fernando when the boy's father died, and, because he admired Thomas Jefferson, sent his new son to study at the University of Virginia. The elder Bolivar penned a letter to the university faculty detailing how he wished Fernando to be educated, expressing appreciation to the institution for taking special care of his every need. The letter now reposes in Alderman Library's manuscript collection. Unfortunately, Fernando was forced to leave when a commercial house that had been managing his funds went bankrupt. James Madison generously offered the distressed student the use of a brick cottage on the university grounds, but Fernando returned to Venezuela, where he built a distinguished diplomatic career. Among his notable achievements were his service as a member of the Venezuelan Congress from 1847 until 1850; and his term as governor of the province of Caracas, Venezuela, in 1853 and 1854. His brief stay was important, not just because he was the University of Virginia's first Latin American student, but also because his attendance would mark the beginning of a long-standing academic relationship between the university and Latin America. Portraits of Fernando and Simon Bolivar, gifts to the university from the Venezuelan government in the 1940s, can be found in the Casa Bolivar.[8] Fernando's memoir, *Recuerdos y Reminiscencias*, was published in Paris in 1873 under the pseudonym "Rivolba," an anagram of Bolivar. In it he describes his days at the University of Virginia, and his admiration for the eminent men Jefferson had secured for the faculty.

Mario Garcia Menocal was another of America's first Latin American students. Son of a Cuban sugar plantation owner, Menocal studied initially at the Institute of Chappaqua, New York, and then the Maryland College of Agriculture, later attending Cornell University, where he graduated in 1888 with an engineering degree. He would become the third president of Cuba, serving from 1913 until 1921.[9]

China

Latin American students were first to arrive in America's colleges, but they were isolated and few in number. When Chinese students came to the United States in the latter half of the nineteenth century, they arrived as a large group and were an unmistakable presence in nineteenth-century Connecticut. In the past 150 years, China has sent more students to earn degrees in America than any other country, and they have influenced every component of American higher education exchange. Today China remains the top foreign supplier of students to US colleges and universities. Therefore, the story of the first Chinese students in America and the circumstances that brought them are covered here with considerable detail.

On the 17th of November 1828, Yung Wing (Rong Hong) was born in the village of Zhuhai near the Portuguese colony of Macao. When he was old enough, his parents broke with Chinese tradition by enrolling him in the nearby Christian missionary school instead of the Confucian school where his older brother had attended. Unforeseen results would emerge from their unorthodox choice. Among other things, their son would become the first Chinese citizen ever to have a "completely Western" education, from primary school through college.

When Yung Wing was seven years old, his father accompanied him to the little missionary school that was run by the flaxen-haired Mrs. Gutzlaff, a robust English lady and wife of Reverend Charles Gutzlaff. Yung Wing would recall the meeting much later in his autobiography, writing that he had trembled with fear at her imposing proportions.[10]

He would spend the next four years at the missionary school, learning English and other subjects, until the news of his father's death arrived, accompanied by a mandate that he return home to his village. With no means of support, his mother needed help to survive, and all of the children were put to work. Yung Wing, the youngest in the family, took on the job of hawking candy throughout his village, rising at three o'clock every morning and often working late into the evening. It was an exhausting routine that netted the equivalent of about 25 cents a day. He later took a job in a rice field, where, as he recorded in his diary, his English skills first proved an advantage. The head gleaner had heard a rumor that Yung Wing, his new hire, could speak a foreign language. Curious about how it might sound, he asked the boy to demonstrate. Standing knee-deep in a rice paddy, Yung Wing complied as ordered, speaking a number of unrelated sentences in English, to the delight of the boss and the surrounding crew. As a reward for the entertainment, the head gleaner gave Yung Wing all the sheaves of rice he could carry home that day.[11]

Yung Wing had little hope of ever returning to school, but an unexpected visit from Dr. Benjamin Hobson, a missionary from Macao, changed everything. Hobson had been searching for the boy for some time, in his effort to honor a request made by Yung Wing's former teacher, Mrs. Gutzlaff. After the completion of her teaching term, before returning to the United States, she implored Dr. Hobson to try to locate one of her former students, an especially bright and amiable boy named Yung Wing. She had seen promise in the boy's abilities and hoped Hobson might visit the child and convince him to continue his education at the Morrison Society School. The school had been named after Robert Morrison, the first Protestant missionary to work in China.

If Yung made the decision to honor Mrs. Gutzlaff's wishes and come to Macao, and if his mother approved, he could work at the local hospital to offset expenses. For Yung Wing the welcome news "had more the sound of heaven in it."[12] With his mother's blessing the boy set out to resume his English studies at the Morrison Society School. It was here he would meet his mentor, Reverend Samuel Robbins Brown, who was a seasoned instructor at the school and a proud graduate of Yale University. Brown was a popular teacher who loved telling stories about his boyhood in faraway America and his happy days at Yale. They were colorful tales that inspired many of the children to wish they could visit this magical place. As Brown completed his tenure and was making arrangements to return to the United States, he surprised everyone by announcing his plan to take a few of his students back to America with him, to continue their education. The reverend asked for any interested students to stand up, and Yung Wing was the first on his feet.

Reverend Brown left the Morrison Society School in the winter of 1847, accompanied by Yung Wing and two of his classmates, Wong Shing and Wong Foon, who were brothers. They set sail for the United States on the *Huntress*. Andrew Shortrede, a Scottish proprietor and editor of *The China*

Mail, and American merchants A.A. Ritchie and A.A. Campbell, were among the generous patrons who provided funding for the boys' living expenses to cover the first two years. Free passage to America on the *Huntress* was provided by the Olyphant brothers from New York, who were in the shipping business. Together with a large cargo of tea, Reverend Brown and the three boys departed from Whampoa on January 4, bound for New York and aided by a strong north wind. Their voyage was long but uneventful, except for a violent electrical storm, an exciting display that Yung Wing recorded in his diary, describing a howling wind that whistled "like a host of invisible Furies." He added that he had enjoyed the wild scene "hugely."[13] The ship would safely dock in New York harbor on April 12. They traveled on to New Haven for a brief meeting with Yale's president, Jeremiah Day, the author of the earlier-mentioned Yale Report.

The party then left for East Windsor, where the Reverend Brown and his wife Elizabeth kept their residence. The boys would reside with Reverend Brown's mother, Mrs. Phoebe Brown, in a small cottage a half mile from the Monson Academy. Using the funds supplied by their benefactors, the boys paid a fee of about $1.25 a week, according to Yung's memoirs, for board and lodging, which included fuel, light, and washing. The boys were responsible for cleaning their rooms, and during the winter they cut, split, and stacked their own firewood.

The two Wong brothers would return to China before the end of their first term, leaving Yung Wing on his own. Funding had been the problem. Both boys were offered additional financing by American church societies, should they agree to use their education to become Christian missionaries, but neither felt such a calling. Their benefactor Andrew Shortrede also offered to help, on the condition they attend the University of Edinburgh to study medicine. He envisioned his homeland, Scotland, training and producing the first Chinese physician. Wong Foon accepted Shortrede's offer. He graduated from the University of Edinburgh's medical school before returning to China, where he would gain a reputation as one of its most skilled surgeons, and for years he administered the London Mission Hospital at Canton (Guangzhou). Wong Shing, the other brother, returned to China because of health reasons, then worked with the London Missionary Society, assisting Dr. James Legge in his translations of Chinese classics.[14]

When it was time for Yung Wing to apply to Yale, his funds were nearly depleted. He was rescued through the generosity of a Southern women's group called the Ladies Association of Savannah, Georgia, an organization in which Reverend Brown's sister was a long-standing member. Now armed with funds to cover the first year, Yung Wing went to New Haven for his entrance examination, then began his studies at Yale in the fall of 1850, the only Chinese in a class of 98 freshmen. His graduation in 1854 was significant in the annals of education exchange history, as he would be the first Chinese ever to earn a college degree in the United States. There is sketchy evidence of a few other Chinese students who studied in the United States between 1817 and 1825. One was recorded as attending a school, although not at the college level, that was established by the American Board of Commissioners for Foreign Missions in Cornwall, Connecticut. Another student named Zeng Laishun is reported to have attended college classes in the United States in the 1840s, but he did not receive a degree.[15]

By the time of his graduation, Yung Wing had been in the United States for almost eight years. Paramount in his mind, he wrote, was the question of how to use American education to modernize China. The lamentable condition of China weighed on his spirit, and in his despondency sometimes wished he had never been educated, as the experience had "revealed to me responsibilities which the sealed eye of ignorance can never see."[16]

The end of the Taiping Rebellion, in 1860, was a turning point for China. The Imperial Palace had been devastated along with the beautiful *Yuanming Yuan*, the Garden of Perfect Brightness. The years of fighting and the leveling of the palace had weakened China, not just economically and militarily, but also emotionally. Western troops had helped China end the rebellion, and Chinese officials, who had witnessed the fighting firsthand, could no longer disavow the superiority of Western forces. Government leaders now conceded that China must acquire new and modern technology from the West in order to survive. In the opinion of historian Y.C. Wang, China's wound was too deep to be ignored and the path was prepared for reform.[17] Even so, the idea that China needed anything from outside its borders was a problematic admission for any official of the Qing court.

For 2000 years, even before the Han dynasty established power in 202 BCE, China had considered itself to be the center of the world. The self-proclaimed Celestial Kingdom, *Khongguo* had for centuries rejected all outside influences as inferior and regarded all citizens from beyond its borders as barbarians.[18] The Qing dynasty, the last of China's long dynastic tradition, had been conventionally unsupportive of any education beyond the Confucian classics. For centuries there had been an occasional acceptance of foreign scholars, *liuxuesheng*, from nearby countries such as Japan and Korea, but that was the extent of China's educational reach. A few Chinese had traveled to other regions of Asia for various types of learning over the centuries, but not until the nineteenth did China begin to seek knowledge from the West. The military defeats of the Opium Wars and the rebellions that followed—the Taiping Rebellion in the south, the Nian Rebellion in the northeast, and the Muslim revolts in the northwest—finally and forever severed the ancient belief that the emperor was nothing less than the Son of Heaven, who governed the world from China.

Further degenerating China was the enforcement of several treaties, including the Treaty of Nanjing that ended the first Opium War in 1845 and the Treaty of Tientsin. Among other things, the treaties demanded huge reparations by the Qing government, rendered China helpless in prohibiting the entrance of Protestant missionaries, and limited the government's right to try Westerners accused of committing crimes in China.[19] To make things worse, treaty terms recognized Western authority over trade in various regions of China and forced the opening of multiple ports along its southern coast for further trading, as Kowloon and Hong Kong were ceded to the British. China was losing its grip of authority over its own affairs, as Britain, France, and America each demanded extraterritoriality.

Something had to be done to strengthen China, and even the most conservative leaders now agreed that advancing education was imperative. Among the options the Chinese government considered was the possibility of importing Western technology.[20] Various approaches were considered. One idea was to establish modern schools in China and bring in foreign experts to teach Western technology and languages. Another idea was to send periodic delegations from China to the West to observe technology in action, witness the secrets of Western wealth and power, and then bring back armaments to study.[21] Around 1863 the Qing court was leaning toward a third option—sending students to Western universities to earn degrees in science and technology. Those in favor pointed out that the time involved in sending students to study in the West was similar to the time required to learn the Confucian classics in preparation for the traditional imperial examinations, which for centuries had prepared students for bureaucratic service. In the same amount of time, proponents argued, Chinese students might acquire far more usable knowledge from the West than if they studied the classics.

Viceroys Zeng Guofan and Li Hongzhang, the Taiping Rebellion war heroes who had since been elevated to positions of government leadership, had already taken a number of important organizational steps designed to lend support to the study-abroad idea. The Bureau of Foreign Affairs, for example, was put into operation in 1861 to aid collaboration with other nations and the College of Foreign Languages, including English, opened in 1862. The School of Western Language and Science was established the year after that.

It was Yung Wing's influence that led the Chinese leaders to choose the United States for their educational experiment. Following the Taiping Rebellion, he worked temporarily at a tea packing company in the port of Kew Keang, then started a commission business. It was here that he saw the first ray of hope—that the educational scheme he had dreamed of since his college life at Yale might materialize. The ray of hope came in a letter from an old friend, Chang Shi Kwei, who had risen to become an assistant to Viceroy Zeng Guofan. In the letter Chang wrote that the viceroy had heard of Yung Wing and wanted to meet him. Fearful that the invitation could have something to do with his near-allegiance with the now-defeated Taiping rebels, Yung Wing declined the invitation, using the excuse that it was tea season and impossible for him to leave.[22]

Two months later a second letter arrived, this time from Li Sien Lan, a distinguished Chinese mathematician Yung had met in Shanghai. Li Sien Lan had told Viceroy Zeng of Yung's unique, completely Western education, and of his great desire to help China prosper through education abroad. This information prompted His Excellency to seek an introduction, with the intention of asking Yung to work in service to the state government in Kgan Khing, to help with a special project. In his memoirs, Yung Wing recorded the meeting, describing Zeng Guofan as a perfect nobleman and gentleman. He agreed to help the viceroy.[23]

Viceroy Zeng's experiments in building China's first steam vessels at the arsenals in Shanghai had provided him with some understanding of the intricate network of technical skills used by the modern militaries of the West. Now he hoped to strengthen China's military by introducing those same technical skills as rapidly as possible, by means of training schools at the arsenal sites.[24] It turned out that the reason Yung and others were summoned had to do with the development of a machine shop in Kow Chang Mew, about four miles northwest of Shanghai. The Viceroy put Yung Wing in charge of finding and purchasing the world's best machines and machine parts to serve as a foundation for the project. Yung was allowed to decide from which country the machines would be purchased—England, France, or the United States. He lost no time in selecting the United States.

Yung crossed the Atlantic in one of the Cunard steamers and landed in New York in the spring of 1864, ten years after his graduation from Yale and just in time to attend the decennial reunion of his class. The American Civil War was still going on, which meant that nearly all of the machine shops in the country, particularly those in New England, were busy filling government orders. After an extensive search, the Putnam Machine Company in Fitchburg, Massachusetts, agreed to fill Yung Wing's order for machines, which they said would take about six months to complete. Yung took advantage of the waiting period to attend his class reunion in New Haven. He also made a side trip to Washington to offer his service as a volunteer courier for the armed services for the six-month duration.[25] Naturalized in 1854, the year he graduated from Yale, Yung was a bona fide American citizen, and he believed it was nothing less than his duty to show his patriotism and loyalty for his adopted country by offering service during a time of war. Brigadier General Barnes of Springfield, Massachusetts, a man Yung had met as a student at Yale, happened to be the man in charge of the Volunteer Department in Washington. He suggested Yung Wing's time would be better spent on his educational mission.

Anson Burlingame

As with most histories, certain individuals stand out as leaders—inspired people who dare to take action and pave definitive paths for others to follow. A man who shared Yung's passion for building stronger ties between China and America was Anson Burlingame. His actions would directly affect Yung's success in channeling China's education trade toward the United States.

After practicing law in Boston, Burlingame developed an interest in politics, and associated himself with the Free Soil party. A popular figure in the region, Burlingame was elected to the state senate; then two years later he was elected to the US House of Representatives on the American Party ballot. In 1855 he changed his political affiliation to help establish the new Republican Party in Massachusetts, after which he served in Congress for three terms, until 1861. President Abraham Lincoln selected Burlingame to be the US minister to Austria, but the Austrian imperial government, which had strongly objected to Burlingame's outspoken support of Sardinian and Hungarian independence, rejected his appointment. In a twist of fate, Burlingame was reassigned to China.[26]

Anson Burlingame's relationship with China would be extraordinary, and he would grow to love the Chinese people. It was his hope to help strengthen Sino-American relations and, recognizing a window of diplomatic opportunity following the Second Opium War, he worked to initiate a reconciliation between the two countries. In Burlingame's view, America's posture of arrogance toward China had served only to support those in the Qing court who were opposed to anything leading to greater contact with the West.[27] In an 1862 letter to Secretary of State William Seward, Burlingame wrote that "If the treaty powers could agree among themselves to the neutrality of China, and together secure order in the treaty ports, and give their moral support to that party in China in favor of order, the interest of humanity would be sub-served."[28] Burlingame's pleas rallied support from important officials, among them China's Ministry of Foreign Affairs, British Consul Robert Hart, and British minister to China, Rutherford Alcock.

Also advocating for Sino-American reconciliation was Xu Jiyu, a member of China's Ministry of Foreign Affairs, who had become an ardent admirer of "kingless America" and George Washington. Xu said the United States "has a territory of ten thousand li, but it does not have princes and dukes ... public affairs are placed before the public ... a truly unprecedented system. What a wonder!"[29] Some of Xu's inspiring words would later be inscribed on a granite block and placed on the Washington Monument. As a gesture of his gratitude, Anson Burlingame presented Xu with a copy of one of Gilbert Stuart's portraits of George Washington.

Supported and befriended by important officials such as Xu, Anson Burlingame's influence and respect reached a high level, so much so that when he stepped down from his America post, the Chinese government asked him to stay in China and assume a new position, this time representing the Chinese government as China's ambassador-at-large. It was unprecedented. Never in its long history had the Celestial Kingdom offered its representation to any non-Chinese. The decision was an extraordinary demonstration of China's desire to improve long-strained Sino-American relations, with the help of a unique individual who genuinely loved and understood both countries.

A humble and grateful Burlingame said that "when the oldest nation in the world, containing one-third of the human race, seeks, for the first time, to come into relations with the West, and requests the youngest nation, through its representative, to act as the medium of such change, the mission is not one to be solicited or rejected."[30] Prince Gong presented Burlingame with the imperial decree, written on heavy yellow parchment (the royal color) and wrapped in yellow satin brocade and encased in a yellow box. Sir Rutherford Alcock affirmed that it was the greatest compliment ever given to any man.

In 1868 Burlingame traveled to the United States, accompanied by a mission from China, to negotiate what was essentially a revision of the 1858 Treaty of Tientsin. Drafted by Secretary of State Seward, and signed on July 28, the resulting agreement was known thereafter as the Burlingame Treaty, or the Burlingame-Seward Treaty.[31] According to its terms, the United States and China were to recognize the inherent and inalienable right of a person to change his home and allegiance, and also the mutual advantage of the free migration and emigration of their citizens and subjects, respectively for purpose of curiosity or as permanent residents. Also included in its terms was an agreement for both nations to respect the territorial sovereignty of the other.[32]

At the insistence of the United States was the inclusion of the free-immigration provision, designed to counter the Chinese government's prohibition of its subjects emigrating. Article VII stated that Chinese subjects should be allowed to enjoy all the privileges of the public educational institutions under the control of the government in the United States.[33] Reciprocal privileges were provided for Americans, making the treaty an important influence in the establishment of the first Sino-American education exchanges.

A Plea to the Imperial Court

Back in New England, Yung Wing's orders for machines had been filled. In the spring of 1865 they were loaded onto a ship in New York harbor, bound for Shanghai. When the machinery arrived in China, Yung went immediately to Zeng Guofan's headquarters to report on the project, and to give him a tour of what had been brought from America. It was the first time the viceroy had seen machinery, or how it worked. During this tour Yung took the opportunity to again initiate a conversation with the viceroy about the future of education in China. Yung convinced Zeng to annex a school next to the arsenal where Chinese students might be taught mechanical engineering, thus enabling China to eliminate, in time, the employment of foreign mechanical engineers and machinists.

Later a translating department was established for the school under the direction of John Fryer, who took on the task of transcribing many of the basic works of the various branches of science into Chinese.[34] Yung Wing's success with the machine project prompted the Qing court to award him the fifth civil rank (there were nine) within the bureaucratic hierarchy, in appreciation for his service. Yung was thus given the privilege of wearing an elegant robe embroidered with silver pheasants at full-dress occasions, accompanied by a hat adorned with a peacock feather, a sign of great honor. His acceptance among the conservative members of the Imperial Court was now decidedly elevated.

Encouraged by his new status, Yung put together a proposal for the Qing court to consider. In it he suggested that the Chinese government select youths to be educated in the West in preparation for public service in China. One hundred and twenty students could be sent, Yung suggested, in increments of 30 students per year, over a period of four years. If the initial dispatches were successful, the venture could be continued indefinitely.

Any official review of Yung's proposals would have to wait, however, because about the same time the document arrived in Peking, Prime Minister Wen Seang's mother passed away. In keeping with Chinese tradition, her death obliged Wen to go into mourning for a period of 27 months and his attention to public affairs was put on hold. Just three months after the passing of his mother, Wen also died, and the official reading of Yung's proposals was again delayed. It would not be until the Tientsin Massacre, in early 1870, that another opportunity for Yung to offer his proposal would present itself.

It was very late one night when Governor Ting sent orders that Yung Wing should be awakened for an important message. Viceroy Zeng and the other commissioners had unanimously agreed to sign their names in supporting Yung's proposal. The news disallowed any further sleep, Yung recorded in his memoirs. "I felt as though I were treading on clouds and walking on air."[35]

The choice to send the first Chinese students to the United States was heavily influenced by the fact that Yung Wing had the advantage of personal experience with the American system, and a first-hand understanding of the problems that Chinese students might confront. The Burlingame Treaty had been another important motivation. Choosing America would demonstrate China's respect for Anson Burlingame's extraordinary efforts toward the promotion of peaceful collaboration and cooperation between the two countries.[36] The decision was not without controversy. Conservatives questioned the wisdom of exposing Chinese youth to Western culture for extended periods of time, and some questioned Yung Wing's patriotism, as he had a close allegiance to the United States.

Viceroy Zeng, in a wise and calculated effort to balance conservative and new perspectives, directed Governor Ting to recommend a man who was known to uphold Confucian ideals. Ting recommended Chin Lan Pin, a member of the Hanlin college who had been educated in the traditional Confucian way. Chin would be chosen to serve as Yung's co-administrator in the operations of the newly authorized mission, thus alleviating any doubt about the nature of the project. Chin could not have been happier. In the winter of 1870, he quit his position at the Board of Punishment in Peking, where he had spent 20 years, and, even though he had almost no practical experience in the world of business or education, assumed his duties as co-commissioner of the new Chinese Educational Mission (CEM). He and Yung Wing were to work as a team, to bring China's first students to America.

With policies basically in place, a preparatory school to accommodate the first 30 boys was begun in Shanghai. Liu Kai Sing, who had served for many years as the viceroy's first secretary in the Department of Memorials, was appointed superintendent upon its completion and through his efforts all four installments of students would be prepared for their trip to America.[37]

Yung Wing's proposal was to be carried out much as he had intended. Students were to be dispatched to America over a period of years, to earn degrees in engineering, business, and the sciences. Because they were dependents of the government, the boys would not have the option of withdrawing from their studies before completion, nor could they seek naturalization abroad or secure their own employment. Those who graduated were allowed a period of two years for travel before they were obliged to return to China and report to the Chinese Foreign Office. Then, awards of official rank and appointments to government service would be issued based on student evaluations submitted by the CEM commissioners, and the new knowledge would be put to good use for China. That was the plan.

THE CHINESE EDUCATIONAL MISSION

The boys chosen for the first dispatch ranged in age from ten to fifteen, and they were all from respectable parentage. Acceptance to the program was based on student evaluations, and a complete medical examination was mandatory. Recruited from various provinces, the boys were provided lessons in English and other subjects and were obliged to attend a preparatory school in Shanghai for at least six months before they were deemed ready for the voyage to America. Once their preparations were complete, the boys would be dispatched in four groups of 30. Students had to secure a signed letter from their parents or guardians, granting them permission to be sent abroad, and agreeing not to hold the Chinese government responsible for anything whatsoever that might go wrong. It was not a small decision, as the children would be gone for a period of perhaps 15 years. They would depart as boys and return as men.

The conservative co-commissioner Chin Lan Pin had been assigned the responsibility of assuring that the boys kept up with their knowledge of China and the Chinese language throughout their stay. After beginning their studies in the United States, they would be expected to undergo quarterly and annual examinations to gauge their progress in Chinese studies and at specific intervals commissioners were to summon the students together to read from the *Sacred Book of Imperial Edicts*. Two teachers, Yeh Shu Tung and Yung Yune Foo, were assigned to provide Chinese studies for the boys and an interpreter, Zeng Laishun, was also assigned to the project.

Financial issues would be handled by both commissioners.[38] The Chinese government had allotted an initial budget of 1,200,000 taels to finance the students' stay, but unanticipated expenses soon raised the figure to 1,489,800. The funds were to be set aside from the receipts of the Imperial Maritime Customs at Shanghai. It was a truly enormous sum for agricultural China to spend on education.[39]

Yale's president Noah Porter was among the first Americans contacted about the project. In February of 1872 Yung penned a letter to Porter, describing the Chinese government's intention to send its first dispatch of students to the United States later that same year. He sought his guidance in finding accommodations for the boys. Without hesitation, Porter agreed to help, and it was with his direction that housing was secured prior to their arrival.[40]

The first dispatch of 30 elegantly dressed Chinese boys, fresh from preparatory school and with baggage in tow, bade farewell to their families and friends and boarded a ship bound for *meiguo*, the beautiful country. From Shanghai there were stops at Nagasaki and Kobe, so it took a full week just to reach the port in Yokohama, Japan. It was during this stop that the boys first witnessed an "iron horse" or steam engine train, the sort that China would not build for another ten years.

Sailing ships had given way to steamships and the establishment of coaling stations in Japan had made possible a considerably faster passage across the Pacific. The party left Yokohama for San Francisco on the paddlewheel steamer *Great Republic*, which crossed the Pacific in three weeks. Almost a third of its first-class cabins were occupied by CEM students and their escorts. Relegated to steerage were about 1000 less fortunate passengers, comprised mostly of Cantonese laborers going to America to look for work or to seek their fortunes. To pass the time the boys were expected to study. They were also obliged to write to their families, letters that were exchanged mid-ocean with a ship going the opposite direction.

By all accounts, the CEM boys were warmly welcomed when they reached America. They stayed in San Francisco for three days, residing at the Occidental Hotel, an elegant facility that sported an elevator and running water, both hot and cold, wonders that boys would document in their journals. Group and individual photographs were taken at the nearby study of Thomas Houseworth and Company, and the boys were introduced to a number of prominent residents (Fig. 4.1).

The weeklong journey from Oakland, California, to Springfield, Massachusetts, was on a railway that had been constructed just a few years earlier, chiefly through the efforts of hundreds of Chinese laborers. The Central Pacific transported the CEM party first to Ogden, Utah, and then they took the Union Pacific on to Omaha. The Chicago and Rock Island took them from Omaha to Chicago, the Lake Shore and Michigan Southern on to Buffalo, New York, and then the New York Central on to Albany. Finally, the Boston and Albany delivered them safely to the station in Springfield. At every stop, luggage and supplies had to be transferred. At long last they arrived in Hartford, Connecticut, and were met at the station by an elated Yung Wing, who was there in advance to make the preparatory arrangements. With the approval of Noah Porter and help from B.G. "Birdsey" Northrop, the commissioner of education for Connecticut, an estimated 120 New England families had come forward to volunteer to host the boys in their homes.[41]

Life in New England would require considerable acclimation. Church was at the center of the lives of most local families, as religion was a significant component of New England society. Church activities were almost unavoidable, and in time most of the CEM boys participated in the various

Fig. 4.1 Chinese Educational Mission boys departing to the United States, 1872

happenings with their American families. Most were members of the Congregationalist Church, the predominant denomination in Connecticut and Massachusetts at the time. A few of the Chinese students converted to Christianity but for the most part the boys enjoyed the events offered by the churches while continuing to adhere to their traditional beliefs. The boys became Americanized rapidly, learning quickly how to communicate in the schoolroom, the churchyard, and on the playground.

Almost immediately the boys wanted to wear Western-style clothing like the other children instead of their assigned gowns, as teasing from their American classmates had reportedly resulted in some hurt feelings and a few black eyes. They would soon shed their gowns, and with them, according to a few reports, some of their dignified Chinese manners. Yung Wing supported the change of dress, as he had encountered the same sort of chiding when he first came to America, even though his conservative co-commissioner was unsupportive. The boys gradually adopted American clothing, but were ordered to maintain their queues, as the long braids symbolized obedience and loyalty to the Qing dynasty. They were allowed, as a compromise, to discontinue shaving their foreheads. A student found guilty of cutting off his braid would be returned to China, a fate that befell two of the CEM boys.[42]

During the CEM years a center of operation was needed. Headquarters were established at 400 Collins Street in Hartford, Connecticut, near the prestigious Nook neighborhood. The large three-story house could accommodate all of the CEM leaders and students at the same time with its meeting hall, sleeping quarters, kitchen facilities, and classrooms. Constructed under the supervision of Springfield architect Eugene C. Gardner, at the cost of about $55,000, the facility attracted Hartford's elite and many of the town's most influential citizens to its events. Connecticut's governor Charles B. Andrew was a guest.

Things were generally in place when the second installment of 30 students arrived in 1873. The third group arrived the following year. The final dispatch of Chinese students reached America in 1875, bringing the grand total to 120. With rare exception the boys progressed through their respective American high schools and academies successfully and began enrolling at Yale and other prominent institutions of higher education, where most continued to excel in and out of the classroom. Many took on some sort of nickname, either self-imposed or cast upon them in a spirit of friendship by their American classmates—"Flounder," Breezy Jack," "Charlie Cold Fish," Ajax," "Fighting Chinee," "Alligator," and "Big Nose," to name a few.[43] The young men participated enthusiastically in popular campus activities and many victories were won by the Orientals, CEM's baseball team at Yale. The Chinese students would leave their footprints on other time-honored bastions of Yale culture, such as the prestigious rowing team. Chung Mun-Yew was the coxswain for Yale's varsity rowing crew in both 1880 and 1881.

In most ways the project seemed idyllic, but its demise was eminent. With the last dispatch had arrived a new commissioner, Ou Ngoh Liang, sent to replace Chin Lan Pin. Then Ou himself was replaced by Woo Tsze Tung, a man Chin Lan pin had personally recommended to Viceroy Li Hongzhang. Woo was a conservative who, even before his arrival in New England, had regarded the CEM as subversive to the principles of Chinese culture. Yung began to suspect that Chin was trying to dismantle the project. It was soon discovered that Chin had been sending lists of grievances to Viceroy Li, alleging that the students were playing more than studying, and were losing their love for China. Yung was outraged. He quickly reassured Li that the stories were no more than malicious misrepresentations of the truth.[44]

But the dye had been cast, and the downfall was begun. It accelerated when Yung submitted a number of applications to the US State Department to seek admission for CEM students to the Military Academy at West Point and to the Naval Academy at Annapolis. From the Chinese perspective, it was understood that when the students were eligible, some would enroll in the military academies to learn America's secrets of military strategy and weaponry. The United States must have understood things differently, because the response from both institutions was the same, and it was clear—the Chinese students would not be admitted.[45] The Burlingame Treaty, enacted only a decade before in a spirit of friendship, was now in Yung's estimation "trampled underfoot unceremoniously and wantonly, and set aside as though no such treaty had ever existed."[46]

The CEM project happened at a time in America's history when prejudice against the Chinese was at an all-time high. The postwar period of acceptance toward immigrants had run its course, as the thousands of coolies and other so-called undesirables flooded into the country. For conservatives in China who had never supported the project, the growing atmosphere of hostility between the United States and China provided a convenient opportunity. Goaded by those in the ranks of the reactionary party who were also pressing for the recall, the viceroy finally yielded and agreed to end the project. The students were ordered to immediately return to China. In July of 1881 the first group of CEM students departed New England. The so-called first wave of Chinese students in America was officially over, and three decades would pass before significant numbers of Chinese students would return.

What Became of the CEM Boys?

Thirty years after the CEM boys were recalled to China, an article appeared in a 1910 issue of *The New York Times*, titled "Graduates of Our Colleges in High Posts in China." Included were stories about some of the CEM students.

Upon their return to China, most of the young men had been assigned to work in one of the new Self-Strengthening Movement (1861–1895) projects that were just getting underway. By this means, many of the CEM students became instrumental in the operations of new enterprises such as the Telegraph Administration, the Kaiping Mines, the Tianjin Naval Academy, the Tianjin Medical School, the Zongli Yamen, and the newly established diplomatic corps. The government also routed CEM students to the various technical colleges and institutions that had been established by Li Hongzhang in Tientsin.[47] It would take years for the young men to gain influence and status, but near the end of the Manchu reign, two former CEM students had risen to the rank of admiral and another had been appointed vice minister of the Chinese Navy. Many former CEM students eventually contributed substantially to China's modernization, according to the article, and some were establishing places of honor in Chinese history. Below are brief accounts of a few.

Jeme "Jimmy" Tien Yau, one of the original 30 CEM boys, would become one of China's most influential and honored engineers, and hailed as "the father of Chinese railroads." Many of the industry standards Jeme established in China during his years with the railroads are still in force today. Another CEM student, Liang Dunyan, became the Director of Beijing-Fengtian Railway. The former southpaw pitcher for the Orientals baseball team at Yale, Liang would also serve as president of Tianjin University, and in this capacity helped prepare students for study in the United States under the Boxer Indemnity program. In 1907 he was appointed comptroller general of Imperial Maritime Customs, then later held the position of vice president of the Board of Foreign Affairs. In 1910 Liang was appointed to minister-at-large for Europe and America, and in 1914 would also serve as minister of communications during the Qing restoration.[48]

First assigned to the Tongshan mines in 1899, Y.T. Woo was appointed assistant director and chief chemist at Kaiping Mining Company, where he would later organize miners to resist the Russian invading forces that were attempting to take over the company. In 1906 he served as assistant examiner for returned students from Europe and America and as adviser to the Board of Education.[49]

Wong "Breezy Jack" Kia-kah was known for his gift of eloquence. Wong had gone to America with the first CEM student detachment, where he attended both West Middle Public School and Hartford High School. At Yale, Wong was a member of the Orientals baseball team, and a member of Kappa Sigma Epsilon Freshmen Society. According to the 1875 *Yale Banner*, on his graduation Wong was one of ten students appointed to give an oration. Wong's first assignment upon returning to China was translator at Shanghai Water Conservancy Bureau and then later would be managing director of China merchants Steam Navigation Company and Government Telegraph Administration. In 1898 Wong was appointed secretary of the Imperial Railway. He also served as secretary to various princely envoys that the Chinese government sent to America and Europe. In 1902, as secretary to the embassy, Wong was sent to England by the imperial government to attend the coronation of King Edward VII. He returned to China via the United States, where he attended the Washington conference and met President Theodore Roosevelt. Wong would accompany Prince Pu Lun to the United States in 1904 to the St. Louis Exposition, to Washington, DC. Wong returned to the United States in 1905 as a member of the Chinese delegation at the Portsmouth Peace Conference in New Hampshire, which concluded the Russo-Japanese War. Wong was later diagnosed with nervous exhaustion and advised to recuperate in a health resort in Japan. While there, he entered a bathroom and was overcome by charcoal fumes, causing him to fall against a stove that overturned and burned him severely. He died a few hours later at Yokohama General Hospital.[50]

In the fourth dispatch in 1875 was 11-year-old Liang Cheng, who would attend Phillips Andover Academy. Liang went on to work with the Ministry of Foreign Affairs and served in Europe and was knighted in England in 1897. A year later he accompanied Prince Chun to Berlin to officially apologize to the Kaiser court for the killing of German subjects in Shandong; then from 1903 to 1907 he served as China's minister to the United States and to Germany from 1910 until the end of the Qing dynasty. During his term as minister to the United States, Liang was instrumental in convincing Theodore Roosevelt to remit the excess portion of the American share of the Boxer indemnity for educational exchange scholarships.[51]

Tang Shaoyi (Tong Shao Yi), another of the former CEM students, went on to gain a high position with the Chinese government. Tang had come to the United States with the third dispatch of CEM students when he was 12 years old, first attending Hooker Street Grammar School in Springfield and then Hartford Public School, where he graduated with honors. He enrolled at Columbia, but after only a brief attendance the mission was recalled, and Tang was obliged to return to China. By 1899 he was chief political adviser to Yuan Shikai in Shandong and head of the provincial trade bureau. He would be in Tianjin during the Boxer Rebellion to help handle both the chaotic aftermath and the foreign claims for reparation. Tang was appointed customs *daotai* at Tianjin in 1901, and from 1903 to 1904 he served as superintendent of Beiyang University. In 1904 he was appointed as a special commissioner for Tibetan affairs and was made minister to the court of St. James for negotiations with the British in Calcutta, and two years later he signed an agreement with the British recognizing Chinese sovereignty over Tibet. As president of the Board of Posts and Communications, Tang replaced Yuan Shikai's control over the telegraphs, railways, and China Merchants Steam Navigation Company.[52]

The so-called Cantonese Clique, which included Tang Shaoyi, Liang Dunyan, Liang Yu-ho, Wo Ting Fan, and other Western-educated officials, commanded such a level of influence that they are credited for being a driving force behind the creation of the new government. Without their influence it would have been impossible, many believe, for Sun Yat-sen and the other revolutionary leaders to establish the Republic of China. In 1912 Tang was appointed premier when Yuan was elected president of the new republic. Their relationship would be tumultuous, as they clashed over conditions governing the negotiation of foreign loans, among other things, and in 1916 Tang joined the opposition to Yuan's dissolution of the National Assembly, turning his support to Sun Yat-sen's political regime in southern China. Tang refused several offers to return to government service and in 1929 was named by Chiang Kai-shek as "superior adviser" to the national government at Nanking. Tang ignored that appointment as well. It was in 1934 that he finally accepted the position of the head of the Zhongshan district. Tang retired at his home in Shanghai later the same year, but shortly afterward was brutally attacked and killed with an ax—reportedly because of rumors that he was secretly negotiating with the Japanese, who were then in control of northern China.[53]

Other former CEM students whose accomplishments were notable included Woo "Big Nose" Chung-yen, who helped in the formation of China's modern army and served as consul general to Yokohama. Chung

"Munny" Men-yew, the "little coxswain" from the Yale rowing team, went on to become secretary to the Legation at Washington, then held the position of chargé d'affaires to Madrid, and later consul general at Manila. Munny supervised the construction of the Shanghai-Nanking Railroad and finally became commissioner of the railway.

Liang Yu Ho "Charlie Cold Fish" rose to high positions in the Korean service and helped to construct a 27-mile branch line of the Peking-Tientsin railways. Liang was later appointed to commissioner of customs in Manchuria, then served as high adviser to the Chinese delegation to the Washington Conference.[54]

Ching Ta Yeh, nicknamed Baby Ta Yeh by his American classmates, established telegraph lines connecting Peking with Mongolia. He became the head of the telegraph service in Kyakhta and Manzhouli and Hei Monggol, in Inner Mongolia. Chu "Flounder" Pao Fay became Managing Director of the Imperial Chinese Telegraph Administration, later serving as director of the Shanghai-Nanking Railroad Administration before being appointed to vice minister of communications in 1907, and then vice president of the Board of Foreign Affairs. CEM student Tong Yuen-chan became China's director general of the Imperial Telegraph Administration. Tong was one of only two CEM boys who had been granted permission to cut off their queues during their time in America, presumably because the long braids interfered with certain machinery they were studying. Lin Yuen Fai became director of Beiyang Hospital, the first chief administrator of a Western-style hospital in China. Kwong King Yang became chief engineer for the Peking-Mukden Railway, the engineer-in-chief of Hankou Railway, Canton section, and then in 1912 was made chief engineer of the Peking-Kalgan-Shiyuan Railway. Tong Kwo On would become the first president of Tsinghua College. Kwong Pin Kong would write a groundbreaking book, *The Metallurgy of Gold and Silver in China*.[55]

It was a remarkable record of achievements. In spite of the early recall of the students, which would stop well short of the original goals set by the Chinese Educational Project, the 120 young students who were sent to America, over time, contributed immeasurably to China's progress. Given the elevation in status of those with American educations, jealousies would inevitably arise. The Mandarin officials, who were Chinese-educated, occupied high positions within the railway, telegraph service, mining industries, and most other critical areas. But these fields were becoming increasingly dependent on Western-trained technicians and engineers to conduct the real business of developing and running the operations.

America's First Immigration Policies

Before the passage of America's first immigration law in 1882, the Chinese Exclusion Act, anyone could come to the United States.[56] Beginning around midcentury, however, Americans were increasingly alarmed at the escalating numbers of immigrants, fears that began with the thousands of unskilled Catholic immigrants who flooded into America as a result of Ireland's potato famine.

The introduction of the steamship in the 1840s also contributed to immigration growth. Prior to the development of steamship travel, immigrants had most often arrived on sailing ships, with voyages from the British Isles to the United States typically lasting five to six weeks. In addition to speed, the new steamships were far more comfortable. Prior to the 1850s, foreign students had arrived in America at any one of the several ports of entry—New York City, Philadelphia, Boston, New Orleans, and Baltimore, primarily. After steamships overtook the seagoing industry, New York City became the main arrival port for immigrants. It was here that America's first immigration facility, Castle Garden, a complex located at the tip of Manhattan, was established. In 1892, it would be replaced by a much larger facility at Ellis Island.

In the early 1870s, public concern about the numbers of immigrants entering the country had resulted in a handful of individual states passing restrictive immigration laws, but each state's policies were unique. Anticipating confusion, the US Supreme Court declared in 1875 that immigration policy should be consolidated under federal control.[57] Congress began to formulate detailed immigration legislation in the 1880s, as the number of immigrants rose.

Most of the new immigration legislation directly targeted the Chinese. California's Gold Rush, which began in 1847, was attracting fortune hunters from the world over, particularly from China. Mostly poor, uneducated, and unskilled, the overwhelming majority failed to strike it rich and many were left with no means of paying their way back to China. Forced to remain in America and find work, thousands would serve as underpaid laborers in order to survive, operating laundries or working as coolies. These laborers are credited for having provided much of the physical work required in building and laying thousands of miles of track, for what would become the nation's economic lifeblood—the first transcontinental railroads. But as America's era of railroad-building came to an end, legions of Chinese laborers were again forced to seek employment, and, as had happened before, American resentment of the "yellow peril" grew. Mainly, the Chinese were blamed for taking needed jobs from US citizens. As a means of self-protection against angry Americans, many Chinese created close-knit communities within American cities, areas that would become known as Chinatowns.[58]

The US government ultimately responded with the passage of the Chinese Exclusion Act of 1882. The legislation prevented any Chinese without family already in the country from entering the United States, effectively stopping almost all new immigration from China. Under its provisions only diplomats, merchants, and students were allowed access. The same year Congress imposed the Immigration Act. More far-reaching, it bolstered the Exclusion Act and levied a head tax of 50 cents on each immigrant likely to become a public charge.[59]

The 1870s and 1880s witnessed growing levels of distrust between China and the United States, in part because of America's new immigration policies. As divisions widened, the Scott Act of 1888 was passed, prohibiting immigration of virtually all Chinese, including those who had gone back to China to visit and had planned to return. In a Chinese Exclusion case in 1889, the Supreme Court ruled (*Chae Chan Ping v. United States*) that an entire ethnic group could be denied entry to the country if the government deemed it difficult to assimilate, regardless of prior treaty.[60]

One result of the new policies was the immediate need to establish an enforcement agency. Until this point, state boards or commissions were responsible for enforcing immigration law with direction from US Treasury Department officials. At the federal level, US Customs Collectors at each port of entry collected the head tax from immigrants, while Chinese inspectors enforced the Chinese Exclusion Act.

In 1891, the Immigration Act was updated to bar polygamists, persons convicted of crimes of moral turpitude, and those suffering from contagious diseases from entering the United States. Congress created the Office of the Superintendent of Immigration around the same time. Housed at the Treasury Department, the Superintendent oversaw the first of the legions of US immigration inspectors stationed at the nation's points of entry. By the 1990s, in compliance with the new laws, the federal government took on the tasks of inspecting, admitting, rejecting, and processing all immigrants seeking admission to the United States.[61]

The new federal immigration station on Ellis Island in New York began its operations on January 2, 1892. The complex housed inspection facilities, hearing and detention rooms, hospitals, cafeterias, administrative offices, railroad ticket offices, and representatives of many immigrant aid societies. Between 1892 and 1953, the facility at Ellis Island would process more than 12 million immigrants. Additional immigrant stations soon appeared at other US points of entry, such as Boston and Philadelphia, efforts financed by an "immigrant fund" that was created from the collection of the "head tax," which remained in effect until 1909. At that point Congress replaced the fund with an annual appropriation. Congress exercised additional federal control over immigration with the Act of March 2, 1895, which upgraded the Office of Immigration to the Bureau of Immigration and changed the administrator's title from Superintendent to Commissioner-General of Immigration. In the course of a decade, the United States had moved from a policy of open borders to one of selected exclusions. And for those not excluded, more documentation would be required.[62]

America's First Students from Japan

Amherst College would play a key role in US higher education exchange by hosting the earliest enrollments of significant numbers of Japanese students. Julius H. Seelye, president of Amherst College from 1870 until 1890, was an ordained minister in the Dutch Reform Church and a member of the American Board of Foreign Missions. In 1871, members of Japan's diplomatic Iwakura Mission were seeking a system of education to support the building of a modern nation. Seelye invited the members to visit Amherst, a visit that was reciprocated when Seelye went to Japan in 1872, where he dined with Emperor Meiji. The visits served to establish a long and friendly association between Amherst College and Japan.

As a result of this relationship, many of America's first Japanese students enrolled at Amherst. One of the first was Niijima Jo, better known as Joseph Hardy Neesima. Born of samurai parents, he was only ten years old when Commodore Perry's arrival altered Japan's isolationist policies, opening doors to Western thinking and religion. Neesima converted to Christianity at age 21, reportedly after reading an abridgement of the Bible, and decided to study theology in the United States. At considerable risk, he left Japan without governmental permission and finally reached the United States by working for his passage on the *Wild Rover*, an American schooner. When the ship arrived in Boston, a man named Alpheus Hardy, who was the ship's owner, agreed to sponsor the young prospective student, and in 1865 enrolled him in Phillips Academy at Andover. Neesima would graduate from Amherst College in 1870 and then from Andover Theological Seminary in 1874, the first Japanese ever to obtain an academic degree in the United States.[63]

Neesima's knowledge was soon put to good use. Through a fortunate opportunity to act as an interpreter for a Japanese embassy in 1871, he was given a formal pardon from Japan for having left the country without authorization. To his delight, he was additionally granted the privilege of teaching Christianity upon his repatriation to his homeland. Neesima returned to Japan in 1874, convinced of the necessity of establishing an institution of higher learning in his own country that was based on Western ideals and Christian teachings. In 1875 he founded Doshisha Eigakko, which would become Doshisha University, in the heart of Kyoto, just across from the imperial palace. He also encouraged the education of Japanese students in America. By 1904, partly through the efforts of Doshisha University, students from Japan accounted for 105 of the 2673 foreign students studying in the United States, according to the US Bureau of Education.[64]

Kanda Naibu, class of 1879, was one of the students who followed Neesima to Amherst. Aided by the Japanese government, which was not yet enamored with Western modernity, Kanda Naibu arrived at Amherst at the age of 14. Seelye arranged his accommodations with a local family, and from there he attended high school, then enrolled at Amherst College. Kanda, like Neesima, devoted his life to Christianity and new education in Japan. Kanda Naibu would become Japan's preeminent authority on English and Latin, and served as president of Japan's English Speaking Society, where he worked to make the study of English an integral part of Japan's national education.

Uchimura Kanzo, Amherst class of 1887, was another of Seelye's disciples. He came to be known as the founder of "Japanese Christianity."[65] Based on his assertions he founded what he called the No Church, or *mukyokai*, movement, the first Japanese Christian sect. Uchimura advocated scholarly study of the Bible rather than organized church services, and he became a popular lecturer. By the 1920s, he was a sharp critic of the American government's exclusion policies that barred Japanese immigration.

Sukenori Kabayama Aisuke, the son of Admiral and Count Kabayama, was another of Amherst's early Japanese students. He served in his country's government and in business after graduating in 1889, then served as president of the Japan-US Friendship Society in Tokyo, where he befriended US Ambassador Joseph Grew. That association would lead to the establishment of the International House of Japan many years later (1966) with the assistance of funds from John D. Rockefeller. From these efforts emerged the Grew Foundation, which provided fellowships to Japanese students for study in American colleges and universities.[66]

Tomo Inouye received her primary and secondary education in Japan, before coming to the United States in 1896. She first entered the Cleveland Municipal Medical College before enrolling at the University of Michigan Medical School in 1899. She would be the University of Michigan's first Japanese woman graduate. In 1901 Inouye opened a medical practice in Tokyo, making her among the first, or perhaps the first, female doctor in Japan.

Notes

1. Stewart Fraser and William W. Brickman, *A History of International and Comparative Education* (Chicago: Scott, Foresman and Company, 1968): 293–295.
2. Ibid.
3. Isaac Fidler, *Observations on Professions, Literature, Manners and Emigration in the United States and Canada Made During a Residence There in 1832* (London: Whittaker, Treacher and Company, 1833): 46–47.
4. Fraser and Brickman, 367.
5. Ibid., 434.
6. Ibid., 436.
7. Michael E. Sadler, "Impressions of American Education," *Educational Review*, Vol. 25 (March 1903): 217–231.
8. University of Virginia, "UVA Names Its Spanish House in Honor of Alumnus Fernando Bolivar, Nephew and Adopted Son of South American Hero Simon Bolivar." Available at: http://www.virginia.edu/topnews/textonlyarchice/November_1996/bolivar.txt.
9. Columbia University, "Mario Garcia Menocal," *The Columbia Encyclopedia*, 6th edition (New York: Columbia University Press, 2001).
10. Wing Yung, *My Life in China and America* (New York: Henry Holt and Company, 1909): 6.
11. Ibid.
12. Thomas E. LaFargue, *China's First Hundred* (Pullman, WA: Washington State University Press, 1987): 18.
13. Yung, 22.
14. LaFargue, 21.

15. From the Yung Wing Project. Available at: http://ywproject.x10.mx/index.htm. Accessed November 1, 2018.
16. Wing Yung, 40.
17. Ibid., 41.
18. Li Dalong, "The Central Kingdom and the Realm Under Heaven Coming to Mean the Same: The Process of the Formation of Territory in Ancient China," *Frontiers of History in China*, Vol. 3, no. 3 (2008).
19. Jonathan D. Spence, *The Search for Modern China* (New York and London: W. W. Norton, 1999): 145–160; also see Jack Gray, *Rebellions and Revolutions: China from the 1880s to the 1980s* (Oxford: Oxford University Press, 1990): 39–92.
20. Stacey Bieler, *Patriots or Traitors?* (Armonk, NY: M.E. Sharp, 2004): 3–4.
21. Wang, 42.
22. Wing Yung, 136.
23. Wing Yung, 136–150; also see Edmund H. Worthy, Jr., "Yung Wing in America," *The Pacific Historical Review*, Vol. 34, no. 3 (August): 265–287.
24. John Fryer, "Chinese Education—Past, Present and Future," *Current Chinese Readings*, Vol. XVIII (1897): 381–382; also see LaFargue, 29.
25. Wing Yung, 157.
26. Tim Brady, "Anson Burlingame: Diplomat, Orator," *Journal of Aviation/Aerospace Education and Research*, Vol. 7, no. 2 (Winter 1997): 15–22.
27. Ning Qian, *Chinese Students Encounter America*, Trans. T.K. Chu (University of Washington Press, 1996): 19.
28. Ibid., 16; also see Frederick Wells Williams, *Anson Burlingame and the First Chinese Mission to Foreign Powers* (New York: Charles Scribner's Sons, 1912): 149–150.
29. Ning Qian, 16.
30. Ibid.
31. Shih-Shan Henry Tsai, *The Chinese Experience in America* (Bloomington: Indiana University Press, 1986).
32. Lu Suping, "Chinese Exclusion Acts: A Brief History of United States Legislation Aimed at Chinese Immigrants," *Readex*, a division of *NewsBank, Inc.*, Vol. 3, no. 2 (April 2008).
33. Paul H. Clyde, *United States Polity Toward China: Diplomatic and Public Documents* (Durham, NC: Duke University Press, 1940): 85.
34. LaFargue, 27.
35. Wing Yung, 180.
36. LaFargue, 32.
37. Teresa B. Bevis, *A History of Higher Education Exchange: China and America* (New York: Routledge, 2014): 41–42.

38. Edward J.M. Rhodes, "In the Shadow of Yung Wing," *Pacific Historical Review*, Vol. 74, no. 1 (February 2005): 19–58.
39. Wang, 43.
40. Judith Ann Schiff, "Where East Meets West," *Yale Alumni Magazine*, November/December 2004.
41. LaFargue, 37.
42. Ibid.
43. LaFargue, 53.
44. Timothy Kao, "Yung Wing and Young Chinese Students in America 1872–1881," *The Chinese Students Memorial Society*. Available at: www.120students.org. Accessed November 1, 2018; also see Yung Wing, 190–196.
45. Wing Yung, 207–209.
46. Wing Yung, 208.
47. LaFargue, 55–56, 67–114; also see Y.C. Wang, 88–90.
48. Bevis, 65–66.
49. Bevis, 68–70.
50. Bevis, 72–74.
51. Ibid.
52. Bevis, 74–76.
53. Ibid.
54. Gand Qian, Jingcao Hu and Liumei Youtong, *Chinese Educational Mission* (Wenhui Publishing, 1985): 5–29.
55. Ibid.
56. Marion Smith, "Overview of INS History," in *A Historical Guide to the U.S. Government*, ed. George T. Kurian (New York: Oxford University Press, 1998).
57. Ibid.
58. Bevis, 55–58.
59. Peggy Pascoe, "At America's Gates: Chinese Immigration During the Exclusion Era," *Journal of Social History*, Vol. 38, no. 3 (Spring 2005): 812–814.
60. Smith.
61. Smith.
62. Thomas M. Pitkin, *Keepers of the Gate: A History of Ellis Island* (New York: University Press, 1975).
63. Jerome Dean Davis, *A Sketch of the Life of Reverend Joseph Hardy Neesima* (Kyoto, Japan: Doshiva University, 1936).
64. Ibid.
65. Janet E. Goff, "Tribute to a Teacher: Uchimura Kanzo's Letter to William Smith Clark," *Monumenta Nipponica*, Vol. 43, no. 1 (Spring 1988).
66. Ray Moore, *Amherst College and Japan* (Amherst College of Asian Languages and Civilizations, 2004).

References

Bevis, Teresa B., and Christopher J. Lucas. 2007. *International Students in American Colleges and Universities, A History*. New York: Palgrave Macmillan.

Bieler, Stacey. 2004. *Patriots or Traitors?* Armonk, NY: M.E. Sharp.

Clyde, Paul H. 1940. *United States Policy Toward China: Diplomatic and Public Documents*. Durham, NC: Duke University Press.

Dalong, Li. 2008. The Central Kingdom and the Realm Under Heaven Coming to Mean the Same: The Process of Formation of Territory in Ancient China. *Frontiers of History in China* 3 (3): 323–352.

Davis, Jerome Dean. 1936. *A Sketch of the Life of Reverend Joseph Hardy Neesima*. Kyoto, Japan: Doshiva University.

Fidler, Isaac. 1833. *Observations on Professions, Literature, Manners and Emigration in the United States and Canada Made During a Residence There in 1832*. London: Whittaker, Treacher and Company.

Fraser, Stewart, and William W. Brickman. 1968. *A History of International and Comparative Education*. Chicago: Scott, Foresman and Company.

Fryer, John. 1897. Chinese Education—Past, Present and Future. *Current Chinese Reading* XVIII: 381–382.

Goff, Janet E. 1988. Tribute to a Teacher: Uchimura Kanzo's Letter to William Smith Clark. *Monumenta Nipponica* 43 (1, Spring): 95–100.

Gray, Jack. 1990. *Rebellions and Revolutions: China from the 1880s to the 1980s*. Oxford University Press.

Kao, Timothy. 1999. Yung Wing and Young Chinese Students in America 1872–1881. *The Chinese Students Memorial Society*. www.120students.org.

LaFargue, Thomas E. 1987. *China's First Hundred*. Pullman, WA: Washington State University Press.

Moore, Ray. 2004. *Amherst College and Japan*. Amherst College of Asian Languages and Civilizations.

Pascoe, Peggy. 2005. At America's Gates: Chinese Immigration During the Exclusion Era. *Journal of Social History* 38 (3, Spring): 812–814.

Pitkin, Thomas M. 1975. *Keepers of the Gate: A History of Ellis Island*. New York: University Press.

Qian, Ning. 1999. *Chinese Students Encounter America*. Translated by T.K. Chu. University of Washington Press.

Qian, Gand, Jingcao Hu, and Liumei Youtong. 1985. *Chinese Educational Mission*. Wenhui Publishing.

Rhodes, Edward J.M. 2005. In the Shadow of Yung Wing. *Pacific Historical Review* 74 (1, Feb.): 19–58.

Sadler, Michael E. 1903. Impressions of American Education. *Educational Review* 25 (Mar.): 217–231.

Schiff, Judith Ann. 2004. Where East Meets West. *Yale Alumni Magazine*, November/December.
Smith, Marion. 1998. Overview of INS History. In *A Historical Guide to the U.S. Government*, ed. George T. Kurian. New York: Oxford University Press.
Spence, Jonathan D. 2012. *The Search for Modern China*. New York and London: W.W. Norton.
Suping, Lu. 2008. Chinese Exclusion Acts: A Brief History of United States Legislation Aimed at Chinese Immigrants. *Readex*, a division of *NewsBank*, Inc. April 2008, Vol. 3, no. 2.
Tsai, Shih-Shan Henry. 1986. *The Chinese Experience in America*. Bloomington, IN: Indiana University Press.
Wang, Y.C. 1966. *Chinese Intellectuals and the West 1872–1949*. Chapel Hill, NC: University of North Carolina Press.
Williams, Frederick Wells. 1912. *Anson Burlingame and the First Chinese Mission to Foreign Powers*. New York: Charles Scribner's Sons.
Yung, Wing. 1909. *My Life in China and America*. New York: Henry Holt and Company.

CHAPTER 5

The Early Twentieth Century

Prior to 1903 American colleges and universities offered no foreign student support services whatsoever. Matters pertaining to academic or social acculturation were most often handled informally by sympathetic faculty members, local churches, the Boards of Mission, the Young Men's and Young Women's Christian Associations, or helpful townspeople. An influx of students from China, a product of Teddy Roosevelt's creative use of Boxer Rebellion indemnities, was adding significantly to the rising foreign student population, elevating the need for services. Among the first organizations to offer formal support was the Association of Cosmopolitan Clubs of America, which defined the job of "foreign student adviser," a position soon adopted in institutions across the United States. The Committee on Friendly Relations Among Foreign Students, founded in 1911, provided the first foreign student census, and a platform for articles on topics related to education exchange. The International House in New York City, which opened in 1928 through the generosity of John D. Rockefeller Jr., would be the first of many foreign student centers.

Governmental Policies and Immigration Laws

From its inception in 1867, the US Department of Education (Office of Education) had been interested in studying and reporting developments in foreign education. Between 1889 and 1905, escalating interest in education abroad led to the establishment of the Division of Foreign School

Systems, later changed to the Division of Comparative Education, and then to the Division of International Educational Relations. While most of the exchange efforts carried on in the United States in the early part of the century were privately sponsored, in at least two instances the government directly involved itself in international education relations. These were regarded later as important precedents for making intercultural relations an integral part of the country's foreign policy objectives. Some of those objectives were defined in the wake of the Boxer Rebellion in China in 1900, and the US government also was influential in initiating educational exchanges with the Hispanic-American republics. Cross-cultural cooperation with the region was attempted as early as 1849 but was unsuccessful. In 1890, the situation began to change, when the International Union of American Republics was established for the maintenance of peace and improvement of commercial relations among the countries of Latin America and the United States. By 1906, the union's successor, the International Bureau of the American Republics, had the added responsibilities of collecting and distributing information regarding education. In 1910, this bureau developed into the Pan-American Union, which, among other things, aided in the strengthening of cultural and intellectual ties among the member nations. All of this led to increasing numbers of Central and South American students attending US colleges.[1]

Over the next several years, the notion of developing America's international education increased in importance, drawing more attention to the tasks of recruiting and attending to both foreign students in the United States and American students traveling abroad. Isaac L. Kandel, author of *United States Activities in International Cultural Relations*, pointed out that both groups of students—foreign and American—would need pertinent information, and advice in the selection of the institutions best adapted to their needs. In the interests of international relations and the promotions of goodwill the exchange of students needed the stimulus of financial assistance in the form of scholarships and fellowships. In the case of teachers, the creation of visiting professorships or other aids should be addressed, Kandel added. Although government-led initiatives fostered educational and cultural ties among the nations of the Americas, the task of furthering this cause was handled largely by nongovernmental enterprises. By 1925, more than 115 private organizations had been established in the United States that were concerned in some way with global education exchange.[2]

Governmental policies relating to immigration had varying effects on education exchange during the early years of the century. While foreign students often had exemptions, America's fluctuating immigration policies would nevertheless have an effect on demographics and attitudes. As the century progressed, immigration became more pointed, and more restrictive. In 1903, the growing list of those barred from entry into the United States included epileptics, professional beggars, and anarchists. Imbeciles, the feeble-minded, those with tuberculosis, persons with physical or mental defects, and persons under age 16 were added. On February 14 of that year, a new immigration act had transferred the administration of the Bureau of Immigration from the Treasury Department to the newly created Department of Commerce and Labor, whose duty it was to put together a fitting roster of undesirables.

A major point of concern was naturalization. An investigation in 1905 reported an absence of uniformity among the nation's more than 5000 naturalization courts. While the process of bestowing citizenship was assigned to Congress by the Constitution, for more than a century it had actually been carried out by any court of record. Congress responded by framing a standardized set of rules, which would become the Basic Naturalization Act of 1906. The act mandated specific naturalization forms and encouraged state and local courts to relinquish their naturalization jurisdiction to federal courts. It then renamed the organization the Bureau of Immigration and Naturalization, to indicate its expanded responsibilities. To further standardize procedures, and to prevent fraud, the new organization called for copies of every naturalization record issued by every naturalization court. Bureau officials took on the duty of rechecking every record—a formidable task, even at this early stage—to be certain that each applicant for US citizenship had been legally admitted. In 1913, when the Department of Commerce and Labor divided into separate cabinet departments, the Bureau of Immigration and Naturalization was likewise divided into the Bureau of Immigration and the Bureau of Naturalization.[3]

The job of immigration enforcement was expanding alongside a quickening pace of new arrivals. In an unprecedented global resettlement, between 1911 and 1920 almost six million people immigrated to the United States. Rising concerns among the American public would result in a series of quotas acts and other policy changes. In 1917 Congress enacted a literacy requirement for all immigrants, and passed the Immigration Act of 1917, which restricted immigration from Asia. In 1921 the Emergency

Quota Act limited immigration from any given country to 3 percent of the number of people from that country living in the United States in 1910. The Immigration Act of 1924 limited annual European immigration to 2 percent of the number of people from that country living in the United States in 1890. Exceptions were made for students wishing to study temporarily in America, but they still had to comply with new procedural requirements and documentation. These duties also fell on the host colleges and universities, which would by necessity begin to develop internal systems that would ensure both student and institutional adherence to the many governmental mandates.

STUDENTS FROM THE PHILIPPINES: THE PENSIONADOS

Among the earliest exchange efforts in the 1900s was the Pensionado program. For around 300 years, the Philippine Islands were controlled by Spain. During this long occupation, most Filipino people had converted to Catholicism, an important component of Spanish colonial rule, and a transformative influence on education. At the end of the nineteenth century, following the Treaty of Paris that ended the Spanish-American War, Spain would cede the Philippines to the United States. In 1902, the United States passed the Philippine Organic Act, setting terms for civil government and endorsing Filipino self-government. At the same time American education was introduced to the Philippines and the English language was mandated for regular use in the school systems. To introduce the new systems, the United States had exported hundreds of teachers, called the "Thomasites" to the Philippines.[4]

The Thomasites, a group of 500 American educators, were so named because they crossed the Pacific on the USS *Thomas*. It was their goal to educate the Filipinos in the "American way" by establishing an updated school system for the island population. They arrived in August 1901, and, after a two-day quarantine, were dispatched to the provinces of Albay, Catanduanes, Camarines Norte, Camarines Sur, and Sorsogon, as well as others.[5] The Thomasites were successful in preparing many Filipino students for college in America, through the new *pensionado* scholarship program.[6]

Championed by W.A. Sutherland, who had been sent to the Philippines the year before as an assistant to William Howard Taft, the pensionado program was adopted in 1903, offering scholarships to bright students who wished to attend universities in the United States. In return for each year of education in the United States, scholarship recipients were required to work for the government in the Philippines for the same length of time. The student recipients, or pensionados, were supposed to be chosen by merit from each Philippine province, but local prominence and connections played a major role in the selection process.[7]

The first group of 100 pensionado students sailed for the United States on October 13 and spent a year studying in high schools in California, where they also learned English. They were then dispersed to colleges and universities, mostly institutions on the East Coast and in the Midwest. In the Chicago area especially, these first students formed a strong and long-lasting association between Filipino students and the state of Illinois. The relationship developed naturally from the presence of so many Filipino students in Illinois during the first decade of the century. Of the 178 pensionados enrolled in US institutions of higher education in January 1906, 42 studied in Illinois. Others enrolled in the State Normal School in San Diego, Berkeley, Cornell, Notre Dame, Purdue, Yale, the University of Wisconsin, Northwestern, Nebraska, Colorado, Indiana, Iowa, Ohio State, Michigan State, the Massachusetts Institute of Technology, and others. Those selected received an allowance of $70 per month, or $80 if the student resided in New York City. The government program paid for college tuition and fees, room and board, books, medical care, clothing, and laundry. In late 1903, three more pensionado students were selected to join the first allotment, bringing the total to 103; then in 1904, another 43 joined them, and the next year, 35 more.[8]

Of the more than 200 students sent by the program, only eight were women. One was Honoria Acosta-Sison, who would become the Philippines' first female physician. Rebelling against traditional Filipino culture, Honoria applied for a government scholarship as a pensionado in the first year of the program's operation and was accepted. After taking preparatory courses first at Drexel Institute and at Brown Preparatory School, she earned a degree from the Woman's Medical College of Pennsylvania, becoming the first Filipino woman physician, and the first Filipino woman to graduate from an American medical school. She was also the first Filipino woman obstetrician.[9] The Philippines' second female physician, Olivia Salamanca, was another of the eight female pensionados. As Acosta-Sison had done, Salamanca graduated from the Woman's Medical College of Pennsylvania, then went on to do important work back home. Today, at the intersection of Taft Avenue and T. M. Kalaw in Manila, one can find Olivia Salamanca Park, and the Dr. Olivia Salamanca Memorial Hospital is located in Cavite City.

Fewer pensionado students were sent to America between 1905 and 1912, in part because the act that had provided for the maintenance of the students in the United States had been amended to apply only to those in graduate programs. The decline was also due to the opening of the University of the Philippines, which was established in 1911. The number of Filipino students sponsored by the government dwindled to only a few each year between 1912 and 1919. The decline coincided with a time of increasing need for well-trained persons to command technical and scientific positions in the Philippines. To fill the growing professional void, in 1918 the Philippine legislature authorized additional funding to again send pensionados to the United States, and by 1919, another 114 government-sponsored students had been sent to earn professional degrees. These later pensionado students were mostly people who had been employed by the Filipino government for a number of years, who had a special field of interest they sought to develop. In 1922 the Bureau of Insular Affairs reported a total of 1156 Filipino students in the United States. By field of study, 280 of those students were enrolled in engineering, 181 in commerce, 149 in medicine, 98 were studying law, 50 were enrolled in agriculture programs, 43 in education, and another 43 in the sciences.[10]

The Barbour Scholarships and Gender Issues

In the early twentieth century student exchange programs that included women were scarce. One of the few initiatives for foreign female students was the Barbour Scholarship program, established at the University of Michigan in 1914, through the efforts of Levi Lewis Barbour, a university regent. It was a "tiny and timid Japanese schoolgirl" named Kameyo, just admitted to study medicine, who inspired Barbour. She wanted to become a doctor but found the process of adjustment to America daunting. She would attend her premed classes, take notes in Japanese, then translate them slowly into English, a process that led to low grades. She reported feeling ashamed of her slow progress, and that she appreciated her professors' patience.[11]

Touched by the challenges she and others were facing, Barbour set about establishing a scholarship program that would help finance, house, and support female foreign students of the highest academic and professional caliber. They would be awarded to students encompassing a region extending from Turkey in the west to Japan and the Philippines in the east, to study modern medicine, mathematics, and other disciplines critical to the development of their native countries. With a gift of $100,000, he formalized the program in 1917, and the tiny and timid Kameyo was the first recipient. The scholarships were specifically designed for females who wanted to study medicine, public health, or teaching, preferably at the college level. At the time of its inception, it was one of the few scholarship programs in the United States implemented expressly for female foreign students. The scholarships continue today through the University of Michigan's Rackham Graduate School. Fellows are chosen on the basis of potential for contribution to their home country as well as academic record. Candidates must not be permanent residents or citizens of the United States and not married to permanent residents or citizens of the United States, and they must be enrolled full-time in a master's or doctoral program.

In 1925, Katy Boyd George, administrator for the Committee on Friendly Relations Among Foreign Students, produced one of the few available commentaries relating to foreign women students in America. A result of several interviews, the report described assorted elements of social and religious life. George concluded that concerns encountered by foreign female students could be organized into a few basic categories, among them racial prejudice, a lack of sincerity on the part of American students, overemphasis on the differences among foreign students, lack of unity in the expression of religion, and perceptions of freedom. According to George's research, racial bias was more frequently encountered when the foreign student was dark-skinned. An East Indian woman reported that she had been turned down at more than 20 boarding houses because of her complexion. Others complained about the American students' seeming lack of consideration for the academic side of college life. "I have no one in my house [dormitory] who has a sympathy for studies."[12] One respondent expressed resentment of what she referred to as an overkindly attitude on the part of Americans. Adjustment to new freedoms was another point of concern. Some had suddenly encountered an environment with choices and options in far greater abundance than they were accustomed to at home. Many respondents described positive aspects as well. Freedom of thought, for example, was listed among the most important benefits of their American education.

Cosmopolitan Clubs

For many American colleges and Universities, Cosmopolitan Clubs were their first formal organization catering exclusively to foreign students. Before 1903, foreign students in American colleges and universities were not provided formal organizations specifically designed to address their unique needs. Despite the evangelical and humanitarian efforts of churches, the Boards of Missions, the Young Men's Christian Association (YMCA), and the Young Women's Christian Association (YWCA), foreign students often had to confront issues pertaining to social adjustment or other concerns without help. The first organized attempt at forming reliable associations capable of attending to the special needs of foreign students was the founding of the Association of Cosmopolitan Clubs of America. More commonly referred to as Cosmopolitan Clubs or International Clubs, these informal enclaves were initiated and developed by the students themselves. For many years these clubs provided a social forum and a support system for nonnationals on campuses across the country.[13]

The University of Wisconsin would be the birthplace of Cosmopolitan Clubs. In March 1903, 16 foreign students, representing 11 different nationalities, met in the modest apartment of Karl Kawakami, a student from Japan, and came up with a plan. An international club was to be organized in which all of the foreigners of the university, rich or poor, were to meet on an equal basis of mutual friendship and brotherhood. No similar organization at any other university furnished them a precedent. It was an action that was both original and unsolicited, wrote Louis Lochner, a student from Illinois who later became the first president of the Association of Cosmopolitan Clubs.[14] The clubs spread quickly to campuses around the country.

Cornell began its club in 1904, and it found immediate success. At its first meeting on November 4, in Barnes Hall, 60 students attended, but at the next meeting, a few weeks later, more than 100 had to squeeze into the tight quarters offered at the law school. International students had come to Cornell from the beginning of the university, and some foreign students, as well as some faculty, created early social organizations for themselves. In 1873 Cornell's Brazilian students published "Aurora Brasileira," a monthly newsletter written in Portuguese, and they established Club Brasileiro. In 1888–1889 Latin American students from Nicaragua, Puerto Rico, Honduras, and Brazil created Alpha Zeta, a short-lived "foreigner's fraternity." In 1894, a Canadian Club appeared, and a Club Latino-Americano flourished for a time. Cornell's Chinese Students Association was founded in 1904, and a Filipino Cornellians group began in 1924.[15] In the early years, countries represented at Cornell included Argentina, Australia, Brazil, Bulgaria, China, England, Germany, India, Ireland, Japan, Mexico, the Netherlands, the Philippines, Peru, Romania, Russia, Scotland, South Africa, Turkey, and Sweden.

The University of Michigan would begin its Cosmopolitan Club in 1905, followed by Purdue (Ohio) and Louisiana, in 1907. "Above All Nations Humanity" was the anthem heard as the University of Illinois at Urbana-Champaign opened its Cosmopolitan Club in 1907. Among its founding members were a newly arrived Russian student, and the son of Indian poet Rabindranath Tagore.[16] In December of 1907 the first convention of the Association of Cosmopolitan Clubs was held in Madison, Wisconsin. By 1912 there were at least 26 clubs nationwide.

The forerunners of the organization had been active somewhat earlier in Europe. The first international student congress convened in Turin in 1889. The association that sprung from that meeting was known as *Corda Fratres* (Brothers in Heart) International Federation of Students and was similar in scope and mission to the Cosmopolitan Clubs. When the American and European groups learned of each other's existence, they arranged to meet and by 1911 had worked on terms of affiliation. While each group retained its autonomy, they worked together to create a central committee, comprised of two delegates from each representative country. Under this aegis, the affiliates could compare notes and plan joint projects.[17]

Most Cosmopolitan Clubs sponsored activities designed to celebrate the foods, music, arts, and dances of various countries. Such an event might be housed in some campus facility or a local church or community hall, and American students were invited to share and learn about the cultures of a school's foreign students. In a time where air travel was not yet an option and few American youths went abroad, local teachers used these opportunities as teaching tools for global education.

Cosmopolitan Clubs offered hands-on assistance for foreign students. They also pushed for more institutional and governmental support. Members and supporting associations lobbied for universities to appoint special advisers for foreign students to help them comply with the various federal and institutional regulations. Clubs were successful in convincing the US Bureau of Education to publish an informational bulletin for the guidance of foreign students who were considering study in the United States. In 1915, the Bureau published *Opportunities for Foreign Students in American Universities*, probably the first official guide for foreign students. It contained information about the features of American colleges and universities, living conditions, college life, as well as details of entrance requirements for 62 institutions.[18]

The growing influence of the Cosmopolitan Clubs paved the way for other changes relating to how schools dealt with foreign students. One exceedingly important development the clubs promoted was the concept of the foreign student adviser (FSA). This fledgling idea varied dramatically from institution to institution. On some campuses, the foreign student adviser was no more than an interested faculty member who made himself or herself available for counsel. At other institutions, formal positions were implemented within the framework of a school's administration. Oberlin College was one of the first to appoint an official foreign student adviser, around 1910.

The concept of offering separate and specialized advisers to address the unique needs of foreign students was described in a 1928 work published by the American Council on Education. "In every institution the foreign student will find an official who is ready to confer with him regarding his special problems," it was asserted. "These may concern his admissions credentials, or the choice of his curriculum, his financial problems, his living conditions, his health, his religious or other quandaries."[19] As foreign study became more regulated, particularly due to changing immigration laws, the need for foreign student advisers increased. Colleges demanded officials who could oversee the admission of foreign students and ensure that those students adhered to both federal and institutional requirements.

In the early part of the twentieth century, responsibilities for overseeing foreign students were shared by the Bureau of Citizenship and Immigration Services and the colleges and universities that foreign students attended. Prior to admitting nonnationals, institutions had to petition the Bureau for accreditation, and then work with the Bureau and make regular reports. Failure to do so put a school at risk of being removed from the Bureau's list of approved institutions. Hence, centralizing knowledgeable administrators for the purpose of maintaining those mandates was in the interest of both the students and the institutions. Although the Cosmopolitan Clubs were instrumental in inaugurating the field of foreign student advising and pioneered many of the intercultural activities now found on most campuses, the association would not last at many institutions, as other agencies and institutional efforts came into play.

The Committee on Friendly Relations Among Foreign Students

In 1911 a small group of far-seeing men in New York sought to create an association focused on foreign students. Their efforts would be led by statesman and student organizer John R. Mott, who later served as General Secretary of the International Committee of Young Men's Christian Associations, Chairman of the World's Student Christian Federation, and Chairman of the International Missionary Council. Other founding members included Cleveland H. Dodge, Andrew Carnegie, George W. Perkins, John W. Foster, Andrew D. White, William Sloane, and Gilbert Beaver. First an independent association, it would later affiliate with the Young Men's Christian Association. D. Willard Lyon served as the first General Secretary. The personnel were drawn from several Christian bodies, including the foreign and student departments of the International Committee, mission boards, the Student Volunteer Movement, and the Committee of Reference and Counsel. Headquarters were in New York City at the offices of the International Committee, at 347 Madison Avenue.[20]

The services of the Committee, according to W. Reginald Wheeler's *The Foreign Student in America* (1925), included an extensive correspondence throughout the world with missionaries and educators, but especially with students who were considering coming to America. Studies were prepared with facts about migrating students, as well as a range of ministries to the students coming in through New York and other ports. The Committee aided students by helping them obtain room, board, and, occasionally, employment. If foreign students intended to remain in New York, they were directed to the local institutions and placed under the care of the Intercollegiate Cosmopolitan Club of New York City. Those bound for colleges elsewhere were assisted by the office in arranging for tickets and the transportation of baggage. Students were given letters of introduction to YMCA secretaries and other friends at their destination. Sometimes telegrams were sent ahead asking that the student be met at the train station. The Committee's representatives at New York, Boston, Seattle, San Francisco, and New Orleans would meet steamers when notified that students were due to arrive. The Friendly Relations committee promoted comradery in the colleges by serving as a clearinghouse of information on activities promoted in the institutions. Foreign students were introduced to the influences of American life through Bible study classes, religious education groups, forums on international questions, Cosmopolitan Club events, international nights, group receptions and parties, local and sectional conferences on student problems, contact with student volunteers and missionary societies, and attendance at summer conferences.

The National Board of the Young Women's Christian Associations provided hospitality, friendship, and service specifically for female foreign women students, as did the Committee. When notified, secretaries of the Committee on Friendly Relations with Foreign Women Students met incoming female students at the dock or station, assisted with finding living spaces, and helped them make connections with people who could assist with adjustment to American life. They might lend a student money when a check from home was delayed. The intention was to help, with finances, illness, social adjustment, or finding work. It was also the desire of the Committee on Foreign Relations Among Foreign Students that the contribution which these foreign students made to America's life should find its way into college groups. The Committee therefore fostered connections for them with groups of American students.[21] Its staff members routinely visited institutions where foreign students were enrolled, to consult with the institutions' foreign student advisers, representatives of student bodies, and the foreign students themselves.

In one of its early handbooks, *The Unofficial Ambassadors*, was a menu of services the Committee on Friendly Relations offered, which included providing advice and assistance in the presentation of scholarship applications, helping with transportation upon arrival, preparation of letters of introduction, help in arranging temporary loans, placement at summer camps, and assistance in finding student conferences. They also helped find activities for students, usually through the YMCA or YWCA or on campus.

In addition, the organization took on a variety of specific activities, such as coordinating campus and community exchanges, refining service programs, and providing educational campus visitations to help institutions better care for their foreign student populations. The committee's efforts were supplemented by its information publications, such as *Living in the United States*, *A Guide for New Visitors*, *Community Resources for Foreign Students*, and *International Campus*, among others. The Committee also initiated a foreign student census, which was begun in 1915 and continued annually for several years.[22]

Foreign Student Enrollments

Before midcentury, when the Institute of International Education (IIE) began its annual census that defined specifically who should be counted as "foreign students" in US higher education, enrollment figures were imprecise. Reports produced by the Committee on Friendly Relations Among Foreign Students, and estimates provided by various annual editions of the World Student Christian Federation's publication, Reports of Student Movements, helped to document the totals as closely as they were able. The Bureau of Education also had been interested in compiling a correct census of foreign students. Discrepancies occurred in determining who should be included. Sometimes high school-level students were counted along with graduate-level students, and in some cases, there were disagreements about which institutions should be considered part of higher education. Therefore, any foreign student counts prior to the IIE data in 1949 are best viewed as approximations.

Foreign students comprised a very small percentage of enrollments in American colleges before World War I. Records vary, as an accurate census of foreign students would not be produced until midcentury, but the population appears to have remained below 5000 until around 1912. The 1904 US Office of Education (also called the Bureau of Education due to a temporary name change) report contained statistics showing 2673 foreign students from 73 countries enrolled in institutions of higher learning in America. This total did not include all-women's colleges. To provide points of comparison, figures in 1904–1905 showed the number of foreign students in Germany to be 8786. Statistics offered by a French writer in 1904 reported that foreign enrollments in France totaled 2046.[23]

By 1911, according to figures provided in the Institute of International Education's publication *Education for One World*, there were 4856 nonnational students enrolled in American higher education institutions. The leading sender was Canada, with 898 students, followed by the West Indies, with 698. China sent 549; Japan 415; Mexico 298; the United Kingdom 251; and Germany 143. India and Ceylon together sent 148; Russia and Finland combined sent 120; Brazil 76; Argentina 51; Peru 28; Colombia 28; Chile 19; and the other South American countries, 72.[24]

In 1920–1921, the Department of the Interior, which oversaw the Bureau of Education, fixed the number of foreign students in American colleges and universities at 8357. This time the biggest sender was China, with 1443, a continuing result of the Boxer Indemnity scholarships. Canada was second with 1294. Other significant representation was the Philippines with 857.[25]

Conventional wisdom held that attention should be paid to providing help and service to this growing population of international students. To determine how well US higher education was doing toward this end, in 1909 the Bureau of Education circulated a letter to 100 institutions, asking for information pertaining to Chinese students. The survey first asked if any Chinese students were enrolled, and, if so, what proof of attainments, or knowledge of English, was accepted in the case of each student. It asked if any scholarships were being made available for Chinese students as inducements to enroll, and if they were permitted to join fraternities or sororities. Other questions focused on finances, asking for an approximation of a Chinese student's annual expenses. What accommodations could be secured by these students? What special care would be exercised over their welfare? And so forth. The questionnaire was circulated among a broad cross-section of institutions of varying types and sizes.[26] A selection of their responses is provided here.

The University of California at Berkeley reported a total of nine Chinese students enrolled for the year 1907–1908, with 19 registered for the 1908 summer session. The institution's department of oriental languages was charged with their special care and guidance. Tuition cost $20 annually, and living expenses were estimated to be about $400 per year. Most of the Chinese students at Berkeley resided with private families rather than on campus, although a few lived in a small clubhouse reserved for Chinese students.

Yale's response to the questionnaire was in narrative form. "We have had a large number of students from China at Yale," it began. "During this past year (1907–1908) there has been an enrollment of about 25. Among the men of distinction who have graduated in the past years have been Jeme Tein Yow, of Peking, and Yu Chuan Chang, who passed first in the great examinations in Peking two years ago."[27] As far as enrollment requirements, in the case of Chinese students a knowledge of the Chinese language and literature was accepted in place of the Greek requirement at Yale, and substitutions of Chinese for Latin in the scientific school. The school made a special point of emphasizing the importance of a good knowledge of English before admission. Degrees from representative Chinese institutions, such as St. John's College, Shanghai, and Tientsin University, were accepted for admission to the graduate school, as were the degrees of American institutions of rank. Regarding scholarships, Yale offered two Williams scholarships for Chinese students, at $100 each per year. Other special scholarships were awarded from time to time. Yale already had in place a special organization of Chinese students, as well as a Cosmopolitan Club, with members from several different nationalities. Yale's cost of tuition at the time was around $155, with rooms on campus available to any student, including Chinese, for about $4 per week. The response continued, "There is a distinct esprit de corps among the Chinese students at the university." There had also developed a high level of interest in China among its traditional students. Yale graduates had founded a collegiate school, with the hope of developing it into a university at Changsha, in Hunan.[28]

The respondent was referring to the Yale-China Association, founded in 1901 by a group of Yale graduates and faculty members, with a goal of furthering knowledge and understanding between America and China. China had been chosen in part to honor Yale graduate Horace Tracy Pitkin, who had died tragically during the Boxer Rebellion. Yale-China had been originally conceived for religious purposes, but under the influence of Dr. Edward Hume it grew to assume a more educational, than evangelical, function. My 1905 Hume's medical clinic in Changsha had grown into an extensive educational compound and would become the site of several preparatory institutions—the Yali Middle School, the College of Yale-in-China, and the Hsiang-Ya Medical College. Yali is a Chinese transliteration of the word Yale.[29]

Indiana University at Bloomington's response to the 1909 survey was more typical of many schools. They had only one Chinese student enrolled, who lived in a private home off campus. The school's annual tuition was reported to be $40 and living expenses were estimated at $300 per year. There were no special provisions. Some large institutions, such as the State University of Iowa at Iowa City, the University of Minnesota at Minneapolis, and Baylor University at Waco, Texas, reported having no Chinese enrollees at all. Wellesley College had only one Chinese enrollee, although three scholarships had been established during the time of a visit by Chinese commissioners in 1906. Tuition at Wellesley was expensive by comparison, around $175 annually. Living costs were around $275 per year. Most colleges that did host Chinese students had some support in place, such as faculty advisers and scholarships, in preparation for a much-anticipated advance of foreign students and scholars. It was easy to conclude from the survey responses that there was little uniformity or definition relating to the education or support of Chinese students in 1909, as admissions standards, English requirements, and living conditions varied dramatically.[30]

The International Houses

"Good morning," Harry Edmonds said casually to a student as he passed. The young Chinese stopped in his tracks, turned to face Edmonds, and said, "I've been in New York three weeks, and you are the first person who has spoken to me."[31] The year was 1909 and Edmonds, then working for the New York YMCA, was unsettled by the young man's remark. Was it possible that foreigners studying in America were truly this isolated? Edmonds soon made it his mission to find out, actively investigating the state of foreign students in New York City. One of his first steps was to author and administer a survey of the estimated 600 foreign students living in the city at the time, to learn first-hand about their experiences, living conditions, and problems. Edmonds discovered an almost universal lack of support services for international enrollees.[32]

Edmonds looked for opportunities to bring together foreign students, faculty, and local citizens for friendly exchanges and Sunday suppers, but he had much grander ideas, plans that would require substantial funding. He imagined impressive brick structures in prominent city locations where foreign students from all over the world would reside, dine, enjoy activities together, and have spaces for meetings or study. These "international houses" would provide a central place for community affairs, banquets, fund-raising events, global education, and cross-cultural interaction. They would encourage and promote international tolerance and understanding. Edmonds appealed to the generosity of John D. Rockefeller Jr., the fifth child and only son of John Davidson Rockefeller, Sr., the founder of Standard Oil. The younger Rockefeller was intrigued.[33] Edmonds also approached the Cleveland H. Dodge family, which had helped found the Committee on Friendly Relations Among Foreign Students. Both parties were convinced of the need for Edmonds' project and agreed to support it.

The first International House opened in 1928 in New York City, at 500 Riverside Drive, with "That Brotherhood May Prevail" boldly inscribed in granite above the main entrance. It instantly became the most sought-after residence and gathering place for foreign graduate students in the New York area, as well as a venue for all sorts of community and social events. Its success made Edmonds and Rockefeller eager to expand the idea, and they soon approached the University of California at Berkeley with a similar plan.

The project was immediately controversial and met resistance from the conservative 1920s Berkeley community, as many people opposed the idea of men and women living together under one roof, as was the practice in New York's International House. On one occasion more than 800 community members assembled to protest racial integration in the proposed facility. The most memorable and influential speaker at that meeting turned out to be an intriguing woman of color named Delilah Beasley, who wrote for the *Oakland Tribune*. Beasley had spent nine years studying black life in California and in 1919 documented her findings in *The Negro Trail-Blazers of California*. Largely through her efforts, the press would discontinue using the offensive terms "darkie" or "nigger" as a reference to people of color, and they began to capitalize the word Negro. Her fame was widespread, and her persuasive remarks at the podium in support of Edmonds' plan proved to be a powerful force in countering the racist views of some of those in attendance.[34]

Bolstered by increasing public support, Edmonds and $1.8 million of Rockefeller money headed to Berkeley to establish a site. He purposefully chose a location on Piedmont Avenue, the traditional home of Berkeley's sorority and fraternity houses, which at that time summarily excluded any foreigners or people of color. By proposing the site, Edmonds sought to strike bigotry and exclusivity, as he put it, right hard in the nose.[35]

The original idea was to keep the facility indigenous (owned by International House) like the New York model, to spare the University of California controversy and to allow the students freedom of movement that might not be possible if the property were under university ownership. But, because of tax issues better addressed through the university, the new International House was set up as a separate corporation whose board of directors was interrelated with the institution. International House Berkeley officially opened on August 18, 1930, offering 338 rooms for men and 115 for women—the single largest student housing complex in the Bay Area and the first coeducational residence west of the Mississippi.[36]

Among the early concerns about the facility was the possibility of attracting overzealous Christian evangelists, which might result in uncomfortable situations for the Buddhists, Hindus, Muslims, Jews, and other non-Christians residing at the house. Berkeley's president, William Wallace Campbell, offered Allen Blaisdell the first director's job, for an annual salary of $5000. A respected educator, Blaisdell had developed a passion for cross-cultural awareness during a teaching assignment in Japan and was an outspoken proponent of international education. Blaisdell accepted the position and agreed upon a starting date of fall 1928. Soon after Blaisdell agreed to take the job, however, it was discovered that he was not only an educator, but also an ordained minister. He remained in the position but was under orders to keep his religion quiet and avoid openly revealing his ties to the Christian ministry.[37]

By all accounts the two International Houses were successful in their mission to provide a centralized "home" for foreign students and international activities. Following the triumphs of these ventures, Harry Edmonds and John D. Rockefeller Jr. collaborated in the establishment of a third International House, this time in Chicago, which opened in 1932. The International Houses in New York, Berkeley, and Chicago served as models for similar projects on campuses across the nation and around the world.

The Institute of International Education

In 1917 Steven Duggan was a professor of government at the College of the City of New York, and a member of a subcommittee on international education relations of the recently formed American Council on Education. He was convinced that World War I had much to do with misunderstandings among the world's cultures, and that the exchange of education and ideas could serve to remedy the situation.

While many American youth had studied painting in Paris or philosophy in Heidelberg, few foreign students had made their way to the United States. Duggan envisioned two-way scholarships between American and foreign universities, and he took his idea to Nicholas Murray Butler. In the fall of 1918, Stephen Duggan, Nicholas Butler, and Elihu Root, who was Secretary of State in Theodore Roosevelt's cabinet, sat together in front of a log fire at the Columbia University Club. The Armistice ending the war had been signed only two weeks before, in a railway coach in the forest of Compiegne. The three men would spend the evening discussing Duggan's ideas for educational exchange and its implications for peace.[38]

Something must be done on a large scale, declared Elihu Root. Like Duggan, Root believed that friction between countries was frequently caused by language barriers and an inadequate acquaintance of individual nations with other cultures. Butler, President of Columbia University and a trustee of the newly founded Carnegie Endowment for International Peace, agreed, adding that even intelligent and educated Americans knew little about international relations. They concluded that the only hope of avoiding future wars was to become internationally minded. A kind of clearinghouse was needed, that could stimulate interest in the study of international relations, and student exchange. By the end of the fireside discussion, the three men had put together a strategy. The plan would give birth to the Institute of International Education (IIE), an organization that in time would become America's foremost organization involved with student exchange. The IIE opened its doors on February 1, 1919, in New York City.[39]

The central goal of the new organization was to promote a two-way exchange of students and scholars between the United States and all other areas of the world, in every field of study. Participants should be selected according to ability, and, upon completion of a program, it was expected that the students would return to, and serve in, their home countries. Scholarships were set up to help support those who had insufficient funds for educational pursuits. Not intending to take on its exchange goals alone, the IIE served primarily as a mediating agency, and in that capacity could establish and manage scholarships, exchange professorships, and take on a wide variety of student programs. Stephen Duggan was appointed IIE's first director, a post he would hold for 28 years.

Armed with a pledge of $60,000 a year from Carnegie, Duggan set to work nurturing alliances between US and European universities, selecting the US students to go abroad on scholarships, finding chaperones for the visiting students, and promoting faculty exchanges. IIE's original staff members included Arthur W. Packard, Director of the Rockefeller Brothers Fund, and Edward R. Murrow, later a renowned radio commentator and vice president of the Columbia Broadcasting System. The impressive list of trustees and the Advisory Council of the Institute included eminent names—Nicholas Butler, Henry Morganthau Sr., John Bassett Moore, Alice D. Miller, John Foster Dulles, Joseph P. Chamberlain, Jane Addams, Henry L. Stimson, Harry Emerson Fosdick, Julius Sachs, Charles Evans Hughes, and Quincy Wright.[40]

Acknowledging the new organization's timely importance, the Ford Foundation provided a grant that helped expand IIE through the establishment of regional offices in the United States. Among IIE's early accomplishments was the publication of the first comprehensive list of scholarship opportunities for foreign students in the United States and for Americans abroad. It produced the first guidebooks for foreign students and the first monthly publication in the United States that dealt exclusively with international education exchange. IIE would pioneer the practice of sending American professors to universities abroad and bringing foreign professors to the United States.

In 1922 IIE assisted in securing a change in the immigration regulations, permitting foreign students to enter the United States on special visas, and it was instrumental in the establishment of "student third class" travel arrangements on ships, later to be called "tourist class." At the same time IIE was working with the US Department of State on establishing a more uniform evaluation of academic credentials from all education systems, as well as the development of binational selection committees, to ensure that only well-qualified applicants would come to the United States or be sent abroad.[41]

The IIE periodically administered a search for dissertations that had to do with various aspects of comparative education, and the published report was made available to its members. These publications, together with the institute's *Educational Yearbook*, served to form a history of world educational developments between World War I and World War II. These many efforts brought forth by IIE and other organizations, in tandem with immigration legislation, would help determine America's approach to education exchange and foreign students for the foreseeable future.

Teachers College

The International Education Board, which had been founded by John D. Rockefeller Jr., contributed a grant that helped lead to the creation of the International Institute of Teachers College (1887) at Columbia University. The institute would be remarkable in its pursuit of international education exchange, and its successes during its infancy were transformative for global learning. It was among the first institutions to demonstrate on a large scale how an American college could adapt its program to fit the needs of foreign students. A number of Boxer Indemnity scholarship recipients, who began the "second wave" of Chinese students coming to the United States in 1909, would study at Teachers College.[42] Its goals included giving special assistance and guidance to the growing body of foreign students enrolled there, and to conduct investigations into educational conditions and tendencies in foreign countries. It would make such investigations available to students of education in the United States and elsewhere, with the hope that pooling information would help advance the cause of education.[43]

Grace Hoadley Dodge had been the inspiration behind Teachers College. In 1880 Dodge created a so-called kitchen garden school in Greenwich Village in New York City, to teach cooking, sewing, hygiene, and other practical skills to poor immigrant women. She soon understood that a new sort of pedagogy was needed—teaching that reflected an understanding of different cultures. By 1887, with the help of Columbia University's Nicholas Murry Butler, and a site at West 120th Street that had been donated by industrialist George Vanderbilt, Dodge's kitchen garden school turned into something much greater—a school devoted to teacher education. In 1892 it was formally incorporated. Its most iconic figure would be John Dewey, a psychologist and education philosopher who served as president of the American Psychological Association. Teachers College launched the nation's first program in comparative and international education.[44] Paul Monroe was named director of Teachers College, and, under his guidance, orientations were provided for foreign students in terms of course selection and programs best suited for their individual needs. Special classes in English were offered, and courses were altered in content and method to provide a superior learning environment for foreign students.

A Second Wave of Chinese Students

After a 30-year absence, since the recall of the Chinese Educational Mission (CEM) in 1881, the early years of the twentieth century witnessed the return of Chinese students to American colleges and universities. The Boxer Rebellion in China, a bloody and violent siege against Christian missionaries and foreign influence, had the effect of triggering a new surge of Chinese enrollments.

When China was defeated by Japan in 1895, European powers responded with a scramble for so-called spheres of interest, which primarily involved holding leases for railway and other commercial privileges in various regions of the country. The Russians took control of Port Arthur; the British acquired the New Territories around Hong Kong; and the Germans were granted a leasehold in Shantung. The American government supported an "open door" policy in China through which many commercial and trade opportunities became available. The enfeebled Imperial Court saw such incursions as a form of foreign occupation, and desperate measures were needed if they were to regain their autonomy. The Empress Dowager had a plan. By quietly funneling aid to a number of underground societies, they could secretly work together to undermine the foreign intruders. Traditionally, these rebellious underground societies had been formed, many in small villages or rural areas, to oppose the imperial government. But antiforeign sentiment was now so pronounced in China that the government and the secret societies decided, at least for the time being, to overlook their differences in a united effort to rid the country of foreigners.[45]

The Empress would begin covert negotiations with one of those secret societies, the Righteous and Harmonious Fists, more commonly known as the Boxers. The society, which had originally rebelled against the imperial government in Shantung in 1898, practiced animistic rituals and cast spells that they believed made them impervious to bullets and pain. In common with the government, they also were convinced that the expulsion of "foreign devils" would begin a new golden age in China. The Boxers' original focus was on the hardships of the 1890s, which they blamed almost entirely on the government, but now the Boxers and the government had a common enemy. With a wink and a nod from the Empress Dowager, the Boxers turned their aggression toward the unwelcome Westerners, with an understanding that government troops would not interfere.[46]

The rebellion that ensued was concentrated in Peking, although it extended to some degree into outlying areas. The Boxers attacked Western missionaries and merchants in the legations, compounds, and neighborhoods where they worked and lived, burning buildings, destroying anything they could, and killing many of the residents. The siege lasted eight weeks, as victims scrambled to send urgent messages to the West. In response, 19,000 troops of the allied armies of the West were sent to end the onslaught. On August 14, the allies captured Peking, rescuing the Westerners and then forcing the imperial government to submit to the terms of the Boxer Protocol of 1901. Under the protocol's provisions, Western powers now had the right to maintain military forces in the Chinese capital, thereby placing the imperial government under what amounted to a form of continuous arrest. Several high-ranking Chinese officials were prosecuted for their roles in the rebellion, and finally China was ordered to pay a sizable indemnity for the human and monetary loss, to various countries, including almost $25 million to the United States. The harsh conditions set by the Boxer Protocol served to put China on a new course of political and educational reforms. Among the first was in

1901, when China's education system was restructured to allow the admission of girls. The curriculum would move from the study of the classics and Confucian theory, toward the study of Western mathematics, science, engineering, and geography.[47]

The United States took a genuine interest in China's educational reform. In 1908 Theodore Roosevelt put forth a plan to revoke a significant portion of the Boxer Indemnity owed to the United States by China, provided that a good portion of the returned money be used for the continuation of China's education reform. Roosevelt suggested that the plan should include education exchange with the United States, asserting that China could be helped in a practical way through the importation of scholarship.[48] With the endorsement of the American government, and the remission of the Boxer Indemnity funds, China was once again motivated to send students to America. In 1899, only about 80 Chinese were studying in American colleges, but by 1912, the count jumped to nearly 800. In 1914, China would include women among the students sent to the United States.[49]

The Board of Trustees of the China Foundation for the Promotion of Education and Culture, which consisted of ten Chinese and five Americans, was one of the groups charged with the distribution of the proceeds of the Boxer Indemnity. They would see that Chinese student recipients moved successfully through the process of getting safely to America, enrolling and graduating. Comprising a selection of well-known educators and dignitaries, board meetings were attended by W.T. Tsur, former president of Tsinghua University; V.K. Wellington Koo, Minister of Foreign Affairs; Chang Poling, President of Nan Kai University, Tientsin; W.W. Yen, Premier of China and Chairman of the Board; and Fan Yuan Lian, President of the National Normal University, Peking. Nearly every Chinese member of the Board of Trustees had at one time studied in the United States. At least one was a former CEM student.[50]

Tsinghua College and the Indemnity Scholarships

Funded by the Boxer Indemnity, Tsinghua (Tsing Hua; Qinghua) College, located in the northwestern suburbs of Peking, was established in 1911 on the site of the Qing Hua Yuan—a former royal garden of the Qing Dynasty. It first functioned as a preparatory school called Tsinghua Xuetang (Tsinghua Imperial College) for students who were sent by the government to study in the United States.[51] The college would be expressly designed to prepare students planning to attend American institutions by means of Boxer Indemnity scholarships. Unlike China's traditional institutions, Tsinghua's first faculty members were recruited almost entirely from the United States. Also unlike traditional Chinese institutions, where professors typically remained for their entire careers, at Tsinghua instructors could be replaced, or moved on their own to other colleges. Rather than close teacher-student relations based on familial or provincial ties, relationships were temporary and less personal, similar to the United States. Teachers at Tsinghua also were better-paid, typically, and enjoyed a higher level of academic freedom than did their colleagues in other Chinese institutions.

The daily schedule at Tsinghua likewise differed from traditional institutions. The school year began each autumn on an American academic calendar, rather than after the lunar New Year, as did traditional colleges. In most Chinese higher learning institutions, students were offered classes that combined history, ethics, and general knowledge, and they could come and go as they pleased, learning at their individual pace. At Tsinghua students were offered a succession of subjects during the day and regular attendance was mandatory. In the early years, the journey to Tsinghua from Beijing was about 45 minutes by donkey. Therefore, both students and faculty lived on campus. A bus route, which ran from Tsinghua to the YMCA building in eastern Beijing, would not begin until 1926.[52]

Tsinghua was also unique in that it was the only college located outside Beijing's city gate, and it would be so until Yanjing University opened in 1926, just a mile away. The campus stood out because most of its buildings had been designed by American architects. In the tradition of the Chinese, however, who put grand entrances in front of simple houses, Tsinghua's imposing front gates, called *Yong En Si* or the Temple of Forever Blessings, were white masonry. Flanked by four grand columns— two Doric and two Corinthian—they led visitors to beautiful gardens and a lotus pond. Tsinghua was well equipped, with materials from the United States, such as laboratory equipment, musical instruments, and something unusual in Chinese colleges—sports gear. The institution would utilize the equipment by adopting sports events that happened to fit well with the wave of nationalism China was experiencing. The students themselves would form the cultural elements of the campus, establishing a student union, leaders, and a yearbook called "The Tsinghuapper," with the college's impressive gate on the cover.[53]

Tsinghua Imperial College opened on April 29, 1911, and among its first duties was the oversight of the examinations and selecting the Indemnity Scholarship students. For its first two years, from 1912 to 1913, Tang Guoan, a native of Guangzhou province and former CEM student, served as president. Between 1912 and 1929 the college sent a fairly steady flow of students to the United States using Boxer Indemnity scholarships. The first group of 16 set sail in 1912. By 1929 some 1268 Tsinghua students had studied in the United States.[54]

Joint memorials of the Board of Education and the *Wai-wu-pu* expected that about 80 percent of the students sent to the United States would study technical subjects, such as agriculture, engineering, commerce, and mining. Another 20 percent were expected to enroll in law, finance, and education. In the years from 1909 to 1929, 32.33 percent were enrolled in engineering, 3.63 percent in agriculture, 16.18 percent in science and medicine, 11 percent in business, 2.77 percent in law, and 5.04 in education. Others studied the humanities or social studies.[55]

There were some obstacles. Soon after the arrival of the first Indemnity scholars in America, it became evident that their English preparation was severely inadequate. There were financial issues as well. Indemnity scholars were provided a stipend of $60, which barely covered living expenses, and finding other funds could be difficult, as working was prohibited. Some did odd jobs or picked fruit during the summers or worked in restaurants illegally. Still, they were generally better off than most students in China, who relied on governmental support, which sometimes was delayed depending on economic conditions. With Indemnity scholarships, the funds were always on time.

Notable Boxer Indemnity Students

This second wave of Chinese students would diminish as China advanced toward communism in the 1930s; nevertheless, not since the 1870s, when the Chinese Educational Mission was in force, had America hosted such a large population of China's students. As did many of the CEM students, Boxer Indemnity graduates went on to do important things.

Hu Shi (Hu Shih) had grown up in a fatherless home, under the strong influence of a traditional mother who supported modern education for her son. Awarded a Boxer Indemnity scholarship in 1910, Hu Shi enrolled at Cornell, and later studied in the Department of Philosophy at Columbia University under John Dewey. In part through Dewey's influence, Hu was led to the conviction that China's modernization had to take place by changing ways of thinking and by writing Chinese—not in the classical style, but as it was spoken. Returning to China in 1917, Hu accepted an appointment at Beijing University and came to be regarded as one of the important intellectuals of his time. He would write for the journal *New Youth*, a publication edited by one of the founders of the Chinese Communist Party, Chen Duxiu. The Sino-Japanese War of 1937 temporarily delayed Hu Shi's scholarly work, when he accepted a post as ambassador to the United States, where he served until 1942. He returned to China as chancellor of Peking University in 1946. In 1949 the advance of Communism forced Hu to flee to the United States, and he remained there until 1958, when he went to Taipei as president of the prestigious Academia Sinica research institute. Due to his contributions to Chinese culture, Hu Shi is sometimes referred to as the "father of the Chinese Literary Revolution." However, because of his criticisms of the Communist Party, today his work is seldom taught in China's schools.[56]

Tao Xingzhi, another Indemnity scholar, studied at Columbia Teachers College and returned home to help modernize China's education. Tao's synthesis of Deweyan and Chinese approaches to progressive education, a text based on his analysis of Chinese life and society, would make him among the most renowned educators in Chinese history.

Another Indemnity scholar, Chen Hegin, studied at Teachers College in 1917 and 1918, then returned to China to become the first Chinese theoretician of early childhood education. In addition to his promotion of early childhood educational opportunities, Chen developed teacher-training programs that emphasized child psychology, education for handicapped children, and family education. Also funded by an Indemnity scholarship, Wong Chin (Wang Jin) would complete his bachelor's degree in chemical engineering at Lehigh University. He returned to his homeland to serve as dean for two major universities—the College of Sciences at Southeast University, and the National Central University. He became a renowned scientist and was invited to form the Academia Sinica and became the first director of its institute of chemistry. He was an original member of the Chinese Science Society. After the Communist Party took control, Wong was sent to Zhejiang Normal College to conduct research in analytical chemistry. Here he edited and reworked the most widely used chemistry textbooks at the time, volumes originally written by Russian scientist Vladimir Nikolaevich Alekseev. Wong also co-founded the Chinese Chemical Industry Society and the Chinese Chemistry Society.[57]

Ho Chieh from Guangdong Province, who studied coal-mining technology at the Colorado School of Mines and then at Lehigh University, was another noteworthy Indemnity scholar. He would become a renowned geologist. Yeh Tingshien from Hunan Province graduated from New York University in 1915 with a master of science degree, would later serve as the chief engineer at the Hunan Electric Light Company, where a new 20-kilowatt electric power plant was built under his leadership, an accomplishment that made Yeh famous throughout central China. Chen Hengzhe (known also as Sophia Chen) was one of the first women to be awarded an Indemnity scholarship, enrolling at Vassar College in 1914. Chen would arouse interest in Chinese poetry through her articles in *Vassar Miscellany Monthly* and as a contributing editor to *Youth*, a magazine of contemporary poetry published by students at Cambridge.[58]

The Critics

To most people in the United States, it seemed obvious that China would benefit from Chinese students returning home with American degrees, but that presumption was not embraced by everyone. In fact, the merits of an American education were vehemently rejected by some conservatives who felt that Western education simply could not effectively find practical use in China. According to an article written by Chiang Yung-chen, then a professor at DePauw University in Indiana, disdain for foreign education had spread across the ideological spectrum in China.

The Chinese were not alone in their concern about the value of Western degrees. American liberals such as John Dewey and Bertrand Russell, who had both taught in China, levied criticisms against modern Chinese education in general, and study abroad in particular. Other notables such as Thomas Read of Beijing University voiced similar disdain, as well as Robert McElroy, the first exchange professor at Tsinghua University; and Selskar M. Gunn, vice president of the Rockefeller Foundation.[59] A central concern was the possibility of China's excessive reliance on foreign theories and methods. What the returned students had learned in foreign countries was not always applicable to China, some contended.

Among the harshest critics was Nathaniel Pfeffer, an American journalist who reported from Shanghai and Beijing, who concluded that as a class the returned scholars were not only a sad disappointment as representatives of their nation but were also not successful despite having favorable opportunities. "Their worst faults are their glib tongues, the mere lip service they give to patriotism, and the superficiality of their views."[60] Similar criticisms appear in *History of Studying Abroad in Modern China, Jindai Zhongguo Liuxueshi*, which was written by Shu Xincheng in the 1920s. Shu accused the returned students of acting like they were in a superior class. He further criticized the students for taking on too many of the characteristics of foreigners and for forming factions promoting self-interest, with the ultimate goal of seizing power.

These were reminiscent of the accusations that had prompted the recall of the Chinese Educational Mission students in the 1880s and, according to Shu, the criticisms were as pertinent as ever. Shu saved his most disparaging accusations for the Chinese government. Since the Qing dynasty, he claimed, when the first students were sent abroad, the Chinese government had no definitive purpose or policy regarding the practice. Further, there were insufficient screening methods and a lack of uniform procedures. The most serious problems were the overly generous stipulations governing self-supported students and the exemption of these students from any screening examinations. It had led to a waste of social resources, Shu claimed, and encouraged students to go abroad for empty documents rather than practical knowledge. Shu held that the concentration of Chinese students in Japan and the United States created a special political social status for the returned scholars that further contributed to the "Japanization" and "Americanization" of Chinese society. Moreover, the quotas of government-funded students sent abroad were unevenly distributed—students from the provinces of Jiangsu, Zhejiang, and Guangdong were sent more often than students from other parts of China.[61]

In *Chinese Intellectuals and the West*, Y.T. Wang extended Shu's argument, applying terms such as "slave education" and "worshipping and fawning on foreign powers."[62] Wang traced the weaknesses of the returned Chinese scholars back to those first led by Yung Wing to America, charging that Yung Wing had deliberately planned from the beginning to disregard the demands of the Qing court. Yung Wing was convinced, Wang believed, that China's future depended on these students abandoning their traditions, fully taking on the science and technology of Western culture. That presumption had effectively betrayed the Chinese government's original purpose of assimilating and using Western technology while preserving traditional culture. The resulting premature recall of the students had, according to Wang, resulted in the mission being a poor investment for China. The arguments on all sides were largely ideologically based.

Notes

1. Teresa B. Bevis and Christopher J. Lucas, *International Students in American Colleges and Universities: A History* (New York: Palgrave Macmillan): 94.
2. Isaac Kandel, *United States Activities in International Cultural Relations*, American Council on Education Studies, series I, vol. IX, no. 23 (Washington, DC: American Council on Education, 1945): 54.
3. Marion Smith, U.S. Citizenship and Immigration Services website: https://www.uscis.gov/about-us/our-history. Accessed December 2018.
4. Stanley Karnow, *In Our Image: America's Empire in the Philippines* (New York: Random House, 1990): 85–86.
5. Susan Evangelista, *Carlos Bulosa and His Poetry: A Biography and Anthology* (Seattle, WA: University of Washington Press, 1985).
6. Stanley Karnow, 106–138.
7. Barbara M. Posadas, *The Filipino Americans*, The New American Series, ed. Ronald H. Bayor (Westport, CT: Greenwood Publishing Group, 1999).
8. Posadas, 3.
9. Anna Liza R. Ong, First Filipino Women Physicians, *Society of Philippine Health History*, 2004. Available at: www.doh.gov.hp/sphh/filipino/women.htm.
10. Wheeler, 20.
11. Kim Clarke, "The Barbour Scholars," The Michigan Difference, University of Michigan Office of Development (Winter 2003). Available at: http://www.giving.umich.edu/leadersbest/winter2003/barbour.htm.
12. Wheeler, 180.
13. Stewart Fraser, *Governmental Policy and International Education* (New York: John Wiley & Sons, 1964): 92.
14. Louis B. Lochner, "Cosmopolitan Clubs in American University Life," *American Review of Reviews*, Vol. 37 (1908): 1.
15. Elaine Engst and Blaine Friedlander, "Cornell Rewind: Above All Nations is Humanity," November 20, 2014.
16. Wheeler, 269–271.
17. L. Glazier and L. Kenschaft, "Welcome to America," *International Educator*, Vol. 11, no. 3 (Summer 2002): 7.
18. Glazier and Kenschaft, 8.
19. Ibid., 9.
20. Teresa B. Bevis and Christopher J. Lucas, *International Students in American Colleges and Universities*, 88.
21. W. Reginald Wheeler, *The Foreign Student in America* (New York: Association Press, 1925): 228–231.

22. Bevis, 89.
23. Wheeler, 11; also see L. Houllevigue, "Les etudiants etranger don nos universities," *Review de Paris* (May 15, 1917).
24. Wheeler, 12.
25. Ibid.
26. John Fryer, "Admission of Chinese Students to American Colleges," *United States Bureau of Education*, Bulletin No. 2, Whole No. 399 (Washington, DC: Government Printing Office, 1909).
27. Ibid.
28. Ibid., 199–200.
29. The Yale-China Association. Available at: www.yalechina.org.
30. Fryer, 215.
31. From the University of California at Berkeley Website, "International House Berkeley Historical Background 2000." Available at: http://ias.berkeley.edu/ihouse/I/History.html.
32. Committee on Friendly Relations Among Foreign Students, *Unofficial Ambassadors* (New York: Author, 1945): 1.
33. David Rockefeller, *Memoirs* (New York: Random House, 2002): 124–125.
34. Analee Allen, "International House Marks 70th Year," *Oakland Tribune*, February 20, 2000. Available at: https://ihouse.berkeley.edu/about/news/Tribune_I-House_Marks_70th_Year.pdf.
35. Ibid.
36. Ibid.
37. J. Ariff, "Oral Interview with A.C. Blaisdell 1928–1961," in *Foreign Students and Berkeley International House* (Berkeley: University of California Press, 1967).
38. "Father and Son," *Time Magazine* (November 4, 1917).
39. Edward Charnwood Cieslak, *The Foreign Student in American Colleges* (Detroit: Wayne University Press): 11.
40. Frasier, 96.
41. Ibid., 97.
42. Bu Liping "International Activism and Comparative Education: Pioneering Efforts of the International Institute of Teachers College, Columbia University," *Comparative Education Review*, Vol. 41, no. 4 (1997): 413–443.
43. Institute of International Education, *Blueprint for Understanding* (New York: Author, 1949).
44. Grace Dodge Hall, *Chemistry Laboratory with Students*, Gottesman Libraries at Teachers College, Columbia University (Ca. 1910).
45. Teresa B. Bevis, *A History of Higher Education Exchange: China and America* (New York: Routledge, 2014): 84–85.

46. Stacey Bieler, *Patriots or Traitors?* (Armonk, NY: M.E. Sharpe, 2003).
47. Bevis, *A History of Higher Education Exchange*, 83–85.
48. Isaac Kandel, *United States Activities in International Cultural Relations*, American Council on Education Studies, series I, vol. IX, no. 23: 2.
49. Bevis, *A History of Higher Education Exchange*, 85–89.
50. Ibid, 65.
51. Beiler, 57–89.
52. Bevis, *A History of Higher Education Exchange*, 91–94.
53. Ibid.
54. Ibid.
55. Ibid.
56. Yi Zhuxian, "Hu Shi, Chinese and Western Culture," *The Journal of Asian Studies*, Vol. 51, no. 4 (November 1992): 915–916.
57. Bevis, *A History of Higher Education Exchange*, 103–105.
58. Ibid.
59. Yung-chen Chiang, *Chinese Studies in History*, Vol. 36, no. 3 (Spring 2003): 38–62.
60. Ibid., 41.
61. Ibid.
62. Y.T. Wang, *Chinese Intellectuals in the West, 1872–1949* (Chapel Hill, NC: University of North Carolina Press, 1966).

References

Allen, Analee. International House Marks 70th Year. *Oakland Tribune*, February 20, 2000. Available at: https://ihouse.berkeley.edu/about/news/Tribune_I-House_Marks_70th_Year.pdf

Ariff, J. 1967. Oral Interview with A.C. Blaisdall 1928–1961. In *Foreign Students and Berkeley International House*. Berkeley: University of California Press.

Bevis, Teresa B. 2014. *A History of Higher Education Exchange: China and America*. New York: Routledge.

Bevis, Teresa B., and Christopher J. Lucas. 2007. *International Students in American Colleges and Universities*. New York: Palgrave Macmillan.

Bieler, Stacey. 2003. *Patriots or Traitors?* Armonk, NY: M.E. Sharpe.

Bu, Liping. 1997. International Activism and Comparative Education: Pioneering Efforts of the International Institute of Teachers College, Columbia University. *Comparative Education Review* 41 (4): 413–434.

Chiang, Yung-chen. 2003. Chinese Students in America in the Early Twentieth Century. *Chinese Studies in History* 36 (3, Spring): 38–62.

Engst, Elaine, and Blain Friedlander. 2014. Cornell Rewind: Above All Nations is Humanity. *Cornell Chronicle*, November 20.

Evangelista, Susan. 1985. *Carlos Bulosa and His Poetry: A Biography and Anthology.* Seattle, WA: University of Washington Press.

Fraser, Stewart. 1964. *Governmental Policy and International Education.* New York: John Wiley & Sons.

Fryer, John. 1909. Admission of Chinese Students to American Colleges. *United States Bureau of Education, Bulletin No. 2.* Washington, DC: Government Printing Office.

Glazier, L., and L. Kenschaft. 2002. Welcome to America. *International Educator* 11 (3, Summer): 5–11.

Hall, Grace Dodge. 1910. *Chemistry Laboratory with Students.* Gottesman Libraries at Teachers College, Columbia University.

Institute of International Education. 1949. *Blueprint for Understanding.* New York: Author.

Kandel, Isaac. 1945. *United States Activities in International Cultural Relations.* American Council on Education Studies, series 1, vol. IX, no. 23. Washington, DC: American Council on Education.

Karnow, Stanley. 1990. *In Our Image: America's Empire in the Philippines.* New York: Random House.

Lochner, Louis. 1908. Cosmopolitan Clubs in American University Life. *American Review of Reviews* 37: 316–321.

Ong, Anna Liza R. 2004. First Filipino Women Physicians. *Society of Philippine Health History.*

Posadras, Barbara M. 1999. The Filipino Americans. In *The New American Series*, ed. Ronald H. Bayor. Westport, CT: Greenwood Publishing Group.

Rockefeller, David. 2002. *Memoirs.* New York: Random House.

Smith, Marion. U.S. Citizenship and Immigration Services website: https://www.uscis.gov/about-us/our-history. Accessed December 2018.

Unofficial Ambassadors. 1945. *Committee on Friendly Relations Among Foreign Students.* New York: Author.

Wang, Y.T. 1966. *Chinese Intellectuals in the West 1872–1949.* Chapel Hill, NC: University of North Carolina Press.

Wheeler, W. Reginald, Henry H. King, and Alexander B. Davidson, eds. 1925. *The Foreign Student in America.* New York: Association Press.

Zhuxian, Yi. 1992. Hu Shi, Chinese and Western Culture. *The Journal of Asian Studies* 51 (4, Nov.): 915–916.

CHAPTER 6

The Student Exchange Boom Following World War II

In the late summer of 1939, educators were concerned about the future of institutions of higher learning, and for Western civilization itself. It was no surprise to most observers that education exchange programs would be early casualties of the events to come. Ironically, these were the very programs whose lofty initiatives were intended, at least in part, to avert the devastation of another global conflict through the promotion of greater intercultural understanding.

Impending threats to student safety were eminent, and there was no question about the need to suspend such programs. The same year an article in *Time Magazine* reflected on the situation in Europe. It mentioned the now-white-haired Stephen Duggan, still director of the Institute of International Education (IIE), who predicted that the war would interfere with the education of 8000 US students abroad, and the 7500 foreign students enrolled in the United States. With regret, he announced that his Institute would cancel the fellowships of 300 US scholars who had planned to go to Europe in the fall. He viewed it as an interlude in IIE's work, adding that they intended to continue stronger than before.[1]

A harbinger of things to come was the influx of academic refugees who escaped Europe during the 1930s, threatened with being stripped of their academic freedom in teaching and writing. The prospect of compulsory service to socialist or fascist governments, prison, or possibly execution caused many of Europe's leading intellectuals to flock to the United States

© The Author(s) 2019
T. B. Bevis, *A World History of Higher Education Exchange*,
https://doi.org/10.1007/978-3-030-12434-2_6

and elsewhere in search of a secure academic haven. Distinguished German professors, many of whom were Jewish, would flee the Nazi regime that had come to power in 1933.

Foreign Student Enrollments

Between 1919 and 1942, whenever a census of foreign students in the United States was compiled, the customary list of schools polled was taken from an Office of Education directory. The first foreign student census had been attempted by the Committee on Friendly Relations Among Foreign Students, using the directory, with the addition of several schools they thought were appropriate for inclusion. In 1942 the Committee reported 8075 foreign students from 95 countries studying in 600 US institutions of higher education. The figures were compiled from the enrollment numbers that were reported by those registrars who responded to the census request.[2]

The following figures from the 1949 issue of *Unofficial Ambassadors*, a publication of the Committee on Friendly Relations, show the overall growth of the foreign student population from 1930 to 1949. The totals reflect early foreign student census figures compiled by the Committee, as well as later counts obtained in collaboration with the IIE.

1949–1950	29,813
1947–1948	17,218
1946–1947	14,942
1944–1945	6954
1939–1940	6154
1936–1937	7036
1930–1931	9643

In 1947, the Committee and the IIE collaborated to conduct a more thorough census, using the same list of institutions. This initial list did not include schools such as hospitals that provided nursing instruction, theological seminaries, and other business and professional schools, such as those operated by private industry, even when the institutions enrolled foreign students. In 1948, the Committee and IIE agreed that some of these institutions should be added to the list, to produce a more accurate count. The final list for the 1948/1949 census of foreign students in US higher education included 2512 institutions.[3]

IIE president Donald Shank reported that, according to the 1948/1949 official census, there were 26,759 foreign students enrolled in US academic institutions, from 151 countries, colonies, dependencies, protectorates, absorbed states, and states, studying fields from architecture to zoology. The top sender was Canada, followed by China, India, and Mexico. As a body, Shank pointed out, they were more representative of the peoples of the world than the United Nations. The population of foreign students in America was of 152 different faiths, and slightly more than one-half of the foreign student body were undergraduates. About one out of every five students from abroad was studying engineering, and around one out of ten were preparing for a career in some branch of medicine. The study of agriculture accounted for only 4 percent of the foreign students, outdistanced by business administration, religion, and education.[4]

As in earlier surveys, foreign students were shown to prefer America's well-known institutions. The largest numbers studied at Columbia (1140), the Universities of California (971), and the University of Michigan (818). The Massachusetts Institute of Technology, Harvard, and Columbia had the largest percentages of foreign student representation among the entire student body—7.1 percent, 5.3 percent, and 4.9 percent, respectively. One striking exception existed to this pattern. Montezuma Seminary in Montezuma, New Mexico, had a foreign student body of 309 (99 percent of its total enrollment) consisting chiefly of Mexicans studying for the priesthood. Because Montezuma was such a special case, IIE omitted it from its college rankings in its annual census.[5]

More than half of the 27,000 foreign students enrolled, according to the 1949 count, were hosted by six states: New York (5000, or 18.7 percent); California (3098, or 11.6 percent); Massachusetts (2019, or 7.5 percent); Michigan (1921, or 7.2 percent), Illinois (1514, or 5.7 percent), and Pennsylvania (1064, or 4.0 percent). That year the cost of room, board, and tuition at an American college or university usually was somewhere between $1500 and $2000 per year—expensive for anyone at the time but particularly for a foreign student who had the added expense of travel. About two-thirds of foreign students were dependent on financial assistance of one form or another, either from their home country, or from an individual, school, foundation, or government agency of the United States. Home-government assistance for foreign students usually took the form of all-expense study grants for students deemed as having exceptional promise. Turkey, India, and the Philippines were especially invested in grants for aspiring scholars, sending more than 2000 students to the United States in 1948 (Tables 6.1 and 6.2).[6]

Table 6.1 Foreign student enrollments for 1948–1949: top countries of origin

Canada and Newfoundland	4197
China	3914
India	1493
Mexico	1344
Cuba	778
Turkey	660
Norway	541
Columbia	537
Iran	446

Source: *Open Doors*, 1948–1949

Table 6.2 Foreign student enrollments for 1948–1949: top ten institutions

Columbia University	1140
University of California	971
University of Michigan	818
New York University	724
Harvard University	631
University of Minnesota	402
Massachusetts Institute of Technology	382
Syracuse University	363
University of Wisconsin	340
University of Illinois	336

Source: *Open Doors*, 1948–1949

Communities promoted education exchange during the postwar years in an unusual variety of ways, including offering discounted tuition, housing supplied by a fraternity or other group, or grants from local Chambers of Commerce or Rotary clubs, to name a few examples. In spite of early Cold War tensions, Americans generously supported student education exchange during the years of postwar recovery. After World War II, as many war-torn institutions in Europe were in the process of reconstruction, globally minded leaders and educators turned to the work of rebuilding international connections. Agencies such as the new Germany Academic Exchange Service, and many others, would be founded to help reinstate and promote the sort of cultural and education efforts that existed in the prewar years. Around the same time, the United Kingdom began inviting German students to apply for Rhodes scholarships and other sources of support for academic sojourns.

Americans were now in almost universal support of institutionalized peacemaking, deeming it essential for the rebuilding and recovery of the economic stability in Europe. Spared the physical destruction suffered by many European countries, the American economy had in fact been stimulated by the war. Now armed with nuclear capabilities, it had remained militarily and economically dominant, a set of circumstances that served to secure America's position as the undisputed world leader. With its global influence in place, the United States was prepared to support the establishment of a successor organization to replace the waning League of Nations. Armed with the wisdom of hindsight, a new global agency might be free of the flaws of Woodrow Wilson's now-weakened initiative. In 1945, some 51 nations attended the founding conference in San Francisco of a new creation—the United Nations. Among its first initiatives would be an array of cultural and educational exchanges.

UNESCO

In 1948 the United Nations Educational, Scientific and Cultural Organization, or UNESCO, brought the first UNESCO Fellows to the United States to study. The organization had begun approximately six years before. As early as 1942, representatives of the Allied governments of Europe met in the United Kingdom for the Conference of Allied Ministers of Education. World War II was far from over, yet those countries were already looking for ways to reconstruct their system of education once peace was restored. As the project gained momentum, more governments, including the United States, elected to join.

A United Nations conference for the establishment of an educational and cultural organization had convened in London in November 1945, gathering representatives from 44 countries. Spurred by France and the United Kingdom, two countries that had suffered tremendous hardship during the war, the delegates conspired to create an organization that would embody a genuine culture of peace. At the close of the conference, 37 countries founded the United Nations Educational, Scientific and Cultural Organization. Its constitution was signed in November 1945 and came into force a year later, after ratification by 20 countries: Australia, Brazil, Canada, China, Czechoslovakia, Denmark., Dominican Republic, Egypt, France, Greece, India, Lebanon, Mexico, New Zealand, Norway, Saudi Arabia, South Africa, Turkey, the United Kingdom, and the United States. Paris hosted the first session of the General Conference of UNESCO, which included the participation of representatives from 30 governments entitled to vote.

The new organization was the only UN body with a mandate to support national capacity-building in higher education. Designed to develop global and regional networks that could assist with a broad range of higher education issues (academic mobility, international exchange, research on education systems and knowledge production, curriculum innovation, leadership roles for women educators, teacher development, and the promotion of quality in higher education), the organization also provided a platform for dialogue on how best to adapt education systems to the new social, cultural, and economic challenges of a globally connected world. Author Archibald MacLeish, the first US member of UNESCO's governing board, wrote the preamble to its 1945 Constitution, using the opening line "Since wars begin in the minds of men, it is in the minds of men that the defenses of peace must be constructed."[7]

Swords into Plowshares: The Fulbright Program

As game day approached, sportswriters picked Southern Methodist University (SMU) by six touchdowns. When the players walked onto the field, more than 2000 spectators had gathered to witness the anticipated slaughter. The Arkansas players, some wearing leather caps and some bareheaded, were nervous. The SMU players were older, larger, and supremely confident, but the Arkansas youngsters were tough. The game turned into a defensive struggle. Operating out of the single wing, Bill Fulbright passed for the only touchdown, sealing the victory with a fourth down field goal late in the game. Fulbright was the archetypal Big Man On Campus in 1924, president of Sigma Chi fraternity and a member of virtually every other important club on campus, even the Glee Club.[8]

Born in 1905 in the small town of Sumner, Missouri, James William Fulbright would attend the nearby University of Arkansas in Fayetteville, the state's largest research facility. Bright and popular, he was the quarterback for the university's Razorback football team, and was awarded a Rhodes scholarship at age 20, which would transport him to Oxford, England. Fulbright later studied law at the George Washington University, where he taught for a short time, and he also served briefly in the Justice Department. By the time he returned to Arkansas in 1936, he was a committed internationalist. Fulbright assumed the administrative leadership of the University of Arkansas, his beloved alma mater, at age 34, making him the youngest president of a major university in America.[9]

His journey on to the senate would be rife with local color. Fulbright's mother Roberta was recognized in the area as an outspoken and progressive editor for the local newspaper the *Northwest Arkansas Times*.

In her articles she had been sharply critical of Arkansas' new governor, Homer Adkins. Convicted perhaps by association, William Fulbright would eventually be compelled to leave his position at the university, by some reports due to ongoing pressure from the governor's office. At least that was Bill Clinton's take on the situation. The former president, a longtime friend and colleague, would detail the incident in his book *My Life*. Without a job and with "nothing better to do," wrote Clinton, Fulbright filed for the open congressional seat in northwest Arkansas, and easily won. In his only term with the House of Representatives, he would sponsor the Fulbright Resolution. In 1944 Fulbright ran for the US Senate. Coincidentally, his main opponent was the same man who had cost him his job with the university, Homer Adkins. Fulbright evened the score, as Clinton put it, by winning the election and serving as a US senator for the next three decades.[10]

In 1945, at the close of World War II, Fulbright introduced a bill in the US Congress that called for the promotion of international goodwill through the exchange of students, in the fields of education, culture, and science. "I just got to thinking one day ... [how] friendship between China and ourselves was greatly influenced by the Boxer Rebellion .... The result was to make them actually feel that we were civilized ... and interested in their welfare. That kind of feeling is fundamental to not having war every twenty years."[11] Such a venture could be financed, he suggested, by selling the surplus materials and properties that had been abandoned since the war. It was an inspired piece of legislation. President Harry S. Truman signed the bill into law on August 1, 1946. It would become the Fulbright Program, the government's flagship international exchange effort. In the decades following the bill's signing, thousands of "Fulbrighters" would participate in the program, from almost every region of the world. The Institute of International Education was approached by the Department of State's Bureau of Educational and Cultural Affairs in 1947 to administer the new Fulbright Educational Exchange Program on its behalf. The duties would be handled in partnership with the Council for International Exchange of Scholars (CIES), a private organization and division of IIE, which would administer the faculty component.

The initial legislation provided no funds designated for bringing international students to America. It would take a separate legislation to allocate the money necessary to make it a two-way flow of student exchange.

Referred to as the Smith-Mundt Act, the United States Information and Educational Exchange Act established a programming mandate that still serves as a foundation for US overseas cultural programs. It was passed into law by President Truman in 1948. Models for distributing its allocations had been earlier exchange efforts, such as the Boxer Indemnity scholarships, which brought students from China to America. Other precedents were the Belgian Relief project in the 1920s and the Finnish World War I debt repayments.

The first agreement for student exchange under the Fulbright initiative was signed in China, on November 9, 1947. Its first student participants, however, were from Burma. Embroiled in a civil war, and under threat of Communist rule, there was not a more unsettled place on earth to begin the Fulbright Program than in Burma. J. Russell Andrus, Second Secretary of the US Embassy in Burma, because of his deep understanding of the region, was asked to guide the program. Andrus had been a Baptist missionary, and a professor of economics at the Baptists' Judson College and later at Rangoon University. The Fulbright Program would be unique in Burma because it was implemented there, and also because it included medical and agricultural education, setting a template for the Point Four technical assistance projects to come.

Initially, the program brought six American students to Burma and also sent several Burmese to study in the United States, simultaneously. The first grants were awarded in 1948. One of the students attended Rangoon University; another went to the famed "Burma Surgeon" Gordon Seagrave's Hospital in the Hills. A third attended Sao Saimong. Because of Dr. Seagrave's affiliation with healthcare education, the first Fulbright scholars to go to the United States were nursing students.[12]

Otto and Helen Hunerwadel headed up a follow-up project, focusing on agricultural education and home economics. The Hunerwadels had adventurous spirits, and, as they traveled to remote areas of Burma to promote education, their stories became the stuff of local legend—so much so that Otto would be the prototype for the hero of the controversial novel *The Ugly American*, published a decade later. The title is misleading. Local residents had dubbed Otto Hunerwadel an "ugly" American as a term of endearment, because it distinguished their beloved teacher from the broader population of self-important, self-serving, and better dressed Americans living in Burma.[13]

By late 1949, 123 Fulbright grants had been awarded in Burma, China, the Philippines, and New Zealand. These included 20 graduate scholarships for Americans to study in China, 6 grants-in-aid for professorships, and 15 for research fellowships in China. There were 26 travel grants for Chinese students to come to the United States, 4 for visiting professorships in Burma, and others. Also in 1949, the Turkish Fulbright Commission was established by a binational agreement signed between the United States and Turkey, and the Australian Fulbright Program was put in place.[14]

Postwar Middle Eastern Exchanges

Saudi Arabia was one of the first Middle Eastern countries to participate with Fulbright scholarships, a decision driven by academic and professional need, largely the result of a new and fledgling oil industry. Americans had stepped in to administer the new enterprise, as there was little expertise in oil production among the local citizens, but the Saudis wanted to change that. The Saudi Minister of Commerce stated that this would be an important role for America. Saudi Arabia would also make use of Aramco scholarships, grants from the Arabian American Oil Company (now the Saudi Arabian Oil Company) as their commitment to education gained momentum.

Few Saudi citizens had studied in America prior to the postwar years. Fadil Gabani was one, traveling to the United States before the war began and then finally graduating in 1954 from the Colorado School of Mines. Gabani would go on to become Saudi Arabia's first deputy minister of petroleum for mineral affairs, and also served as Saudi Arabia's representative to the European Atomic Energy Commission in Vienna. In 1978 and 1979 he was chairman for the board of governors of the International Atomic Energy Agency. Another war-era student, Abdullah Tariki, earned a master's degree in geology and petroleum engineering in Texas in 1947, then later became Saudi Arabia's first minister of petroleum. Ali Abdullah Alireza attended Berkeley in 1945, the year representatives of 46 nations were to meet in San Francisco to draft the United Nations charter. King Abdulaziz himself requested that the 23-year-old take time off from school to join the Saudi Arabian delegation at the conference. Ali would later become Saudi Arabia's ambassador to the United States.[15]

Saudi Arabia was investing in education. In April 1948 the official government newspaper published the national budget for the period from November 25, 1947 to November 13, 1948, which reported that 7,022,224 Saudi riyals were allotted for education, 3.2 percent of the national expenditure of 214,586,500 riyals. Following years would see a similar allotment, funds that resulted in the establishment of several educational institutions. Saudi Arabia's first technical secondary school and institute of higher learning, the College of Sharia, was founded in 1949. It would later become Umm Al Qura University. Three more colleges—the Teachers College, the College of Sharia in Riyadh, and the College of Arabic Language in Riyadh—were granted charters in 1952, 1953, and 1954, respectively.[16]

The creation of the Saudi Arabian Cultural Mission in 1951 would allow for the administration of programs and policies relating to Saudi students in America. It would also function as the intermediary between educational institutions in the United States and the kingdom, regarding issues relating to culture, education, or science. First headquartered at the Saudi Arabian Mission to the United Nations in New York, it would relocate to an independent space under the name Saudi Cultural Office in America. The mission would begin by supervising the welfare of the 48 Saudi students already enrolled in the United States. By the 1970s an estimated 11,000 students were sponsored by the Saudi Mission, enrolled in English-language institutes, colleges, and universities in more than 550 American cities. With them were several hundred offspring, who attended American elementary and secondary schools.[17]

Adding to Saudi enrollments were students sponsored by the Saudi armed forces, and by *Saudia*, the kingdom's national airline, and more Saudi students were coming to the United States on Fulbright and Aramco scholarships. From the late 1940s to the late 1970s, their numbers increased ten-fold, according to historian Abdul Latif Tibawi. It was significant, he said, that in 1978 seven out of the ten US alumni serving in the cabinet had also served as faculty or administrators in one of Saudi Arabia's own universities after their graduation. Saudi leaders had set examples in support of the education exchange effort. King Faisal sent seven of his eight sons to the preparatory Hun School in Princeton, New Jersey, or nearby Lawrenceville School, and each would go on to attend college in the United States or in England.[18]

AMIDEAST

Hitler's eyes "had the peculiar shine which often distinguishes geniuses, alcoholics and hysterics.... In less than 50 seconds I was quite sure I was not [meeting the next chancellor of Germany]."[19] He was not to be taken seriously, concluded American foreign correspondent Dorothy Thompson in 1931, after she interviewed the controversial Hitler for a news article. It was a monumental error in judgment, but others had made the same mistake, and even those who correctly predicted the future were often unheeded. Writers such as Edgar Ansel Mowrer of the *Chicago Daily News* were warning Jews to leave Germany, but most failed to recognize the severity of the situation until it was too late.[20]

Dorothy Thompson was a glamorous war correspondent who became a national celebrity, famous in part for having been the first American journalist kicked out of Germany by Adolph Hitler. In 1934, typing from her post in Berlin, Thompson had been unrelenting in her outspoken opinions until an exasperated Hitler finally had the Gestapo march her straight out of the country. But the event did not end her career. Back in America her many articles and stories in nationwide publications propelled her to national and international fame and in 1939 *Time Magazine* proclaimed Dorothy Thompson to be one of the two most influential women in the United States. The other was Eleanor Roosevelt. Thompson was the inspiration behind the character played by Katherine Hepburn in the 1942 movie *Woman of the Year*. She would marry the acclaimed writer Sinclair Lewis.[21]

After World War II, Thompson contributed a thrice-weekly column in the *New York Herald Tribune*, a piece that was syndicated and distributed nationwide. In postwar years she was a passionate supporter of the Zionist cause, in part because she had seen the atrocities against the Jews at the hands of the Nazis, first-hand. A trip to Palestine, however, allowed her to witness something else—the reality of the conditions there. From that point on, Dorothy Thompson became an outspoken advocate for the Arabs. She watched her career vanish almost overnight, as the media companies, many owned by those sympathetic to Jewish causes, now refused to print her work. Thompson's writings virtually disappeared from American journalism, but the reversal of fortune did not dampen her resolve. Working in concert with 22 other distinguished educators, theologians, and writers, Thompson turned her attention to the founding of an organization that would be committed to peace and to lessening the tensions in the Middle East. The members of this new organization would choose a name that stated its theme, the American Friends of the Middle East, or AFME. Founding members included William Aiken, professor of history at Lehigh University, Millar Burrows of Yale, H.H. Fisher of Stanford University, Philip K. Hitti of Princeton, and John A. Wilson of the University of Chicago. Others included George Kamp Keiser, chair of the board of governors of the Middle East Institute in Washington, DC; William Eddy, former US minister to Afghanistan; Wallace Murry, former US ambassador to Iran; Daniel Bliss; ex-missionary Samuel Zwemer; Dorothy Kenyon; Vincent Sheean; George Britt; Leigh White; Harold Lamb; Garland Evans Hopkins; W.L. White; Harry Emerson Fosdick; and David R. Sellers.[22]

At the 1950 Domestic Convention, Thompson declared that the AFME would seek to implement goodwill. Above all the organization sought to demonstrate that the Middle East, from Pakistan and Iran, across the Arab World to Morocco, had friends in the United States. AFME quickly attracted widespread interest and over the next decade succeeded in establishing a network of overseas field offices and organized educational and cultural exchange programs. Among its first official projects were visitor exchanges and exhibition tours for leading contemporary artists. It hosted an international conference of theologians in 1954, the Muslim-Christian Convocation, to encourage constructive dialogue on issues of common concern.

Scholarships for education exchange were soon developed and awarded. In the early 1950s the AFME worked alongside exchange organizations such as the National Association of Foreign Student Advisers (NAFSA), arranging tours of the Middle East for selected college advisers, and organizing programs to help ease student transitions into US institutions. It opened student advising centers in Tehran and Baghdad in 1953 and established country offices in various parts of the Middle East, to provide information about American academic programs to prospective students. In 1956 a job placement service was added. By the 1960s the AFME was working on new programs that would advance technical and administrative skills of working professionals in the region. In the 1960–1961 academic year more than 10,000 students visited AFME's country offices and about 2000 were placed in American universities, some with scholarships that the organization helped them secure.[23]

In 1969 the Department of State Bureau of Educational and Cultural Affairs awarded AFME the administration component of the Fulbright

Foreign Student Program for parts of the MENA (Middle East and North Africa) region. At the same time the organization also began managing a faculty development program through the University of Libya, which would bring 387 of their doctoral candidates to the United States. Soon thereafter, the AFME was renamed America-Mideast Educational and Training Services, Inc., more commonly known by the capitalized acronym AMIDEAST.

The Institute of International Education in the Postwar Years

In 1946, after more than a quarter-century as director of IIE, Stephen Duggan retired. During his administration the institute had placed more than 3000 Europeans, Asians, and Latin Americans in US universities, and had sent more than 2300 US students abroad. Duggan was succeeded by his son, the scholar Laurence Duggan, graduate of Exeter and Harvard's class of 1925. Laurence Duggan was chosen for the $15,000-a-year-job not by his father, but by a special committee whose members included Stephen Duggan's former assistant, Edward R. Murrow, who was now president of Columbia Broadcasting System. As the younger Duggan took over the leadership of IIE, student scholarships were largely a one-way street.[24] In 1946, the institute brought about 1000 foreign students to the United States but sent only 65 US students abroad. The institute was wary about sending American students to European universities until Europe's rebuilding had progressed further. Other options, such as attempts to arrange exchanges with Russia, had failed, and few US students had opted to go to Latin American universities.

After serving only two years as director, Laurence Duggan's life came to an untimely end when he fell from the window of his 16th-story office onto New York's 45th Street. Police investigators were unable to establish the cause of his death. Duggan's brown tweed overcoat and his briefcase, which had contained a ticket for an airplane trip to Washington the next day, were found in his office, his left shoe was still on the floor, and one of the two windows of his office was open—leading to speculation about foul play. Alger Hiss, president of the Carnegie Endowment for International Peace and assistant to Franklin Roosevelt at Yalta when the United Nations was created, had been indicted for perjury by a federal grand jury just five days before. Republican Congressman Karl E. Mundt revealed that Laurence Duggan had attended a secret hearing held by the

House Un-American Activities Committee early in December, where Russian-born Isaac Don Levine claimed to have overheard him collaborating with ex-Communist and Soviet spy Whittaker Chambers.[25]

Some thought the Federal Bureau of Investigation (FBI) had pressured Duggan for information about the charge and he had jumped to his death. Many came to Duggan's defense, including his friend Edward R. Murrow, who at the time was serving as chairman of IIE's board of trustees. There was little solid evidence to prove that Duggan had knowing contact with Communist spies. Richard Nixon, then a California congressman, said that, in his view, Whittaker Chambers' statement of denial had cleared Duggan of any implication in the espionage ring. Nevertheless, Laurence Duggan's death remained unexplained.[26]

In spite of controversy, IIE pressed on, accomplishing many milestones during the postwar years. In 1947, IIE and CIES were asked by the US government to administer the Fulbright Education Exchange Program. They subsequently arranged for more than 4000 Americans to go to Europe to aid in reconstruction. In 1948 the first UNESCO Fellows, foreign students brought to the United States for study, were placed and counseled by IIE. That same year IIE signed an agreement with the Department of the Army to bring students from occupied areas of Germany, Japan, and Austria to the United States on exchange programs, as part of the postwar reconstruction efforts. In 1950 IIE aided Hungarian refugee students, arranging scholarships for more than 700 freedom fighters to study in the United States. Because the flow of international students nearly doubled during the decade, IIE established a network of US offices to serve the growing numbers of students.

In 1951 IIE's regional offices opened in Chicago, Houston, Denver, and San Francisco, with support from the Ford Foundation. The following year IIE initiated the International Music Competition Project, then in 1954 published its first annual *Open Doors* report, which was, and still is, the foremost source for international student exchange census data.

In 1958 IIE's president traveled to Moscow to develop exchanges between the United States and Russia, and the Department for East-West Exchanges was established. The same year IIE launched the Counsel of Higher Education in the American Republics. The following year the Young Artists Project, designed to bring young foreign talent in the creative arts to the United States for study and travel, was begun. In 1960 IIE established overseas offices in Asia, Africa, and Latin America.[27]

NAFSA

The National Association of Foreign Student Advisers (NAFSA) had been conceived and organized in the years preceding World War II, but their impact would become significant after the restoration of peace. NAFSA's first conference, which took place in Cleveland on April 28–30, 1942, was under the auspices of the Institute of International Education in cooperation with the Department of State, the US Office of Education, and the Office of the Coordinator of Inter-American Affairs (renamed the Office of Inter-American Affairs in 1945). The scope of the conference was broad, covering topics that emphasized issues and problems that resulted from the war and that foreign students now faced, such as difficulties in transportation, selective service regulations, the evacuation of Japanese-American students from the West Coast, and the need for funds and work opportunities for stranded students. The first conference also addressed special problems relating to Latin American students due to the interest in Pan Americanism and the large enrollments from Latin American countries in the United States. At this first conference, only a few persons were formally identified as foreign student advisers (FSAs). At the next convocation, held in Chicago in 1947, the number of FSAs exceeded 30, but those were barely enough to adequately take care of the ever-increasing postwar enrollments. In 1947 there were 10,341 students from 91 countries enrolled in colleges and universities in the United States, with 19 institutions hosting more than 100 nonnationals on their campuses.[28]

Also sponsored by IIE and the Department of State was the 1947 Chicago conference, which sought to establish a Conference Steering Committee to guide future conferences. Attendees adopted a resolution to form a Committee on By-Laws for a "National Association." There was discussion about what to name the new association, as well as about issues pertaining to membership qualification and the structure of the organization, all of which were to be voted on at the next conference. At the 1948 Ann Arbor Conference on International Student Exchange, assisted by the W. K. Kellogg Foundation, the new National Association of Foreign Student Advisers was officially born. By this time, 43 of the 224 conference attendees had titles that could be interpreted as "foreign student adviser."[29]

By the end of the conference, the bylaws had been discussed, modified, and passed, and officers were elected. Professor Clarence Linton, Advisor to Students from Other Lands at Teachers College, Columbia University, was named president. Allen C. Blaisdell, Advisor to Foreign Students and Director of International House, Berkeley, became vice president. Other officers included Harry H. Pierson, Director of Programs for the Institute of International Education, as secretary, and Joe W. Neal, Adviser, Foreign Students' Advisory Office, University of Texas, as treasurer. Twenty-four others were elected to the board of directors, including Laurence Duggan, President of the Institute of International Education, and J. Benjamin Schmoker, general secretary of the Committee on Friendly Relations Among Foreign Students.[30]

Foreign student advisers, teachers of English, and community groups were now joined in a combined effort through membership in NAFSA to better serve students from abroad. Article II of the new association's bylaws stated that the purpose of this association would be to promote the professional preparation, appointment, and service of foreign student advisers in colleges and universities and in other agencies concerned with student interchange; to serve more effectively the interests and needs of exchange students; to coordinate plans for student interchange through comprehensive voluntary cooperation of all agencies and individuals concerned with exchange students. To fulfill that purpose the organization would initiate, promote, and execute such systematic studies, cooperative experiments, conferences, and other similar enterprises as were required to that end.[31]

A central concern was the quality of the foreign student experience in the United States, both in the classroom and out. People responsible for creating a good experience for foreign enrollees were largely student advisers and English teachers, and turnover tended to be high among those groups, so to improve the situation, NAFSA focused on in-service training. Publications to support those efforts were also put in place. Established in 1949 with Katherine Bang as its first editor, the widely circulated *NAFSA Newsletter* provided the first vehicle for the dissemination of written information among professionals who advised and otherwise served foreign students.

Four years after its founding NAFSA's first grant for travel abroad was established, with assistance from the American Friends of the Middle East. Other NAFSA services and contributions have included its government liaison activities, the development of relationships with educational and cultural officers of foreign embassies, its cooperative relationships with other organizations interested in international education exchange, the reporting of relevant research, and the development of a code of ethics for practitioners in the field.

Fields of Study

In 1955–1956, a total of 6033 foreign physicians from 84 countries were training in American hospitals as interns or residents, representing an increase of nearly 1000 over the previous academic year. The majority of foreign doctors training in US hospitals were from the Far East, Europe, and Latin America, but large numbers were also coming from the Near and Middle East and Canada. Almost universally shared was the dream of earning a medical degree from a prestigious school in the United States. Most of the visiting physicians in the mid- and late 1950s were taking advanced training as residents (69 percent), a pattern that held true for almost all nationality groups. Of the total number of physicians, 13 percent were women. The Philippines accounted for 38 percent of all foreign female doctors enrolled. In fact the largest number of internationals training to be physicians in the mid-1950s was from the Philippines, with a total of 1065 students enrolled in US institutions. Canada was next, with 584; followed by Mexico, with 489; Germany, 364; Turkey, 320; Italy, 260; Greece, 232; Korea, 216; and India, 208.[32]

In 1956 foreign physicians were enrolled for training in 44 states, the District of Columbia, the Canal Zone, and Hawaii. One-quarter of the total was concentrated in the state of New York and another quarter was training, collectively, in Ohio, Pennsylvania, New Jersey, Massachusetts, Illinois, Missouri, Maryland, Michigan, and Minnesota. Eleven hospitals, mostly concentrated in the east, had more than 40 foreign doctors in training on their house staffs. Bellevue Hospital Center in New York City hosted the most, with 101. The Mayo Foundation in Rochester had 97, and Jersey City Hospital was hosting 75.

The most popular field of study for foreign students in the United States in 1956 was not medicine, however. Engineering was the leading field, accounting for 22 percent of the total, or 8089 students, and the most frequently reported field of study for students from Columbia, Iran, Greece, Venezuela, Jordan, China, India, Israel, Cuba, and Iraq. The second most popular area was the humanities, with a total of 7585 foreign enrollees (21 percent of the foreign enrollment), followed by the social sciences, with 15 percent. As for academic level, more than half of all foreign students enrolled in the United States, about 56 percent, were undergraduates. More than one-third (37.4 percent) were studying at the graduate level.[33]

EVALUATING INTERNATIONAL STUDENT CREDENTIALS

Admissions officers in American colleges and universities faced one of the most complex challenges in the postwar era. When applying to US institutions, foreign students presented many types of academic credentials, from a vast array of different educational systems, and admissions officers were charged with the unenviable task of determining whether each nonnational applicant qualified for admission to American institutions of higher learning. Credentials differed from country to country. Sets of standards were needed to help determine the qualifications of international students.

From the end of World War II and through the early 1950s, American collegiate admissions personnel could call for governmental assistance if they had difficulty with credentials evaluation. Admissions personnel could contact the division of International Educational Relations in the US Office of Education if they found things confusing. Established in 1918, the division was comprised of a small staff of specialists to aid and advise in the processing of evaluating any foreign student's record. In its first year of operation there was just one call for help. In 1924, there were 81 requests for assistance, and in 1928, the number increased to 299. By 1948 the division was handling nearly 3000 requests from college admissions officers. Besides the Office (now Department) of Education, there were other agencies that assisted with foreign student credential evaluation, such as the Institute of International Education, the Department of Education of the Methodist Church, the American Association of Collegiate Registrars and Admissions Officers, and the National Association of Foreign Student Advisers.[34]

The admission of a foreign student into a college or university involved a series of steps that began with collecting a student's education records and evaluating the records' equivalency to the requirements of the institutions to which the student was applying. Each student's country of origin and the characteristics of that country's education system had to be considered during the admissions process. Often complex, the process usually entailed interviews of the applicant and a determination of his or her ability to communicate effectively in English. Complicating things further, American colleges themselves had differing standards. Since 1935, to provide an example, Iran had implemented an education system based on six years of elementary school followed by six years of secondary school, which was divided into two cycles of five years and one year. Each cycle was concluded by a state examination. When considering an Iranian student's qualifications for admission, many American institutions required a certificate indicating the completion of the fifth year, while other US institutions required the certificate identifying the completion of the sixth year. There was disagreement among advisers about which level of achievement met American expectations for a high school education.

India is another example. In the 1950s its public educational system consisted of four years of primary school, a four-year middle school, and then two years of high school. After the ten-year program, students took either the "school leaving examination" or an Indian university's matriculation examination. After two years of university work, students were required to take the intermediate examination, followed by an additional two years of college to attain a bachelor's degree. American admissions officers took various approaches in evaluating the credentials of Indian students, depending on the institution. Some US institutions required a certificate of completion of the middle school, while others required the certificate of the school leaving examination. Others wanted the Indian university matriculation examination.[35]

Transfers between institutions created similar frustrations. All colleges required a statement of grades and credit points earned, but institutions varied in their requirements regarding advance-standing credit, secondary school units, scholastic aptitude test scores, achievement tests, or personal interests. Postwar era surveys often showed a high degree of dissatisfaction among foreign students, regarding the admissions process. NAFSA would work to provide training and to establish workable standards.

Postwar Chinese Enrollments

"From now on, the Chinese people have stood up!" declared Mao Zedong at Tiananmen Square on October 1, 1949. But those who did quickly discovered that they could stand only on their own soil. When the People's Republic of China took control in 1949, an isolationist policy was strictly enforced, and education systems and requirements were changed. No more would China's students be allowed to study in the West, proclaimed Mao.[36]

Thanks in part to the use of Boxer Rebellion Indemnity funds, China had sent increasing numbers of students to the United States in the early decades of the twentieth century. The defeat of China's Nationalist government, its retreat to Taiwan, and the triumphant establishment of the Maoist People's Republic of China would change everything. When Chinese students again ventured into American colleges and universities, admissions officials were faced with evaluating mixed sets of academic records. Sometimes a student's records would have spanned the two distinct systems. English-language proficiency was often the chief obstacle for Chinese students.

As China's civil war wound down and Communist forces prepared to occupy Peking (Beijing), most of the Chinese students enrolled in American colleges and universities instantly found themselves cut off from any source of support, and in 1949, six months after the fall of Peking to Communism, more than 2000 students reported extreme financial exigency. In the Boston area alone, 97 were declared to be in acute distress. The burden of assisting these stranded students fell on the host colleges and universities, and scholarship funds were made available wherever possible. Emergency loans were granted, and tuition payments were deferred. Churches, civic organizations, and businesses donated both time and money to help the students. The Chinese Embassy in Washington also contributed what it could from its rapidly declining funds.[37]

These combined efforts were not enough to meet either the immediate or the ongoing needs of the students, and the US government increased aid for stranded postwar Chinese. The Department of State, through the Office of Education and the China Institute in America, allocated around $8000 for distribution to a limited number of students.[38] Over the next several years, that figure increased to almost $8 million. The funds would be distributed to the 3517 Chinese students and 119 Chinese scholars and visiting professors in institutions of colleges and universities across America. Funding recipients were required to sign a pledge stating that upon completion of his or her education they would return to China and make their skills useful—a condition that had to be dropped when the loss of the mainland to the Communists made a safe return to China impossible.

An additional $4 million was made available by Congress, as part of the Foreign Aid Appropriation Act of 1950 (Public Law 327); then in June 1950, an additional $6 million was provided under the China Area Aid Act (Public Law 535). These funds were administered by the Division of Exchange of Persons in the State Department. Congressional appropriations were authorized to enable Chinese students and scholars to achieve a meaningful educational objective, after which they could either return to their home country or, with authorization from the Immigration and Naturalization Service, accept employment in the United States to support themselves until such time a return home was feasible. To qualify for aid, Chinese students had to be citizens of China as evidenced by a passport or other identifying document; in financial need as certified by their official campus representatives and references; enrolled in an institution of higher learning approved by the Secretary of State; in good standing and working full time for an academic degree; and residing in the United States before January 1, 1950.[39]

Normally, foreign students were restricted from working while in the United States, but to help offset the cost of the funding program an amendment was made to the China Area Aid Act of 1950, authorizing the Commissioner of Immigration and Naturalization to promulgate a general regulation permitting Chinese students to take jobs. Of the estimated 1300 Chinese students who departed the country, the travel expenses of about 930 were paid in whole or part by the US government. The greatest number of Chinese students (2894) was aided by these funds the following year, but numbers steadily declined after that, and within five years the program was closed. In 1950 and 1951, the Immigration Service of the Department of Justice (DOJ), acting under legislation relating to national emergencies, issued approximately 150 orders temporarily preventing the departure of certain Chinese from the United States. The actions were initiated by the presidential proclamation of a state of emergency in late 1950, at a time when few Chinese had publicly stated desire to return to their homeland. Those detained were mostly students and scholars and limited to individuals who had skills that the DOJ determined might be of use to the Chinese Communist regime.[40]

The detention gathered widespread publicity. One case that received worldwide attention was in September 1951, when nine Chinese, on their way to Asia, were physically removed from the *S.S. President Cleveland* in Honolulu.[41] Little media coverage was given, however, to the millions of dollars contributed by American taxpayers for Chinese student support.

China wanted its students back. At the first Geneva Conference, Chou En-Lai accused the United States of detaining Chinese students in order to keep new technological skills from benefiting China. The Chinese government began to register names of the remaining students' families in preparation for a "letters from home" offensive. Chinese families were mandated to send messages to their sons and daughters in America, strongly urging them to return. Not only did China need the skills of these refugees, it also hoped to avoid what could become a dangerous group of well-educated counter-revolutionaries. Chinese students who remained in America were living in limbo, with no legal status and an indefinite time to stay in the country.

The detention orders were gradually lifted during 1954 and 1955, a reversal of policy that was not necessarily good news for all Chinese detainees. Just a few, at this point, expressed any desire to go back through the "bamboo curtain" to China. Many reported having used the detainment policies as a sort of insurance against Communist pressure. Being legally restrained from returning home allowed them to both appease the Chinese government and to remain in America. Only 39 of those previously detained exercised their privilege of returning to China by the end of 1955.[42]

At some points the Department of State and the Immigration Service found themselves working at cross-purposes. While the State Department was operating under legislation enacted to assist Chinese students in completing their education in the United States, the Immigration Service was trying to enforce increasingly complex immigration statutes implemented in response to the situation with Korea. At the Geneva Conference in 1954, China pushed for a solution to the problem of what to do about the Chinese still in the United States, but American officials were reluctant to authorize a third-party investigation. The chief concern was that any identification of the remaining students and scholars could result in retaliatory action by the Chinese Communist government. India attempted to help resolve the problem by providing a neutral channel through which Chinese citizens, on their own initiative, could seek assistance if they felt passage back to China had been obstructed, or was problematic. In 1955, a year later, the State Department reported that the Indian Embassy had not represented a single Chinese with departure concerns.[43]

The revocation of detention policies would not be the end of the story of the stranded Chinese. The problem of finding satisfactory employment for these Chinese refugees lingered for years and was complicated by the often-daunting task of bringing their families from China to join them. Some shifted to permanent residence status under the provisions of the Refugee Relief Act of 1953, and others married Americans, which increased their preferential status as quota immigrants. In the end the vast majority of detained postwar Chinese and their descendants chose to make the United States their home.

McCarthyism, the Cold War, and the McCarran Act

Communism was on the march everywhere, it seemed to alarmed observers, consuming country after hapless country, and the litany of victims was growing: Czechoslovakia, East Germany, Hungary, Yugoslavia, Romania,

Bulgaria, Estonia, Latvia, Ukraine, Poland, China, Cambodia, Albania, Laos, Vietnam, and others. In the United States, many feared that Communist sympathizers and other assorted leftists would burrow into the foundations of American institutional life itself, undermining the government, subverting business and industry, and corrupting universities.

In response to a rising outcry, Wisconsin Senator Joseph McCarthy spearheaded a campaign to root out all communists, socialists, assorted leftists, and any other subversives who posed a threat to American security. Most legislators were unwilling to publicly raise an opposing voice. An exception was William Fulbright of Arkansas, who said that he hated sanctimonious demagogues parading as patriots. Fulbright cast the only vote in the Senate against giving McCarthy's special investigative subcommittee more money.[44]

American colleges and universities became especially tempting targets during the "McCarthy Era." So-called witch-hunts were conducted across the nation in search of disloyal professors, administrators, and students. Foreign students, scholars, and faculty, especially those from countries sympathetic to Communist ideals, were doubly scrutinized. Some institutions were less willing to enforce the investigation for "un-American" suspects than others. An article in *The Harvard Crimson* recalls the institution's legendary protection of its faculty and students during the "Red Scare" and Harvard's proud position of defiance.[45] Closer scrutiny reveals a public facade not quite consistent with reality. As Harvard's leaders resolved to stand firm against government pressure, at the same time they privately conducted their own investigations, and a few faculty members were relieved of their positions soon thereafter.

The McCarran-Walker Act, Public Law 82-414, otherwise known as the Immigration and Nationality Act (INA), was adopted in 1952. The new law imposed more rigid restrictions on entry quotas to the United States and codified the scattered provisions of several earlier legislative works—the National Origins Act of 1924 for example. It tightened controls over aliens and immigrants, removed racial barriers, and made citizenship available to people of all origins for the first time. It also required screening of aliens to help eliminate suspected security risks. Its statutes addressed questions pertaining to political asylum, deportation, refugee status, intercountry adoptions, replacement of immigration documents, visas, family- and employment-related immigration, foreign student authorizations, travel documentation, lawful permanent residency, employment restrictions, and a host of other provisions. The Immigration and Nationality Act allowed students to come to the United States as temporary residents, but the McCarran legislation increased dramatically the extent of evaluation and documentation required.[46]

Critics voiced disapproval of some of the INA's features, such as the restrictions against student work, but also the limitations placed on global education exchange. The National Research Council of the National Academy of Sciences' American Association for the Advancement of Science (AAAS) was among the vocal opponents. It released a statement, saying that the Council was profoundly disturbed over the present world conditions, which were severely impeding the free interchange of knowledge, even among friendly nations. The Council acknowledged the need for measures which would safeguard security but was troubled over the manner in which such measures, in particular the McCarran Act, were being administered.

The year the McCarran bill was enacted, there were 29,813 students from abroad studying in American institutions of higher education, from 121 countries. Canada topped the list with 4498 internationals students, and China took second place, with 3549. Germany was in third place with 1264, and the Philippine Islands had sent 839.[47]

During the 1940s, students from the Western Hemisphere accounted for more than half of all international students living and studying in the United States, but by 1950 the numbers of South American students had substantially decreased. The number of students from the Western Hemisphere remained around 10,000, but the total number of students from Europe suddenly increased by more than 1500, making Europe the second-largest contributor of students.

Regarding gender, during the early 1950s the number of female foreign students accounted for roughly one-fourth of the total foreign student population attending US institutions. In 1953, for example, of the 34,000 foreign students enrolled in higher education in the United States, approximately 8000 were women. Philippine students had the highest ratio of women (44 percent of total Filipino students). French and German students also included higher percentages of females, while India and Iran had the lowest percentage of females represented. By the late 1950s, the ratio of men to women foreign students was closer to three-to-one, with females making up 47 percent of all Filipino students, 39 percent of Jamaican students, 34 percent of French students, and 32 percent of Chinese students.[48]

The overall growth of the foreign student population, the changing student migration patterns, the ongoing process of postwar reconstruction, and America's new legislation all presented new challenges for America's colleges and universities. Postwar America had become much more self-conscious about its relationship with foreign students.[49]

THE 1955–1956 FOREIGN STUDENT CENSUS

The foreign student census released in 1956 was significant because it marked the last time a count of foreign students in the United States was conducted as a cooperative enterprise of the Committee on Friendly Relations Among Foreign Students and the Institute of International Education. The statistical nature of the census itself, combined with the growth of the foreign student population, resulted in the decision to centralize the census-taking process at the IIE. From that point the Institute conducted the annual census alone (Table 6.3).

The international student enrollment in US higher education had reached a total of 36,494 students representing 132 nations, according to the 1955/1956 report. Thirty percent of the total were from the Far East, 23 percent from Latin America, 15 percent from Europe, 14 percent from

Table 6.3 Foreign student enrollments for 1955–1956: top countries of origin

Canada	4990
China	2637
India	1818
Korea	1815
Philippines	1703
Japan	1678
Mexico	1303
Iran	1011
Greece	962
Venezuela	941
Germany	778
United Kingdom	745
Israel	708
Cuba	690
Thailand	659
Iraq	654
Jordan	581
France	548
Jamaica	500

Source: *Open Doors*, 1955–1956

North America (Canada and Bermuda), and 13 percent from the Near and Middle Eastern countries. The nation showing the most growth was Korean. From 203 students enrolled in 1948–1949, the size of this group increased to a total of 1815, taking it from eighth to fourth place in one year. Student enrollments from the Philippines also increased significantly, from 660 in 1948–1949 to 1703 in 1955–1956. Indian and Japanese enrollments increased too, although Japan's rank fell from fourth to sixth place. The only leading nationality group whose enrollments decreased was Colombia. The other large Latin American group, Mexican students, continued to increase in size, and of the European countries, Greece sent the largest group. The number of German students, which had averaged 1250 annually between 1950 and 1953, fell to just under 800 students in 1955–1956. Iranians composed the strongest representation of students from the Middle East, with a total of 1011, double its 1948 enrollment of 466.[50]

Foreign students were reported in all 48 states, the District of Columbia, Alaska, Hawaii, and Puerto Rico. Concentrations were found in certain states, with the largest numbers enrolled in New York (5046). California was second with 4598, followed by Michigan, with 2687; Massachusetts hosted 2643; Illinois, 2299; Pennsylvania, 1559; Texas, 1341; and Indiana, 1173. The District of Columbia, with 1159 students, and Ohio, with 1090, completed the top ten list.

By institution, the University of California hosted the most foreign students, with a total of 1392. Others included Columbia University, with 1224; the University of Michigan, with 1070; New York University, 776; and Harvard University, 729. Completing the top ten were the Massachusetts Institute of Technology (658), the University of Illinois (633); the University of Texas (533); Cornell University (526); and the University of Minnesota (518).[51]

American educational institutions were not yet, by world standards, overcrowded with foreign students. Of the nearly three million students enrolled in American higher education in 1955–1956, only 1 in 70, less than 1.5 percent, were foreign, distributed among some 1630 institutions. Only 12 institutions hosted more than 400. Just to compare, the same year Oxford University hosted a foreign student population that comprised nearly 13 percent of their total enrollments. The foreign student population at the University of Geneva in Switzerland was around 14 percent.[52]

The 1960s and 1970s

John F. Kennedy, who had studied abroad himself, was genuinely concerned with the welfare of the nearly 50,000 foreign students hosted by America's colleges and universities. Reminded that the United States did not have an office in its government that concerned itself solely with the guidance and welfare of foreign students, he wrote a letter to the Secretary of State, suggesting that this should be remedied.[53] During the early 1960s the US government itself contributed a surprisingly small share of the funding for student exchange, providing only partial sponsorship for just 5000 foreign students.

By 1960, 48,486 foreign students were enrolled at 1712 institutions of higher learning in the United States, a 2.6 percent increase over the previous year. The following data are from IIE's 1959–1960 *Open Doors* annual report. As in the preceding years, Canada was the largest sender, representing 12 percent of the total foreign student enrollment. Chinese students constituted 9 percent, followed by India (Table 6.4).

Table 6.4 Foreign student enrollments for 1959–1960: top countries of origin

Canada	5679
China	4546
India	3772
Iran	2507
Korea	2474
Japan	2168
Philippines	1722
Mexico	1352
Venezuela	1126
Greece	1095
Thailand	1006
United Kingdom	993
Cuba	935
Jamaica	902
Turkey	835
Israel	807
Germany	720
Colombia	687
Iraq	675
Lebanon	590
France	572
Jordan	556

Source: *Open Doors*, 1959–1960

By academic level, 24,100 students were enrolled as undergraduates, and 18,114 were studying in graduate programs. The remaining 4266 were unclassified. Academic levels varied according to world region. There were more undergraduate, than graduate, students from Latin and North America, the Near and Middle East, and Africa. European students were almost equally divided between graduates and undergraduates, but four countries—Cuba, Mexico, Venezuela, and Iran—had more than 75 percent of their students enrolled as undergraduates. The largest percentage of graduate students from any one country was India (67 percent), followed by 62 percent of students from the United Kingdom, 60 percent from the Philippines, 55 percent from France, and 52 percent from Japan. Engineering was again the top field of study among foreign students (11,279 enrolled), followed by the humanities and the natural sciences.[54]

All 50 states and the District of Columbia reported hosting international students, with California and New York hosting the lion's share (6457 and 6069 students, respectively, more than 25 percent of the total foreign student population in America). Other states hosting large numbers of internationals were Michigan (3259), Massachusetts (3136), Illinois (2889), the District of Columbia (2020), and Indiana (1819). Eighteen institutions reported having more than 400 foreign students in attendance. The University of California, for the third consecutive year, enrolled the largest number of foreign students. Howard University had the largest percentage of foreign students in relations to its total enrollment.[55]

President Lyndon Johnson would carry on Kennedy's work in promoting and caring for international students. A 1964 gathering on the White House grounds was attended by 800 foreign students from 71 countries, where Johnson told them: "I am glad you have had this chance to see America, to know its people, to understand its problems as well as its achievements. For, like your own countries, we are an unfinished society." In his Special Message to the Congress Proposing International Education and Health Programs, Johnson urged legislators to share his vision. He supported the passage of the International Education and Health Acts of 1966, saying it would be shortsighted to confine the country's vision to its shorelines.[56]

Providing educational rewards to the African countries was now a focus, as enrollments from that region were on the rise. For African students, earning an American degree could be life-changing. In Kenya, as an example, higher education was synonymous with *uhuru* (freedom), and applications for US scholarships flooded American institutions every year. African students had, for the most part, been left on their own to find ways to get to America. The expense was more than many could afford, which sometimes led to students taking dangerous chances. The need for travel assistance, which sparked a political dispute between the Kennedy and Nixon camps, led to the "African Airlift."[57]

The effort was launched when the African-American Students Foundation lined up scholarships to US colleges and universities for 250 students from Kenya and other British-controlled areas of Africa. Kenyan labor leader Tom Mboya, who had organized the students, needed money to get them to America. After repeated rejections from the US State Department, Mboya sought an audience with presidential candidate Richard Nixon. But the State Department turned Nixon down too. The intrepid Mboya then arranged to meet President Kennedy, who agreed to help. Rather than wait for Congress, Kennedy funded the request with family money. Sargent Shriver, Kennedy's brother-in-law and director of the family foundation, suggested funding the entire $100,000. Hearing of the arrangement, Nixon again involved himself with the project, as others joined in. Jackie Robinson, former baseball star, called Nixon and urged his active participation in helping the African students. William Fulbright, then chairman of the Foreign Relations Committee, also was on board, and questioned the State Department's decision to deny support. Presumably through these and other efforts, the State Department reversed their decision and granted the needed $100,000 to the African Airlift project. Airlifts had been arranged on a limited basis since 1959, but this new project was considerably larger in scope.[58]

Another program focused on Africa was developed by Harvard's Dean of Admissions, David Henry, in 1961. This brought 250 students, most from West Africa, to some 150 US campuses. Coordinated by the African-American Institute, the Henry Program included a rigorous selection system, transportation, scholarships, and living expenses, all paid for by the International Cooperation Administration.

The IIE continued their work throughout this period. For one example, IIE undertook administration of the Venezuelan government's Fundacion Gran Mariscal de Ayacucho Scholarship Program, which assisted nearly 4000 promising Venezuelans, many from under-advantaged backgrounds, to study in the United States, in fields related to national development. Also during the 1970s IIE assumed responsibility for a portion of the United States Information Agency's (USIA's) International

Visitor Program, and began administering the ITT (International Telephone and Telegraph) International Fellowship Program, which for many years served as a model for corporate involvement in international education exchange. Then in 1979, IIE established the landmark South Africa Education Program to increase higher opportunities for black South Africans.[59]

Working with the White House and USIA, IIE helped plan the innovative Hubert H. Humphrey Fellowship Program, which brought accomplished professionals from designated countries of Africa, Asia, Latin America, the Caribbean, the Middle East, Europe, and Eurasia to the United States at a midpoint in their careers for a year of study and professional experience. Operating as a Fulbright exchange activity, the Humphrey Program was funded by the US Congress through the Bureau of Educational and Cultural Affairs of the US Department of State. The J. William Fulbright Scholarship Board (FSB), appointed by the President of the United States to oversee and supervise the educational exchanges of the Fulbright Program, had overall responsibility for the final selection of Humphrey Fellows. The fellowships were limited to one academic year, preceded, if appropriate, by a period of English-language training.[60]

THE 1969–1970 FOREIGN STUDENT CENSUS

In 1969–1970, nearly 135,000 international students were enrolled in US colleges and universities, according to the Institute of International Education's *Open Doors* annual report (Table 6.5).

Table 6.5 Foreign student enrollments for 1969–1970: top countries of origin

Canada	13,313
India	11,327
China, Republic of	8566
Hong Kong	7202
Iran	5175
Cuba	4487
Thailand	4372
United Kingdom	4216
Japan	4156
Korea	3991

Source: *Open Doors*, 1969–1970

As in previous years, male foreign students outnumbered females by about three-to-one, although varying from region to region. The ratio of male to female students sent from the Near and Middle East and Africa was about six-to-one. California, New York, and Illinois enrolled the most international students in 1969, followed closely by Michigan. More than 46,000 of the foreign students in the United States that year were self-supporting. As in earlier years, students from the Near and Middle East (40 percent) and the Far East (35 percent) were self-funded. About 25,000 foreign students were funded in whole or in part by US colleges and universities, while private organizations provided financial assistance for about 10,000. The US government provided funding for about 7000 foreign students, and foreign governments helped fund around 6500.[61]

Research on higher education exchange increased during the 1970s. Among the studies and reports were: I.T. Sanders and J.G. Ward's *Bridges to Understanding* (1970); Helm's *Cultures in Conflict: Arab Students in American Universities* (1978); and Pruitt's *The Adaptation of Africans to American Society* (1978). W. Frank Hull's study of foreign students centered on acclimation. As other researchers had revealed, Hill found that foreign students from lesser-known areas and those most easily distinguishable as "foreign" were the ones less able to integrate. According to Singh (1976), adjustment to the learning environment was the most critical area of concern. Spaulding and Flack (1976) agreed. Culture shock, according to Shogren and Shearer (1973), could manifest itself as hostility toward the host country. Chongolnee (1978) agreed that Asians, in general, achieved better overall academic performance than others. Overall, interest in international education exchange was escalating among academics, and related research and publications were becoming more commonplace, and narrower in scope.

Notes

1. *Time Magazine*, "Alarums and Excursions," Vol. XXXIV, no. 12 (September 18, 1939).
2. Unofficial Ambassadors, *Committee on Friendly Relations Among Foreign Students* (New York: Author, 1942).
3. *Open Doors Annual Report* (Institute of International Education, 1949).
4. Ibid., 7.
5. Ibid, 21.
6. Ibid.

7. US Department of Education, UNESCO, United Nations Educational, Scientific and Cultural Organization. Available at: https://www2.ed.gov/about/inits/ed/internationaled/unesco.html.
8. Randall Bennett Woods, *Fulbright, A Biography* (Cambridge University Press, 1995): 14–15.
9. Ibid., 19–43.
10. Bill Clinton, *My Life* (Alfred A. Knopf, 2004): 98–99.
11. Richard T. Arndt and David Lee Rubin, eds., *The Fulbright Difference 1948–1992: Studies on Cultural Diplomacy and the Fulbright Experience* (New Brunswick, NJ: Transaction Publishers, 1993): 1–3.
12. Arndt and Rubin, 3–10.
13. Teresa B. Bevis and Christopher J. Lucas, *International Students in American Colleges and Universities* (New York: Palgrave Macmillan, 2007): 107.
14. Ibid.
15. Katrina Thomas, "America as Alma Mater," *Saudi Aramco World* (May/June 1979): 2–11.
16. George T. Trial and R. Bayly Winder, "Modern Education in Saudi Arabia," *History of Education Journal*, Vol. 1, no. 3 (Spring 1950): 121–133.
17. Ibid.
18. Teresa B. Bevis, *Higher Education Exchange between America and the Middle East through the Twentieth Century* (New York: Palgrave Macmillan, 2016): 115.
19. Jeff Nillson, "The Real Woman of the Year," *The Saturday Evening Post* (July 9, 2011). Available at: http://www.saturdayeveningpost.com/2011/04/21/opinion/dusting-off-first-drafts-of-history.html.
20. Andrew Nagorski, "Dusting Off First Drafts of History," *The New York Times* (April 20, 2012). Available at: www.nytimes.com/2012/04/21/opinion/dusting-off-first-drafts-of-history.html.
21. Nillson.
22. Paul Garrett and Kathleen A. Purpura, *Frank Maria: A Search for Justice and Peace in the Middle East* (Bloomington, IN: AuthorHouse, 2007): 130.
23. Bevis, 208.
24. *Time Magazine*, "The Confidence Game," Vol. LXVIII, no. 2 (July 9, 1956).
25. *Time Magazine*, "The Man in the Window," Vol. LIII, no. 1 (January 3, 1949).
26. Ibid.
27. *Open Doors* 1960, Report on International Education Exchange (New York: Author, 1960).
28. Edward Charnwood Cieslak, *The Foreign Student in American Colleges* (Detroit, MI: Wayne University Press, 1955): 15.

29. Stewart Fraser, *Governmental Policy and International Education* (New York: John Wiley and Sons, 1964): 103.
30. Cieslak.
31. Ibid.
32. *Open Doors Annual Report* (Institute of International Education, 1956).
33. Ibid.
34. Cieslak, 39–60.
35. Ibid.
36. Ning Qian, *Chinese Students Encounter America*, trans. T.K. Chu (University of Washington Press, 1999).
37. Committee on Educational Interchange Policy, *Chinese Students in the United States, 1948–1955* (New York: Author, 1956).
38. Ibid.
39. Committee on Educational Interchange Policy, 7.
40. Ibid.
41. Ibid., 10.
42. Committee on Educational Interchange Policy, 11.
43. Ibid., 12.
44. Clinton, 100.
45. Nathan J. Heller and Jessica R. Rubin-Wills, Crimson Staff Writers, "Trying Times, Harvard Takes Safe Road," *The Harvard Crimson* (June 5, 2003).
46. Ibid.
47. Open Doors 1950 Report on International Education Exchange Institute of International Education (New York: Author, 1951): 9.
48. Ibid.
49. M. Brewster Smith, "Features of Foreign Student Adjustment," *Journal of Higher Education*, Vol. 26, no. 5 (1955): 234.
50. *Open Doors* 1955, Report on International Education Exchange (New York: Author, 1955).
51. Ibid.
52. Ibid.
53. The JFK Presidential Library and Museum, Image Archives, August 8, 1961, Memorandum to the Secretary of State. Available at: https://www.jfklibrary.org/search?search=memorandum+to+the+secretary+of+state+1961. Accessed November 30, 2018.
54. *Open Doors* 1959–1960 Annual Report.
55. Ibid.
56. Woolley and Peters, *The American Presidency Project*, Lyndon B. Johnson, Special Message to Congress Proposing International Education and Health Programs (February 2, 1966). Available at: http://www.presidency.ucsb.edu. Accessed November 30, 2018.

57. George M. Houser, "Meeting Africa's Challenge: The Story of the American Committee on Africa," *A Journal of Opinion*, Vol. 6, nos. 2–3 (Summer–Autumn, 1976): 16–26.
58. "John F. Kennedy and the Student Airlift," John F. Kennedy Presidential Library. Available at: https://www.jfklibrary.org/learn/about-jfk/jfk-in-history/john-f-kennedy-and-the-student-airlift.
59. Institute of International Education, *Opening Minds to the World*, "Timeline and Institute Highlights." Available at: http://www.iie.org.
60. Hubert H. Humphrey Fellowship Program 2001–2002, "Humphrey Fellows." Available at: https://www.humphreyfellowship.org/node/106. Accessed November 30, 2018.
61. *Open Doors* 1969–1970 Annual Report.

REFERENCES

Arndt, Richard T., and David Lee Rubin, eds. 1993. *The Fulbright Difference, 1948–1992: Studies on Cultural Diplomacy and the Fulbright Experience.* New Brunswick, NJ: Transaction Publishers.
Bevis, Teresa B. 2016. *Higher Education Exchange between America and the Middle East through the Twentieth Century.* New York: Palgrave Macmillan.
Bevis, Teresa B., and Christopher J. Lucas. 2007. *International Students in American Colleges and Universities, a History.* New York: Palgrave Macmillan.
Cieslak, Edward Charnwood. 1955. *The Foreign Student in American Colleges.* Detroit, MI: Wayne University Press.
Clinton, Bill. 2004. *My Life.* New York: Alfred A. Knopf.
Committee on Educational Exchange Policy. 1956. *Chinese Students in the United States 1948–1955.* New York: Author.
Fraser, Stewart, and William W. Brickman. 1968. *A History of International and Comparative Education.* Chicago: Scott, Foresman and Company.
Garrett, Paul, and Kathleen A. Purpura. 2007. *Frank Maria: A Search for Justice and Peace in the Middle East.* Bloomington, IN: AuthorHouse.
Heller, Nathan J., and Jessica R. Rubin-Wills 2003. Trying Times, Harvard Takes Safe Road. *The Harvard Crimson*, June 5.
Houser, George M. 1976. Meeting Africa's Challenge: The Story of the American Committee on Africa. *A Journal of Opinion* 6 (2–3, Summer–Autumn): 16–26.
Institute of International Education. 1949. *Open Doors.*
———. 1950. *Open Doors.*
———. 1956. *Open Doors.*
———. 1960. *Open Doors.*
———. 1979a. South Africa Education Program. *Opening Minds to the World.* https://p.widencdn.net/egleca/1979-IIE-Annual-Report.
———. 1979b. Timeline and Institute Highlights. In *Opening Minds to the World.* http://www.iie.org.

Nagorski, Andrew. 2012. Dusting Off First Drafts of History. *The New York Times*, April 20.
Qian, Ning. 1999. *Chinese Students Encounter America*. Translated by T.K. Chu. University of Washington Press.
Smith, M. Brewster. 1955. Features of Foreign Student Adjustment. *Journal of Higher Education* 26 (5): 231–241.
The Hubert H. Humphrey Fellowship Program website. https://www.humphreyfellowship.org/node/106. Accessed December 2018.
Thomas, Katrina. 1979.America as Alma Mater. *Saudi Aramco World*, May/June.
Time Magazine. 1939. Alarums and Excursions. XXXIV (12), September 18.
———. 1949. The Man in the Window. LIII (1), January 3.
———. 1956. The Confidence Game. XLVIII (2), July 9.
Trial, George T., and R. Bayly Winder. 1950. Modern Education in Saudi Arabia. *History of Education Journal* 1 (3, Spring): 121–133.
Unofficial Ambassadors. 1942. *Committee on Friendly Relations Among Foreign Students*. New York: Author.
Woolley and Peters. 1966. The American Presidency Project, Lyndon B. Johnson, Special Message to Congress Proposing International and Health Programs. University of California Santa Barbara, February 2. http://www.presidency.ucsb.edu.

CHAPTER 7

The Late Twentieth Century (1979–1999)

A total of 286,340 international students from 185 countries were enrolled in colleges and universities in the United States in 1979–1980, according to Institute of International Education's (IIE's) *Open Doors* annual census. The Middle East was well-represented. Iran was now the leading sender of students to America. Two other Middle Eastern countries, Saudi Arabia and Jordan, were in the top 15. Middle Eastern enrollments had reached an all-time high, from the region in general but especially from the Organization of the Petroleum Exporting Countries (OPEC), whose presence had escalated at a remarkable rate since its implementation in the 1950s.[1] The trend would be abruptly redirected in 1979, when the Iran Hostage Crisis would result in the severing of ties between America and Iran (Table 7.1).

James Earl Carter, Jr., soft-spoken Southerner and Washington outsider, had been embraced by the American people, who elected him president in 1977. His term would prove to be a time of extraordinary trials, for Carter and also for America.

The Shah of Iran had been reinstated by the coup of 1953. His regime, fiercely anti-Soviet, was well-positioned to ally themselves with the United States. In the 25 years that followed, the Shah earned a reputation for being ruthless when dealing with anyone he considered disloyal, and Savak, the Shah's heavy-handed secret service, had reportedly committed many human rights violations. Nonetheless, during his visit to Iran in

Table 7.1 Foreign students in the United States from OPEC for selected years

	1954–1955	1964–1965	1974–1975	1979–1980
Algeria	1	83	240	1560
Iran	997	3719	13,780	51,310
Iraq	650	919	420	1220
Kuwait	0	214	960	2670
Libya	4	74	980	3030
Qatar	0	4	120	630
Saudi Arabia	40	552	1540	9540
United Arab Emirates	0	1	0	740
Total	1692	5566	18,000	70,700

Source: IIE, *Open Doors*, 1979–1980

1977, Carter publicly proclaimed the country to be an "island of stability" and praised the Shah for his wisdom and sensitivity. His controversial show of support would remain resolute.[2]

In late 1978, with political tensions at an all-time high in Iran, protests denouncing the Shah's regime as anti-Islamic broke out in the city of Qom. By January 1979, the situation had become so perilous that the Shah and his family were forced to flee to Egypt as the exiled Ayatollah Ruhollah Khomeini, who had inspired the revolt from afar, triumphantly returned to Tehran. His thousands of supporters, none apparently remembering America's role in assuring Iran's independence after World War II, shouted "Death to the Three Spreaders of Corruption, Sadat, Carter and Begin!" and "Death to the Great Satan," meaning America.[3]

Iran declared a new republic, and there was little chance for negotiation. Terminally ill with cancer, the exiled Shah was permitted to go to the United States for treatment, which only amplified the wrath of Iranians. In an act of retaliation, on November 4, 1979, hundreds of Iranian college students, with posters of Khomeini and shouting *Allahu Akbar*, scaled the walls of the US Embassy in Tehran. Ransacking the chancery and the residences, they captured 66 Americans as hostages, including diplomats, administrative staff, US Marine guards, and CIA officials. For their release, the kidnappers demanded the Shah's extradition, the transfer of his holdings to Iran, and a public apology from Jimmy Carter.

Carter's response was Operation Eagle Claw, a secret mission to rescue the hostages. Landing in the Iranian desert on April 24, Delta Force and Ranger troops were preparing to refuel when a sudden and violent sandstorm moved into the area. Two of the helicopters crashed and were consumed by flames, causing the mission to be aborted. Seven helicopters, some housing classified documents, were abandoned and left behind. The bodies of eight American servicemen who had been killed in the crash were put on public display. It was a scene eerily reminiscent of the Barbary Wars (1801–1805) during Thomas Jefferson's administration, when the Pasha of Tripoli ordered a display of the remains of Americans sacrificed on the *Intrepid*. A devastated Carter addressed the nation, accepting full responsibility.[4]

Sacrificed also was the exchange of scholarship between the United States and Iran. The loss was significant, because at the time there were more than 51,000 Iranian students enrolled in US colleges and universities.

Under the Ayatollah, Islamic law was integrated into every aspect of the government and military, and education. Khomeini worked to remove any American influence whatsoever from Iran, while he praised and rewarded all acts of terrorism against the West. These actions had the effect of curbing one-fifth of the OPEC production capability, causing a worldwide strain on the oil market. In response, the United States enforced an embargo against Iran, an executive order in 1980 that put a block on properties and investments of the Iranian government. The impact of these events on higher education exchange was immediate. In 1979, Iranians had comprised 29.2 percent of America's total foreign student population—61.3 percent of all Middle Eastern enrollments. By the 1981–1982 IIE census, the region's enrollments had declined by 12.2, the largest overall drop in Middle Eastern enrollments since 1971. Looking at the region as a whole, the numbers can be a bit deceiving. If one excludes the Iranians and looks only at the rest of the Middle Eastern countries, enrollments in American higher education actually rose 3.7 percent over the previous year. The dynamics had shifted. Saudi Arabia was now the leading sender from the region, and for the first time in 27 years, Israel was not on the list of top Middle Eastern senders.[5]

As a group, the 13 members of the Organization of the Petroleum Exporting Countries (OPEC)—Algeria, Ecuador, Gabon, Indonesia, Iran, Iraq, Kuwait, Libya, Nigeria, Qatar, Saudi Arabia, the UAE, and Venezuela—were especially impacted by the events in Iran. In 1979, foreign students from these countries had been increasing in numbers at a much higher rate than students from all other countries, around 12.6 percent. The next year, the 1980–1981 student census showed that the number of enrollments from OPEC increased only 1.3 percent, not the substantial rise exhibited in the previous two years.[6]

The decrease had to do with the new policies put in place after Khomeini took power, but there were deterrents from the American side too. Many were slow to forget the 1979 crisis. "I think it's an absolute disgrace that those people are now going to our schools when the head of the country is saying in effect it is at war with the United States," said Republican John D. Bradley of South Carolina in the *Spartanburg Herald*.[7] Another report in the *Lodi News Sentinel* (Jackson, Mississippi, United Press International) reported that around 500 Iranian college students could be forced to leave Mississippi unless a federal court set aside a selective tuition increase. The tuition increase had been directed at Iranian students only, under an act approved by Mississippi Legislature, but was later challenged by the American Civil Liberties Union on constitutional grounds.

Rebuilding Middle Eastern Enrollments

Actions taken by the IIE and AMIDEAST (America-Mideast Educational and Training Services, Inc.) were especially important in the recovery of Middle Eastern students after 1979. Since the 1970s, AMIDEAST administered scholarship programs in the region for study in the United States, many funded by Arab governments. The Royal Palace of Jordan, the Dubai Petroleum Company and the H.H. Sheik Maktoum Educational Scholarship Program, were among those that sponsored dozens of students for study in the United States. Oman would use the organization's services to operate its own student scholarship program.

A cooperative venture combining AMIDEAST, the Africa-America Institute, the Asia Foundation, and the Experiment in International Living, resulted in the formation of Partners for International Education and Training in 1982. Each of the organizations contributed region-specific expertise in international education exchange to administer the United States Agency for International Development's worldwide participant training program. During the 15 years this venture was in operation, AMIDEAST provided US-based training to more than 6700 participants from the MENA (Middle East and North Africa) region. The organization published the Directory of Academic and Technical Training Programs in Selected Middle East and North African Countries, in English, French, and Arabic, in 1985. The following year their offices in Lebanon established the Center for English Language Education to improve the quality of English-language instruction in that country, in spite of growing security risks.[8]

AMIDEAST also provided testing services. In addition to the Test of English as a Foreign Language (TOEFL), it administered the Scholastic Aptitude Test, Graduate Record Examination, Graduate Management Admissions Test, and the new Institutional TOEFL, registering well over 20,000 exam applicants annually through the rest of the decade. A branch office was also set up to serve Palestinians in the Gaza Strip. In 1989, the organization's office in Tunis initiated a program to help Tunisian graduates of US colleges and universities find positions upon their return home.

In the 1980s, AMIDEAST was hired by the United States Information Agency (USIA) to provide training and support for the educational advisers serving at its posts in the Gulf. Under a grant from the USIA it began publishing *The Advising Quarterly*, which reported trends, issues, and resources in international education advising. A quarterly publication called *Membernews*, which covered educational developments in the Middle East, was first made available in 1990. During the 1980s, AMIDEAST also published informational materials for American students who were considering studying abroad in the MENA region. Two texts, *Study and Research Opportunities in the Middle East and North Africa* and *Teaching Opportunities in the Middle East and North Africa*, were updated to address increasing interest in the region's academic, cultural, and job offerings. *Education in the Middle East* was another. It surveyed educational institutions in the region and was often referred to by foreign student advisers and admissions officers. AMIDEAST's collaboration with the Experiment in International Living, later called World Learning, was renewed in 1988, with the organization of semester abroad programs in Morocco.[9]

Around the same time AMIDEAST contributed its critically acclaimed videotape and instructional guidebook, *Introduction to the Arab World*, designed to educate Americans about the region. The video won an award at the 1989 National Educational Film and Video Festival and was aired on broadcast and cable television across the United States, as thousands of copies were distributed to schools, libraries, and interested groups. The same year, the organization launched a new periodical teaching resource, *Arab World Almanac*, which assisted high school teachers in providing students with insights about the Arab world.

With the help of USIA grants, other organizations also developed videotapes and accompanying materials for use by educational advisers overseas. The National Association of Foreign Student Advisers (NAFSA) was awarded one such grant and used the funds to produce "Where Will I Live," which showed various housing alternatives for students coming to the United States for the first time.

Grants from the USIA supported AMIDEAST's "Study in the United States," a series of videos on engineering, humanities, the social sciences, and graduate medical studies, which were produced in Arabic, French, and Spanish and distributed to advising centers worldwide. In cooperation with the US State Department, the organization would continue to administer the Fulbright Student Program for the MENA region. Under its management, more than 2400 students from Algeria, Bahrain, Egypt, Iraq, Jordan, Lebanon, Libya, Morocco, Oman, Saudi Arabia, Syria, Tunisia, the UAE, the West Bank/Gaza, and Yemen were placed in graduate programs across the United States.[10]

Circumstances in 1991 found the United States at war with Iraq, with some 400,000 troops on the ground in the Persian Gulf. As the conflict progressed, orders for educational materials on the Arab world surged. With endorsements from the United States and host governments, AMIDEAST began operating full-service advising centers in Bahrain and Kuwait, which included English-language training. An office in the UAE was opened a few years later. A rising demand for high-quality English-language training led to the introduction of such training in other countries, which in some cases offered language instruction designed for a broader purpose, such as "legal English" for participants in the Legal Rights Project in Egypt, or for legal scholars in Lebanon. The organization would eventually provide English instruction in all of its field offices. AMIDEAST would also design and produce curricula and teacher recruitment materials for the Military Language Institute in the UAE.

Demand soared for highly specialized, short-term training programs. AMIDEAST was chosen by the USIA in 1992 to administer the Israeli-Arab Scholarship Program, an initiative designed to afford Palestine citizens of Israel an opportunity to pursue advanced degrees in the United States. Such initiatives were linked with greater efforts to close the gap between university study and widespread unemployment, or underemployment. Around 1995, the organization published an annotated bibliography on career planning and advising, distributing it first in the region and then worldwide. Adding to the recruitment efforts, job fairs would become important. Job ConneXion pioneered a job fair in Jordan.

In the late 1990s, with a grant from NAFSA, AMIDEAST developed an online Guide to Study in the MENA region for students considering enrolling in the region's institutions. It then launched the Arab Heritage

Fund to create an endowment that could support rapid development of new information, and its distribution to precollege educators throughout the United States. In 1998 the organization's newest video, "Young Voices from the Arab World" received acclaim and national awards, and by 2000 its catalog, with more than 130 offerings, was reaching an audience of at least 100,000 educators annually.

Initiatives and recruitment efforts in the 1990s also included the University of the Middle East Project (UMEP), which built educational bridges among societies and cultures in the Middle East, North Africa, North America, and Europe. The project sought to empower progressive secondary school teachers through teacher training. The UMEP has since contributed to the creation of inclusive classrooms across the MENA region, with support from organizations such as the United Nations Educational, Scientific and Cultural Organization (UNESCO), the United Nations Alliance of Civilizations, the US Department of State, and the Spanish Ministry of Foreign Affairs. The program would implement 37 academic programs in the United States, Spain, Lebanon, Morocco, Jordan, and Egypt.[11]

Middle East Studies

Also serving to encourage MENA region enrollments was the continuing advance of Middle East Studies in American universities. Forty years after the establishment of the first full-fledged Middle East Studies program at Princeton (1947), American interest in the region was again rising. By the late 1980s, 124 American colleges and universities were listed on the Middle East Studies Association (MESA) roster.[12] In addition to MESA, another important organization involved in the promotion of research and instruction related to the region was the Middle East Institute, organized after World War II.

After midcentury there had been a proliferation of large, multidisciplinary programs. Following Princeton, other frontrunners were the University of California at Berkeley and at Los Angeles, the University of Chicago, Columbia, Harvard, the University of Michigan, and the University of Pennsylvania. A more telling indication of the growth of Middle Eastern studies was the addition of programs to smaller institutions, such as St. Cloud State University, the University of Massachusetts at Amherst, Western Connecticut State University, Wayne State University, and many others. Some were initiated through donations from Middle Eastern countries. The King Fahd Center for Middle East Studies at the University of Arkansas, one example, was established in 1994 with a gift of $18 million from Saudi Arabia. It was at the time the largest single gift in the university's history, one generated by then-governor Bill Clinton's 1991 proposal for a Middle East studies program in Arkansas. By the end of the decade, about a third of the programs on the MESA list offered degrees in Middle East studies, mostly at the graduate level.[13]

In addition to the many programs and courses offered in the 124 institutions on the MESA list, a wide variety of individual courses on the Middle East were by now being offered on the majority of American campuses. Things had changed since World War II, when the study of the Middle East was centered solely in departments or programs of religious or cultural studies. By the 1990s, the Middle East was being studied in almost every field of the social sciences and humanities.

A study initiated by Rutgers in 1987, designed to survey existing Middle East programs and courses at accredited institutions of higher education in the United States, offered some interesting findings. Among other things, the survey determined that most of the nation's Middle East studies had been established in the 1970s, most within existing liberal arts programs. The inclusion of countries also varied from institution to institution. Most programs listed history, political science, and religion as essential to a sufficient understanding of the region. Many of the programs included language training. The fields of psychology, philosophy, and geography were considered least important. Another finding was that five institutions offered Middle East area specializations and degrees through their departments of Judaic studies, while only one, Arizona State University, offered courses through its department of Islamic studies. It was the only university with a department devoted to or organized around the study of Islam, in contrast with several with Judaism at their epistemological center. Specialized studies focused on Islam were offered at five other universities, according to the study—the Aga Khan Program for Islamic Architecture at Harvard, the Islamic and Arabian Development Program at Duke, Hartford Seminary's Center for the Study of Islam and Christian-Muslim Relations, the programs in the Middle Eastern and Islamic studies at the University of North Carolina at Chapel, and the University of Minnesota.[14]

A New Wave of Chinese Students

As commander of the Second and Third Field Armies in China, Deng Xiaoping's troops had fearlessly crossed the Changjiang and succeeded in breaking through the Guomindang line of defense. The victory would initiate the collapse of the Nationalist government. Deng had been made first secretary of the East China Bureau, and in this capacity had been present at the famous 1949 gathering at Tiananmen Square. It was here that Chairman Mao Zedong announced the birth of the People's Republic of China (PRC), effectively closing its doors to the West. Three decades later, when Deng himself assumed power, one of the first tasks on his list was to reopen China's borders to American education exchange.

An early effort toward reconciliation was the formation of the Committee on Scholarly Communication with the People's Republic of China (CSCPRC), initiated when the Joint Committee on Contemporary China met to discuss the possibilities of reopening communications between American and Chinese scholars. The formation of the committee was motivated in part by academics who would, because of their professions, benefit by having more access to China's culture and history. There were perhaps more consequential motivations. In 1962, the detonation of China's first atomic bomb made clear to the world that its scientific capabilities had become vastly more sophisticated. Acknowledging China's new importance, scientists affiliated with the National Academy of Sciences look for a means of convincing its leaders to participate in the Pugwash Disarmament Conferences, meetings that would include the United States and the Soviet Union.[15]

In the mid-1960s, academic and scientific communities had explored the possibilities of establishing a committee on China that would also include government representatives and key figures. John Lindbeck, a professor of political science at Columbia University and chairman of the Joint Committee on Contemporary China; and Harrison Brown, foreign secretary of the National Academy of Sciences, were among those discussing those possibilities. Their alliance soon grew to include social scientists, humanists, and natural scientists, who worked as a team to provide leverage for access to China. The CSCPRC was officially adopted in 1966 and headquartered at the National Academy of Sciences in Washington, DC, where it would be active for the next 30 years. The American Council of Learned Societies in New York and the Social Science Research Council were included as equal sponsoring partners. With China in the throes of its Cultural Revolution, the CSCPRC had made attempts at advancing communication. One example was a letter, hand-delivered in 1971 by the committee's executive director Anne Keatley to the president of the Chinese Academy of Sciences. In the letter, the CSCPRC offered to initiate an exchange of scholars. The following year the president of the United States himself would step in.[16]

Richard Nixon would call it "the week that changed the world." Early in 1972, the President and Mrs. Nixon left by helicopter to Andrews Air Force Base for a flight to Hawaii, then from there to the People's Republic of China. At Capital Airport near Peking, they were greeted by Premier Chou En-lai and his party, and everyone stood for the playing of the national anthems of the two countries. That afternoon, President Nixon met with Chairman Mao.

Secretary of State Cyrus Vance and national security adviser Zbigniew Brzezinski also traveled to China on separate occasions in 1977 and 1978 to negotiate the possibilities of resuming diplomatic relations with the United States. Ultimately, the United States announced its agreement to accept the three conditions set forth by China for the resumption of diplomatic relations—the severance of American diplomatic relations with Taiwan, abrogation of the mutual defense treaty between the United States and Taiwan, and the withdrawal of all US forces from the island. Leonard Woodcock, chief of the US Liaison Office in China, was to conduct detailed negotiations with the Chinese side. It was a turning point in Sino-American relations, and it also resulted in an agreement to initiate an exchange of academic delegations.[17]

Seventy-three such delegations were sent from both countries. It was during these month-long visits that the American members of the delegations began to fully recognize the magnitude of damage incurred by Chinese education as a result of the Cultural Revolution. Many of the Chinese visitors had little capacity for negotiating the sophisticated learning environments they encountered in America. Useful results emerged from the delegations nevertheless, including the book *Cancer in China*, an important contribution based on the country's striking epidemiological patterns of different kinds of cancer, and the significance of diet.

Jimmy Carter and Deng Xiaoping

Jimmy Carter had first visited China in 1949, as a young naval officer on an American submarine. He would turn 25 that year, the same day Mao Zedong announced the birth of the People's Republic of China. Many years later, in a speech at the Li Xiannian Library Hong'an, Carter said he was proud his birthday had fallen on such an important date. Three decades later President Jimmy Carter and Deng Xiaoping, who assumed China's leadership following Mao, would meet in Washington, DC. The friendship that arose between the two men was genuine, and it would be an important influence in initiating a third and on-going wave of Chinese student enrollments in the United States.

Carter described the meeting as one the most delightful experiences of his presidency. He judged Deng to be smart, intelligent, tough, frank, courageous, personable, self-assured, and friendly—and they had in common an understanding of the importance of education exchange between their two countries. Their amiable talks would become policy, launching a new era of Sino-American education exchange that continues today. Neither Carter nor Deng could have predicted the magnitude of China's extraordinary economic and military growth in the years to follow, nor the extent to which American higher education had enabled those changes.

In China, most attributed the reopening of China's borders to the efforts of Deng Xiaoping. The claim was difficult to dispute. Few reforms in the post-Mao era were as important to Deng as the opening of China's doors, and he envisioned Chinese people scouring the world for new ideas in science, technology, and management. He rushed to hold national entrance examinations and reopened universities that had been shut down during Mao's Cultural Revolution. To reach his educational goals for China, Deng was willing to listen to new ideas, even Western ones. On many occasions, he was known to invite renowned scientists for long discussions, during which he would earnestly seek their advice and ask, How can China catch up?[18]

Some suggested ramping up higher education exchange with the United States, and Deng took heed. When Jimmy Carter's science adviser Frank Press was thereafter dispatched on a diplomatic mission to China, he was caught by surprise. Deng unexpectedly proposed China send many more students and scholars to America than was first considered. In a late-night call to Washington, DC, Press advised the president of Deng's unexpected proposal, and asked how he should respond. Carter said to accept the offer immediately.

The Understanding on Educational Exchanges, signed in October 1978, was an agreement that provided for scholars to undertake study and research in China and in the United States. Then on January 31, 1979, Vice Premier Deng Xiaoping and Fang Yi, director of the State Science and Technology Commission, signed the Agreement on Cooperation in Science and Technology, a landmark accord that provided an umbrella under which scientific, technological, and other educational exchanges could occur. The signing took place during Deng Xiaoping's meeting with Jimmy Carter in Washington, DC. Soon the United States authorized the granting of an unlimited number of academic visas to Chinese students and scholars who were accepted at American institutions of higher education. During the Mao era, China had been involved in study-abroad programs with the Soviet Union, but these were fundamentally different, as the Soviets had demanded a strict numerical equality of "person-months."[19]

The CSCPRC went to work to establish and provide single-year grants for individual research in China, which emphasized Chinese studies and the natural sciences. Shortly thereafter, the committee began administering the reciprocal Distinguished Scholar Exchange Program, a multinational, peer-reviewed competition. Within just a few years, many diverse exchange programs were added by the CSCPRC but also by a growing list of public and private organizations. Some offered multi-year grants and others offered opportunities for collaborative research. By the mid-1980s, the many initiatives comprised a relatively comprehensive framework for academic exchange.[20]

Hong Kong and Taiwanese Enrollments

When the People's Republic of China (PRC) was instated in 1949, declaring itself the new government, the Nationalist leaders fled to the neighboring island of Taiwan (Formosa). The United States had maintained a strong informal relationship with Taiwan, as Mao closed mainland China's borders, for the next three decades. In the census conducted for the 1978–1979 academic year, just before Deng Xiaoping's reopening of China's borders to Sino-American exchange, IIE reported Taiwanese enrollments to be 17,560. Hong Kong had sent 9900 that year. There were fewer than 1000 students from the People's Republic of China.

THE LATE TWENTIETH CENTURY (1979-1999)   183

Within one year after Deng's announcement, enrollments from mainland China nearly tripled to 2770. By 1981, PRC enrollments had risen to 4350. Students from the PRC would quickly overtake Taiwanese enrollments and by 1985 the United States was hosting around 14,000 students from mainland China.

Hong Kong, despite its small size and distance from the Chinese capital, has always had a strong educational connection with the United States. The first Chinese Educational Mission (CEM) group in 1872 included boys who attended school there. Other prominent Chinese had been schooled in Hong Kong, such as Sun Yat-sen, who studied at Hong Kong Medical College, and Nobel Laureate Daniel Chee Tsui, who graduated from Hong Kong Pui Ching Middle School before enrolling at the University of Chicago. Hong Kong universities had actively recruited American-trained staff into its system.

According to Leo A. Orleans' 1988 book *Chinese Students in America: Policies, Issues and Numbers*, a precise census during the first years of the third wave of Chinese enrollments in America is rife with contradictions. In 1979, *China Education Almanac* reported a total of 1750 Chinese students enrolled in US colleges and universities, while the official count from the Chinese government was 1277. Some of the discrepancies were due to what was not included—the Chinese government count did not include students who studied in the United States using private funds. Another book, *A Relationship Restored*, agreed with Orleans' assessment that the figures were sometimes inaccurate. It reported that during the period 1979–1983, scholarly exchange visas were issued to 19,872 mainland Chinese, 63 percent in the J-1 category. The remaining were issued F-1 visas. But factors had skewed the total. Some scholars, for example, went back to China during that period, and when they later returned, were again counted as incoming students.[21]

In IIE's annual 1998–1999 international student census, 20 years after the resumption of US-China education exchange, there were 51,001 students from the People's Republic of China enrolled in US higher education. Taiwan sent 30,855 and 9665 were from Hong Kong, altogether a total of 91,951. Ten years later, in 2009–2010 would again reflect a sharp rise. A total of 127,628 students were enrolled from China, 26,685 from Taiwan, and 8034 from Hong Kong, a grand total of 162,347.[22]

THE WORLD COMPETES FOR INTERNATIONAL STUDENTS

In 1995, Australian universities were forecasting a five-fold increase in fee-paying foreign students over the next 15 years.[23] The report was based on a study by the International Development Program, the overseas marketing arm of the Australian Vice-Chancellor's committee. It went on to say that the enrollment gain was predicted to add an estimated four and a half billion US dollars per year to the Australian economy.

Australia was in the business of attracting more foreign students. Britain, Canada and others were too, all competing with the United States for a greater share of internationally mobile students. Recruiting efforts included marketing their institutions globally, through information offices and state-sponsored campaigns. Australia presented itself as an affordable alternative to study in the United States, particularly with regard to the Australian dollar, which had declined in value against the US dollar by almost a third. For many cost-conscious Asians, the Australian's presentation was irresistible. Also enticing for prospective students was the promise of fewer immigration regulations, making them eligible for permanent residency immediately after graduation.[24]

The United States was faced with the prospect of losing growing numbers of foreign students, so to address the problem, in September 1998 the Director of the United States Information Agency (USIA) and the President of Educational Testing Service convened a summit at the State Department. What came to be called the Summit on U.S. Leadership in International Education included representatives from various institutions of higher education, US corporations, nonprofit organizations, and government entities.

The conference participants, with the help of USIA, sought to identify barriers to international educational exchange between the United States and other countries. The hope was to formulate a plan for maintaining America's competitive position. By the end of the conference, the participants had concluded that intensified competition from other English-speaking countries was only one of several reasons for the United States should be concerned. A number of factors were identified, including what appeared to be complacency on the part of US institutions of higher education in promoting themselves to prospective foreign students. There was a failure of state and federal governments to facilitate a robust and well-coordinated spirit of entrepreneurship in international education. In addition, there were diminishing federal funds to support overseas educational advising centers (affiliated with the USIA).[25]

An added concern was the lack of coordination at the federal level between the State Department and the Immigration and Naturalization Service (INS), as evidenced by burdensome visa regulations. Officers of the INS often had overly heavy caseloads, a condition that resulted in visa interviews that could shortchange foreign applicants. If the United States was to regain and retain its position of dominance in this very important area, it should consider emulating the enlightened policies of other advanced nations who were looking to the future. A framework for a broad-based, clearly defined strategy, was needed.

In years past, the United States had depended on its overseas educational advisement centers, supported by the USIA, to communicate the strengths of American higher education to the local populations. As federal funds to support these centers diminished, some had little choice but to eliminate staff or shut down completely. Spending cuts had likewise affected Fulbright and other exchange programs. At the state level, the conference reported a need for alliances between the various administrative areas, such as state university boards, state governments, and commerce officials, to reinforce effective planning and promotion of student exchanges.

Along with conclusions and recommendations, points were raised. Among them was the fact that in 1998 the half million foreign students in the United States had contributed more than $8 billion to the economy. To provide some comparisons, foreign students in Australia had contributed more than $1 billion to the Australian economy and in the United Kingdom foreign students contributed about $2 billion. Distance learning technology, which was rapidly creating new outlets for the marketing of education, was another consideration. Also, the strength or weakness of the various economies relative to that of the United States affected the ability of students to afford schooling. This was evidenced by a mid-1990s financial crisis in Asian countries, which caused a reduction of education exchange. To cap it off, the ability of foreign students to study in the United States, according to the conference report, was further inhibited by a more complex regulatory environment than most of the competing countries.[26]

Conference attendees were in support of a clear federal policy on international education. They suggested also that an alliance in support of international education be created; that a public awareness campaign should be implemented; and that a comprehensive and extensive marketing strategy be developed for the promotion of American higher education.

Research on Foreign Students

Conventional wisdom demands that those attending to international students (admissions personnel, support services, faculty, advisers, etc.) should have a deep and genuine understanding of the distinctive characteristics that define this complex and diverse group. In the latter part of the century, efforts were made to review, update, and consolidate research on foreign students and education exchange.

Concerns most commonly reported by international students, according to most of the studies, included homesickness, finance, housing and food, English language proficiency, adjusting to the American classroom environment, preparing written and oral reports, understanding American customs, making friends, forming relationships with members of the opposite sex, and being accepted by social groups. Variables affecting students were revealed through a variety of studies, and institutions worked to address the issues by providing on-campus intensive English classes, international student organizations, special activities, and host family programs, among other services.[27]

Compilations of comprehensive sources for research related to international students appeared in the mid-1980s, such as one produced by Philip Altbach, David Kelly, and Y. Lulat in 1985.[28] A follow-up by Altbach and Jing Wang was published four years later.[29] An extensive review of research on foreign students was produced by Paul Marion in 1986 and published in *New Directions for Student Services*.[30] Some studies looked specifically at the attitudes and characteristics of foreign students with the intention of discovering how international students, as a group and within various categories, differed from the general American student population.

For the most part, the studies agreed that the academic achievement of foreign students was affected by their attitudes and adjustment. An international student's immediate needs usually related to the process of getting settled, becoming accustomed to the campus climate and the surrounding community, joining appropriate campus activities, and adjusting to new academic practices and expectations. It took different amounts of time and varying approaches for internationals to make positive adjustments, the studies further revealed, and adjustments were usually influenced by any combination of an array of factors, such as English language ability, personality characteristics, previous foreign travel, financial status, academic success, cultural differences, race, foreign appearance, living arrangements, age, length of stay, graduate or undergraduate status, preconceptions and expectations, socioeconomic background, and future job prospects upon their return home. Legal and immigrations issues could also affect international students.

Making acclimation more complex were some students' discomfort with being regarded as "foreign" by their classmates. Studies showed that the students who were most academically well adjusted were those who had the most frequent interaction with American students and with faculty and they also revealed that most foreign students desired close relationships with their professors. Different learning styles sometimes created obstacles in the academic adjustment process in the classroom. Writing in *The Handbook of Foreign Student Advising* in 1984, NASFA president Gary Althen pointed out that whatever their educational differences, most foreign students in the United States found certain aspects of American education to be different from what they had experienced in their home countries.[31]

Dealing with the often-complex systems for registering for classes each term was difficult for some foreign students, and selecting from a number of possible courses, rather than following a prescribed curriculum, was for some a new challenge. Programs often required taking courses outside one's field in order to obtain a "liberal" education. In such cases, the student's assigned academic adviser was invaluable.

For some, objective-type tests, such as true-false or multiple choice, were different from the subjective-type examinations to which they were accustomed. Some international students reported having difficulty analyzing and synthesizing materials and were reluctant to raise questions or participate in class discussions. The expectation of extensive library use was new for some, as well as the competitiveness among students, especially at the graduate level. Being held liable to punishment for activities deemed to constitute cheating or plagiarism may also have been different from the system from which they came. Being assigned menial tasks in laboratory courses was a new experience for some students.[32]

Most studies agreed that a foreign student's country of origin was an important factor in the student's ability to adjust to all of these issues. Canadian and Western European students usually reported the fewest overall adjustment problems, while Asians experienced the most. This was attributed both to English language abilities and cultural differences. Looking at regions, Latin and European students tended to be more generally satisfied with their US educational experience, interacted more frequently with American and other students than did those from other world regions, and had the fewest reported problems. Asians interacted the least, and many reported feelings of isolation or non-inclusion. Many Asian students, especially those from the People's Republic of China, tended to remain within their own cultural enclaves while on campus.[33]

Regardless of the country of origin, studies generally agreed that international students who were involved in extracurricular activities early in their college career, such as student programs or interactions with their American peers, faculty, or students from other cultures, were the most satisfied with their college experience. They also tended to remain enrolled at that institution. An example is Abe, Talbot, and Geelhoed's 1998 study, which surveyed newly admitted international students participating in an International Peer Program. Participants, it was shown, experienced significantly higher social adjustment scores than non-participants.

Marion's literature review revealed that insufficient studies had been conducted to determine the needs of foreign students returning home, or re-entry issues. Literature designed to inform both practitioners and students about re-entry issues was often country-specific. *Returning to Russia*, for example, published in 1998 by the American Chamber of Commerce in Russia, provided statistical data about returnees and advice about the Russian job market. There was also little follow-up research about whether American education had met their occupational needs. An exception was a 1993 study by Hansel that tracked the readjustment experiences of 49 students who returned home to India after graduating with a US degree. Interviews revealed that most had experienced stress or other difficulties, with problems ranging from moderate anxiety about getting a job to frustration upon returning to the crowded conditions, pollution, and poor services, after having become accustomed to the United States. A few reported depression and alienation.[34]

Some international graduates had an easier time than others in finding an appropriate job upon re-entry, depending on their field. In some parts of Asia, returning students with degrees in computer science from the United States could often find a job right away. Asian students with degrees in the arts, education, or other fields, however, reported having more trouble finding a professional niche where they could appropriately translate their US study to fit their home environment. In some studies, international graduates who had previous educational experience in the United States indicated that a longer stay in America, and more practical experiences in their academic programs, may have made their re-entry experience more manageable. Optional Practical Training, or Curricular

Practical Training, provided the chance for many internationals to experience the American workforce before either returning home or becoming a permanent US resident. Most agreed that was a benefit.

Few comprehensive nationwide studies were designed to compare international and US student attitudes and characteristics. One was conducted by the American Council on Education. The results of its 1994 Cooperative Institutional Research Program (CIRP) Freshman Survey, which were published in the 1996 issue of *Open Doors*, enumerated important differences between the two student populations.[35]

Among other things, the CIRP Freshman Survey reported that, in general, foreign students were better academically prepared for the collegiate experience than American students. More than 40 percent of foreign freshmen had earned top grades in high school, and international students also reported excellent preparation in the sciences, compared with American students. The only areas where the proportion of American students reported stronger preparation than foreign students were in English and American history. Foreign students, more than American students, saw college as an opportunity to become more broadly educated individuals, and more than 60 percent of foreign students looked to college as a place to become a more cultured person, as compared with only 36 percent of US students. Americans wanted a college degree for more practical reasons, and more than 76 percent of US students viewed college as a means of securing a better job and earning more money, according to the survey.

The CIRP survey also showed that, in general, internationals came from households that were either quite poor or quite wealthy, while most American students were from middle-class backgrounds. However, foreign freshmen tended to be less concerned about financing their college experience than American students. Forty percent of international students reported having no concerns at all, compared with 30 percent of US students. International students' reasons form selecting institutions also differed between the two freshmen groups. Americans made their selection not just on academic reputation but also on the cost of tuition and the institution's proximity to home. Foreign students selected colleges and universities on the basis of academic reputation (62 percent) and whether or not a school's students were accepted into America's top graduate schools (35 percent). Occupationally, the aspirations of foreign freshmen were often higher than those of incoming American students, and a greater proportion of foreign students planned on earning a graduate degree than did Americans. American students, according to the survey responses, placed greater importance on religion in their daily lives than foreign students, and viewed themselves as being above average for such characteristics as stubbornness, cooperativeness, and physical appearance. US students were more likely to drink alcohol, "hook up" with short-time acquaintances, feel overwhelmed, stay up all night, and fail to complete assignments.[36]

LATE-CENTURY ENROLLMENTS, EVENTS, AND IMMIGRATION ISSUES

In the closing years of the twentieth century, California colleges had more spaces for students than did all of China. The United States had four million more spaces in its colleges than did the entire European Union. Yet, wrote Allan Goodman, academic dean of the School of Foreign Service at Georgetown University (now president of IIE), only about 10 percent of American colleges reported foreign student enrollments larger than 5 percent, and only a handful were guided by mission statements that committed to the promotion of international affairs courses as part of their liberal arts core, or to increasing opportunities for foreign study by students or faculty members. Few institutions placed high importance on foreign student recruitment, Goodman added.[37]

International students now accounted for about 3 percent of the 14 million graduate and undergraduate students in American colleges and universities. While America's share of international students was large by world standards, in real terms the numbers seemed small to many in higher education. Given the popularity of American institutions and the limited number of seats for college students elsewhere, the 3 percent figure was surprising, even considering the relatively high cost of postsecondary education in the United States. Many hoped to increase America's percentage of international students, but catastrophic events in 1993 would make the challenge more complicated.

On Friday, February 26, 1993, a bomb left a hundred-foot crater, several stories deep, beneath the World Trade Center in New York City. Six people were killed instantly, and a thousand others were severely hurt in the panic that ensued. The Federal Bureau of Investigation (FBI) and its partners on the New York Joint Terrorism Task Force staffed a command center and prepared for a full investigation. The FBI had been tracking

Islamic fundamentalists in New York City for some time. The investigation that followed uncovered the damning evidence in the rubble—a vehicle identification number. The number belonged to Mohammad Salemeh, who had rented the vehicle for the attack. He was arrested by an FBI SWAT (Special Weapons and Tactics) team when he tried to get his $400 deposit back. Soon three others were in custody—Nidal Ayyad, Mahmoud Abouhalima, and Ahmed Ajaj. The apartment where the bomb had been built was discovered, along with a storage locker with enough cyanide to wipe out a small town. The four men were tried, convicted, and sentenced to life imprisonment. The task force thereafter uncovered a second plot to bomb several of New York's most iconic landmarks, including the Holland and Lincoln Tunnels.[38]

Still on the run was Ramzi Yousef, the mastermind of the World Trade Center attack. Within weeks he was planning more, including the simultaneous bombing of about a dozen US international flights. It was later learned that his plan had been to topple the World Trade Center, and he hoped the falling debris might damage or destroy the second tower. He was captured in Pakistan in February 1995 and returned to the United States, where he was convicted along with 26-year-old Jordanian Eyad Ismoil, who had driven the van. Ismoil entered the United States on a student visa in 1989 to study engineering at Wichita State University in Kansas. A seventh attacker, Abdul Yasin, remained at large.[39]

There was public outcry for the enhancement of governmental systems that tracked and monitored people allowed into the United States. President Bill Clinton signed the Illegal Immigrant Reform and Immigrant Responsibility Act (IIRIRA) of 1996 into law. The new legislation would affect every international student and scholar in America, as well as most of the college officials who served their needs, as documentation, tracking, and reporting demands were suddenly implemented. The final piece of legislation was vast, more than 200 pages, divided into six broad sections: Title I involved improvements to border control, the facility of legal entry, and interior enforcement. Title II enhanced enforcement and penalties against alien smuggling and document fraud. Title III related to inspections, apprehension, detention, adjudication, and removal of inadmissible and deportable aliens, and Title IV was concerned with restrictions against employment. Title V addressed restrictions on benefits for aliens, and Title VI was for miscellaneous provisions.[40]

An immediate impact was the significant increase in the number of Border Patrol agents. Twelve million dollars was allocated for a 14-mile triple fence along the US border from San Diego eastward, as entry and exit from the United States became more controlled. Border-crossing identification cards had to be issued and put in use before the year 2000, along with "biometric identifiers," such as fingerprints or handprints. To comply with IIRIRA, the Attorney General was to develop an automated entry-exit control system. Pre-inspection stations would be set up in at least five of the foreign airports sending the greatest number of inadmissible aliens to the United States, as Immigration and Naturalization Service's internal enforcement efforts gained momentum.

Especially concerning to international students were new provisions affecting F-1 and J-1 exchange visitors, conditions that created grounds for exclusion for certain students considered "visa abusers." Under Section 346 and 625 of IIRIRA 96 (1996), students were inadmissible if they sought to attend a public elementary or adult education program, other than a college or university program. They were likewise inadmissible if they sought to attend a secondary school for more than one year without reimbursing the local school district for the full, unsubsidized per capita cost of the alien's school attendance. Those who entered the United States on an F-1 visa to attend a private elementary, secondary, or language school, and then left that school to attend a public education program, could be removed if the 12-month limit and the tuition reimbursement requirements were not met.[41]

Student visas fall into a few different categories. An F-1 visa is for full-time students enrolled in an academic or language program. F-1 students may remain in the United States for the full length of their academic program, plus 60 days. F-1 students are required to maintain a full-time course load and must complete their studies before the expiration date listed on their I-20 form, otherwise known as the Certificate of Eligibility for Students Status. An I-20 is issued by an educational institution in the United States to a prospective student from another country.

Coming to America is a multi-step process. First, a student applies to an educational institution, which then examines the educational credentials and financial standing. If the criteria are met, the student receives a letter of admission and an I-20. Next, the student takes the I-20 to the US embassy in their home country and applies for a visa. One cannot apply for a student visa without an I-20 but having an I-20 is no guarantee that he or she will receive one.

An F-2 visa is issued for a spouse or child of an F-1 visitor. A J-1 visa is issued to research scholars, professors and exchange visitors participating in programs involving cultural exchange, and for medical or business training. The issuance of a J-1 visa obligates visitors to return to their home country for a minimum of two years after the end of their studies in the United States, before they can apply for permanent residence. A J-2 visa is for the spouse or child of a J-1 visitor. An M-1 visa is issued for students attending non-academic trade or vocational schools, and an M-2 is for their spouse or child. With the passage of the new law, colleges and universities and exchange visitor program sponsors now had to collect and retain a substantial amount of documentation, including contact information and visa status. Schools failing to provide the required information would be barred from sponsoring F, M, or J visas. According to IIRIRA directives, beginning on April 1, 1997, the INS could require F, M, and J visa sponsors to collect fees of up to $100 from the affected aliens.[42]

Most agreed that pilot programs for new documentation systems had to be tested, as the existing system was considered, according to Jackie Dednarz of the INS, to be obsolete, flawed, and ineffective. The Coordinated Interagency Partnership Regulating International Students (CIPRIS), a federal task force assembled in 1995, began testing a pilot version of its computerized tracking system in cooperation with 21 universities in Alabama, Georgia, North Carolina, and South Carolina. The pilot program called for students to obtain identity cards that included a photograph and a print of the student's right index finger. For reasons of national security, the INS was asked to determine if there was a foolproof system for controlling foreign students. They concluded there was not.[43] Some worried that the new tracking system would have the effect of turning them into INS agents, saying it would be difficult to both counsel international students and scholars, and at the same time regularly report information on them to the immigration service.

The US Internal Revenue Service (IRS) would be accused of imposing unfair burdens on foreign students, a criticism made in a 1997 issue of *The Chronicle of Higher Education*. The tax laws were also sometimes misunderstood. To illustrate, the article included a story about a student from Indonesia, who was pursuing an undergraduate degree from Lewis and Clark College. Her entire financial support, money for tuition, books, room, board, and spending money, was provided by her family in Jakarta. Because she had no paying job or US income of any kind and received no financial aid, the student assumed she need not file an income-tax return in the United States.[44]

In fact, the IRS required two highly detailed tax forms from every student, even those with no income whatsoever to report, and failure to return the forms could subject students to fines and get them into trouble with immigration authorities. The forms themselves sometimes required information that was difficult for the student to obtain, particularly in an unfamiliar environment, calling for a passport number, visa number, taxpayer identification number, type of US visa, foreign address, and their reason for coming to the United States. To receive a tax identification number, students with no income had to appear in person before an IRS employee, prove their identity, and make an application. Students sometimes waited a full month before receiving the ID number. Then they could finally file a return, forms that in many cases contained zeroes in every operative line.[45]

International students were required to disclose information about any scholarships or fellowships; the name, address, and phone number of the director of their academic program; and the exact number of days spent in the United States during each of the past three years. Many international students either filed incorrectly or gave up altogether. Educators such as John Bogdanski, professor of law at Lewis and Clark Law School and former member of the Commissioner's Advisory Group of the Internal Revenue Service, said it was "gobbledygook" and called for simplified systems.[46]

In June 2000, the congressionally appointed, ten-member National Commission on Terrorism (NCT), which had been established in 1998 after the bombings of two US embassies in Africa, endorsed the idea of monitoring foreign students in the United States even more closely than before. Its report included several specific proposals. Among them was using the existing computer-based program as the model for a new $45 million nationwide tracking system, to be overseen by the Immigration and Naturalization Service. In June 1997, the INS had implemented a pilot project, the Coordinated Interagency Partnership Regulating International Students (CIPRIS), to test the feasibility of an electronic reporting system.

The successor program, called the Student and Exchange Visitor Information System, or SEVIS, would be developed with modifications from the original CIPRIS database, and was considerably more ambitious in scope and detail than its earlier incarnation. Mandatory computerized records would now identify the place of residence of all foreign students, the schools they attended, their academic majors, course loads, and expected graduation dates—detailed data to be supplied by every US academic institution admitting foreigners. Students themselves would be required to bear part of the cost of the system's operation and updating through a separate processing fee or surcharge levied when seeking admission to study at a US institution of higher learning.

With considerable understatement, the NCT report added that even with all the mandated documentation, the United States lacked the nationwide ability to exactly monitor the immigration status of all students, and there was still no mechanism for ensuring terrorism would not happen again. Much was made of the revelation that it was possible for a terrorist to drop out of school yet remain in the country illegally. "We're under no illusions that anything you do with foreign students makes a serious dent in the security of a country's borders," said L. Paul Bremer III, the commissioner's chair. He likened the proposed tracking to a home security system, with locks on the doors and bars on the windows. Each precaution provides an additional degree of security, but no guarantee. Opponents pointed to the high cost of its implementation, time consumption, and the potential violation of students' privacy. Marlene M. Johnson, executive director of NAFSA, said that the commission had not provided new data on the potential threat represented by foreign students, apart from the World Trade Center example. Others contended that surveillance was a necessary evil in today's world, and that filling out forms and paying a tuition surcharge was warranted if it afforded everyone a greater measure of security.[47]

THE 1999–2000 CENSUS

At the close of the millennium, there were 514,723 international students studying in US colleges and universities, an increase of 4.8 percent over the previous year. International students represented 3.8 percent of all US higher education enrollments but were enrolled in much greater proportions at higher academic levels, making up 12.9 percent of all US graduate enrollments, according to IIE's *Open Doors* report. By academic level, a total of 177,381 internationals were enrolled in bachelor's programs and 218,219 foreign students were studying in graduate programs. Two-year colleges hosted 59,830, or 1.2 percent of the total enrollment (Table 7.2).[48]

In the 1999–2000 count, Asian students made up more than half of international enrollments, or about 54 percent. Next were Europeans, who comprised about 15 percent of international enrollments in the United States. Canada ranked sixth among the country senders, with more than 23,000 students in the United States. As for destinations, New York

Table 7.2 Foreign student enrollments for 1999–2000: top places of origin

	Number enrolled	% of total foreign students in the United States
World total	514,723	
China	54,466	10.6
Japan	46,466	9.1
India	37,482	8.2
Korea, Republic of	31,191	8.0
Taiwan	29,234	5.7
Canada	23,544	4.6
Indonesia	11,300	2.2
Thailand	10,993	2.1
Mexico	10,607	2.1
Turkey	10,100	2.0

Source: *Open Doors*, 1999–2000

University remained the leading host, followed by the University of Southern California, Columbia, and the University of Wisconsin.

By country, China topped the list, but enrollments from India had increased substantially, accelerating at more than twice the overall rate. One reason was because many prospective Indian students felt that the standard of higher education in India had not kept pace with change. According to a 1998 UNESCO report, even though India was now home to more than 260 universities comprising some 8000 colleges, many lacked up-to-date facilities, a result of insufficient funding. Few changes had in fact been implemented since the educational system was set up during the British era, and educational institutions, which were largely state-aided, were still suffering from years of federal budget cutbacks. Most Indian colleges had been stagnating since the 1970s, according to New York University researcher Virul Acharya, and in 1998, some did not even have the Internet.[49] It had become a familiar sight to the residents of Madras and other large Indian cities to see scores of young people standing in line outside US embassies or consulates, waiting to be interviewed. Indian students coming to the United States or England in the 1980s and 1990s were mostly from middle-class families, many of whom were seeking elevated social status by sending their children abroad. In the past, British universities attracted the preponderance of Indian students because of the historical and colonial ties between the two countries. Drastic cuts in the number of scholarships in Britain during the 1970s had helped to reroute these students' migration toward America.

Notes

1. *Open Doors* (Institute of International Education, 1979).
2. Teresa B. Bevis, *Higher Education Exchange between America and the Middle East Through the Twentieth Century* (New York: Palgrave Macmillan, 2016): 138–141.
3. Michael B. Oren, *Power, Faith and Fantasy* (W.W. Norton, 2008).
4. Ibid.
5. Institute of International Education, *Open Doors*, Annual Report (1980); also see Bevis, 141–142.
6. Ibid.
7. From the *Spartanburg Herald*, Columbia AP (January 1980): B1.
8. AMIDEAST's 60th Anniversary 1951–2011. Available at: https://apply.amideast.org/flash/60th/60th.htm.
9. Ibid.
10. Bevis, 145.
11. University of Middle East Project. Available at: https://www.ume.org/about-ume/general.
12. Hooshang Amirahadi, ed., *The United States and the Middle East: A Search for a New Perspective* (Albany: State University of New York Press, 1993).
13. Ibid.
14. Tareq Y. Ismael, ed., *Middle East Studies: International Perspectives on the State of the Art* (New York: Praeger, 1990): 17.
15. Mary Brown Bullock, "Mission Accomplished: The Influence of the CSCPRC on Educational Relations with China," in *Bridging Minds across the Pacific*, ed. Cheng Li (Lanham, MD: Lexington Books, 2005): 49–68.
16. Ibid.
17. Ministry of Foreign Affairs of the People's Republic of China, The Establishment of Sino-U.S. Diplomatic Relations and Vice Premier Deng Xiaoping's Visit to the United States (2001). Available at: https://www.fmprc.gov.cn/mfa_eng/ziliao_665539/3602_665543/3604_665547/t18007.shtml. Accessed December 14, 2018.
18. Ezra F. Vogel, *Deng Xiaoping and the Transformation of China* (Cambridge, MA: Belknap Press of Harvard University Press, 2011).
19. Ibid.
20. David Lampton, *A Relationship Restored* (National Academy Press, 1986): 70–72.
21. Ibid., 32.
22. *Open Doors* (Institute of International Education, 1999).
23. Geoffrey Maslan, "Big Growth in Foreign Students Predicted for Australia," *The Chronicle of Higher Education* (December 15, 1995).
24. Paul Desruisseaux, "Intense Competition for Foreign Students Sparks Concerns about U.S. Standing," *The Chronicle of Higher Education*, Vol. 45, no. 7 (October 9, 1998): A55.

25. Ibid.
26. From U.S. Leadership in International Education, "The Lost Edge," Conference Report and Action Agenda (Washington, DC: United States Information Agency and Educational Testing Service, 1998).
27. Christine F. Meloni, *Adjustment Problems of Foreign Students in U.S. Colleges and Universities* (ERIC #ED276296).
28. Philip Altbach, David Kelly and Y. Lulat, *Research on Foreign Students and International Study* (New York: Praeger, 1985).
29. Philip Altbach and Jing Wang, *Foreign Students and International Study 1984–1988* (University Press of America, 1989).
30. Paul Marion, "Research on Foreign Students at Colleges and Universities in the United States," *New Directions for Student Services*, Vol. 36 (1986): 65–82.
31. Gary Althen, *The Handbook of Foreign Student Advising* (Washington, DC: NAFSA, 1984).
32. Ibid.
33. Marion, 65–82.
34. Ibid.
35. Institute of International Education, *Open Doors*, Report on International Education Exchange (New York: Author, 1996).
36. Ibid.
37. Allan E. Goodman, "What Foreign Students Contribute," *The Chronicle of Higher Education*, Vol. 42, no. 23 (February 16, 1996).
38. World Trade Center Bombing 1993, Federer Bureau of Investigation. Available at: https://www.fbi.gov/history/famous-cases/world-trade-center-bombing-1993.
39. Ibid.
40. The Immigration Law Portal, IIRIRA 96: A Summary of the New Immigration Bill. Available at: http://www.visalaw.com/iirira-96-a-summary-of-the-new-immigration-bill/. Accessed December 14, 2018.
41. Ibid.
42. Ibid.
43. Amy Magaro Rubin, "U.S. Tests a New System to Track Foreign Students," *The Chronicle of Higher Education* (September 19, 1997): A49.
44. John A. Bogdanski, "The IRS Imposes a Ridiculous Burden on Foreign Students," *The Chronicle of Higher Education*, May 2, 1997.
45. Ibid.
46. Ibid.
47. McMurtrie, A49.
48. *Open Doors* (Institute of International Education, 2000).
49. Beth McMurtrie, "American Colleges Experience a Surge in Enrollments from India," *The Chronicle of Higher Education*, Vol. 48, no. 12 (December 10, 1999).

References

Altbach, Philip, David Kelly, and Y. Lulat. 1985. *Research on Foreign Students and International Study*. New York: Praeger.
Altbach, Philip, and Jing Wang. 1989. *Foreign Students and International Study 1984–1988*. University Press of America.
Althen, Gary. 1984. *The Handbook of Foreign Student Advising*. Washington, DC: NAFSA.
Amirahadi, Hooshang, ed. 1993. *The United States and the Middle East: A Search for a New Perspective*. Albany: State University of New York Press.
Bogdanski, John A. 1997. The IRS Imposes a Ridiculous Burden on Foreign Students. *The Chronicle of Higher Education*, May 2.
Bullock, Mary Brown. 2005. Mission Accomplished: The Influence of the CSCPRC on Educational Relations with China. In *Bridging Minds across the Pacific*, ed. Ching Li. Lanham, MD: Lexington Books.
Desruisseaux, Paul. 1998. Intense Competition for Foreign Students Sparks Concerns about U.S. Standing. *The Chronicle of Higher Education* 45 (7), October 9.
Goodman, Allan E. 1996. What Foreign Students Contribute. *The Chronicle of Higher Education* 42 (23), February 16.
Institute of International Education. 1996. *Open Doors Report on International Education Exchange*. New York: Author.
———. 2000. *Open Doors Report on International Education*. New York: Author.
Ismael, Tareq Y., ed. 1990. *Middle East Studies: International Perspectives on the State of the Art*. New York: Praeger.
Lampton, David. 1986. *A Relationship Restored*. National Academies Press.
Marion, Paul. 1986. Research on Foreign Students at Colleges and Universities in the United States. *New Directions for Student Services* 1986 (36): 65–82.
Maslan, Geoffrey. 1995. Big Growth in Foreign Students Predicted for Australia. *The Chronicle of Higher Education*, December 15.
McMurtrie, Beth. 1999. American Colleges Experience a Surge in Enrollments from India. *The Chronicle of Higher Education* 48 (12), December 10.
Meloni, Christine F. 1986. Adjustment Problems of Foreign Students in U.S. Colleges and Universities. ERIC #ED276269.
Ministry of Foreign Affairs of the People's Republic of China. 2001. The Establishment of Sino-U.S. Diplomatic Relations and Vice Premier Deng Xiaoping's Visit to the United States. www.fmprc.gov.cn.
Oren, Michael B. 2008. *Power, Faith and Fantasy*. W.W. Norton.
Rubin, Amy M. 1997. U.S. Tests a New System to Track Foreign Students. *The Chronicle of Higher Education*, September 19.

The Immigration Law Portal. 1996. IIRIRA 96: A Summary of the New Immigration Bill. www.visalaw.com/96nov.3nov96.html. Accessed December 2018.

U.S. Leadership in International Education. 1998. The Lost Edge. Conference Report and Action Agenda. Washington, DC: United States Information Agency and Educational Testing Service.

Vogel, Ezra F. 2011. *Deng Xiaoping and the Transformation of China*. Cambridge, MA: Belknap Press of Harvard University.

CHAPTER 8

September 11 and Student Mobility

Khalid Sheikh Mohammed, the professed mastermind of the September 11, 2001, attacks, had come to America 20 years before on a student visa to attend Chowan College—a small, southern, two-year Baptist school located in North Carolina. It may have seemed an odd choice for the son of an imam who had been a member of the Muslim Brotherhood as a teenager, but like others had done, Khalid Sheikh Mohammed was assumedly using it as a springboard into an American university. Small or community colleges have typically been a necessity, rather than a first choice, for international students. For many, such colleges were the only institutions that would accept their limited credentials. Of the 54 students in Khalid Sheikh Mohammed's class at Chowan, 29 were from the Middle East. Foreign students such as Mohammed were attracted to institutions like Chowan because they did not require applicants to take an English proficiency exam. Students could be admitted with a limited understanding of English and could survive by taking a lot of math and chemistry as they worked to improve their language skills. Then they could qualify to move to another institution.[1]

After improving his English skills at Chowan, Mohammed was admitted to North Carolina A&T State University in Greenville, where he studied mechanical engineering. He resided with other Middle Eastern students in a group of houses on a nearby residential street. One of the houses had been converted for use as a makeshift mosque. According to reports, he existed in a sort of self-imposed isolation, associating only with other devout Muslims and avoiding college activities. He would not listen to music, recalled a classmate from Kuwait, who said he barely recognized the disheveled and balding man who was photographed after his capture in Pakistan. The CIA later reported that Khalid Sheikh Mohammed's experiences in America, including a short stay in jail for being involved in an accident while driving without a license, may have helped propel him on his path to terrorism. But the truth is that Mohammed never experienced America. Finishing his mechanical engineering degree in two and a half years, he went at once to Afghanistan, where he joined the *mujahedeen*. He would be linked to every terrorist attack between 1993 and 2003, until his capture in Rawalpindi, Pakistan.

In hindsight, others involved in the attack on America on September 11, 2001, might also have seemed unlikely candidates to participate in a violent act of terrorism. Of the four men believed to have been pilots in the hijacking conspiracy that claimed thousands of lives, Hani Hanjour stands out. Hanjour, who was 29 years old at the time, shared the view of the Islamic extremists, that anyone with different beliefs—men, women, or children—should be destroyed by any means possible. Violent methods appear to have been preferred. Hanjour was a perfect candidate for recruitment. He was so unambitious as a teenager in Saudi Arabia that he considered dropping out of school and becoming a flight attendant. Of small stature, he was known to be withdrawn and socially isolated. Recognizing his photograph as the person who crashed American Airlines Flight 77 into the Pentagon, his family claimed to be incredulous. "We were in shock" said his older brother, "we thought he liked the USA ..."[2] Unlike Mohammed Atta, the likely leader of the plot, who was described as outwardly arrogant and intense, Hanjour's meek and introverted manner fit a recurrent pattern in al-Qaeda's network of recruits—unsophisticated young men, who fit the personality to be manipulated and brainwashed. He would be one of just two hijackers who held a student visa.

Most of the 9/11 hijackers had been issued B visas, which allowed enrollment in a short recreational course of study, not for credit for a degree or academic certification. Study leading to a US-conferred degree or certificate was not permitted on a B visa, even if it was a short duration. A student in a distance learning program, for example, that required a period of time on the institution's US campus, must obtain a visa (F or M) before entering the country. The 9/11 hijackers started submitting visa applications in 1997. Initially 24 applied, and by 2000 all but one had received their visas. Two were issued in Berlin, two in the UAE, and the rest were granted by Saudi Arabia.

In each case, state consular offices reportedly followed standard operating procedures, performing name checks using their outlook database, which included the terrorist watch list. None of the applicants, based on the identities given in their passports, were listed on the database. From later investigations it was discovered that most of the applications were incomplete in some sections, but they were processed anyway. In fact, such omissions were common. Hani Hanjour, for example, was denied an application in September 2000 for insufficient information, but after he produced additional evidence of support his student visa was approved. Two others were known to have submitted false statements. Saeed al Ghamdi and Khalid as Mihdhar both said they had not previously applied for a US visa, which was not true.

His visa secured, Hanjour enrolled at the English as a Second Language (ESL) Center, a school in Princeton, New Jersey, but never showed up for class, according to Associated Press reports. When he later enrolled in an Arizona flight school, its officials were immediately concerned. Hanjour seemed to lack the English language and flying skills necessary to have the commercial pilot's license he already possessed. "I couldn't believe he had a commercial pilot's license of any kind with the skills he had," said Federal Aviation Administration (FAA) spokeswoman Laura Brown. Records later revealed that Hani Hanjour had obtained a license in 1999 in Scottsdale. A poor student, he failed in 1996 and 1997 to secure a license from other schools. Ultimately, the administrators told him he would not qualify for the advanced certificate, but Hanjour continued to pay in order to train on a simulator for Boeing 737 jets. The now-defunct JetTech flight school alerted Federal aviation authorities of their apprehensions in early 2001, and in response a Federal Aviation Administration (FAA) inspector was sent to investigate the situation. After reviewing Hanjour's records, and observing the soon-to-be hijacker in class, the inspector concluded no other action was warranted, but school officials remained concerned. Hanjour never completed his studies and eventually left the school.[3]

On the morning of September 11, 2001, Hani Hanjour and 18 other Arab militants, all now affiliated with Osama bin Laden's Islamic extremist group al-Qaeda, carried out suicide assaults against targets in the United States. After hijacking four commercial airliners, two were flown into the World Trade Center towers in New York City, another hit the Pentagon in Washington, DC, and the fourth crashed into a field in rural Pennsylvania, falling short of its target. More than 3000 people lost their lives, among them more than 400 firefighters and police officers. When Hanjour's name became public, the Arizona flight school manager reported that the FAA inspector called, saying, "Your worst nightmare has just been realized." Much was made, especially in the academic community, about the revelation that two of the pilots were international students, who may have entered the United States through the issuance of F-1 visas.[4]

SEVIS

The emotional weeks that followed 9/11 came with growing demands that the Immigration and Naturalization Service (INS) accelerate the installation of its highly touted but long-delayed computerized tracking system. Senator Diane Feinstein of California urged a six-month moratorium on new student visas and an allocation of $32 million to allow the INS to get the student identification system up and running. New and stringent entry requirements and time-consuming barriers, most erected in the name of national security, were repeatedly proposed, as was legislation mandating more restricted visa policies. The welcome mat for international students was being withdrawn, and bitter recriminations were heard across the globe.[5]

Five months before the 9/11 attack, the American Council on Education (ACE), an organization whose membership included the presidents of 1800 institutions, had sent a letter to the INS. In it they rejected the Coordinated Interagency Partnership Regulating International Students (CIPRIS) effort, describing its potential implementation as a looming disaster for higher education. It would have the effect of closing off options for many foreign students who might want to study in America, said Terry Hartle, the Council's senior vice president for government and public affairs. Such a system would not only stifle foreign enrollments, but would also pose an unfair hardship to students from the poorest regions. Nevertheless, America's mood of acceptance had changed.[6]

In October 2001, President George Bush issued the Homeland Security Directive, which called for measures to end the abuse of student visas, with the intention of preventing certain international students from receiving education and training in sensitive areas. The directive came on the heels of the Patriot Act, which called for the full implementation of the controversial Illegal Immigration Reform and Immigrant Responsibility Act that had been enacted in 1996. Bush's directive initiated the rewriting of the US immigration policy, particularly regarding international students seeking higher education or other special training in America. More than a half million international students were enrolled in colleges and universities in the United States at the time, and all would be affected. As foreign enrollments came under the increasingly watchful eye of the Bush administration, colleges and universities across the United States stepped up efforts to protect their own. Most backed off opposition to a computerized system being developed to track foreign students more efficiently, even as advocates for foreign exchange programs argued that such a plan by the Immigration and Naturalization Service would send an unwelcoming message to foreign students with honest intentions.[7]

On September 24, 2002, in a statement before the Joint House Subcommittee, American Council on Education president David Ward referred to SEVIS (Student and Exchange Visitor Information System) as the single most important step that the government could take toward national security. He added that it should be implemented as soon as possible.[8]

From an economic standpoint, a major decrease in international student enrollments could have deleterious consequences. Unlike other student populations, foreign students usually paid full tuition. Another concern was that fewer students might threaten the existence of certain short-term academic programs such as summer or single-term intensive English. Without foreign students, courses taken by small numbers of US collegians might also be endangered. Temple University's director of international student services said that without foreign students, areas of study such as business, engineering, and computer technology, courses that did not typically attract large enrollments from US students, might have to be cut drastically or even eliminated.

National Association of Foreign Student Advisers (NAFSA) had been among the leading critics of increased foreign student monitoring and restricted visas, and declared that such changes would be expensive to enforce, and would accomplish little. But recognizing the prevailing demand for action, the organization likewise understood that it would be difficult to convince Congress that such a system was not needed.

Part of the National Security Investigations Division, the Student and Exchange Visitor Program (SEVP) acted as a bridge for governmental organizations and had an interest in information on nonimmigrants whose primary reason for coming to the United States was for study. On behalf of the Department of Homeland Security (DHS), SEVP managed schools, nonimmigrant students and their dependents in the F and M visa classifications. It was the responsibility of the Department of State (DOS) to manage Exchange Visitor Programs, nonimmigrant exchange visitors in the J visa classification and their dependents. Both the SEVP and the DOS employed the SEVIS process, and together would track and monitor these programs and visa classification systems. Under the SEVIS system, international students and schools hosting foreign enrollments were listed in a database available for Immigrations and Customs Enforcement and other law enforcement agencies.[9]

The new Immigration and Customs Enforcement (ICE) agency was a creation of the 2003 Homeland Security Act. Congress had granted ICE a unique combination of civil and criminal authorities to better protect national security, in answer to the events of 9/11. Its primary mission would be to promote homeland security and public safety through the enforcement of federal laws governing border control, trade, and immigration. As of December 2009, ICE had some 8.1 million people recorded on its database.

The SEVIS tracking operation was documented and transferred electronically, and the many mandates for information required continuous updating. To admit a student, a university entered several pages of information about them into the government's database. From that point on, the admitting institutions were obliged to track the student's actions on behalf of the government, until their exit from the country. Course enrollments, address changes, and even personal financial information were constantly updated. The start of classes, a failure to enroll, students who dropped subjects below a full course load, or early graduation added to the list of required documentations. Typically, students who dropped their courses were either detained or deported.

As mentioned, upon admission to a US college or university, an I-20 was issued by the university and then sent to the student. The student then would visit the US consulate or embassy in his or her home country, which confirmed through SEVIS that the I-20 was valid. Upon arrival in the United States, a DHS officer was to report the arrival to SEVIS. When the student arrived on campus, it was again notified. The institution would at that point be required to provide regular electronic reports to the DHS, such as information on practical training, extensions of stay, off-campus employment, and academic progress, throughout the student's academic career. At the time of its enforcement, SEVIS mandated reports included the following:

- Enrollment status for the current semester
- Student's completion date
- School transfers

- Employment authorizations
- Reinstatement of status
- Change of the student's or dependent's legal name or address
- Academic or disciplinary actions taken due to criminal conviction
- Students who drop below a full course of study without prior authorization from the designated school official (DSO) or the international student adviser
- Termination date and reason for termination
- Any student who failed to maintain status or complete the program—this could include dropping below full-time enrollment without prior approval from the DSO; failure to apply for a timely transfer; or an I-20 extension or change in level of study; unauthorized employment; or failure to report a change of address within ten days of relocating
- Other dates generated by standard procedures such as program extensions, changes in level of study, employment authorizations, or reinstatement

Students also had a list of mandates. Those failing to stay in compliance lost the privileges of their student status and were subject to deportation. Consequences might include denial of re-entry to the United States, inability to move from undergraduate to graduate status, rejections of requests for practical training, inability to change visa status, or possibly the refusal of all future visa applications. To regain status, if the violation was beyond the student's control, they could apply to the DHS for reinstatement. They could not apply for reinstatement if they were out of status longer than five months, and if the DHS denied the request for reinstatement, the student could not appeal.[10]

Colleges and universities were hard-pressed to meet the January 2003 deadline for full implementation of the SEVIS requirements. Little time had been allowed to hire and train adequate numbers of employees who could manage the system, and many international admissions offices needed to be differently funded or restructured to amend staffing shortages. In a hearing before the Subcommittee on twenty-first Century Competitiveness in 2002, the American Association of State Colleges and Universities complained about the rapid implementation of the system as well as the costs, expenses that included training, software licenses, staffing, and many other now-necessary things.

Most schools were in the position of carrying out the new policies without the benefit of any budget increases. Fees to cover the process inevitably surfaced, and when they did, some students protested. A case in point was the University of Massachusetts at Amherst, where more than 200 international students refused to pay a new $65 fee charged to allay expenses incurred by the new system. The fee was wrong on two counts, they said. It was folly to have to pay for one's own surveillance, and by extension, why should they bear the burden of supplementing the budget for the international student office? Led by the Graduate Employment Organization, a campus union representing about a thousand international graduate students staged a rowdy protest outside the administrative offices and began a petition condemning the new charges. The university responded by sending out reminders to the students that to be in good standing, they must meet this financial obligation by the published deadlines. The consequences of not doing so could include cancellation of class registration, eviction from the residence hall and administrative withdrawal from the University of Massachusetts. The response was clear. There was no choice.[11]

The State Department was similarly understaffed and unprepared to quickly implement and carry out the new system, as consular offices around the world scrambled to institute the changes necessary to phase it in, and in some cases they fell short. In 2003, the Bureau of Resource management released their Performance and Accountability Report, which found Consular Affairs to be deficient in what they expected to be a fundamental re-adjustment regarding visa issuance. Accompanying the report was a recommendation from the Office of the Inspector General that the department assess and reallocate consular workloads worldwide. For prospective students, a consequence of these internal overhauls within the Consular Affairs offices was long delays in the visa issuance process, and some were unable to proceed until the transitions were complete.[12]

Reminiscent of the Cold War era, in May 2002, all American visa officers received a memo from the State Department, instructing them to watch for applicants whose area of study appeared on the "technology alert list," or the "sensitive major list." SEVIS was implemented to prevent the abuse of student visas, but it was also intended to prevent certain international students from receiving education and training in sensitive areas. Murky interpretations of those rosters led to sweeping effects as they expanded to include topics as seemingly harmless as urban planning and landscape design. Another problem was that the scrutiny disregarded most students not connected with the list of sensitive areas. Nor was it concerned with undergraduate students who had yet to declare majors. Theoretically, anyone could pursue sensitive technology if the study began at the undergraduate level, or if the student changed majors after arrival. Changing majors would presumably be documented by the college as part of the SEVIS requirements. In reality, this sort of change happened often and was infrequently acted upon by the DHS.[13]

Many still questioned whether policy shifts focusing on student exchange could have much of an effect on preventing terrorism, since there were far easier ways to enter the country, both legally and illegally. The government was policing the one means of entry that already presented the most challenges. Nonimmigrant students applying to colleges and universities in the United States had to begin the process months, sometimes years in advance. Tests had to be taken, many forms needed to be completed, and fees paid, combined with a willingness to take on the tasks assigned to them by a bureaucratic university admissions office. With few exceptions, foreign students in the United States had been a peaceful lot.

Post-9/11 Enrollments

It was widely predicted that concerns over borders and documentation would translate into a reduction of the foreign student population in America. An article in *The Chronicle of Higher Education*, titled "No Longer Dreaming of America," reported that for the 2002–2003 academic year, the total number of foreign students increased, but at a rate less than 1 percent compared to previous years, when the increases were around 5 percent. Countries such as China were recognizing opportunities. They began to invest more of their own resources in new academic programs, making the idea of studying at home more appealing. India, a major exporter of students to the United States, was at the same time experiencing an escalating economy that might encourage graduates to remain at home and enter the local workforce rather than pursuing advanced studies overseas.[14]

Surveys conducted by NAFSA, the Association of American Universities, the National Association of State Universities and Land-Grant Colleges, the Institute of International Education, and the Council of Graduate Schools, were released in March 2004. They found that 47 percent of the 250 colleges and universities that responded received far fewer graduate applications for the fall term of 2004 than they had the year before— among them were 19 of the 25 US research institutions that enrolled the largest number of international students. The declining rates appeared to be connected in part to the actions taken by the US government to make it progressively more difficult for people to enter the country, said Victor Johnson of NAFSA.[15]

In September 2004, the Council of Graduate Schools released the results of a second survey, this time including 126 institutions. The sobering data indicated an 18 percent decrease in foreign student admissions between the fall of 2004 and the previous fall. The largest enrollment drops reported were from China (34 percent), India (19 percent), and South Korea (12 percent), the three countries that had been sending the most students.[16]

In the end, almost everyone conceded that the events of September 11 had changed everything. In the 50 years since the end of World War II, American educators and US policy had enthusiastically supported international and intercultural information exchange, with the heartfelt belief that, if people understood and appreciated each other, there would be no need for war. It was a romantic, high-minded notion that inspired the continuation or creation of organizations such as the Institute of International Education, the Fulbright program, AMIDEAST (America-Mideast Educational and Training Services, Inc.), and many others. The world instead seemed to be entering an unprecedented time of international insecurity, dominated by political and religious intolerance. There was nevertheless a commonly advanced declaration on behalf of the importance of hosting even greater numbers of foreign students.

The liveliest debate of the period revolved around a series of critiques that threw into question the rationale underlying international education exchange, such as the 2002 publication of Evaluation of the Foreign Student Program by Harvard economist George Borjas under the imprimatur of the Center for Immigration Studies (CIS). An excerpted version had appeared a few weeks before in the *National Review*. Soon afterward, the CIS convened a panel on which Borjas was joined by the American Council on Education's Terry Hartle and other educational luminaries. The agenda included discussions of Borjas' attack on international education exchange, as well as the practical importance of foreign students.

In the *National Review* report, Borjas opened with the observation that by the year 2000 the State Department was issuing more than 315,000 student visas annually. But he also asserted that the program was riddled with corruption. The INS did not know, he claimed, how many foreign students were in the country, or where they all were. Borjas contended that the foreign student program had been spinning out of control for years, and that there were few checks and balances to keep the number of foreign students at a manageable level, or to prevent foreigners from using the many loopholes to enter the country for reasons other than education. Perhaps most important, he added, was that the program had grown so explosively without anyone asking the most basic question. Is such a large-scale foreign student program in America's interest? What does it buy us? What does it cost us?

Borjas claimed that the financial incentives of large research universities did not necessarily align well with national security. Institutions need low-cost workers to staff laboratories and they depend on minimal-wage graduate teaching assistants to instruct large undergraduate classes. Foreign students provide a nearly unlimited supply of willing workers who have not undergone any meaningful screening or background checks. Meanwhile, he added, corruption abroad was rampant, notably illustrated by a thriving industry of consulting firms that supply bogus letters of recommendation, faked evidence of economic self-sufficiency, and even professional actors who could stand in for an applicant during a counselor interview. Borjas dismissed panegyrics touting the supposed benefits of hosting foreign students as nothing more than unsubstantiated rhetoric. Nor was he impressed with the frequent claim that America benefitted by skimming the best talent from other countries, as there was no warrant for assuming that those who remained were necessarily talented. "It's not politically correct to say so, but the foreign student program may not be all that beneficial," said Borjas. "Once we stop humming the Ode to Diversity that plays such a central role in the modern secular liturgy, we will recognize that the time has come for a fundamental reevaluation of the program."[17]

Notes

1. Dina Temple-Raston, "Khalid Sheikh Mohammed's Isolated U.S. College Days," *National Public Radio* (November 18, 2009). Available at: www.npr.org/templates/story/story.php?storyId=120516152. Accessed December 14, 2018.
2. Amy Goldstein, Lena H. Sun, and George Lardner, Jr., "Hanjour, a Study in Paradox," *The Washington Post* (October 15, 2001).
3. Jim Yardley, "A Trainee Noted for Incompetence," *The New York Times* (May 4, 2002). Available at: https://www.nytimes.com/2002/05/04/us/a-trainee-noted-for-incompetence.html. Accessed December 14, 2018.

4. Ibid.
5. Victor C. Johnson, "Taking Stock, Making Strides," *International Educator*, Vol. 14, no. 1 (March–April 2005): 4; also see Olga Gain and William K. Cummings, "Where Have the International Students Gone?," *International Instructor*, Vol. 14 (March–April 2005): 20.
6. M. Allison Witt, "Closed Borders and Closed Minds: Immigration Policy Changes after 9/11 and U.S. Higher Education," *Journal of Educational Controversy*, Vol. 3, no. 1 (2008): Art. 5.
7. James M. O'Neill, "Foreign Students May Bear Brunt of Terrorism with Stricter Visas," *Knight Rider Tribune News Service* (September 27, 2001).
8. "Dealing with Foreign Students and Scholars in an Age of Terrorism: Visa Backlogs and Tracking systems," From the Hearing before the Committee on Science, House of Representatives, 108th Congress, First Session (March 26, 2003).
9. "U.S. Immigration and Customs Enforcement, Student and Exchange Visitor Program." Available at: https://www.ice.gov/sevis#wcm-survey-target-id.
10. Ibid.
11. Jenna Russell, "Foreign Students Protest Fee at UMass," *The Boston Globe* (March 21, 2004).
12. U.S. Department of State, Review of Nonimmigrant Visa Issuance Policy and Procedures (2003). Available at: http://www.state.gov/s/d/rm/rls/perfrpt/2003/index.htm. Accessed December 14, 2018.
13. Y. Zhou, "The Visa Trap," *The New York Times* (January 18, 2004): 4A, 32.
14. Paul Mooney and Shialaja Neelakantan, "No Longer Dreaming of America," *The Chronicle of Higher Education*, Vol. 51 (October 8, 2004): A41.
15. Yudhijit Bhattacharjee, "Foreign Graduate Student Applications Drop," *Science*, Vol. 303 (March 5, 2004): A41.
16. Victor Johnson, "The Perils of Homeland Security," *The Chronicle of Higher Education*, Vol. 49 (April 11, 2003): B7.
17. Ibid.

References

Goldstein, Amy, Lena H. Sun, and George Lardner, Jr. 2001. Hanjour, a Study in Paradox. *The Washington Post*, October 15.

Johnson, Victor. 2003. The Perils of Homeland Security. *The Chronicle of Higher Education* 49, April 11.

Johnson, Victor C. 2005. Taking Stock, Making Strides. *International Educator* 14 (1), March–April.

Mooney, Paul, and Shialaia Neelakantan. 2004. No Longer Dreaming of America. *The Chronicle of Higher Education* 51, October 8.

O'Neill, James M. 2001. Foreign Students May Bear Brunt of Terrorism with Stricter Visas. *Knight Rider Tribune News Service*, September 27.

Temple-Raston, Dina. 2009. Khalid Sheikh Mohammed's Isolated U.S. College Days. *National Public Radio*, November 18. www.npr.org/templates/story/story.php?storyId=120516152.

U.S. Department of State. 2003. Review of Nonimmigrant Visa Issuance Policy and Procedures. http://www.state.gov/s/d/rm/rls/perfrpt/2003/index.htm.

Witt, M. Allison. 2008. Closed Borders and Closed Minds: Immigration Policy Changes after 9/11 and U.S. Higher Education. *Journal of Educational Controversy* 3(1): Art. 5. https://cedar.wwu.edu/jec/vol3/iss1/5.

Yardley, Jim. 2002. A Trainee Noted for Incompetence. *The New York Times*, May 4.

Yudhijit, Bhattacharjee. 2004. Foreign Graduate Student Applications Drop. *Science* 303, March 5.

Zhou, Y. 2004. The Visa Trap. *The New York Times*, January 18.

CHAPTER 9

Escalation of Exchange with Asia

At the close of the first decade of the new millennium, 723,277 international students were enrolled in colleges and universities in the United States, a 4.7 percent increase from the previous year (690,923). By region, Asia was the largest sender. China was the top country of origin, comprising more than 21 percent of the foreign population, followed by India, which accounted for 14.4 percent. South Korea was third, contributing 10 percent (Table 9.1).[1]

In 2009, India's enrollments began to decline, a trend that would continue for the next three years. Between 2009 and 2013, the number of undergraduate Indian students in America declined by 16 percent, from 15,192 to 12,740. Similarly, the number of graduate Indian students declined by 20 percent, from 68,290 in 2009 to 54,607 in 2013. Of the top senders, Japan experienced the sharpest decline in 2010/2011, compared to the previous year.

China

Turning out a well-educated and successful offspring, especially after the adoption of the one-child policy, took on a special urgency in China. In the decades after Deng Xiaoping reopened China's borders to education exchange, earning an American degree became a national obsession. Since 1979, Chinese enrollments in US colleges and universities have been escalating more or less consistently, and China has held the position of top

Table 9.1 Foreign student enrollments in the United States 2009–2010 and 2010–2011: Asia

	2009–2010	2010–2011	% total	% change
China	127,822	157,558	21.8	23.3
India	104,897	103,895	14.4	−1.0
South Korea	72,153	73,351	10.1	1.7
Taiwan	26,685	24,818	3.4	−7.0
Japan	24,842	21,290	2.9	−14.3
Vietnam	13,112	14,888	2.1	13.5
Thailand	8531	8236	1.1	−3.5
Hong Kong	8034	8136	1.1	1.3

Source: *Open Doors*, 2010–2011

sender for most of those years. Efforts to continue that escalation have emerged more recently, as well as initiatives designed to promote American study abroad in China, such as President Obama's 100,000 Strong Initiative. Meanwhile, China's own initiatives, such as the cultivation of its "Ivy League" of elite universities, have altered the course of Sino-American higher education exchange.

Since Yale graduated America's first Chinese student in 1854, there have been three distinct migrations. The Chinese Educational Mission initiated the first Sino-American exchanges in the latter half of the nineteenth century; then in the early twentieth century, a subsequent wave of Chinese students came to the United States on Boxer Indemnity scholarships. A third and still-continuing surge of students and scholars began when Deng Xiaoping took power in 1979 and reopened China's borders to education exchange. China and Chinese students have played important roles in the development of exchange programs and study abroad opportunities. The prominence of Chinese students has influenced the rise of Asian studies courses in universities, the expansion of ESL (English as a Second Language) services, the development of international student organizations, and other components of foreign student support.

While the advantages of intercultural learning have most often been cited as the reason for America's favorable attitude toward Chinese students, a more practical benefit has been these students' profitability. The preponderance of Chinese students enrolled in US institutions are self-funded. Another motivation for America's interest in education trade with China has been the opportunity to exert so-called soft power. Teddy

Roosevelt was one who embraced that idea. Through education exchange, American philosophies and Christian values could be subtly and peacefully transferred to the Chinese. While the United States has reaped the monetary benefits generated by hundreds of thousands of profitable customers, there have also been opportunities to export American ideals. China has in turn used the transfer of science and technology as a means of accelerating their economy and strengthening their military, goals they have accomplished to a remarkable degree. This was China's strategy from the beginning.

Enrollments 2000–2010

Between 2000 and 2010, China's enrollments in the United States more than doubled, with the greatest increases after 2006. During the same period, the number of American students enrolled in Chinese institutions of higher learning increased more than four-fold. China's broad investment in its own institutions during the opening years of the millennium was paying off in terms of foreign enrollments, not just from the United States but from countries around the world (Table 9.2).

Table 9.2 Chinese students in the United States and Americans studying in China 2000–2010

	# *Chinese students in the United States*	*% change from previous year*	# *American students in China*
2009–2010	127,822	29.9	13,910
2008–2009	98,235	21.1	13,674
2007–2008	81,127	19.8	13,188
2006–2007	62,723	19.8	13,188
2005–2006	62,582	8.2	11,064
2004–2005	62,523	1.2	6391
2003–2004	61,765	−4.6	4737
2002–2003	64,757	2.4	2493
2001–2002	63,211	5.5	3911
2000–2001	59,939	10.0	2942
1999–2000	54,466	6.8	2949

Source: IIE *Open Doors*, 1999–2010

The Allure of China

In the opening years of the millennium, students and scholars in the United States were increasingly charmed by China. The attraction was in part a result of the American media coverage of its exploding economic power. The Olympics in Beijing, China's issues in Tibet and a host of other China-related topics were front-page headlines.

Colleges across America were experiencing a surge of interest in programs relating to the Chinese. The Inter-University Program for Chinese Language Studies, a consortium of 13 American universities, is a case in point. The program's applicants skyrocketed during the first millennial decade, according to program director Tom Gold, a professor at the University of California. When he assumed the position in 2000, the program accepted about 97 percent of the students who applied, but by 2008 they were only accepting one in three. At Syracuse University, one China program proved insufficient to meet student demand and in 2006 it started a Beijing program in collaboration with Tsinghua University. State University of New York at Oswego went from one small exchange docket in Beijing to seven partner destinations throughout China, supplemented by two faculty-led short-term programs, one on business and another on Chinese culture.[2]

For 150 years, Sino-American knowledge trade had been almost entirely one-way. Thousands of China's students were eager to earn degrees in prestigious US Universities, but few Americans were inclined to seek instruction from the far-less-developed Chinese institutions. Now, Americans would begin to be drawn to China. Since the 1990s China was on a course to upgrade higher education, and since then the Chinese government has dedicated ever-increasing sums toward its improvement—money made available with the escalation of its economy. Backed by expanded funds, China's colleges and universities quickly elevated their status in the world's higher education market, attracting increasingly greater shares of the world's international student enrollments. The allure of vastly upgraded institutions in a beautiful and exotic country, combined with the lessening of border restrictions, proved to be irresistible for growing numbers of international students and scholars. China's Ministry of Education reported in 2010 that foreign enrollments had risen markedly, hitting a record high of 240,000 students—a striking contrast from 60 years prior when there were just 20 foreign university students in all of China.[3]

As with the medieval universities of Europe, when centers of higher learning in China developed academic reputations sufficient to draw foreign students from faraway places, only then were they regarded as true universities. Chinese facilities were now in that exclusive league, and it had taken a long time to get there. The formal establishment of a cohesive higher education system in China is a relatively recent event. China's first modern, American-type institution of higher education was Peiyang University (now Tianjin University), which was established in 1895, not long after the end of the Sino-Japanese War. The devastating surrender to Japan had revitalized imperial interest in education reform and the Qing emperor sanctioned a proposal to carry out those changes. Drawn up by Sheng Xuanhuai, the plan outlined a long-range strategy designed to strengthen China's economic and military power through the development of its universities. With assistance from Charles Tenney, an American educator, Shang set in place the founding of the first fundamentally modern university in China, The Peiyang Western Study School, the first institution to fully adopt a Western system.[4]

Peiyang operated according to an American model, for the most part teaching Western learning in the areas of law, civil engineering, mining, metallurgy, and mechanics, using books and equipment purchased from the United States and Germany. The majority of its first instructors had been recruited from the United States, graduates of Harvard, Stanford and other high-ranking universities, effectively making Peiyang's first faculty competitive with many top-tier American institutions. In 1899, the university awarded its First Imperially Written Diploma to Wang Chonghui—a milestone for Chinese education. Wang would later become a judge to the international court. Other important graduates from Peiyang's early years include Liu Ruiheng, founder of the Chinese public health system, and Ma Yinchu, who was the first person in China to be awarded a PhD in economics. The Peiyang Western Study School would become Peiyang University, and then would merge with Hebei Technical College to become Tianjin University.[5]

Founded in 1898, Peking University (known colloquially as Beida) was originally known as the Imperial University of Peking and was the first national university offering comprehensive disciplines in China. In 1912, the university adopted its present name. It would merge with Beijing Medical University in 2000.

Nanjing University dates from 1902, when it was known as Sanjiang Normal School and Fudan University, whose name translates as "heavenly light shines day after day" had its start in 1905. Harbin Institute of

Technology opened in 1920. By 1949, when Mao Zedong and the Communist Party took control, there existed at least 200 institutions of higher education in mainland China. It was not until after the ascension of Deng Xiaoping that a uniform system of enrollments and operations was implemented. Among Deng's early decisions regarding education had been the resumption of a national examination system for college admissions, and three such examinations were held between 1977 and the end of 1979. An estimated 18 million high school graduates participated and about 880,000 of them were accepted into China's colleges and universities.[6]

China did not have a fully developed academic degree system in the modern sense, and prior to Deng's reforms only about 30 percent of its university faculty had earned postsecondary degrees. With the resumption of a formalized national college entrance examination, Chinese higher education began to upgrade its universities and it would soon produce a home-grown instructional staff.

In 1993, the Central Committee of the Chinese Communist Party and the State Council jointly issued the Program for Educational Reform that once again allowed private universities to operate in China. Fresh facilities, funded by nongovernment entities, were allowed to emerge—a major change for a system that had previously been under the direct control of the central government. This move would help expand China's college and university enrollments over the next several years. According to China's Ministry of Education, in 1990 less than 4 percent of citizens aged 18–23 were enrolled in Chinese higher education institutions, compared to 22 percent in 2005.[7]

China's Project 211 had begun in 1995. Designed for university building, it would afford special funding for a select group of 100 higher education institutions to help improve their overall performance. The Ministry of Education launched a follow-up program in 1998, called Project 985, which narrowed the focus to nine elite Chinese universities, the so-called C9 League. The project's intention was to make the C-9 League the top-ranked in the world by the early twenty-first century. In 2004, the effort expanded to include additional institutions. By that time many of China's remaining Soviet-style subject colleges had been combined into comprehensive institutions that more closely resembled American universities.

An Ivy League in China

Over the centuries, wars and natural disasters sometimes enfeebled China, but rarely for long. China has historically rebounded to successfully address its weaknesses, and the academic arena has been no exception. On May 4, 1998, on the 100th anniversary of the founding of Peking University, President Jiang Zemin proclaimed with great pride that, in order to realize China's modernization, it would build several universities into world class status.

The following year the sum of one billion yuan, or about $162 million, was given to each of nine colleges, with the mandate to build new facilities and to generally improve. These chosen institutions, the so-called C9 League, were slated to become China's elite institutions of higher education for the twenty-first century, directly competitive with the finest universities in the United States or Western Europe. While they would lack the sports teams that initially linked America's eight elite colleges, this group of nine aspired to become China's own "Ivy League." The effort was conducive to the country's construction of high-quality colleges, cultivation of top-notch talents and enhanced cooperation and exchanges between Chinese universities and their foreign counterparts, said Education Ministry spokeswoman Xu Mei.[8]

On the C9 list are some of China's oldest and most respected institutions, among them Tsinghua University. Tsinghua had already enjoyed a long and prestigious history and a deep relationship with education exchange and the United States. At its centennial celebration in 2011, Yale's president Richard C. Levin hailed the university's many accomplishments. In its first century, Tsinghua played an integral role in the development of China and many of its 170,000 graduates became leaders in their fields, said Levin, with a reminder that the first two Chinese to be awarded the Nobel Prize, Chen Ning Yang and T.D. Lee, were both educated at Tsinghua. Four of the first five presidents of Tsinghua studied at Yale, he added.[9] Tsinghua's other collaborations with American universities have included MIT, Johns Hopkins, the University of Michigan, Columbia and others. Tsinghua was also successful in implementing collaborations with industry leaders such as Toyota, Boeing, and United Technologies to form joint research centers.

Other members of the C9 League include Peking University, Zhejiang University in Hangzhou, the Harbin Institute of Technology, Fudan University, Shanghai Jiao Tong University, Nanjiang University, the University of Science and Technology of China, Xi'an Jiaotong University, and a military school in Hefei. Cooperative agreements among the schools feature flexible student programs, close collaboration on the training of postgraduates, and the establishment of a system which allows students to earn credits by attending classes at the member universities—important steps in the C9 plan. But there have been serious challenges.

China's goal to produce world-class research institutions in an environment where open inquiry and access to information remains severely limited, conditions generally inhospitable to true scientific study, has so far been unrealized. China's ability to effectively balance governmental constraints with academic freedom has been repeatedly questioned. The newly formed C9 League was beginning to consider these and other issues in 2001, just as China gained admission to the World Trade Organization. Among other things, the organization would impact China's quest for international enrollments by providing opportunities for exchange programs with more countries.[10]

As Westernization and internationalization of its academic system moved forward, as late as 2005 China's higher education was still under the influence of the Soviet model. In 2008, Wen Jiabao chaired an executive committee that drafted an education development plan designed to balance the influences of each model—Western, Soviet, and Chinese. It was a pragmatic decision with a vision to the future. In 2012, in a work report delivered to the People's Congress, Wen announced that the government expenditure would begin allotting no less than 4 percent of the gross national product toward the advancement of higher education and academic exchange. Xie Xuren, China's finance minister, promised that the logistics of the budgeted disbursement would be accomplished that same year, a boost in funding that held the promise of even more academic expansion.

China attracted steadily increasing numbers of Americans after the turn of the millennium, drawn naturally to its rich and ancient history, but also to the opportunities emerging from its economic rise. The number of Americans studying in China grew 30 percent between 2001 and 2007 and by 2012, according to Institute of International Education's (IIE's) *Open Doors* report, about 15,000 Americans were enrolled in China's colleges and universities. Supporting the trend, in 2005 Joe Lieberman and

Lamar Alexander had introduced the United States-China Cultural Engagement Act, authorizing $1.3 billion in federal funds to provide for Chinese-language instruction in American schools. The funds also increased consular activity supporting American commercial ventures and provided for physical and virtual exchanges between the two countries. A *New York Times* article quoted IIE president Allan E. Goodman, who confirmed that interest in China was growing dramatically. People used to go to China to study the history and language, he said, but with China looming so large in all our futures, there's been a shift. Now more students go there to understand China economically and politically.[11]

Traditional study-abroad locations still attracted the most Americans in 2008, but by 2012 China had become the fifth most popular destination, after Great Britain, Italy, Spain, and France. In the second decade of the new millennium, there were still about ten times more Chinese students coming to the United States for education programs than Americans going to China, and about 600 times more Chinese studying English than there were Americans studying Mandarin. But those gaps have narrowed. By the year 2020, China plans to be hosting at least a half million foreign students in its universities, including a substantial population of Americans.[12]

Little Emperors and Migrant Children

Three publishers refused to print Jame Liang's book, *Too Many People in China*, citing the topic's sensitivity. Its thesis was that the demographic changes brought about by the one-child policy would challenge China's goal of moving from being the factory of the world to a more entrepreneurial economy. For the first time in history, according to World Bank in 2014, a country is getting old before it has gotten rich. While it took the United States and Europe about a century to become "aging societies," in China it took fewer than 40 years.[13]

According to China's National Population and Family Planning Commission, the one-child policy enacted in 1979 had averted a surge in births that would have added an estimated 400 million Chinese to a population that already exceeded 1.3 billion. Some would question that claim, among them Weng Feng, senior fellow at the Brookings-Tsinghua Center for Public Policy at Tsinghua University. The attitudes that gave birth to the one-child policy date to the period immediately following the Cultural Revolution, explained Weng, when the country suffered food shortages and food rationing. And, it was generally believed that Chinese wanted large families. In the mid-1960s, before the policy was enforced, Chinese couples had an average of about 6 children, compared to 1.5 children in 2013. Demographers at the time predicted that China's population would peak in 2030 at about 1.4 billion.[14]

Enforced with a heavy hand, there were numerous exceptions to the one-child rule. Rural couples whose first child was female were allowed to have a second, and parents who were both only children could also have two offspring. Even with relaxations in the policy since 1979, it has remained a topic of controversy, in part due to its dark history of forced abortions. In recent years, social media has brought far more attention to the issue, in one case posting a disturbing photograph of a 22-year-old woman from Shanxi Province who, at seven months pregnant, was pressured by government officials to have an abortion. The image of the dead fetus, lying next to the traumatized mother, went viral on Weibo, China's Twitter.[15]

China's one-child policy would have effects other than a reduction in population. It also produced new generations of so-called little emperors, a term referring to the only children of doting parents. With just one offspring to lead the family toward a prosperous future, many children were overindulged and spoiled, with every family resource slated for their education and future success. Study abroad in the United States or other Western destinations was often on the agenda. Girls became little emperors too in most respects, but so far have remained behind males in professional success, largely due to social traditions and fewer opportunities available for women. After the implementation of the one-child policy, female enrollments in China's higher education institutions, as well as in their participation in study-abroad programs, increased significantly.

The aging of China's population and a lowered birth rate has altered its future workforce, and its approach to education. Complicating the issue has been the burgeoning number of Chinese children who receive a subpar education. According to some experts, its rising population of impoverished "migrant children" could be a deterrent to the nation's ability to develop the educational levels and the workforce it will need.

Migrant children earned that designation due to their parents' decision to move from the countryside into the city without official approval. In China one may not relocate without governmental permission, a policy aimed at keeping China's population evenly distributed. Nonetheless, in recent decades hundreds of millions have fled rural areas without obtaining permission, desperate to find work and a better life. Because of their status as unofficial migrants, municipal governments were often unwilling or unable to provide public services such as health care or education. Based on information from *The Hechinger Report*, a publication of Teachers College at Columbia University, a 2012 article in *Time World* described private schools in southern China that have taken on the task of educating some of the country's most disadvantaged students. Many nonprofit agencies, nongovernmental organizations, and private citizens have worked to set up thousands of schools, most at the elementary level. On shoestring budgets, such schools are typically understaffed, their teachers are oftentimes less than fully qualified, and most depend on volunteers for their existence. Warnings have emerged that the subpar education being loosely administered to such a large population of young citizens will affect China's overall productivity in the long run.[16]

Stanford University's Rural Education Action Project, an organization formed to help reduce China's growing rural-urban academic achievement gap, judged it to be an enormous problem, one that would require the immediate attention of China's national authorities. For China to maintain its new superpower status, its workforce must be more literate and better educated. The achievement gap between migrant children and the students enrolled in China's public schools was and is concerning, even as its published record shows great improvement over the past couple of decades.

China's published record can sometimes be questioned. In 2010, the world was stunned as Shanghai's 15-year-olds beat their peers around the world on international assessments in reading, math, and science. Americans of the same age finished in the bottom half of the countries examined. What is important to note, however, is that China's scores were generated from its public schools. They did not include millions of less-attended-to migrant students. In America, all children are provided an education regardless of their situation, and its assessment scores were comprehensive. Studies have shown that, even though migrant students in private city schools outperformed those living in poor rural areas, they remained academically inferior to those attending urban public schools. China's public schools clearly had the ability to turn out highly capable students, but without a similar level of academic training for all of its youth, the result could be millions of virtually unemployable adults.

Henan Cheng of Loyola University in Chicago, a researcher who studied migrant education in Kunming in Yunnan Province, believed the problem could have a far-reaching effect. Some nonprofits estimated that more than

22.5 million migrants were living in Chinese cities at the time, about 10 percent of them children. China should brace for as many as 350 million migrants by 2050, according to some authorities on population growth. As early as 2006 China was taking steps to curb the problem, first by allowing migrant children to enroll in some public schools and by subsidizing many of the private schools to help with their expenses. The process of enrolling migrant children in public schools could be daunting, however. Students were required to obtain as many as seven official certificates in some cities, documenting things like birthplace. Education was provided free for city-born children, but migrant students sometimes paid tuition as high as 1000 yuan per semester, or about $150, a sizable fee for most of the families. Migrant children frequently exhibited behavioral problems, a common by-product of poverty and hardship, a condition that added to the difficulties.[17]

China's Ten-Year Plan

Plans put forth by China's Ministry of Education, strategies to improve the country's system of education from its kindergartens to its universities, have been underway. The Outline of China's National Plan for Medium and Long-Term Education Reform and Development (2010–2020) took two years to draw up, and underwent about 40 revisions, before it was officially adopted.[18] The plan set a series of goals to be achieved by 2020, including the universalizing of preschool education, improving nine-year compulsory education, and raising the senior high school gross enrollment rate to 90 percent. In higher education, among other things the plan called for the creation of world-class universities, as well as improved teaching and research and greater freedom for institutions of higher learning to set their academic goals. It sought to revise China's entrance examination system and to achieve a 40 percent enrollment rate in higher education.[19] Both UNESCO (United Nations Educational, Scientific and Cultural Organization) and the World Bank commended the plan as farsighted and ambitious.

The ten-year plan also sought to attract more world-class scholars and researchers to work in China, to import better instructional materials and to establish 250 of its Confucius Institutes in 80 countries. More scholarships would be offered, expanded language programs were to be supported, and more courses were to be taught in English. The plan endorsed sending greater numbers of Chinese students to study abroad and set the goal of attracting a half million international students to its own colleges and universities by 2020.

In a report developed by China's Ministry of Finance, the Development Research Center of the State Council, and the World Bank, titled *China 2030: Building a Modern, Harmonious, and Creative High-Income Society*, it was recommended that China approach midcentury by building upon its strengths—high savings, increasing numbers of skilled professionals, and the potential for further urbanization. China should capitalize on external opportunities, the report suggested, including continued globalization, the growth of other emerging economies, and the promise of new technologies. China would also need to address some significant challenges, including its aging society, rising inequality, and a growing environmental deficit.

Six basic strategies for China's future development were recommended, including the rethinking of the role of the state and the private sector to build competition. It encouraged the adoption of an open innovation system with links to global research and development networks. Third, China should look to green development as a new avenue of growth and fourth, equality of opportunity and social protection should be provided for all of its citizens. The systems should be strengthened along with the improvement of fiscal sustainability, the report recommended, and lastly, China should integrate with global markets. These efforts must be approached within an environment of greater transparency, and to heighten China's credibility in the eyes of the rest of the world, a concerted effort was needed to lessen fraudulence.[20]

President Obama's 100,000 Strong Initiative

In a speech at Howard University, First Lady Michelle Obama referred to education exchange as a key component of the administration's foreign policy agenda. It was President Barack Obama's stated aim to substantially increase the number of Americans studying in China, in part, to prepare the next generation of American experts on that country. He especially hoped to increase the levels of student groups who went overseas less frequently, such as minority groups or students attending community colleges. The goal was tempered with worries about its practicality and achievability.[21]

Such a goal would necessitate considerable change, including an expansion of foreign-study programs and of curricular offerings in Chinese language, culture, and politics on American campuses, and these would take time to implement. Once in force, would China have the capacity to host the larger American enrollments? It was a bold venture, commented IIE president Goodman, and realizable, but he also cautioned that his comment was not without reservations. The 100,000 Strong Initiative would complement successful study-abroad and language-study programs already in force through the State Department's Bureau of Educational and Cultural Affairs, the Department of Education, and the Department of Defense. It sought to rely fully on private-sector philanthropic support to direct funds to existing US-China educational-exchange programs that want to expand.[22]

The 100,000 Strong Initiative was launched in 2009 and Secretary of State Hillary Clinton officially announced its operation in Beijing the following year. The initiative drew enthusiastic support from the Chinese government. The Chinese Ministry of Education, along with the China Scholarship Council, quickly committed 10,000 "Bridge Scholarships" for American students to study in China's institutions. The scholarships were offered under the U.S.-China Consultation on People-to-People Exchange (CPE), and were made available to students with schools accepting credit transfer from their institution's partner university. China would provide positive assistance to the US initiative to send 100,000 students to study in China over the next four years, said State Councilor Liu Yangdong to Secretary Clinton. She added that both countries could benefit from exploring new avenues of cultural exchange. In support of the initiative, China would increase the number of government-funded scholarships for Chinese who want to pursue doctorates in the United States.[23]

For China, it was an effort to support its ten-year national education outline, and an important component of the country's diplomatic work to show Chinese culture to the global community, stated Zhang Xiuqin, director-general of the ministry's Department of International Cooperation and Exchange. Zhang was referring to the National Outline for Medium and Long-Term Education Reform and Development, 2010–2020, and its strategies for expanding international cooperation and higher learning exchange. By 2012, American students were eligible for CPE scholarships in 40 Chinese universities.[24]

The 100,000 Strong Initiative encountered a few problems. One made an early appearance in the admissions process. When the initiative was first launched, the taking of the Scholastic Aptitude Test (SAT) was still prohibited in mainland China, a relic of an earlier time. Some American-based tests had long been permitted, such as the Advance Placement examinations that allowed high school students to earn college credit. Students wanting to take the college entrance SAT exams, however, had to travel to Hong Kong. Unlike Mainland China, the former British colony was allowed to administer SAT examinations. Or they could go to South Korea, Taiwan, Macao, or other locations where the test was administered. In a 2011 *Business Week* interview, a 20-year-old Chinese student summed it up. It was a hassle. Some were concerned it could be politically invasive but the need for efficiency won out. After an effective campaign for policy change the nonprofit College Board, which owns the Preliminary Scholastic Aptitude Test (PSAT), SAT, and Advanced placement tests, began offering the PSAT in China in 2012. Within mainland China, however, the SAT was at that point still only administered within schools for dependents of foreign personnel, or international schools.[25]

Since its implementation the 100,000 Strong Initiative has inspired other programs and policies supporting the expansion of Sino-American academic exchange. In 2011, the Institute of International Education announced that ten US institutions would participate in the International Academic Partnerships Program, a project supported by the Department of Education's Fund for the Improvement of Postsecondary Education and managed by IIE's Center for International Partnerships in Higher Education. Participating schools included Greenville Technical College, Jacksonville State University, Lake Washington Technical College, Marymount Manhattan College, Saginaw Valley State University, Southern Methodist University, State University of New York at Fredonia, College of New Jersey, the University of Southern Indiana, and Utah Valley University.[26]

The Institute of International Education would sponsor other efforts in its support for President Obama's 100,000 Strong Initiative, among them the relaunching of the Freeman Awards for Study in Asia (Freeman-Asia), a venture supported with a substantial grant of $2 million from the Freeman Foundation. The institute also published *Study Abroad in China*, a special edition in its series of study-abroad directories, listing 350 programs open to American graduate and undergraduate students, offered by the two governments, third party providers, private foundations, and US higher education institutions.[27]

American Higher Education in China

Since 2000, more American institutions have brought their campuses to China. Combined with China's efforts to create more sophisticated institutions of their own, this recent abundance of good-quality institutions in China is attracting greater numbers of students from the United States and also keeping many Chinese home. With occupational opportunities expanding in China, higher percentages of American-educated Chinese students are opting to return home after graduation.

A joint venture with Johns Hopkins University is among the most well-developed and extensive Sino-American university collaborations. The Johns Hopkins University-Nanjing University Center for Chinese and American Studies was established in 1986, even before China's millennial push for domestic academic opportunities. The center was the creation of its president Steven Muller and Nanjing University president Kuang Yaming. In this setting, midcareer professionals from China and the West could live and study together in one of a variety of fields, including law, journalism, government, or business, experiences designed to deepen their understanding of each other's cultures and to enrich their academic backgrounds in topics relating to international relations. With burgeoning interest in China, in 2006 the center underwent a $21 million campus expansion and introduced a new two-year Master of Arts in International Studies program. At the time the Hopkins-Nanjing Center was the only joint academic program to offer a master's degree fully accredited in China and the United States. Credit transfer agreements and mutual recognition of academic credentials, at this point signed by at least 34 countries, were an important part of realizing the plan.[28]

Duke University opened a campus in Kunshan, Harvard started a Senior Executive Program in Shanghai, and Auburn University opened a facility in Danyang. In 2010 the University of Chicago opened a research center in Beijing, quickly followed by Stanford's center, and in 2012 officials broke ground on the construction site for Wenzhou Kean University in Zhejiang Province. The following year an agreement was signed with New York University (NYU) to set up a campus in Shanghai in collaboration with a Chinese institution—China's first Sino-American university.[29]

New York University Shanghai (NYU Shanghai) scheduled its opening for 2013, with the expectation that about 51 percent of enrollments would come from the Chinese mainland, while 49 percent would be international students. Applicants for NYU Shanghai were required to demonstrate the same talent required of them by top universities around the world, said NYU president John Sexton. The syllabi and curricula of NYU Shanghai followed the example of the world's leading universities, featuring a well-rounded education, English lectures, and small classes to encourage open discussion. By 2012, about 200 faculty members of NYU and about 100 scholars worldwide voiced an interest in becoming part of NYU Shanghai.[30]

Other collaborations in the early years of the millennium included Liaoning Normal University (LNU) and Missouri State University (MSU), which created the LNU-MSU College of International Business in Dalian, China, in 2000. University of Maryland's Robert H. Smither School of Business opened in Beijing and Shanghai and Ohio University set up operations in Hong Kong and University of Dayton has a campus in Shanghai. In 2009, Yale University partnered with Tsinghua in international healthcare management as part of Goldman Sachs' 10,000 Women Initiative, a program designed to train 500 female students from rural China. The list of partnerships has since continued to grow. A multilateral approach was emphasized in order to build up the network of exchanges, said China's Ministry of Education's Shen Yang.[31]

As academic collaborations have emerged, so have subtle complications. An article in *Forbes* cautioned that US institutions should "prepare for interesting times" when dealing with local Chinese authorities. Dealing with the government would be unlike any experience most universities have had before. They will need to have representatives on the ground in China with strong local and cultural savvy and shrewd negotiating skills, to navigate the labyrinths of bureaus, approvals, and permits.[32]

Finding enough faculty to fill the growing number of positions in Chinese institutions was also a formidable task. An economic downturn in the United States around 2008, combined with these new opportunities, tempted quite a few academics to pack their bags for an extended term in China, and the Chinese welcomed them with open arms. More recently, the Chinese government has further enticed foreigners with new opportunities that offer a range of incentives. In 2011 the Thousand Foreign Experts program was announced, designed to attract up to 1000 foreign academics and entrepreneurs to China over a period of 10 years. An extension of the 2008 Thousand Talent initiative, this new program drew hundreds of applicants from the United States, Japan, Germany, and a host of other countries, according to Xinhua, China's official news agency.[33]

China needs to continue to attract more foreign academics to help lift its international competitiveness, said Li Jun, assistant professor at the Department of International Education and Lifelong Learning at the Hong Kong Institute of Education. They can use that to recruit students and to get recognition from the public, Li added. The presence of top foreign academics helped Chinese universities attract more research funding and made it easier for them to connect with the international academic community at large. Chinese institutions should be most interested in attracting academics who specialize in the so-called STEM subjects (science, technology, engineering, and mathematics) said Alex Katsomitros, a research analyst at the Observatory on Borderless Higher Education in London. He added that the social sciences and humanities academics are understandably less willing to move to China.

CRITICS

What the world was witnessing now was nothing less than a reversal of ideals. China was actively embracing the traditional values of American education and its penchant for encouraging individuality, innovation, and nonconformity. China was beginning to understand what America's real academic strength had been. It brought diversity and unexpected perspectives to any sort of problem or situation, building students' abilities to adapt rapidly to change. By not standardizing anything, graduates could handle everything. The United States appeared to be moving further away from its own historical archetypes. In a 2012 article in *The Chronicle of Higher Education*, Brian Coppola, University of Michigan professor and associate director of the UM-Peking University Joint Institute, warned that the education systems in China and the United States appeared to be heading in opposite directions. Both seemed to be aimed squarely at what the other system was trying to give up.[34]

In the United States, new programs such as No Child Left Behind, Race to the Top, and Common Core led to increasing calls for more standardization and accountability. In response to the calls, and in concert with other factors, America was beginning to embrace the sort of regimented, uniform, standards-based, test-driven education that has weighed down China's education system for centuries.

China was now trying to distance itself from a long history of Confucian-based, then Russian-influenced, inflexible, standards-based education. As the American founding fathers had done, Chinese leaders were recognizing and finding value in the core principles of a true liberal-arts education. China was seeking to avoid the inherent problems that have always accompanied its traditional approach to education. These were problems that America was now in danger of adopting. In the United States, there was growing evidence of an escalation in something the Chinese call *gaofen dineng*, a term referring to a schooled population that exhibits high scores with low ability. Somehow misplaced have been studies done by respected researchers, well-documenting the correlation between high standardized test scores and low understanding. In China's enthusiasm to emulate America's educational strengths, they are holding a compellingly interesting mirror, reflecting precisely the things that have made the United States preeminent for so long.[35]

East-West higher education collaborations have been permeated with philosophical and political divides and the Johns Hopkins University-Nanjing University Center for Chinese and American Studies labors under this reality. America has academic freedom, and therefore open discussion in classrooms, but this is not the case in China. Carolyn Townsley, director of the Hopkins-Nanjing Center in Washington, DC, pointed out that they were not trying to be investigators. In an interview about the teaching of sensitive subjects, such as Tibet or the Tiananmen Square incident, she affirmed that the mission of the center was to build better relations with the Chinese. They had no intention of stirring things up.[36]

Unfettered access to information remains a struggle for American institutions in China. New York University promised that their Shanghai campus would have unblocked Internet use, even though no one outside the Chinese Communist Party actually has completely unrestricted access. For the rest of China, content in Facebook, Twitter, some Western newspapers, and even basic scholarly sources are regularly unavailable, blocked by the Great Firewall, China's censorship network. Cheng Li, a China expert at the Brookings Institution, said that the idea that Duke or NYU could maintain comparable academic freedom in China was self-deceiving and completely out of touch with reality.[37]

China's handling of intellectual-freedom issues has sometimes been extreme. In the case of the Xinjiang 13, to provide an example, a group of American university encountered considerable backlash when they co-authored *Xingiang: China's Muslim Borderland*, published in 2004. The Chinese government subsequently denied them permission to re-enter China and prohibited them from flying on a Chinese airline. They were repeatedly pressured to publicly express pro-China views. To appease the officials, two of the authors presented written statements in which they disavowed support for the independence movement in Xinjiang Province. The colleges that employed the Xinjiang scholars, reportedly reluctant to press Chinese authorities about the individual cases, took no collective action. Dru Gladney, an anthropology professor at Pomona College in California and one of the "Xinjiang 13" authors, was disappointed with their inaction. Colleges are so eager to jump on the China bandwagon, he lamented, that they have put financial interests ahead of academic freedom.[38]

Already some of America's most prominent Chinese scholars are banned in Beijing. People engaged in perfectly legitimate scholarly pursuits can have their careers stymied or even destroyed, said Tim Reiser, foreign policy adviser to US Senator Patrick Leahy. Perry Ling, professor emeritus at Princeton University, has not been able to enter China since 1995. One of Ling's offenses was smuggling an astrophysicist into the US Embassy in Beijing for protection during the 1989 Tiananmen Square uprising. He had also helped edit the Tiananmen Papers, a collection of leaked internal documents released in 2001. Others on China's blacklist roster have included Columbia University professor Andrew Nathan, and Robert Barnett, who, after ignoring two warnings from Chinese officials that his comments should lean more in China's direction, encountered unexplained roadblocks when applying for visas in 2008 and 2009.[39]

At a lecture in 2011 at Tsinghua University, 82-year-old Zhu Rongji, China's premier from 1998 to 2003 and the founding dean of Tsinghua University's school of economics and management, publicly criticized China's educational path. Zhu dismissed the Outline of China's National Plan for Medium and Long-term Education Reform and Development 2010–2020 as "empty talk."[40] In China, criticisms of governmental policy from such a prominent figure have been extremely rare. Among his concerns was the too rapid expansion of college and university enrollments, which increased six-fold between 1998 and 2011. It was all intended to stimulate the economy, Zhu added, but instead the effort had led to rampant academic plagiarism, declining academic morality and rising unemployment of university graduates. Insufficient state support for education in rural China added to his criticisms. Zhu's comments circulated on the Chinese blog site *Sina Weibo*. They would not be published by official media.

Criticisms such as Zhu's may have little impact on policy in China, according to Hong Kong University of Science and Technology professor Ding Xueliang. Anyone seeking to make meaningful reforms will face objections or obstacles posed by university bureaucrats, he suggested, since reforms are likely to take away their control of resources. For this reason, university bureaucrats work to limit any freedom left to university presidents, faculty, or deans, Ding explained to *University World News*. In some respects, the higher education sector in China had remained old-fashioned, unlike the economic realm, where many state-owned entities have successfully undergone far-reaching reforms to break away from bureaucratic control.[41]

At the same time has been the central government's ongoing resolve to avoid a repeat of the 1989 student-led Tiananmen Square incident. There had been waves of student activism on campus, interactions between professors and students, and visits by overseas academics, prior to the incident, conditions that were well remembered by the Chinese government.

CONFUCIUS INSTITUTES AND SOFT POWER

Since 2004, dozens of American colleges and universities have accepted millions of dollars from a Chinese government-affiliated body known as Hanban, money intended for the purpose of establishing Confucius Institutes on their campuses. Hanban, an acronym for the officials at the Office of Chinese Language Council International, states in its bylaws that their Confucius Institutes should be, above all else, governed by principles of mutual respect, friendly negotiations, and mutual benefit.

China should enhance culture as part of its campaign of soft power, said President Hu Jintao in his 2007 address to the seventeenth Communist Party congress. The agenda was both subtle and resolute. Subtlety demanded that the Confucius Institutes not act as overt purveyors of the party's political viewpoints. The important thing was for the world to be given a "correct" understanding of China, said Hanban officials. In spite of the name Confucius Institutes, the promotion of Confucian ideals has not been the aim. The Confucius reference is instead used symbolically. Rather than a philosophical outlook, it serves to symbolize a sort of avuncular Chinese-ness.[42]

Since 2004, the Confucius Institutes have opened more than 500 outposts around the world, including 110 in US colleges and universities, to mixed reviews. Alongside Confucius Institutes are more than 500 Confucius Classrooms (the elementary, middle school, junior high and high school component) now in operation across the American landscape.

The University of Maryland was among the first institutions in the United States to partner with Hanban, More would follow, including Stanford and Columbia and dozens of others that accepted Hanban's generous offer of money in return for welcoming Confucius Institutes onto their campuses. Not all such offers were well received. The University of Pennsylvania and Dickinson State College in North Dakota are examples of American institutions that flatly declined the proposition. The proponents' point of view holds that Confucius Institutes provide American students an opportunity to learn about China, not from textbooks or videos, but from the Chinese themselves. Supporters see them as a godsend. They bring with them Beijing-trained and Chinese-financed language teachers and materials, as well as funding sufficient to cover a director's salary and a program of public events. They were an easy, ready-made partner, said the executive director of the London School of Economics' new Confucius Institute.[43]

When the Confucius Institutes were begun in 2004, participation involved a reciprocal agreement. Colleges and universities agreeing to host Confucius Institutes were expected to provide premises and a faculty member to serve as administrator. In return, Hanban provided the school $100,000 annually—figures varied depending on the institution—as well as visiting instructors, teaching materials, and an open invitation to apply for even more money. For many the offer was irresistible, but there were strings attached. Should a university sign the agreement and collect the funds, they were faced with the probability of self-imposed censorship, to comply with Communist Party ideals. The University of Pennsylvania's East Asian Studies faculty voted unanimously to reject the offer of a Confucius Institute, citing such censorship as an unacceptable breech of American higher education tradition. Freedom of speech was a fundamental American right that in their view should not be sacrificed in exchange for money from China. In light of most universities' never-ending quests for funding, refusing such an offer in an effort to protect academic freedom might be considered nothing less than an act of patriotism. Others justify compliance by contending that the Confucian Institute's agenda, even with the constraints on their college's academic freedom is sufficiently offset by the benefits of in-person intercultural interaction, and the cash that the institutes bring with them.[44]

Colleges or universities that take on a Confucius Institute, or American high schools that host Confucius Classrooms, agree to a second set of opinions and authority that is answerable to the Chinese Communist Party and not subject to scholarly review. Agreement to host a Confucius Institute comes with a lengthy list of proscribed subjects, a roster of topics that are forbidden. Strictly off limits are any discussions on the Dalai Lama, Tibet, Taiwan, the 1989 Tiananmen Square incident, or China's military buildup.

Attempts to establish Confucius Institutes have by some accounts been aggressive. Stanford was offered $4 million to open a Confucius Institute, along with the endowment of a professorship, on the condition that the professor would never discuss Tibet. Stanford at first refused due to objections among its faculty and administration, but they were finally convinced to accept the money anyway, which they used to endow a chair in classical Chinese poetry. By contrast, Columbia University accepted the money on the spot and implemented its Confucius Institute with little objection from its faculty or administration.

A 2012 policy directive, sent by the State Department to universities that sponsor Confucius Institutes, suggested that the language and cultural centers would have to change how they operate, or risk falling afoul of American visa laws. The memorandum, first released in an article in *The Chronicle of Higher Education,* stated that Confucius Institute instructors teaching in America's K-12 schools on university-sponsored visas were in violation of regulations governing J-1 visas. This had apparently been overlooked for almost a decade, but according to the memorandum the instructors would need to leave the country at the end of the academic year. A preliminary review by the State Department determined that institute members teaching in Confucius Classrooms must obtain American K-12 accreditation in order to continue to serve as teachers at those levels. If the State Department intended to implement the charges, their decision would affect the qualifications and placement of about 600 educators.[45]

It was not spelled out how the centers could be accredited nor did the memorandum offer a time frame, although stand-alone and university-based language components can be verified through the Accrediting Council for Continuing Education and Training or the Commission on English Language Program Accreditation. Foreign professors and students at the university level are prohibited from teaching in American elementary and secondary schools without appropriate certification, so teachers would have to reapply for the correct visa and then return to the United States and find a new sponsor. It was a process of securing approval that could exceed one year. Not surprisingly, the memorandum caused alarm on many American campuses and also in China, where the situation made headlines. Any action to remove a teacher, declared an official with Hanban, could do harm to Sino-American exchanges. Within a week of the published memorandum, the US State Department seemed to back down.[46] Spokeswoman Victoria Nuland said in a news briefing that department officials were going to do their best to fix the problem without forcing anyone to leave, and an investigation would be conducted.

The memorandum had been in part a response to an escalating number of alerts from American teachers who were worried about the content of some of Hanban's teaching materials. A subsequent investigation into the instructional methods uncovered serious issues with the accuracy and intent of some of the information being presented by the Chinese instructors. At the same time, the investigation revealed the visa and credentials issues.

Among the examples uncovered was an educational website called "The War to Resist U.S. Aggression and Aid Korea." Classified as a teaching tool, the webpage appeared in the "Kids" section of the site used for teaching Chinese history in American classrooms. The website taught that during the Korean War, China had triumphantly crushed America's imperial and aggressive ambitions—a viewpoint closely hewn to the Chinese Communist Party's official narrative, and the only explanation allowed in China's classrooms. The video went on to explain that the United States had manipulated the United Nations Security Council to pass a resolution to organize a United Nations Command, consisting mainly of American troops, with the intention of expanding aggression against Korea. The video went on to explain to the class that the US military then tried to seize the entire peninsula, affirming that Americans bombed Chinese villages near the Chinese-Korean border. China had no choice but to enter the conflict as "volunteers," forced to protect the motherland. China's volunteers then defeated the United Nations forces beyond the 38th parallel, turning the war around and achieving relative stability for the advance of New China. The video concluded with a victorious Chairman Mao crossing the screen.[47]

The video did not follow the facts as recorded by thousands of participants, observers, and historians. The Korean War Veterans Association labeled it as strictly propaganda. "I was there," said Korean War veteran Frank Cohee. The page was purged by Hanban, deleted the day after Christopher Hughes, a professor at the London School of Economics, forwarded the discovered link to a group of colleagues who had met to discuss Confucius Institute teaching materials. The deleted video was only one of a series of similar teaching tools, clearly intended for propaganda rather than any teaching of authentic history. Associate professor of Asian studies at the University of Manitoba, Terence Russell, characterized the materials as scary, adding that some materials do not meet the most basic criteria for neutrality. June Teufel Dreyer, professor at the University of Miami, in an analysis of the videos concluded that many were outrageous distortions.[48]

Nevertheless, many of the Confucius Institutes' language and cultural programs have been extremely well received on campuses and in communities, and it can be argued that learning has been significantly advanced through their efforts, in spite of its propagandistic tactics. According to most reports, the many Chinese teachers who visit and instruct in American schools have for the most part been capable and devoted educators, genuinely interested in sharing the richness of China's history. The advance of Confucius Institutes has shown little sign of slowing down, as they continue to partner with American colleges and universities—institutions convinced they can balance the monetary and manpower advantages against the sacrifice of free expression in their classrooms.

In November 2018 the China-US International Education Delegation, at the invitation of the Confucius Institute Headquarters, visited the Ministry of Education in Beijing. Fang Jun, Deputy Director-General of the Department of International Cooperation and Exchanges welcomed the delegation. Exchanges in education are of great significance, said Fang, adding that there are around 35 million college students in China. In 1979, before the opening of China's borders, only about 4 percent of Chinese students went to college, but now the percentage is 42.7 percent. China's goal, said Fang, was not to provide more access for students, but to improve the quality and fairness of education. Fang noted the differences in the education systems of China and the United States and spoke of exchanges and cooperation in the field of education, including the Social and Cultural Dialogue proposal based on the meeting between Donald Trump and Xi Jinping at Mar-a-Lago. There are more than 280 cooperative education projects between China and the United States, he continued, and the demand for Chinese language teaching in America is rising, making the Chinese Institutes a necessity in the local community.[49] Matthew Salmon, a member of the delegation and Vice President of Arizona State University, said that China-US relations are among the most important in the world, and that the two countries should focus on common goals rather than differences. He hoped that through exchanges the countries can creatively strengthen bilateral relations.

Notes

1. *Open Doors*, Annual Report (Institute of International Education, 2010).
2. Tamar Lewin, "Study Abroad Flourishes, China Attracts More American Students," *The New York Times* (November 18, 2008).
3. Chen Jia, "China Looks to Attract More Foreign Students," *China Daily* (September 28, 2010). Available at: http://english.peopledaily.com.

4. Guo-hua Wang, "China's Higher Education Reform," *China Currents*. Available at: www.chinacurrents.com/spring_2010/cc_wang.htm.
5. Teresa B. Bevis, *A History of Higher Education Exchange: China and America* (New York: Palgrave Macmillan, 2014): 154–155.
6. Ibid.
7. Ibid.
8. "Formation of China's Ivy League Hailed," *People's Daily Online* (October 30, 2009). Available at: http://en.people.cn/90001/90776/90882/6794654.html.
9. "Greetings on the Occasion of the Tsinghua University Centennial Celebration," A Speech by Yale president Richard C. Levin in Beijing, China (April 23, 2011). Available at: http://communications.yale.edu/president/speeches/2011/o4/23/greetings-occasion-tsihghua-university-centennial-celebration.
10. Michael Sainsbury, "China Establishes Group of Ivy League Universities," *The Australian* (November 4, 2009). Available at: www.theaustralian.com.au/news/world/china.
11. Tamar Lewin, "China Attracts More American Students," *The New York Times* (November 18, 2008).
12. Ibid.
13. Dexter Roberts, "The End of China's One-Child Policy?," *Businessweek* (April 19, 2012).
14. Ibid.
15. Ibid.
16. Sarah Butrimowitz, "Can China Successfully Educate Its Future Workforce?," *Time World* (February 9, 2012).
17. Ibid.
18. "China's New National Education Plan Aims to Build a Country with Rich Human Resources," China's Ministry of Education (July 30, 2010). Available at: www.moe.edu.cn.
19. Ibid.
20. The World Bank, "China 2030, Building a Modern, Harmonious and Creative High-Income Society" (February 2, 2012). Available at www.worldbank.org.
21. Karen Fischer, "As White House Pushes Study Abroad in China, Educators Question the Logistics," *The Chronicle of Higher Education* (January 19, 2011).
22. Ibid.
23. "China, U.S. to Scale Up Student Exchange Programs" (May 26, 2010). Available at: www.chinaassistor.com.
24. Chen Jia.

25. Daniel Golden, "The SAT Is to America as ___ Is to China Mainland. Applicants Have to Take Abroad. The U.S. College Board Wants to Change That," *Business Week* (February 3, 2011). Available at: www.businessweek.com/magazine/content/11_07/b4215014259071.htm.
26. "The Institute of International Education Leads Higher Education Delegation to Build Academic Partnership between China and the United States," Institute of International Education (May 15, 2011).
27. Ibid.
28. "Seven Decades of Educating Global Leaders, Johns Hopkins University." Available at: http://nanjing.jhu.edu/about/index.htm.
29. "China's First Sino-American University Opening in 2013," *People's Daily* (April 6, 2012). Available at: http://english.peopledaily.com.ch/203691/7779455.html.
30. Ibid.
31. Yojana Sharma, "CHINA: Ambitious Plans to Attract Foreign Students," *University World News*, no. 162 (March 13, 2011).
32. "China Needs American Education: Here's How to Bring it There," *Forbes*, June 20, 2012. Available at: https://www.forbes.com/sites/forbesleadershipforum/2012/06/20/china-needs-american-education-heres-how-tobring-it-there/#455e8ff015.
33. Liz Gooch, "Chinese Universities Send Big Signals to Foreigners," *The New York Times* (March 11, 2012).
34. B.P. Coppola and Yi Zhou, "U.S. Education in Chinese Lockstep? Bad Move," *The Chronicle of Higher Education* (February 5, 2012).
35. Ibid.
36. Ibid.
37. Ibid.
38. Danial Golden and Oliver Stanley, "China Banning U.S. Professors Elicits Silence from Colleges," *Bloomberg* (August 11, 2011). Available at: https://www.bloomberg.com/news/articles/2011-08-11/china-banning-u-s-professors-elicits-silence-from-colleges.
39. Ibid.
40. Linda Yeung, "CHINA: Ex-premier Criticizes Higher Education Reform," *University World News* (May 1, 2011). Available at: http://www.universityworldnews.com/article.php?story=20110429170813946.
41. Ibid.
42. Daniel Golden, "China Says No Talking Tibet as Confucius Funds U.S. Universities," *Bloomberg* (November 1, 2011). Available at: www.bloomberg.com.
43. Ibid.
44. Ibid.
45. Karen Fischer, "State Department Directive Could Disrupt Teaching Activities of Campus-Based Confucius Institutes," *The Chronicle of Higher Education* (May 21, 2012).

46. Karen Fischer, "State Department Hopes to 'Fix' Visa Problems Without Forcing Chinese Teachers to Leave," *The Chronicle of Higher Education* (May 23, 2012).
47. Matthew Robertson, "Chinese History According to the Confucius Institute," *The Epoch Times*, October 1, 2015. Available at: http://www.theepochtimes.com/n2/china-news/chinese-history-according-to-the-confucius-institute-255366.html.
48. Ibid.
49. "China-US International Education Delegation Visits Ministry of Education," Confucius Institute Headquarters (Hanban) (November 16, 2018). Available at: http://english.hanban.org/article/2018-11/16/content_752657.htm. Accessed November 29, 2018.

References

Butrimowitz. 2019. Can China Successfully Educate Its Future Workforce? *Time World*, February 9.
China Needs American Education: Here's How to Bring it There. 2012. *Forbes*, June 20. Available at: https://www.forbes.com/sites/forbesleadershipforum/2012/06/20/china-needs-american-education-heres-how-tobring-it-there/#455e8ff015.
China Says No Talking Tibet as Confucius Funds U.S. Universities. 2011. *Bloomberg*, November 1.
China-US International Education Delegation Visits Ministry of Education. 2018. Confucius Institute Headquarters (Hanban), November 16. http://english.hanban.org/article/2018-11/16/content_752657.html.
China's First Sino-American University Opening in 2013. 2012. *People's Daily*, April 6. http://english.peopledaily.com.ch/203691/7779455.html.
Coppola, B.P., and Yi Zhou. 2012. U.S. Education in Chinese Lockstep? Bad Move. *The Chronicle of Higher Education*, February 5.
Fischer, Karen. 2011. As White House Pushes Study Abroad in China, Educators Question the Logistics. *The Chronicle of Higher Education*, January 19.
———. 2012a. State Department Directive Could Disrupt Teaching Activities of Campus-Based Confucius Institutes. *The Chronicle of Higher Education*, May 21.
———. 2012b. State Department Hopes to 'Fix' Visa Problems without Forcing Chinese Teachers to Leave. *The Chronicle of Higher Education*, May 23.
Formation of China's Ivy League Hailed. 2009. *People's Daily Online*. October 27. http://en.people.cn/90001/90776/90882/6794654.html.
Golden, Daniel. 2011. The SAT is to America as ____ is to China Mainland. Applicants Have to Take Abroad. The U.S. College Board Wants to Change That. *Business Week*, February 3.

Gooch, Liz. 2012. Chinese Universities Send Big Signals to Foreigners. *The New York Times*, March 11.
Jia, Chen. 2010. China Looks to Attract More Foreign Students. *China Daily*, September 28.
Levin, Richard C. 2011. Greetings on the Occasion of the Tsinghua University Centennial Celebration. A Speech Given in Beijing, China, April 23.
Lewin, Tamar. 2008a. Study Abroad Flourishes, China Attracts More American Students. *The New York Times*, November 18.
———. 2008b. China Attracts More American Students. *The New York Times*, November 18.
Matthew Robertson. 2015. Chinese History According to the Confucius Institute. *The Epoch Times*, October 1. http://www.theepochtimes.com/n2/china-news/Chinese-history-according-to-the-confucius-institute-255366.html.
Ministry of Education for the People's Republic of China. 2010. China's New Education Plan Aims to Build a Country with Rich Human Resources, July 30. http://old.moe.gov.cn/publicfiles/business/htmlfiles/moe/moe_2862/201010/109031.html.
Rectification of Statutes. 2011. *The Economist*, January 20. www.economist.comnode/17969895.
Roberts, Dexter. 2012. The End of China's One-Child Policy? *Businessweek*, April 19.
Sainsbury, Michael. 2009. China Establishes Group of Ivy League Universities. *The Australian*, November 4. www.theaustralian.com.au/news/world/china
Seven Decades of Educating Global Leaders. Johns Hopkins University. http://nanjing.jhu.edu/about/index.htm.
Sharma, Yojana 2011. CHINA: Ambitious Plans to Attract Foreign Students. *University World News*, no. 162, March 13.
The World Bank. 2012. China 2030, Building a Modern, Harmonious and Creative High-Income Society. www.worldbank.org.
Wang, Guo-hua. China's Higher Education Reform. *China Currents*. www.chinacurrents.com/spriing_2010/cc_wang.htm.
Yeung. 2011. CHINA: Ex-premier Criticizes Higher Education Reform. *University World News*, May 1. http://www.universityworldnews.com/article.php?story=20110429170813956.

CHAPTER 10

US-Middle East Exchange in the Early Twenty-First Century

The loss of foreign student enrollments had been an immediate effect of 9/11, mostly from Iran, but also from neighboring Middle Eastern countries. To recover the losses, recruitment efforts were soon launched by the US government and by private enterprises, often with the cooperation of international organizations such as AMIDEAST (America-Mideast Educational and Training Services, Inc.) or UNESCO (United Nations Educational, Scientific and Cultural Organization). These included the Bush administration's Middle East Partnership Initiative (MEPI), the Ford Foundation's Discovery Program, the Exxon-Mobile Middle East and North Africa Scholars Program, the Middle East and North Africa Peace Scholarships, and the Lift-off Initiative, to name just a few. Some Middle Eastern countries were also interested in recovering the losses and advancing the level of education exchange with America. Saudi Arabia, for example, began allotting generous funds to the availability of exchange scholarships with the United States. In a span of five years (2005–2010), Middle Eastern enrollments rose from 33,000 to 51,000, making Saudi Arabia the top sender from the region.

In recent decades, the Arab World, indeed much of the Middle East, has experienced a quiet yet multidimensional revolution, a rise in higher education along with privatization and internationalization. In 1940, only about ten universities existed in the region. By 2000, there were an estimated 140, and by 2007 the number had reached 260. In Saudi Arabia, 8 universities were operating in 2003, but 100 or more additional institutions have been created since. By 2007 Saudi Arabia's annual budget for higher education was an estimated $15 billion, for its 23 million inhabitants. The UAE and Qatar were also frontrunners, establishing 40 foreign branches of Western universities between the turn of the millennium and 2013. Others in the MENA (Middle East and North Africa) region have followed suit.

AMERICAN OUTPOSTS

Especially since the turn of the millennium, American higher education has expanded its institutional presence in the Middle East by establishing branch campuses and academic collaborations. These efforts have been reminiscent of America's early history of founding schools in the Arab region. Some American colleges were established as early as the mid-1800s, most through the efforts of well-intended missionaries who were aided by funds from the federal government and other interested parties. American Christian missionaries in the nineteenth century successfully opened and operated hundreds of primary, secondary and vocational schools in the Middle East, in addition to a number of American-style universities, many of which are still in operation.

Despite having "American" in their names, these first missionary-led universities were not affiliated with the US government. With no central governing body, each was free to develop its own mission and curriculum, but common to these early colleges was a focus on critical thinking and the American liberal arts approach.[1]

American schools would differ from national and private universities in the Arab region in a number of important ways. Compared with national universities, for example, where students typically took classes only within their discipline, the American-style liberal arts education included courses outside their field of study. American universities also tended to attract a diverse faculty, many with terminal degrees from institutions in the United States. The American University in Cairo's faculty, for example, came from 29 different countries, a practical advantage in providing global perspectives.

Another difference between American universities and universities indigenous to the region has been the issue of accreditation. Even in the United Kingdom, evaluation had never reached the level of institutionalization and formalization it had in the United States. The present-day structure of accreditation in the United States can be traced back to 1905, when the new Carnegie Foundation for the Advancement of Teaching set the requirements it would seek in the institutions of higher education to which it would provide funding. The first official list of accredited institutions was prepared by the American Association of Universities (AAU) in 1914, and regional accreditation boards were established by colleges and universities. Professional organizations also joined the process, led by the American Medical Association, which began accrediting medical schools in 1910. The importance of university accreditation cannot be overstated, as the acceptance of its authority affects a wide range of decisions. The G.I. Bill of Rights, for example, enacted in 1944, stipulated that to be eligible for financial support under federal law, veterans had to enroll in institutions deemed "accredited."[2]

From these roots, today's system evolved. It basically consists of two parts. Specialized accreditation is discipline-specific, carried out by professional organizations. Institutional accreditation evaluates the institution as a whole, in terms of compatibility and sustainability of its resources with its mission. Since 1949 institutional accreditation has been carried out by six regional associations, which were founded by the institutions themselves. With the reauthorization of the Higher Education Act of 1992, standards and procedures were set for institutional accreditation, and the US Department of Education (DOE) was designated to supervise regional boards. The Council for Higher Education Accreditation is a private, nongovernmental national coordinating body for national, regional, and specialized accreditation. Some American universities in the Middle East are accredited in the United States. However, in the Middle East, just because an institution has "American" in its title does not necessarily mean it is accredited.

A fourth difference has to do with admissions requirements. At national universities, placement was often based solely on the results of comprehensive high school examination, but admissions offices at American universities looked at the total person, evaluating the applicant's statement of purpose, letters of recommendation, transcripts, record of extracurricular activities, in addition to standardized test scores. Another important difference was cost. An American university in the Middle East can be cost-prohibitive for many students, as they have tended to be more expensive than most national universities in the region.

In recent decades, internationalization has risen high on the agenda for most American-style universities in the MENA region, as well as universities in the United States, fueled by the intention to help students prepare for a globalized world. Especially since 9/11 there was an urgency to connect education in a global way, through the exchange of students but also through the establishment of a greater American institutional presence in the Middle East. Colleges and universities across America, even those whose primary goal was to educate the immediate community, began turning their attention to global education and the establishment of programs in foreign regions. The prestige of having a foreign campus spurred the rush to set up outposts, in the Middle East and around the world.

Overseas programs were increasingly viewed as an effective means for American universities to elevate their profiles, build international relationships, attract the best available talent, and encourage the granting of funds to their projects. New pools of potential tuition-paying students could also be courted. In common was a thread of hope, that educational and intercultural interaction would promote worldwide peace. Cornell president David J. Skorton believed that higher education was America's single most important diplomatic asset. Education exchange would surely reduce friction between countries and cultures, he added. Real or assumed, such benefits prompted America's number of branch campuses in the Middle East to rise as globalization gained importance within university missions.[3]

And, there was money to be made. In what some might term an educational "gold rush," American universities competed to set up outposts in various world regions, particularly those with otherwise limited opportunities for higher education. Top-rated US institutions were eager to build a global presence through study-abroad sites, research collaborations, faculty exchanges, joint degree programs and other partnerships with foreign institutions. Yale had been a pioneer of this concept of educational collaboration, having established dozens of research partnerships with Chinese universities. But in the opening years of the twenty-first century, the focus of expansion for many institutions was now the Middle East, and the demand was enormous.

Institutions across America dreamed of full-fledged foreign branch campuses, especially in the oil-rich countries of the Middle East. By 2005, students in Qatar could attend an American university locally, without the expense of travel, and without encountering the post 9/11 visa problems, or the backlash against Muslims which had risen in America since the attack. In Education City at Doha, students could study medicine at Weill Medical College of Cornell University, or international affairs at Georgetown, without leaving the comforts of home. Business and computer science could be learned at Carnegie Mellon, or fine arts from Virginia Commonwealth, or engineering at Texas A&M—right there in

Doha. A program for journalism from Northwestern added to the growing roster of choices. In Dubai, Michigan State University and Rochester Institute of Technology began offering classes in 2008. George Mason University was another frontrunner.[4]

New and innovative centers of knowledge were emerging, especially in the United Arab Emirates. Before the end of the first decade of the new millennium, both Education City in Qatar and the extravagant Knowledge Village in the UAE were boasting branch campuses operated by American, Australian, British and Irish universities. With a broad international presence, these "university cities" attracted faculties and students from around the world, and the trend was infectious. Harvard University announced its plans to open a branch medical school in the UAE, as Boston University considered doing the same. Other outposts established in the Middle East during this period included New York University (NYU), which opened a comprehensive liberal arts branch campus in the Persian Gulf in 2010, with the help of a $50 million gift from an Arab investor.[5]

As with any venture of this magnitude, there would be problems, and some reported that the setting up of branch campuses was more complicated than expected. George Mason University, for example, had difficulty finding enough interested students with SAT scores and English skills that qualified for admission. Even the task of ordering books took months, in part because of government censors, and local licensing was also time consuming and rigorous.

George Mason's academic dean Abul R. Hasan viewed it from a business perspective, pointing out that an institution could only take losses for so long. Their goal was to have 2000 students by 2013, but what made it especially difficult was that if the institution was to award a George Mason degree, it could not lower its standards. Whether or not the degree actually reflected George Mason was, in the beginning stages, open to question. At first none of the original faculty members were from George Mason University, although that has since been appended. Regarding students, George Mason's initial enrollments at their Middle Eastern facility consisted mostly of foreigners—Bangladeshis, Palestinians, Egyptians, Indians, Iraqis, Lebanese, Syrians, and others, mostly from comfortably wealthy families. Comparatively few students who initially enrolled were from the emirates.[6]

As earlier mentioned, an important collaboration in the first decade of the millennium was with New York University. In 2007 the government of Abu Dhabi, the richest of the emirates, partnered with NYU to build and operate a campus there. The venture would be central to how the university would approach its future, said NYU president John Sexton. Both campuses would grow together, with the goal of establishing both NYU and NYU-Abu Dhabi among the world's top ten universities by 2020. It was a bold plan. To demonstrate his support and commitment for the idea, Sexton offered to teach a course, even before the campus was built. Every other Friday evening he boarded a plane to Abu Dhabi. Arriving on Saturday, he would teach on Sunday and then return to New York early on Monday. It was a grand gesture that the crown prince, equally enthusiastic about the prospects of growing an international center of education, is said to have greatly appreciated.[7]

Other Middle Eastern countries were moving in the same academic direction. In February 2005, *Gulf News* announced Kuwait's new plans to reform its educational system, emphasizing tolerance and moderation in its school curriculum in an effort not only to improve the system, but also to squelch destructive extremist ideology. The parliamentary committee on education included constitutional studies and human rights as subjects in schools as well. An emphasis on tolerance and moderation in the updated curriculum would become a beacon under which the government would fight extremism and terror, said Sheikh Nasser Mohammad Al Ahmad Al Sabah. Arabic language and religious textbooks were likewise updated, as the government approved 5.5 million dinars to combat extremist ideology, earmarking 195 million to construct new schools and refurbish old ones. Kuwait, said the sheikh, was determined to fight individuals and groups that were now in the destructive grip of extremist thinking.[8]

With private higher education previously banned in the country, the state-owned Kuwait University had for years been the only option for students who wanted to earn a college degree at home, but as demand grew, the single university could not keep up, and the ban on private institutions was lifted. There were conditions. One was a stipulation that any new private higher education institutions must have a foreign partner university. Several recognizable US universities have since partnered with Kuwait's private institutions, such as the University of Missouri at St. Louis, which paired with the Gulf University for Science and Technology. Dartmouth paired with the American University of Kuwait.

Competition for Middle Eastern Enrollments

The United Kingdom and Australia have for decades vied with the United States for a larger share of international students, and over time they have been joined by even more competitors—Singapore, Malaysia, India, China and others—all in the business of trying to lure globally mobile students to their own institutions. After the events of 9/11, increased surveillance and restrictions in the United States, along with newly imposed fees, were encouraging growing numbers of Middle Eastern students to reconsider their study abroad plans, and competing countries were quick to take advantage of the opportunity. The United Kingdom and Canada intensified recruitment activities in the Middle East, particularly in the Gulf region, where the United States had been losing the greatest number of students. The relaxed visa restrictions in both countries also made it easier to remain there after graduation, an important benefit for many potential international students. Sometimes it was simply proximity. Increasing numbers of students from Kuwait, for example, were now choosing Britain because of its geographic location as well as its shorter academic programs, according to the British Council. Enrollments from the UAE in British institutions were also on the rise, bolstered by aggressive marketing and promotional activities.

Australia was enjoying similar growth from the MENA region, enrolling a total of 1466 Middle Eastern students in 2003, mostly from the UAE and Saudi Arabia. As with Britain, recruitment was becoming more aggressive, as the Australian government budgeted about $75 million to advance international higher education. Malaysia, which had been actively promoting itself as a center of educational excellence, was making plans to increase its share of international students from an estimated 36,000 to at least 50,000 by 2005. Malaysian recruiters were especially active in targeting students from the UAE, Oman, Yemen, Saudi Arabia, and Lebanon. Malaysia's allotment of students from the Arab region increased steadily in the years following 9/11, especially at the International Islamic University.[9]

In response to growing competition, the United States bolstered its own recruiting efforts around the world, especially in the MENA region. Organizations soon partnered with colleges and universities to recruit qualified students from the MENA region and within a few years were bringing thousands of promising students to recruitment fairs across the Middle East. Global Vision, which solicited enrollments among undergraduate and graduate students from ten Middle Eastern countries, was among the recruitment leaders. Originally founded in 1996 as Bridge International, Global Vision USA would establish a headquarters in Amman, Jordan, in 2009.

Quality assurance was a critical consideration regarding the recruitment and placement of international students. Founded in 2008, the American International Recruitment Council was begun by senior administrators from a number of American postsecondary institutions. A nonprofit membership association, the council was recognized by the US Department of Justice and the Federal Trade Commission as a Standards Development Organization. Its members have included representatives from accredited US postsecondary institutions, pathway programs, student recruitment agencies, secondary schools, and non-US educational institutions, all working together to establish quality standards for international student placement in the United States.[10]

Publications focused on student recruiting also appeared during these years. An example is *Al Jamiat*, an education news publication based in the Middle East that reports on universities, government offices, and key decision makers around the world, information provided free of charge to libraries, placement agencies, and counseling centers. *Al Jamiat* had a circulation of 50,000 in 14 countries at the end of 2010, including Saudi Arabia, Kuwait, the UAE, Oman, Yemen, Egypt, Jordan, Bahrain, Qatar, Syria, Lebanon, Tunisia, Algeria, and Morocco. Their publications were also distributed through AMIDEAST's advising and counseling centers throughout the Arab World. *Al Jamiat* has also sponsored many recruiting fairs in the Middle East.

A few recruitment initiatives emanated from institutions some would find unlikely, such as elite women's colleges. Representatives from Barnard, Bryn Mawr, Mount Holyoke, Smith and Wellesley Colleges received hearty welcomes, according to a 2008 article in *The Chronicle of Higher Education*, when they traveled to Bahrain, Jordan, Kuwait, Oman, and the UAE to talk about their long history of successes in training female leaders. Some local parents said they were more at ease with the idea of sending their daughters to a women's college rather than a coeducational institution in the United States, but there was a counter-concern. Such colleges had a reputation for being politically and socially liberal.[11]

There were recruitment efforts on the student level too. According to a 2006 article in *The Harvard Crimson*, the university's Society of Arab Students (SAS) was laying groundwork for a recruiting network in the Middle East region and had already spoken to more than a thousand high school students about admission to Harvard University. An expedition funded by the Kennedy School of Government was the first-ever student-led recruitment group to the Middle East. Eight SAS student representatives visited between 30 and 40 secondary schools in nine countries, and along the way met with Jordan's minister of education and Lebanon's cultural minister. They talked with individuals and groups about Harvard, what makes it unique, and about the things that were specifically tailored to international students. Relationships with secondary school counselors were established across the region, which served to advance communication and provide platforms for more interaction and discussion.[12]

Among the topics of discussion was the rapidly growing population of young people in the Middle East. The first years of the new millennium coincided with a time of demographic change in the Middle East, a trend referred to as the "youth bulge." In 2001, young people under the age of 21 already comprised a majority of the population in some Middle Eastern countries. Unemployment was rising, with some countries reporting as high as 25 percent by the end of the first decade, and future implications were alarming. Education was a key factor, but occupational opportunities, once learning was accomplished, were equally critical if the region was to progress economically. While access to education is an essential pathway out of poverty, in countries such as Algeria and Morocco, university graduates were less likely to find employment than citizens with only a primary or secondary education.

Initiatives

The Middle East Partnership Initiative (MEPI) was established in 2002 to create educational and economic opportunities and to help foster private sector development. It was also intended to help strengthen civil society and the rule of law throughout the region by providing a framework to develop four pillars of the organization—economic, political, education, and the empowerment of women. The same year the Bush administration committed $29 million for education, economic, and political reform projects, and $100 million in 2003. In 2004, another $89.5 million was allotted and in 2005 Congress approved $74.4 million.[13]

The Middle East Partnership Initiative also worked to secure coordinating donors from the private sector. At the regional level, MEPI cooperated with training-based projects, exchange programs, regional networks, and scholarship opportunities, through its Washington, DC based grants.

Their exchange programs provided students and professionals with opportunities to learn about the United States firsthand, in the hope that they would return home with a greater understanding of America and a desire to build constructive partnerships. It would also be active in responding to the economic and educational needs of women across the MENA region, by providing training to enhance their capabilities in advancing their countries. The US-MEPI Supporting Women initiative was designed specifically to create those opportunities.

In 2009 another initiative was announced by Secretary of State Hillary Rodham Clinton, this time a million-dollar scholarship program to help Palestinian students enroll at Palestinian or American universities. Speaking from Ramallah during a visit to the West Bank, Secretary Clinton said that the four-year program would support about ten scholarships each year for disadvantaged students to attend four-year courses at Palestinian universities. Also offered were 25 "opportunity grants" to American-accredited institutions in the United States or in the Middle East.[14]

A number of established international exchange organizations also accelerated their efforts to recover foreign student enrollments in the United States in the early years of the millennium. At the same time, they sought to build deeper intercultural connections with the countries of the MENA region, and to broaden the scope of knowledge exchange. The Institute of International Exchange, for example, developed a strong set of services for the MENA region, some in cooperation with the US government or with other exchange organizations. Since Institute of International Education's (IIE's) establishment of its MENA Region Office and its Center for Leadership Excellence in Cairo in 2005, it has administered and supported a variety of programs.

One was the Discovery Program, which was launched in 2006. Offering semester-long extracurricular programs of leadership learning activities, it was designed for public university students in Egypt and made possible through a grant by the Ford Foundation's regional office in Cairo. Another was the Egypt Fellowships Program, established by the Arab Republic of Egypt in cooperation with Harvard University, their aim to provide bright Egyptians the opportunity to advance their graduate studies in government, public health, education or urban development. The Massachusetts Institute of Technology also became a partner in the program, providing opportunities for graduate study in engineering or economics.[15]

The Exxon Mobile Middle East and North Africa Scholars Program was developed to provide student leaders from the MENA region access to scholarships toward the completion of a degree at a US college or university, and also has provided scholarship opportunities to pursue a master's degree in geoscience. The Lift-Off Initiative was another, begun at the end of the decade in 2010, to foster a culture of entrepreneurship among youth across northern Africa. Implemented by the IIE regional office in Cairo in partnership with Endeavor Egypt, it targets MENA region youth from 16 to 35 years of age to promote and support entrepreneurship as a viable career choice.

The LOTUS Scholarship Program was begun near the end of the decade, funded by the US government through the United States Agency for International Development (USAID). It was available to Egyptian applicants who had outstanding credentials as well as great financial need. The Middle East and North Africa Peace Scholarships Program operated from 2007 to September 2010, a cooperation between program sponsors USAID and the Office of Middle East Programs. The goals were to foster leadership among undergraduates in the MENA countries, to provide a greater understanding of US culture, politics, economic structure, and viewpoints, and to promote opportunities for academic excellence. The YELLA program, or Youth Enrichment for Leadership, Learning and Action, was begun to provide preparatory and secondary schools, youth centers, and university career centers, both public and private, a curriculum of leadership and resources.

Adding to IIE's array of programs was AMIDEAST, which was also busy developing opportunities for educational and intercultural exchanges. Founded shortly after World War II, its half-century of service had already built a broad array of programs. In 2001, the organization had planned to celebrate its 50 years of success with an international conference, but the events of September 11 would overshadow any festivities. A new urgency would arise within its outreach mission, as it quickly expanded its offerings concerning the region, especially materials on the subject of Islam. With funds from the US Department of State (DOS), AMIDEAST organized a student colloquium on US-Arab relations that brought together Arab Fulbright students and graduate students at the University of Maryland. Also, in cooperation with the US DOS, AMIDEAST developed Arab-language materials to help explain the new visa restrictions, as their advising staff accelerated outreach activities in response to the many misperceptions. By 2005 more than 250,000 individuals had sought information from its Education USA advising centers, a significant rebound from the 197,000 low in 2002.

The MENA component of the Fulbright Foreign Student Program, which had been administered by AMIDEAST since 1969, also underwent expansion. Despite deteriorating conditions, in 2003 AMIDEAST opened an office in Iraq, making it the 12th country in which it had a presence, then in 2004 began an English-language program to provide underserved youth in the region with opportunities to study English. Around the same time, the US DOS-funded English Access Microscholarship Program was activated. By 2005, AMIDEAST was supporting programs that enabled almost 2000 students from the MENA region to participate in study opportunities in the United States. Offices would open in Oman in 2007 and in Saudi Arabia in 2009, as training centers were established in Tunisia, Morocco, Jordan, and the West Bank. AMIDEAST also contributed to the building of institutional capacity by helping the region's governments and organizations design development programs in three key areas—democracy and governance, the strengthening of the role of civil society and nongovernmental organizations (NGOs), and the development of human resources. The US Business Internship Program for Young Middle Eastern Women, and Middle East Entrepreneur Training in the United States were also implemented.[16]

After 9/11, AMIDEAST had continued to support the Administration of the Justice I Project that had begun in 1996, providing Egypt's Ministry of Justice with technical assistance and support, then in 2004 it partnered with the Open Society Institute to offer the Palestinian Rule of Law program. In cooperation with Lebanon's Ministry of Justice, in 2008 AMIDEAST helped expand the training of judges, and worked to improve efficiency and transparency in the courts and legal process, and to solidify frameworks.

AMIDEAST helped build capacity in the region's education sector by working with Emirati counterparts on the Military Language Institute project, which offered advisory and support services in institutional development, program design, staff management, monitoring, and evaluation. In Egypt it assisted in improving teaching skills under the USAID-funded Integrated English Language Program. Elsewhere the Palestine Faculty Development Program was launched in cooperation with USAID and the Open Society Institute, an $11.4 million project designed to introduce reforms in teaching and learning at institutions of higher education in the West Bank and Gaza. AMIDEAST also began partnerships with companies such as the Boeing Company and the GE Foundation to provide teacher development programs.[17]

In Saudi Arabia, AMIDEAST cooperated with the King Faisal Foundation to develop and manage the University Preparatory Program, which opened in 2007 at King Faisal University. The program was fashioned to provide a bridge to university education for promising graduates of Saudi high schools who needed extra preparation in order to enter and succeed in selective universities in Saudi Arabia and elsewhere. The preparatory program offered a curriculum strong in the sciences, mathematics and other subjects, taught using the latest in educational technology and teaching methods, while emphasizing study skills needed for success in Western systems.

Two US DOS-funded programs, the US Business Internship Program for Middle Eastern Women and the Legal and Business Fellowship Program, were provided for young women professionals in law and business. These two initiatives afforded 20–40 women annually the opportunity to receive executive training at top US business and law schools, followed by fellowships at Fortune 500 companies, or at top-tier law firms. At the same time, AMIDEAST expanded its capacity to provide training to help aspiring entrepreneurs, launching the first Cisco Entrepreneur Institute in Lebanon in 2010.

MIDDLE EASTERN ENROLLMENTS 2000–2010

The number of Middle Eastern exchange students in American higher education reached an overall low of less than 33,000 in 2005, but it would begin to rise. By 2010, the total number of MENA students enrolled in colleges and universities in the United States exceeded 51,000. Turkey was the largest sender until 2010, when Saudi Arabian enrollments took the top position.[18]

Also notable were Iraq's increases, an indication of a reverse of the country's politics and the end of a 20-year period under the leadership of Saddam Hussein, when students were denied access to education exchange. The war in 1991 and the trade embargos had damaged Iraqi education on all levels. Hundreds of schools were damaged or were short on supplies, and the quality of instruction declined. Only a small percentage of the 15,000 faculty had any training that qualified them for the roles to which they were assigned, said California Polytechnic Pomona professor and Iraqi expatriate Farouk Darweesh. Iraq pledged to double the number of Fulbright scholarships in 2009. With $2.5 million in additional funding, scholarships would be available for about 70 Iraqi students, on the condition that they would return to Iraq after completing their degrees and remain for a minimum of two years. This would exceed the number of awards in any other Middle Eastern country, according to Deputy Prime Minister Barham Selah.[19]

The number of students from Saudi Arabia had jumped four-fold since the events of 9/11. While non-immigrant visas from Saudi Arabia dropped between 2001 and 2010, education visas skyrocketed. A total of 26,744 Saudi students received visas in 2010, a substantial rise from the 2001 total of 6836. The numbers increased partly because of the King Abdullah Scholarship program. Established in 2005 and administered by the Ministry of Higher Education, it was the result of an agreement between King Abdullah and President George Bush, which allowed an increase in the number of Saudi Arabian students in the United States. The scholarships are generous, covering full tuition and fees, as well as a monthly stipend for the students, their spouses and children. Medical and dental expenses are covered, and round-trip tickets provided for students and their families. Allowances are provided for books, clothing, private tutoring, scientific materials, or special needs. Scholarship recipients are also rewarded for maintaining high grade point averages (GPAs). Only Saudi citizens with high GPAs are eligible. While scholarships are awarded to both male and female Saudis, a female must have a male guardian to travel with her, required to stay with her through graduation. His expenses are also covered (Table 10.1).[20]

Middle Eastern Studies in American Universities

A fresh enchantment with the Middle East has spread among American college students in the new millennium. American students elect to go into Middle Eastern studies for a number of reasons. For some there is a familial connection, while others see it as a shrewd occupational move, or perhaps because they intend to seek international work. The preponderance of faculty and students in the field also claim to have fascination that stems from the politics of the region. "What I hear from students from all backgrounds is they want to make things better ... even if that sounds trite," said Georgetown University's Osama Abi-Mershed, director of the Center for Contemporary Arab Studies.[21]

For American policymakers, who for decades had lamented how few people in the United States study the Middle East or its languages, the increase in numbers of Americans studying the Arab World was good

Table 10.1 Foreign student enrollments: MENA region (2005–2010)

Country	2005–2006	2006–2007	2007–2008	2008–2009	2009–2010
Algeria	152	145	179	172	178
Egypt	1509	1664	1766	1915	2271
Libya	38	93	155	667	1064
Morocco	1502	1202	1132	1169	1120
Tunisia	277	274	402	306	308
Bahrain	373	392	394	431	415
Iran	2420	2795	3060	3533	4751
Iraq	190	262	307	599	423
Israel	3419	3269	3004	3060	2778
Jordan	1733	1726	1799	2225	1995
Kuwait	1703	1633	1823	2031	2442
Lebanon	1950	1852	1807	1823	1608
Oman	337	254	361	271	286
Palestinian Territories	309	361	249	362	304
Qatar	254	296	345	463	663
Saudi Arabia	3448	7886	9873	12,661	15,810
Syria	446	412	517	454	424
Turkey	11,622	11,506	12,030	12,148	12,397
UAE	978	885	983	1218	1653
Yemen	246	248	233	249	265
Total	32,886	37,155	40,419	45,517	51,135

Source: IIE *Open Doors*, issues from 2005 to 2010

news. There were shortages of Americans who could speak Arabic and other Middle Eastern languages, or who were well-versed in the culture, skills needed in the intelligence services and diplomatic corps. Edward Djerejian, former ambassador to Israel and Syria, said in a testimony to Congress that the State Department had only five diplomats with Arabic skills strong enough to defend US policies on Arab television. Arabic is typically a challenge for Western students, who must learn not only the Modern Standard Arab that is used from Iraq to Morocco, but also local variants that people speak on an everyday basis. Plus, a knowledge of classical Arabic is needed to read literature or the Quran. By the end of the first decade of the new millennium, with increasing violence again turning attention to the MENA region, American interest in the Middle East and its languages soared. Similarly, after the Cold War many Americans studied the Russian language. Arabic was the new Russian.[22]

Fewer than 3600 students were learning Arabic at American colleges in 1990, according to a survey by the Modern Language Association. In 2002, there were an estimated 10,600 and by 2004 that number jumped to 35,000. Still small in comparison with the numbers of Americans pursuing Spanish (about 865,000), or French (216,000), the increase in American interest in Arabic was striking nonetheless. At the University of Chicago, the director of the Center for Middle Eastern Studies said that just after 9/11 they were expecting about 30 students but 80 signed up.[23]

The previously limited number of American students who were interested in Arabic reflected something of a blind spot in American higher education, considering the Arab World's long history of conflict and its 280 million people. In January 2006, at the United States Presidents' Summit, George Bush announced the National Security Language Initiative. With an initial investment of $114 million from the DOS and the Department of Education (DOE), the Department of Defense (DOD) planned to add another $705 million between 2007 and 2009. A collaborative effort, the new Office of the Director of National Intelligence would also be involved. The result was an array of more than 20 centers, offices, and programs.[24]

Among the many efforts was the Critical Language Scholarship Program, begun in 2006 by the State Department. Set up to encourage American college-age students to study Arabic, as well as 12 other languages, the program had 12,000 applications at its inception, resulting in 800 awards. Others included the Defense Language and National Security Education Office, operated by the DOD, the Foreign Language Assistance Program (operated by the DOE), the Fulbright Foreign Language Teaching Assistant Program (DOS), the Language Flagship Programs (DOD), Startalk (Intelligence), the National Middle East Language Resource Center (DOE), Fulbright Critical Language Enhancement Awards (DOS), and the Bowen Awards (DOD).[25]

Interest in studying Arabic was experienced in Middle Eastern institutions as well. The director of American University in Cairo's Center for Arabic Studies Abroad said that not only were the numbers rising, but so was the overall standard. Five years ago, half of their applicants could not finish the entrance exam but this year, every single question was answered in Arabic.

Intercultural and Recruitment Programs in High Schools

In the first decade of the new millennium, programs were initiated to advance international education exchange at the precollege level. For many Middle Eastern teenagers, these programs would serve as introductions to the possibilities of higher education exchange in US institutions. They offered early training in an intercultural setting while serving as a recruiting tool for international students who would soon be choosing their colleges.

A model for these post-9/11 high school programs had been implemented more than 30 years before. The American Institute for Foreign Study (AIFS) Foundation, an independent not-for-profit public charity, was established in 1967 with the assistance of the late Senator Robert Kennedy. Its intention was to help young people from many nations and diverse cultures better understand each other. Using that model and similar in principle was the Kennedy-Lugar Youth Exchange and Study (YES) program, established by the US Congress in 2002, as a response to 9/11. Sponsored by the Bureau of Educational and Cultural Affairs and administered by the Department of State, it was designed to provide scholarships for high school students from countries with significant Muslim populations, allowing them to spend up to one academic year in the United States. The first class of YES students were from Egypt, Gaza, Indonesia, Jordan, Kuwait, Lebanon, Malaysia, Nigeria, Pakistan, Syria, Tunisia, Turkey, the West Bank, and Yemen, and other countries were soon added. The teenage recipients of these scholarships lived with American host families, attended local high schools, and engaged in activities that taught them about American culture and values.[26]

American Study Abroad in the Middle East: "The 9/11 Kids"

Interviewed after spending six months in Morocco, an American study-abroad student reported that he had genuinely enjoyed watching the bottom fall out of every one of his preconceived ideas about the Muslim world.[27] Beginning in the early years of the new millennium, growing numbers of American study-abroad students were looking to increase their understanding of the Middle East. Instead of choosing the typical venue for a term abroad, such as the Sorbonne, Oxford, or an art institute in Italy, many were now choosing the American University in Cairo, or some other well-known Middle Eastern school, to study Arabic and experience regional culture. The American University in Cairo referred to the first arrivals as "September 11 kids."

For some, the decision was more personal than academic. After her brother was deployed to Iraq, one student reported that she had chosen to study in the Middle East to be closer, and to also get a firsthand look at the reality of the situation—partly, she said, because she did not trust the information reported by the US media. Then as now, tensions in the Middle Eastern region were a concern to everyone, and study abroad programs were sometimes suspended as a precaution.[28]

Program suspensions imposed by some institutions may have been more precautionary than necessary. In fact, few students reported encountering anti-American sentiment, other than some heated discussions about foreign policy. For the most part, local residents in Cairo, Aswan, Amman, or Damascus rarely wanted to discuss the struggles. Instead they preferred talking about common interests, family, sports, or music. In truth, while the students' perspectives were admirable, they were accompanied by a degree of youthful naivety. The reality was that quite a few young Americans in the Middle East were studying in classrooms that were near war zones. Universities worry about the welfare of their students and the legal accountability of the institution, as they well should. Proximity alone has remained a legitimate concern, even in the nearby peaceful countries, for parents as well as the colleges.

Some have taken a cautious approach, while others have left things more to fate. American University in Washington, DC, which had a 400 percent increase in the number of students studying in the Middle East after 2004, stopped sending students to Beirut after 2006, explaining that getting students out during a war was very difficult. Brandeis University set a different example. Rather than stop sending their students to Beirut, it instead provided them with a special type of emergency evacuation insurance. Fordham University was especially watchful. Fordham typically sends more than a third of their students abroad during their undergraduate careers. Its study abroad office, with the support of the US Bureau of Overseas Advisory Council, closely monitors safety and security. Evacuation has been rare, Fordham explains in their website, and would not occur unless recommended or required by either the US Embassy or the State Department. Fordham's international office encourages study abroad students to register with the US State Department Smart Traveler Enrollment Program, which provides up-to-date information should a crisis arise.[29]

Such situations have happened from time to time. A case in point occurred in Jordan, when *daesh* (the self-proclaimed Islamic State of Iraq and Syria or ISIS) released a horrific video of a captured Jordanian pilot being tortured and burned. King Abdullah II immediately launched an attack in retaliation for the brutal act, during which Fordham students were advised about the circumstances and classes were cancelled. *USA Today* reported another incident on July 22, 2014, this time involving Georgetown University students who were studying in Israel when tensions were ignited after three young Israeli students were kidnapped and murdered. One student commented that witnessing the local reaction to the violent incident had helped her cope with and accept a new reality, as the locals had done. Even in the face of escalating conflict, daily life in Jerusalem carried on, she observed.[30]

Middlebury College was another that preferred to err on the side of caution. Citing the US DOS travel warnings regarding Egypt, it suspended its Egypt program in 2013, rerouting its students to Amman, Jordan. Talks of American airstrikes in Syria the same year elevated the warnings for the region and Middlebury was joined by Georgetown University and Northwestern University in suspending some of its programs.[31]

There are many other examples. A wave of revolutionary demonstrations, protests, and riots that began in Tunisia in late 2010, the so-called Arab Spring, spread to the countries of the Arab League and beyond and had the effect of increasing the level of interest in the MENA region, but there were now fewer "safe" places to study. Egypt has been one of the MENA countries hit hardest with education exchange suspensions. A 2013 article in *Huffington Post* reported that colleges across the United States, most notably the entire University of California system, had suspended their study abroad programs in Cairo. "The situation in Egypt deteriorated very quickly," said the director of health safety and emergency response at the University of California's Education Abroad Program.[32] The US State Department issued a travel warning telling American citizens to avoid visiting Egypt due to the country's political and social unrest, and in response the University of California system blocked 22 students who were planning to take classes in advanced Arabic at the American University in Cairo that fall. Ten University of California Davis students and staff members on a faculty-led program in Cairo were airlifted from the city and flown to Europe.

Cancellations were not always due to impending violence. California State University chancellor Timothy P. White announced that the study abroad programs in Israel were cancelled for the fall 2014 semester, and there was an accompanying mandate not to approve student travel.[33] The University of Haifa was 150 kilometers from Gaza and was not itself affected by the ensuing violence. The problem was that the university's insurance carrier had indicated that travel to Tel Aviv and south would not be covered, making it difficult for students to get to many places they hoped to see. California later reinstated the programs in Israel.[34]

According to IIE figures, the number of American students studying in Arabic-speaking countries increased six-fold to 3399 in 2007, from 562 just five years before. While those numbers may seem small when compared with the more than 33,000 American students who went to the United Kingdom in 2007, or the 13,000 who studied in China, in the first decade of the millennium MENA represented the fastest-growing region for study abroad in the world. It was the Obama administration's hope to expand American study abroad in the Middle East still further. In a speech in 2009, President Obama declared that for more than a thousand years, Al-Azhar has stood as a beacon of Islamic learning. He hoped to expand exchange programs and increase scholarships "like the one that brought my father to America," encouraging more Americans to study in Muslim countries.[35]

In 2011, there was a significant decline of students going to Egypt, down 43 percent from the previous year. At the same time, Israel was recovering rapidly from a 16 percent enrollment drop the year before. By contrast, Turkey's growth of nearly 1500 percent over a ten-year period was a major global success story for study abroad. In 2012, numbers were predicted to decline due to the changing circumstances, for countries such as Syria, Bahrain, and perhaps Turkey. More American students were predicted to attend universities in the UAE.[36]

By region, in 2017 there were 6901 American students enrolled in higher education institutions in the Middle East and North Africa, according to IIE's *Open Doors*, a 14.2 percent increase over the previous year. To provide a regional comparison, 181,145 American students had chosen to study abroad in Europe.[37]

Online Learning

A few types of distance education were available in the Middle East in the first decade of the new millennium. Syria was the first country in the region to offer an online undergraduate education when it launched the Syrian Virtual University in 2007. Saudi Arabia followed with the Knowledge International University, which offered online courses toward bachelor of arts degrees in Islamic Studies for both Arabic and non-Arabic speakers. The for-profit University of Phoenix had operated a branch in Dubai in 2007 but it was closed after a few years of operation. In 2009 the UAE would launch its own public online venture, the Hamdan Bin Mohammed Smart University. In Lebanon, Talal Abu-Ghazaleh University offered online bachelor's degrees in collaboration with universities in the United States and India.[38] In 2011, the new Saudi Electric University focused on finance, computer science, and health sciences. For Saudi Arabian women the online option was especially attractive, since until recently they were not allowed to drive. Online education eliminated travel expense getting to and from class, and they could remain at home.

Some of the early online programs in the region, such as the Arab Open University, have been blended, hybrid e-learning models that require school visits, so the students can meet with faculty. Headquartered in Kuwait, it opened branches in Saudi Arabia, Bahrain, Oman, Lebanon, Jordan, and Egypt. In addition to fully online institutions and programs, in many cases traditional on-ground courses in Middle Eastern universities were supplementing their learning activities with online work.

International education exchange was in a period of growth in the Middle East, but there were many students who simply could not afford to travel to another country for scholarship. One affordable solution was offered by Connect, operated by Soliya, the nonprofit organization behind the program. Begun in 2003, Connect offered multi-week programs of facilitated online discussions among students from Western and Muslim countries. Within a few years it was serving more than 3000 students from 80 universities and 25 countries. After logging on to the Connect program students enter a videoconference with several other students, in different countries. Discussion topics might include terrorism, Islamophobia, current events, or the significance of the veil. There is no expectation that everyone will agree. The goals are communication and understanding.[39]

Designed for both undergraduate and graduate students, Connect developed its own extensive curriculum that included a final project, and could integrate into traditional classes in fields such as international relations or mass communications. American institutions such as Georgetown University and Western Kentucky University have used their programs, and institutional participants from the Middle East have included universities in Turkey, the UAE, and others. Language is a challenge for the program and some students lament that only English speakers can participate. Technical issues have been problematic, as well as the challenge of setting up schedules, keeping in mind the widely different time zones. For the most part the Connect program has been reliant upon institutional grants to operate. Supporters have included the Norwegian Ministry of Foreign Affairs, the Ford Foundation, the Al Waleed bin Talal Foundation, and the Qatar Foundation. It was also awarded a $1.25 million grant from the Middle East Partnership Initiative.

The more recent introduction of massive open online courses, or MOOCs, added an entirely new and global component to online education. In 2013, Queen Rania al Abdullah of Jordan announced the formation of a partnership between the Queen Rania Foundation and edX, the virtual education platform founded jointly by Harvard and MIT. "We desperately need quality education, and online learning is our opportunity," she added.[40] According to an article in *The Harvard Crimson*, the initiative would provide the first massive open online course portal to the Arab World. Powered by Open edX, the new Edraak was designed to deliver high-quality online education from top Arab instructors as well as Arabic-translated courses from prestigious universities from across the globe. An Arabic preceptor at Harvard, Sami M. Alkyam, said Edraak was important for the development of the Middle East, needed in the Arab World and by Arab youths. Problems in the Middle East require risk-taking, effective partnerships and an efficient use of sources of knowledge, and he believed Edraak could cultivate all of that.

MOOCs are a fairly recent phenomenon. What sets them apart from online courses typically offered in colleges and universities is that they are free, open to the public, earn no credit, and are open to as many students as wish to enroll. As the name indicates, course enrollments can be massive. Interestingly, from the outset MOOCs have attracted some of the world's finest professors, some of whom have earned a "rock star" following of students from around the world. One might ask why a student would choose to take a MOOC when it earns no credit toward a degree. An obvious reason is simply to gain knowledge. Another motivation pertains to education exchange. Taking a MOOC can serve well as a free and straightforward test drive—a risk-free introduction to the American classroom environment.

MOOCs originated with programs such as Coursera and edX, which began at Harvard, and it has evolved to encompass a broad array of subjects and objectives. In the case of Queen Rania's initiative, MOOCs promised the availability of education that was fresh, relevant, and, most importantly, in Arabic.[41] Edraak constructed its own courses in Arabic in league with leading Arab faculty members and education professionals, and offered Arabic translations of selected courses from the 29 xConsortium partners to Arab-speaking students at no cost.

"MOOC camps" soon developed. Hosted at US embassies, consulates, and other public spaces around the world, the camps were designed to facilitate discussions. They were led by alumni who participated in US government exchange programs, such as the Fulbright program, and US embassy staff who were familiar with the course materials. Subjects have ranged from entrepreneurship and college writing to science and technology with course content drawn from major MOOC providers—mainly Coursea, edX, and Udacity. The newer MOOCs have not quite lived up to the hype of 2012 but they are proving to offer worthwhile services, and their future potential seems almost unlimited.

NOTES

1. Vicki Valosik, "5 Facts About American Style Universities in the Arab Region," *U.S. News and World Report* (January 2015). Available at: www.usnews.com/education/best-arab-region-universities/articles/2015/01/07/5-facts-about-american-style-universities-in-the-arab-region?int=a02308.
2. Kemal Guruz, *Higher Education and International Student Mobility in the Global Knowledge Economy* (State University of New York Press, 2011): 71.
3. Tamar Lewin, "U.S. Universities Rush to Set Up Outposts Abroad," *The New York Times* (February 10, 2008).
4. Ibid.
5. Ibid.
6. Ibid.
7. Ibid.
8. Nirmala Janssen, "Kuwait to Reform Education System," *Gulf News* (February 26, 2005).
9. America International Recruitment Council, "Who We Are—Overview, Mission, Vision, Governance, Quick Facts." Available at: http://airc-education.org/about-airc.
10. Ibid.

11. Tamar Lewin, "Sisters Colleges See a Bounty in the Middle East," *The New York Times* (June 3, 2008).
12. Laurence H.M. Holland, "Students Recruit in the Middle East," *Harvard Crimson* (February 15, 2006).
13. "Middle East Partnership Initiative," Available at: https://mepi.state.gov/; also see Teresa B. Bevis, *Higher Education Exchange between America and the Middle East in the Twenty-First Century* (New York: Palgrave Macmillan, 2016): 75–75.
14. Matthew Kalman, "Clinton Announces Million-Dollar Scholarship Program for Palestinian Students," *The Chronicle of Higher Education* (March 9, 2009).
15. Teresa Bevis, *Higher Education Exchange between America and the Middle East in the Twenty-First Century* (New York: Palgrave Macmillan, 2016): 77–81; also see Institute of International Education, Programs. Available at: https://www.iie.org/Why-IIE/Offices/Cairo/Programs.
16. AMIDEAST 60th Anniversary 1951–2011. Available at: https://apply.amideast.org/flash/60th/60th.htm.
17. Ibid.
18. *Open Doors*, Annual Reports 2005 and 2010 (Institute of International Education).
19. Rima Merriman, "Iraqi Students in U.S. Face Unique Challenges," *The Daily Star*, Lebanon (March 25, 2004).
20. Garrett Haake and Robert Windrem, "After 9/11 U.S. Gave More Visas to Saudi Students," *NBC News*. Available at: http://investigations.nbcnews.com/news/2011/02/04/6014237-after-911-us-gave-more-visas-to-saudi-students.
21. Richard Parez-Pena, "More American Jewish Students Take Up the Study of Arabic and the Arab World," *The New York Times* (October 18, 2013): 14.
22. Ibid.
23. Ibid.
24. Robert Sedgwick, "Middle Eastern Students Find Options at Home and Elsewhere" (November 1, 2004). Available at: https://wenr.wes.org/2004/11/wenr-novemberdecember-2004-middle-eastern-students-find-options-at-home-and-elsewhere.
25. Ibid.
26. "Kennedy Lugar YES Program." Available at: https://www.yesprograms.org/about/about-us.
27. Jennifer Conlin, "For American Students, Life Lessons in the Mideast," *The New York Times* (August 6, 2010).
28. Will Rasmussen, "American Students Seek True View of Middle East," *Reuters* (November 14, 2007).

29. Cailin McKenna, "Abroad in a War Zone: Students Amid Global Conflict," *The Fordham Ram* (March 11, 2015). Available at: http://fordhamram.com/2015/03/11/hold-abroad-in-a-war-zone/.
30. Ibid.
31. Akane Otani, "Middle East Unrest Puts Study Abroad Programs on Edge," *USA Today* (September 10, 2013).
32. Aaron Sankin, "Egypt Study Abroad Programs Suspended in Wake of Ongoing Unrest," *Huffington Post* (July 15, 2013).
33. Correspondence from the California State University Office of the Chancellor (August 21, 2014). Available at: www.sjsu.edu/studyabroad/docs/Memo-Israel-Fall2014-082114.pdf.
34. Amanda Borschel-Dan, "California State University Reinstates Israel Study Abroad Program," *The Times of Israel* (February 21, 2012). Available at: https://www.timesofisrael.com/california-state-university-reinstates-israel-study-abroad-program/.
35. "Text of Barak Obama's Speech in Cairo," *The New York Times* (June 4, 2009). Available at: www.nytimes.com/2009/06/04/us/politics/04obama.text.html.
36. *Open Doors*, "Profile of U.S. Study Abroad Students, 2000/01–2010/11" (Institute of International Education, 2012). Available at: www.iie.org/opendoors.
37. *Open Doors*, 2017–2018 Annual Report (Institute of International Education).
38. "Arab Universities Chart New Course between Research, Job Training," *U.S. News and World Report* (November 4, 2014).
39. Ursula Lindsey, "Online Program Connects Students across Cultural and National Borders," *The Chronicle of Higher Education* (December 5, 2010).
40. "Queen Rania Foundation Partners with edX to Create First MOOC Portal for the Arab World," *PR Newswire* (November 8, 2013). Available at: https://www.prnewswire.com/news-releases/queen-rania-foundation-partners-with-edx-to-create-first-mooc-portal-for-the-arab-world-231127691.html.
41. Ibid.

References

American International Recruitment Council website. Who We Are. https://www.airceducation.org/content.asp?contentid=134. Accessed December 2018.

Borschel-Dan, Amanda. 2012. California State University Reinstates Israel Study Abroad Program. *The Times of Israel*, February 21. https://www.timesofisrael.com/california-state-university-reinstates-israel-study-abroad-program/.

Conlin, Jennifer. 2010. For American Students, Life Lessons in the Mideast. *The New York Times*, August 6.

Guruz, Kemal. 2011. *Higher Education and International Student Mobility in the Global Knowledge Economy*. State University of New York Press.

Haake, Garrett, and Robert Windrem. 2011. After 9/11 U.S. Gave More Visas to Saudi Students. *NBC News*, February 4.

Holland, Laurence H.M. 2006. Students Recruit in the Middle East. *The Harvard Crimson*, February 15.

Institute of International Education *Open Doors* 2012. 2012. Profile of U.S. Study Abroad Students, 2000/01–2010/11.

Janssen, Nirmala. 2005. Kuwait to Reform Education System. *Gulf News*, February 26.

Kalman, Matthew. 2009. Clinton Announces Million-Dollar Scholarship Program for Palestinian Students. *The Chronicle of Higher Education*, March 9.

Lewin, Tamar. 2008a. U.S. Universities Rush to Set Up Outposts Abroad. *The New York Times*, February 10.

———. 2008b. Sisters Colleges See a Bounty in the Middle East. *The New York Times*, June 3.

McKenna, Cailin. 2015. Abroad in a War Zone: Students Amid Global Conflict. *The Fordham Ram*, March 11.

Merriman, Rima. 2004. Iraqi Students in U.S. Face Unique Challenges. *The Daily Star*, Lebanon, March 25. http://www.dailystar.com.lb/News/Middle-East/2004/Mar-25/62658-iraqi-fulbright-students-in-us-face-unique-challenges.ashx.

Otani, Akane. 2013. Middle East Unrest Puts Study Abroad Programs on Edge. *USA Today*, September 10.

Rasmussen. 2007. American Students Seek True View of Middle East. *Reuters*, November 14.

Sankin, Aaron. 2013. Egypt Study Abroad Programs Suspended in Wake of Ongoing Unrest. *Huffington Post*, July 15.

Sedgwick, Robert. 2004. Middle Eastern Students Find Options at Home and Elsewhere. *World Education News and Reviews*, November 1. https://wenr.wes.org/2004/11/wenr-novemberdecember-2004-middle-eastern-students-find-options-at-home-and-elsewhere.

Text of Barack Obama's Speech in Cairo. 2009. *The New York Times*, June 4. www.nytimes.com/2009/06/04/us/politics/04obama.text.html.

United States Department of State, Bureau of Educational and Cultural Affairs, MOOC Camps website: https://eca.state.gov/programs-and-initiatives/initiatives/mooc-camp. Accessed December 2018.

Valosik, Vicki. 2015. 5 Facts About American Style Universities in the Arab Region. *U.S. News and World Report*, January 7. https://www.usnews.com/education/best-arab-region-universities/articles/2015/01/07/5-facts-about-american-style-universities-in-the-arab-region.

CHAPTER 11

World Leaders with American Degrees

Kings, queens, prime ministers, presidents, diplomats, and dignitaries around the world have studied or have sent their offspring to study in the United States, preferably in an Ivy League or other elite school. American colleges and universities, in the judgment of many of the world's leaders, have been the best places to prepare for positions of power and influence. Thousands of America's foreign graduates have gone on to become heads of government, top academicians or champions of business and industry, achievements that have cemented the global legacy of American higher education. A review of the educational backgrounds of past and current heads of government and other influential world leaders identifies those educated in the United States, their institutional preferences, and fields of study. The many monetary, academic, and ideological contributions that have sprung from these influential alumni are also reviewed.

No formal analysis of this academic exchange relationship is endeavored, nor is there an attempt to measure the extent to which US higher education has affected attitudes or policies in countries with American-educated leaders. This is intended instead to offer the reader a glimpse into the vast proliferation of American higher education among the world's elite by examining the long rosters of notable foreign alumni from a cross-section of top universities. Also explored are the international rankings of national and international universities, measurements that influence the academic path of those at top levels of government and society.

Through higher education exchange, more diplomats and heads of state hold degrees from the United States than from any other country. American colleges have been graduating heads of state since it first opened its doors to education exchange, and lists of world leaders fill the alumni rosters of every one of America's elite universities. Many of these illustrious graduates have led adventurous and colorful lives, and have contributed significantly to the world, giving testament to the richness of their higher-learning abilities. As discussed in Chap. 4, Latin American students were among the pioneers. Venezuelan revolutionary Francisco de Miranda may have been Yale's first foreign student in 1784, although records are vague. If he was America's first foreign student, he was also the first American-educated head-of-state, as he later took command of patriot forces and served for a time as dictator. Also noted is Fernando Bolivar, adopted son of Simon Bolivar, who studied at the University of Virginia in the mid-1800s. He would go on to build a distinguished diplomatic career and serve as governor of the province of Caracas. Mario Garcia Menocal, after his 1888 graduation from Cornell, would go on to become president of Cuba.

Royals, Diplomats, and Dignitaries

The House of Al Saud traces its origins to the eighteenth century. Muhammad ibn Saud's family has ruled large parts of the Arabian Peninsula for over 300 years. The modern House of Saud was established in 1932, when descendant Abdul Aziz (Abdulaziz) Al Saud founded the Kingdom of Saudi Arabia and pronounced himself monarch. From then on, only his descendants have been considered part of the legitimate family line and eligible to ascend the throne. The line of succession began with the oldest surviving son, Saud, followed by the second eldest, Faisal (1964–1975). The current ruler is King Salman bin Abdulaziz Al Saud.[1]

Faisal's sons received exceptional education compared to other princes born to Saudi monarchs. Prince Turki received his formal education in New Jersey and later attended the Edmund A. Walsh School of Foreign Service at Georgetown University. He would graduate in 1968 alongside future US president Bill Clinton. His brother Prince Saud is an alumnus of Princeton University. Both sons have held important positions in the Saudi government.

Of all Middle Eastern countries, the Hashemite Kingdom of Jordan may have the closest ties to US higher education. Many in the royal family have studied in or hold advanced degrees from American colleges and universities. Jordan's current ruler, King Abdullah II, is the eldest son of King Hussein Bin Talal and Princess Muna Al Hussein. Born in 1962, he is the namesake of his great-grandfather King Abdullah I, the founder of modern Jordan. King Abdullah II began his education at the Islamic Educational College in Amman. He later attended St. Edmund's School in Surrey, England, then concluded his high school education at Deerfield Academy in the United States. He pursued advanced studies at Pembroke College in Oxford, England, and at Georgetown University in the United States. King Abdullah II's son, Crown Prince Hussein, is his and Queen Rania's eldest child. Like his father, he attended Georgetown University, as did his younger sister, Princess Iman bint Abdullah.[2]

Others in Jordan's royal family have also studied in the United States; Prince Hamzah bin Hussein, for example, the first child of Hussein I and Queen Noor. He attended Sandhurst in England and then continued his education at Harvard. Born a year later, Prince Hashim bin Hussein is the eldest son of Prince Mohammad and his wife, Princess Firyal. He attended Harrow School and Sandhurst in the United Kingdom and later graduated from Georgetown University's School of Foreign Service. Prince Ghazi bin Muhammad, the youngest offspring of Prince Mohammed and his first wife Firyal, was educated at Princeton University. He currently serves as adviser to King Abdullah II for Religions and Cultural Affairs and is his majesty's personal envoy. Adding to these examples, at least three of Jordan's prime ministers were educated in America.

In Iraq, American-educated Ghazi Mashal Ajil al-Yawer served as interim president from 2004 to 2005. He first enrolled in an English-language program at American University in Washington, DC, and then received his master's degree from George Washington University in the 1980s. Two other Iraqi presidents and prime ministers were also educated in the United States.

Israel's prime minister Benjamin Netanyahu was another. Born in 1949 to historian Benzion Netanyahu, his family moved to Philadelphia in 1963. Benjamin studied at MIT, earning a master's degree in business administration in 1976. As a member of the Israeli military, in the elite special operations unit Sayeret Matcal, he took time off from his studies to fight in the Yom Kippur War in Israel in 1973. Prime Minister Shimon Perez had also attended college in the United States, first at New York University and then at Harvard.

Born in the Sharqia Governorate in Northern Egypt, Mohammad Morsi was one of at least three Egyptian presidents who were educated in

America. Egypt's current president, Abdel Fattah el-Sisi, attended the US Army War College in Pennsylvania in 2006.[3]

In Asia, at least six Japanese presidents, including the current Prime Minister Shinzo Abe, were schooled in the United States, as well as more than ten Korean and South Korean presidents and prime ministers. Around a dozen Republic of China prime ministers earned their college degrees in America, and the United States has graduated six presidents of Afghanistan. There are many more examples, and the list continues to grow.

A Penchant for the Ivy League

The preferred destinations for international royalty and heads of states include most of America's original colonial colleges—Harvard, Yale, Princeton, Brown, Rutgers, University of Pennsylvania, Columbia, and Dartmouth—with the addition of Cornell, Stanford, and the Massachusetts Institute of Technology. Other institutions frequently chosen by foreign leaders and dignitaries include the University of California system, Georgetown University, American University, George Washington University, the University of Texas, and others. As a group, these are among the best universities in the world. The rich histories of these schools and their impressive alumni have continued to attract the most discriminating students.

This chapter looks at prominent foreign alumni who have become world leaders or heads of state, from a cross-section of top American institutions. Where possible, the year or years of graduation or attendance, sometimes approximated, have been indicated next to the name, in parentheses. For the most part, information pertaining to the institution and the lists of notable alumni were harvested from the universities' own websites.

Harvard University

The really important fact about Harvard College was that it was absolutely necessary if the colonies were to build an independent society and identity. Puritan Massachusetts simply could not have done without it. The New World had been charged with a remarkable mission, but it did not lack humility, and the sense of pride which strengthened it was rigorous in its demands. Accepting the motto *veritas*, Harvard would be America's first college. In 1642, its first commencement graduated nine students.

In 1776, eight of the men who signed the Declaration of Independence had been educated at Harvard. Just a year before, in 1775, Continental soldiers had been quartered on its campus. In 1783 the Harvard Medical School opened, and Harvard Law School in 1817. Today, Harvard enrolls around 36,000 students and boasts a faculty of 2400. Since its chartering in 1636, Harvard has produced at least 48 Nobel Laureates, 32 Heads of State, and 48 Pulitzer Prize winners. In its 280-year history, it has graduated several American presidents, including Teddy Roosevelt, Franklin Delano Roosevelt, and John Kennedy, as well as heads of state and dignitaries across the globe. A number are listed below[4]:

William Lyon Mackenzie King (1898)	Prime Minister of Canada
Syngman Rhee (1908)	First President of South Korea
Fan S. Noli (1912)	Prime Minister of Albania
Andreas Papandreou (1943)	Prime Minister of Greece
Pierre Trudeau (1945)	Prime Minister of Canada
Shimon Peres (early 1950s)	President of Israel
Miguel de la Madrid (1965)	President of Mexico
Birendra of Nepal (1968)	11th King of Nepal
Mary Teresa Robinson (1970s)	President of Ireland
Ellen Johnson-Sirleaf (1971)	President of Liberia
Benazir Bhutto (1973)	Prime Minister of Pakistan
Sebastian Pinera (1976)	President of Chile
Lee Hsien Loong (1980)	Prime Minister of Singapore
Morgan Tsvangirai (1980)	Prime Minister of Zimbabwe
Eduardo Rodurquez (1980)	President of Bolivia
Ma Ying-jeou (1981)	President of Taiwan
Juan Manuel Santos (1981)	President of Colombia
Jamil Mahuad (1989)	President of Ecuador
John Key (1980s)	Prime Minister of New Zealand
Jose Maria Figueres Olsen (1991)	President of Costa Rica
Tsakhiagjin Elbegdorj (2002)	President of Mongolia

Yale University

Yale traces its beginnings to the 1640s, when clergymen in the American colonies led an effort to establish a local college to preserve the tradition of European liberal education in the New World. A charter was granted for the school in 1701. Yale College became official in 1718, named in honor of Welsh merchant Elihu Yale, who had donated a good deal of money along with 417 books. The institution has a long history of international education exchange, and of graduating foreign students who became heads of state. Yung Wing, the first Chinese ever to graduate from an American university (1854) attended Yale. Since then the university has attracted an impressive list of dignitaries, royalty, and heads of state across the globe, as noted below[5]:

Jose P. Laurel (1920s)	President of Second Philippine Republic 1943–1945
Victoria, Crown Princess of Sweden (2000)	Heir apparent
Karl Carstens (1949)	President of the Federal Republic of Germany
Salvador Roman Hidalgo Laurel (1960)	Vice President of the Second Philippine Republic
Mario Monti (1967)	Prime Minister of Italy 2011–2013
Abdul Karim Ali Al-Iryani (1968)	Prime Minister of Yemen
Lee Hong Koo (1968)	Prime Minister of the Republic of Korea
Peter Mutharika (1969)	President of Malawi 2014
Tansu Ciller (1970)	Prime Minister of Turkey
Stavros Lambrindis (1988)	Minister of Foreign Affairs for Greece

Princeton University

Privately endowed Princeton University was founded in 1746 as the College of New Jersey, making it the fourth oldest institution of higher education in the United States. It was in Princeton's Nassau Hall that General George Washington received the formal thanks of the Continental Congress for his conduct in the American Revolution. Two US presidents graduated from Princeton—James Madison and Woodrow Wilson. Wilson served as president of Princeton from 1902 to 1910. More recent alumni include Nobel Laureate Richard Feynman, one of America's renowned physicists, who took part in the development of the atom bomb.

The school's name changed from the College of New Jersey to Princeton University in 1896, and its graduate school opened four years later, in 1900. One of Princeton's students, although he did not graduate, was F. Scott Fitzgerald, who did much to popularize the college's image as a bastion of upper-class white male privilege. Since 1969, however, the institution has accepted women. Princeton's first coeducational freshman class included Lisa Najeeb Halaby, the future Queen Noor of Jordan. Other notable alumni are listed below[6]:

Syngman Rhee (1910)	First President of South Korea
Paul van Zeeland (1921)	Premier of Belgium
Pedro Pablo Kuczynski (1961)	President of Peru
Josephat Nijunga Karanja (1962)	Vice President of Kenya
Prince Saud Al-Faisal Ibn Abdul Aziz Al-Saud (1964)	Minister of Finance Saudi Arabia
Fakhruddin Ahmet (1975)	Interim Prime Minister of Bangladesh
Chung Un-chan (1978)	Prime Minister of South Korea
Prince Moulay Hicham of Morocco (1985)	
Prince Ghazi bin Muhammad of Jordan (1988)	Adviser to King Abdullah II
Prince Ali bin Hussein of Jordan (1999)	
Idrissa Seck (2004)	Prime Minister of Senegal

Columbia University

Columbia University was founded in 1754 as King's College, by royal charter of King George II of England. It is the oldest institution of higher learning in the state of New York, and the fifth oldest in the United States. In July 1754, Samuel Johnson held the first classes in the schoolhouse adjoining Trinity Church, on what is now lower Broadway in Manhattan. One early manifestation of the institution's goals was the establishment in 1767 of the first American medical school. Among the earliest trustees of King's College were John Jay, the first chief justice of the United States and Alexander Hamilton, the first secretary of the treasury. In 1776, the American Revolution would suspend instruction for a period of eight years. When it reopened in 1784 it was renamed Columbia, representing the embodiment of the patriotic fervor that inspired the nation's independence. Among its notable foreign matriculants were the following[7]:

Tang Shaoyi (1880)	Prime Minister of the Republic of China
Wellington Koo (1880)	Premier of China
Zhou Ziqi (1890)	Premier and President of the Republic of China
Juan Bautista Sacasa (1901)	President of Nicaragua
Sun Fo (1917)	Premier of the Republic of China
T. V. Soong (1920)	Premier of the Republic of China
Charles Swart (1922)	State President of the Republic of South Africa
Chen Gongbo (1925)	President of the Republic of China
Gaston Eyskens (1927)	Prime Minister of Belgium
Lee Huan (1930)	Premier of the Republic of China

(*continued*)

(continued)

Muhammad Fadhel al-Jamali (1930)	Prime Minister of Iraq
Prince Abyssinia Akweke Nwafor Orizu (1930s)	Acting President of Nigeria
Nur Mohammad Taraki (1930s)	3rd President and 12th Prime Minister of Afghanistan
Abdul Zahir (1940)	Prime Minister of Afghanistan
Mohammad Musa Shafiq (1950s)	Prime Minister of Afghanistan
Boutros Boutros-Ghali (1954–1955)	Secretary-General of the United Nations
Kassim al-Rimawi (1956)	Prime Minister of Jordan
Mark Eyskens (1957)	Prime Minister of Belgium
Salim Ahmed Salim (1960s)	Prime Minister of Tanzania; President of UN General Assembly
Hafzullah Amin (1962)	13th Prime Minister and 4th President of Afghanistan
Giuliano Amato (1963)	Prime Minister of Italy
Benjamin Mkapa (1963)	President of Tanzania
Ernesto Samper (1970s)	President of Colombia
Hans-Gert Pottering (1970s)	23rd President of European Parliament
Marek Belka (1970s)	Prime Minister of Poland
Radovan Karadzic (1975)	President of Republika Srpska
Toomas Hendrik Ilyes (1976)	President of Estonia
Ashraf Ghani (1977)	President of Afghanistan
Jose Ramos Horta (1983)	President of East Timor
Mikhail Saakashvili (1994)	President of Georgia
Vaclav Havel (2006)	President of the Czech Republic

Cornell University

Ezra Cornell was working for Samuel Morse when he devised a way to use electricity and magnetism to string telegraph wires on glass-insulated poles above ground. Cornell took much of his pay in stocks and eventually became the largest stockholder of Western Union. The success of the telegraph enabled him to found Cornell University in 1865. When President Abraham Lincoln signed the Morrill Act into law, New York State's Governor Fenton signed the Cornell Charter, and together these signatures established Cornell as New York's first land grant university. Some of Cornell's international graduates became important world leaders, among them Mario Garcia Menocal, one of America's first foreign students from South America, who would be president of Cuba from 1913 to 1921. Cornell alumni Lee Teng-hui (1968) would serve as president of Taiwan from 1988 to 2000, and Jamshid Amuzegar, who received his PhD in the 1940s, would be president of Iran in 1977 and 1978. Tsai Ing-wen (1980) was president of China, and Vaclav Klaus (1969) served as president of the Czech Republic.[8]

The University of Michigan

The University of Michigan was founded in 1817, 20 years before the territory became a state, as the Catholepistemiad or University of Michigania. In 1821, it was officially renamed the University of Michigan. Originally located in Detroit, the institution moved its home to Ann Arbor in 1837. The first Ann Arbor classes were taught in 1841 and its first commencement in 1845 recognized the graduation of 11 men. Women were first admitted in 1870. Today, the University has grown to include 19 schools and colleges; in 2017, its total enrollment was 46,002.

In 1847, within the first decade of its founding in Ann Arbor, the University of Michigan enrolled its first foreign students—one from Mexico and one from Wales. Students began arriving from Asia as early as 1872, with the matriculation of Saiske Tagai of Japan. The 1890s saw a great rise in the population of international students at the University, with the arrival of the first Chinese, South American, and Middle Eastern students. University president James B. Angell had much to do with the institution's early international enrollments. Having served as US Minister to China (1880–1881) and Turkey (1897–1898), he was interested in creating an international atmosphere at the University of Michigan. J. Raleigh Nelson, founder of the Nelson International House wrote in 1935 that cosmopolitanism was a Michigan tradition, going back to the beginning of its history. It would graduate many foreign students who would go on to assume positions of leadership[9]:

Pratap Singh Kairon (1925)	Chief Minister of Punjab
Lamberto Dini (1950s)	Prime Minister of Italy
Kamal Ahmed al-Ganzouri (1958)	Prime Minister of Egypt
Lester Bird (1959)	Prime Minister of Antigua and Barbuda
Alfonso Bustamante (1960s)	Prime Minister of Peru
Abdullah Ensour (1960s)	Prime Minister of Jordan
Edgardo Angara (1964)	President of the Senate of the Philippine
Arif Alvi (1975)	President of Pakistan
Simeon Djankov (1975)	Deputy Prime Minister of Finance of Bulgaria
Henry Tang Ying-yen (1975)	Chief Secretary of Hong Kong
HRH Sheikh Saud Bin Saqr al Qasimi (1978)	Ruler of Ras al-Khaimah in the UAE
Luis Guillermo Solis (1985)	President of Costa Rica
Kim Dong-yeon (1993)	Deputy Prime Minister of South Korea

The George Washington University

The George Washington University is a private research university in Washington, DC. Chartered by an act of the US Congress in 1821, it was founded on the wishes of President George Washington. Washington had advocated the establishment of a national university in the US capital in his first State of the Union address in 1790, an idea he continued to promote throughout his career. His vision was never realized as such but in his will Washington left shares of the Potomac Company to endow a university that would bear his name. It was one of only five universities in the United States with a congressional charter.

It would be a backdrop to several momentous events in the twentieth century. In 1906 it inaugurated college basketball, and in 1939 a conference on George Washington's campus revealed that Otto Hahn had successfully split the atom. The university's colors, buff and blue, are reminders of the hues worn by George Washington in battle. In its almost two centuries of operation, it has graduated an impressive list of world leaders:

Shahid Khagan Abbasi (1985)	Prime Minister of Pakistan
Ghazi Mashal Ajil al-Yawer (1985)	Interim President of Iraq
Song Yo Chan (1940)	Prime Minister of South Korea
Syngman Rhee (1907)	First President of South Korea
Lee Myung-bak (2011)	17th President of South Korea

(continued)

(continued)

Faure Gnassingbe (1990)	President of Togo
Yasmine Pahlavi (1990)	Crown Princess of Iran in exile
Mikhail Saakashvili (1995)	President of Georgia
Chimediin Saikhanbileg (1995)	Prime Minister of Mongolia
Nematullah Shahrani (1969)	Vice President of the Afghan Transitional Administration
Edward David Burt (2002)	Premier of Bermuda
HH Prince Talal Arslan (1880s)	Head of House of Arslan and the Lebanese Democratic Party

American University

American University in Washington, DC has a strong tradition of undergraduate and graduate education with a focus on experiential learning, global leadership, and public service. It was founded by John Fletcher Hurst, a Methodist bishop who dreamed of creating a university that trained public servants for the future. Chartered in 1893, the university's policies were groundbreaking. Before women could vote, they were attending American University, and when Washington, DC, was still segregated, 400 African Americans called the institution home.

During World War II, its students shared the campus with the US Navy, which used it for research and training. In the period following the war, the university founded the Washington Semester Program in 1947, a program of semester internships in the nation's capital that began drawing students from the nation and then from the world. American University has graduated many royals and heads of state:

Pongpol Adireksarn (1966)	Deputy Prime Minister of the Kingdom of Thailand
Ousmane Issoufi Maiga (1968)	Prime Minister of the Republic of Mali
Nizar Bin Obaid Madani (1971)	Deputy Foreign Minister of the Kingdom of Saudi Arabia
Kantathi Suphamongkhon (1976)	Foreign Minister of the Kingdom of Thailand
Abdul Ilah Khatib (1978)	Minister of Foreign Affairs of Jordan; UN Special Envoy to Libya
Keith Mitchell (1979)	Prime Minister of Grenada
Dessima Williams (1980)	Ambassador of Grenada to the United Nations
Princess Iman (2007)	

(*continued*)

(continued)

Ghazi Mashal Ajil al-Yawer (1980s)	President of Iraq
Samuel Lewis Navarro (1981)	Vice President and Foreign Minister of Panama
Mauricio Pimiento (1985)	Senator of Colombia; Governor of Cesar Department of Columbia
Julius Maada Bio (1988)	President of Sierra Leone
Prince Sheikh Isa bin Salman Al Khalifa (1992)	Crown Prince and Prime Minister of Bahrain
Yabshi Pan Rinzinwangmo (2003)	Daughter of Choekyi Gyaltsen—tenth Panchen Lama of Tibet

University of California, Berkeley

The University of California was born on March 23, 1868, using land proceeds to establish new schools, one of Abraham Lincoln's lasting legacies. Berkeley, its first campus, is today a distinguished public facility, guided by the motto *Fiat Lux*, the duty to bring new knowledge to light. Today the University of California at Berkeley is a top-ranked research facility, serving as the flagship institution of the ten research universities affiliated with the University of California system. It hosts over 40,000 students in approximately 350 undergraduate and graduate degree programs and a wide range of disciplines. Their many international graduates of note include Pedro Nel Ospina Vazquez, who graduated from Berkeley in 1882, then went on to become the president of Colombia. Fancisco I. Madero, who studied at Berkeley in 1892 and 1893, became president of Mexico. Other alumni included Princess Laurentien of the Netherlands (1991), Prince Johan-Friso of Orange-Nassau (1986–1988), and Crown Prince Haakon Magnus of Norway (1999). Sun Fo, who served as Premier of the Republic of China, attended Berkeley in 1916, as had Zulfikar Ali Bhutto (1950) who would be president of Pakistan. Alumnus Miguel Angel Rodriquez (1966) would become president of Costa Rica and Pedro Nel Ospina Vazquez (1882) would go on to be president of Colombia.[10]

University of Southern California

In the early 1870s, Los Angeles was a frontier town, where a group of citizens led by Judge Robert Maclay Widney first conceived the idea for a university in the region. A decade later, the vision would become a reality, with a generous donation of land from prominent members of the community. The donation provided the location for the campus and also served as a source of endowment. The University of Southern California opened its doors in 1880, a time when the town still lacked paved streets and electric lights, with 53 students and 10 teachers. Today, it is home to more than 44,000 students and over 4800 full-time faculty, in a thriving metropolis.

Among the University of Southern California's prominent graduates is Mohamed Morsi, who earned his PhD in materials science from USC in 1982. The son of a farmer and the eldest of five brothers, Morsi says he remembers being taken to school on the back of a donkey. Morsi was the first of Egypt's presidents to have an American education. After receiving a degree in engineering from Cairo University in the 1960s, he was awarded a government scholarship that allowed him to attend school in the United States. He later served as an assistant professor at California State University in Northridge until 1985, then returning to Egypt he taught at Zagazig University. After the 2011 Egyptian Revolution, the Muslim Brotherhood would establish the Freedom and Justice Party, with Morsi as its president. He would serve as president of Egypt from June 2012 until July 2013, when he was removed from office during the coup d'etat that followed the Egyptian protests. Other notable University of Southern California alumni include Takeo Miki, prime minister of Japan, who graduated in 1930. Shinzo Abe, Japan's current head of state, attended in 1978 and 1979. Other alumni include: Kang Young-Hoon (1973), prime minister of the Republic of Korea; Zulfikar Ali Bhutto (1947–1949), prime minister of Pakistan; Abdurrahim El-Keib (1976), interim prime minister of Libya; Marouf al-Baksit (1982), prime minister of Jordan; Fayez Al-Tarawneh (1980), prime minister of Jordan; and Ljupco Jordanovski (1985), acting president of the Republic of Macedonia.[11]

Georgetown University

Among the important reasons that royals and future heads of state have chosen Georgetown University is its world-renowned Edmund A. Walsh School of Foreign Service, which offers both undergraduate and graduate programs. The university has developed an especially close relationship with Greece, as well as with Jordan. Family members of the House of Hashemites have often attended Georgetown University, Princeton University, or both. In addition to others on the list below, Jordan's current monarch, King Abdullah II, studied at Georgetown. A recent royal graduate was Prince Philippos of Greece and Denmark, eldest son of exiled monarch King Constantine II. His older brother Crown Prince Pavlos had attended Georgetown in the early 1990s, graduating with a master's in international relations and economics. While at Georgetown, he roomed with his cousin Felipe, Prince of Asturias, who was heir apparent to the Spanish throne. Georgetown University would be an excellent place for Americans to meet or marry a royal. It could give the term "homecoming queen" a whole new meaning. Below is a partial list of royals and other leaders who studied at Georgetown[12]:

Galo Plaza (1929)	President of Ecuador
Prince Turki al-Faisal (1968)	Ambassador of Saudi Arabia to the United States
Gloria Macapagal Arroyo (1968)	President of the Philippines
Prince Turki bin Faisal Al Saud (1968)	Director of Saudi Arabian Intelligence
Prince Mohammed bin Nawaf Al-Saud (1981)	Foreign Minister of Thailand
Zeliko Komsic (1982)	Tripartite President of Bosnia
Nasser Judeh (1983)	Deputy Prime Minister and Minister of Foreign Affairs, Jordan
Ahn Ho-Young (1983)	Ambassador of the Republic of Korea to the United States
Taro Kono (1985)	Minister of Foreign Affairs of Japan
Princess Ghida Talal (1989)	Member of the House of Hashemites
Prince Talalbin Muhammad (1989)	Special Adviser to King Abdullah II, Jordan
Saad Hariri (1992)	Prime Minister of Lebanon
King Felipe VI of Spain (1995)	King of Spain
Prince Pavlos, Crown Prince of Greece (1995)	Son of Constantine II
Prince Hashim bin Hussein (2005)	Son of King Hussein and Queen Noor of Jordan
Prince Philippos, Prince of Greece and Denmark (2008)	Son of King Constantine II
HRH Sheikh Abdullan bi Hamad Al-thani (2010)	Deputy Emir of Qatar

New York University

In 1831, the distinguished statesman Albert Gallatin, who served as Secretary of State under Presidents Thomas Jefferson and James Madison, announced his hope to establish a system of rational and practical education. It was a time when most students in American colleges and universities were members of the privileged classes. Gallatin and the university fathers envisioned a center of higher learning that was open to all, regardless of national origin, social background, or religious beliefs. Today, the student body has risen from 158 to more than 50,000, hosted on three campuses in New York City. Students from 133 countries attend New York University. A private nonprofit research institution, it has graduated many foreign dignitaries and world leaders through education exchange[13]:

Shimon Peres (1940s)	President of Israel 2007–2014; Prime Minister of Israel
Rodney Vandergert (1950s)	Permanent Secretary of Ministry of Foreign Affairs of Sri Lanka
Guillermo Endara Galimany (1950s)	President of Panama
Ahmed Zaki Yamani (1955)	Saudi Arabian Minister of Oil and Mineral Resources
Muhammad Hassanein (1966)	Minister of Finance, Arab Republic of Egypt
Mohammed Elbaradei (1967)	Vice President of Egypt
Eugene Chien (1973)	Foreign Minister of Taiwan
Mohamed ElBaradei (1974)	Vice President of Egypt
Ying-jeou Ma (1976)	President of the Republic of China
Ernst Joseph Walch (1981)	Minister of Foreign Affairs for Liechtenstein
Queen Sylvia of Buganda (1985)	Queen consort of Buganda, in central Uganda
Dai-whan Chang (1987)	Prime Minister of South Korea
Dae-whan Chang (1987)	Prime Minister of South Korea
John F. Kennedy, Jr. (1989)	Son of President John F. Kennedy

The Rankings

Times Higher Education recently released its third annual ranking of top colleges and universities. Their 2019 World University Rankings was based on a review of 1250 institutions. In its list of top 20 universities, 15 were American.[14]

1. University of Oxford
2. University of Cambridge
3. Stanford University
4. Massachusetts Institute of Technology
5. California Institute of Technology
6. Harvard University
7. Princeton University
8. Yale University
9. Imperial College London
10. University of Chicago
11. ETH Zurich
12. Johns Hopkins University
13. University of Pennsylvania
14. UCL United Kingdom
15. University of California, Berkeley
16. Columbia University
17. University of California, Los Angeles
18. Duke University
19. Cornell University
20. University of Michigan

Of these top 20 universities, the institutions with the highest percentages of foreign students were Imperial College London (56 percent), University of Oxford (40 percent), Columbia University (37 percent), ETH Zurich (39 percent), MIT (34 percent), and California Institute of Technology (29 percent).[15]

The Times Higher Education's 2019 report also ranked universities in the United States. The list of top institutions is below. It is noteworthy that almost all of America's original colonial colleges are included here.

1. Harvard University
2. Massachusetts Institute of Technology
3. Yale University
4. Columbia University
5. California Institute of Technology
6. Stanford University
7. Brown University
8. Duke University
9. Princeton University

10. University of Pennsylvania
11. Cornell University
12. Dartmouth University
13. Northwestern University
14. University of Chicago
15. Rice University
16. Carnegie Mellon University
17. University of Southern California
18. Washington University St. Louis
19. Vanderbilt University
20. Emory University

A second set of college and university rankings for 2019 was released by the *U.S. News & World Report*. While its annual findings typically do not exactly match with those produced by Times Higher Education, both reports are widely read and referenced[16]:

1. Princeton University
2. Harvard University
3. Columbia University
4. Massachusetts Institute of Technology
5. University of Chicago
6. Yale University
7. Stanford University
8. University of Pennsylvania
9. Johns Hopkins University
10. Northwestern University
11. California Institute of Technology
12. Dartmouth College
13. Brown University
14. Vanderbilt University
15. Cornell University
16. Rice University
17. University of Notre Dame
18. University of California Los Angeles
19. Washington University St. Louis
20. Emory University

It should be noted that there are some inaccuracies in the number sequence. For example, Columbia, MIT, the University of Chicago, and Yale were all tied for third place. For most purposes it may be best to consider whether an individual institution is in the "top 10," or "top 20," rather than attach too much significance to the assigned number.

The *U.S. News and World Report* rankings for international institutions of higher education also differed from the Times Higher Education roster. These are the top 15, based on their review of 1250 institutions[17]:

1. Harvard University
2. Massachusetts Institute of Technology
3. Stanford University
4. University of California, Berkeley
5. University of Oxford
6. California Institute of Technology
7. University of Cambridge
8. Columbia University
9. Princeton University
10. Johns Hopkins University
11. University of Washington
12. Yale University
13. University of California, Los Angeles
14. University of Chicago
15. University of California, San Francisco

Of the top 15 universities, 13 were in the United States, according to the *U.S. News and World Report* analysis. While the various rankings differ to some degree, the preponderance of top higher education institutions in the world today are American.

Wealthy Foreign Alumni = Generous Gifts

A by-product of higher education exchange in the United States has been the generous monetary donations given to the alma maters of foreign graduates, either as heartfelt contributions to scholarship or as a means of immortalizing the family name on a university building or program. While many view such donations as an investment in education, others worry that they could provide a means of gaining underlying influence and intellectual control over American colleges. Foreign donations are typically welcomed by universities, which have in common the perpetual need for private funds, but some have raised concerns about what seems to be an escalating trend.

Since 1636, only two surnames had ever graced the name of a Harvard school. One was John Harvard's, the college's original namesake, and the other was John F. Kennedy, whose name was given to the Kennedy School of Government. But in 2014, when Harvard received a $350 million gift from foreign alumnus Gerald Chan, the largest alumni donation in its 378-year history, that changed. Now, the School of Public Health would become the Chan School of Public Health as a tribute to Chan's father. The difference in the naming of this building was not just the uncommonly large monetary contribution—it was different because it did not fit the archetypical mold of the traditional Harvard alumni donor.[18]

Chan's generous donation fit with a growing trend of international donors, many from Hong Kong and China. According to *The Harvard Crimson*, alumni donations contribute greatly to Harvard's endowment of more than $30 billion. Donations to Harvard had totaled almost $600 million in 2010 alone. Until Gerald Chan's 2014 gift, Harvard's largest contribution had been from American billionaire Kenneth Griffin, who pledged $150 million toward financial aid. His name then appeared on the financial aid office and also on 200 graduate scholarships.[19]

A *Wall Street Journal* analysis of the US Department of Education data revealed that Hong Kong was the top international source of large gifts to US colleges, contributing a total of 17 percent of the world's total donations to American higher education. According to their review of contributions, which covered the period from 2007 to 2013, Hong Kong donated $181 million to US colleges and universities. China also figures prominently on the list of top sources, with a contribution total of $60.4 million. By far, the largest benefactors have been the elite colleges—Harvard, Yale, Princeton, Stanford, the University of California at Berkeley—the same institutions that have been the preferred destinations for the sons and daughters of foreign dignitaries, and future heads-of-state.[20]

The rising trend of such donations can be attributed to the academic preeminence of the United States. Simply put, the more wealthy international students who come to the United States to receive higher education, the more they donate to their alma maters. Gerald Chan had received his doctorate from Harvard. There was a strong affinity, he explained in an interview, between Hong Kong and the United States through generations of education exchange. His brother, Ronnie Chan, pledged $20 million to the University of Southern California. Hong Kong billionaire Gordon Wu donated $100 million to Princeton in 1995. According to the report, Hong Kong residents accounted for a total of 163 disclosed gifts during 2007 alone, with an average donation of $1.1 million.

In China, in 2010, Zhang Lei of Hillhouse Capital Group gave $8,888,888 in cash to the Yale School of Management—the largest gift the university had ever received from a young alumnus at that time—and he added another $3.9 million in 2013. Many in China were reportedly enraged. The next year Zhang Xin and Pan Shiyi, founders of SOHO China, gave a $15 million gift to Harvard. There are many more examples. Contributors have reported some backlash. Wealthy Chinese who donate to American universities are sometimes seen as unpatriotic, causing many to be reluctant to donate. Criticism was especially fierce on Weibo, China's Twitter. "Why don't you donate to our own colleges, traitor?" one user asked. Another respondent claimed, "They take money from Chinese, and benefit Americans."[21] Why were China's rich not contributing to poor areas of China instead, where higher education enrollment lags behind the national average? Even in the face of such criticism, Chinese donations to US universities have escalated. Some donors see an advantage in having their names associated with elite education, especially as they expand their business empires outside China. The country's recent economic gains, and the growing wealth of the elite, have contributed to this trend.

In 2014, Chinese real estate tycoon Pan Shiyi and his wife Zhang Xin donated $15 million to Harvard to establish a scholarship program aimed at sending poor Chinese students there to study. In spite of its focus on scholarship, this donation also gathered criticism. In an August 21 interview with state-run *China Daily*, economist Yao Shujie accused Pan of forgetting that "his skin was yellow."[22]

In 2016, a $115 million donation was given to California Institute of Technology (Caltech) from the Chinese billionaire Chen Tiangiao and his wife Chrissy Luo. Later in the year, it was announced that another gift would fund the creation of an Institute for Neuroscience at Caltech, which was to be named for the donors. Other donations in 2016 included a $30 million gift to Yale Law School from the Tsai family to honor the late Paul Tsai, a Yale Law School alumnus from Taiwan, earmarked for the Law School's China Center. The same year, Chen Yidan, co-founder of China's

Tencent media and investment company, announced a $7.6 million annual award recognizing outstanding research in education. Smaller donations in 2016 included $1 million from Hong Kong's Victor and William Fung Foundation, given to Massachusetts Institute of Technology to support global education opportunities, which added to a similar sum given in 2011. The donation allowed around 300 so-called Fung Scholars to study abroad.[23]

Adding to the accusations of being unpatriotic, Chinese billionaires with a desire to fund education sometimes hesitate to invest in Chinese universities because of the lack of transparency. According to Cui Yongyuan, a former state television host and public intellectual, "If we donate to domestic colleges, how much money will actually be used on education?" A Weibo user noted that when Chinese colleges are managed as well as Harvard, then many more will be willing to donate. It was pointed out in *Southern Weekly*, a liberal newspaper in the metropolis of Guangzhou, that 29 top administrators from well-known Chinese universities had lost their jobs because of corruption since 2012. In response to the many criticisms, and mourning the loss of potential private donations, the Ministry of Education announced that it would augment colleges' public disclosures with auditing from third party agencies. So far, these proposed measures have not curbed the rise in Asian donations to American Colleges.[24]

Donations to American universities from Middle Eastern alumni have also been under scrutiny. In April 2011, the Department of Education published an updated report of foreign gifts to American colleges and universities, which was cumulative dating back to 1995, when Congress required the accumulation and publication of such data. Looking at all gifts from the Middle East, Malaysia, and Indonesia, all of which are predominantly Muslim, the data focused on gifts that totaled $50,000 or more, and contracts in excess of $5 million. The record showed that there had been 11 gifts or contracts which met those criteria from Arab states to American universities, from June 2010 to 2014. None were from Malaysia or Indonesia, Kuwait or Jordan. The totals in the report did not include endowments made prior to the period of the search, although they may have been funding professorships and other university personnel or functions. The largest donor, according to the report, was the Qatar Foundation, and the largest recipient was Georgetown University. It appeared that Qatar was spending a great deal to jumpstart its educational program and was purchasing intellectual capital from the universities with which it contracted.[25]

In addition to buildings and endowments, another product of these growing donations from international alumni has been an overall increase in American university staff that are dedicated to international fundraising. This is especially true among the elite universities. The more foreign contributions they receive, the more those institutions work to engage with their international alumni, to encourage them to keep giving—necessary labor if universities hope to successfully foster new generations of donors.

Notes

1. House of Saud, Available at: https://houseofsaud.com/king-salman-bin-abdulaziz-al-saud/.
2. Teresa B. Bevis, *Higher Education Exchange between America and the Middle East in the Twenty-First Century* (New York: Palgrave Macmillan, 2016): 127–129.
3. Ibid.
4. Donn M. Kurtz II, "Oxford and Harvard: The World's Political Universities," *Foreign Policy Journal* (May 9, 2010).
5. World Scholarship Forum, Available at: https://worldscholarshipforum.com/50-notable-alumni-of-yale-university-usa/.
6. 100 Notable Alumni of the Graduate School, Princeton University, Available at: https://www.princeton.edu/~paw/archive_new/PAW00-01/08-0124/features3.html.
7. Columbia Alumni Association, Available at: https://alumni.columbia.edu/; also see Wikipedia, List of Columbia University Personnel, Available at: https://en.wikipedia.org/wiki/List_of_Columbia_University_people.
8. Cornell University Alumni, Available at: alumni.columbia.edu; also see Wikipedia Cornell University, Available at: https://en.wikipedia.org/wiki/List_of_Cornell_University_alumni.
9. Wilfred Byron Shaw, *The University of Michigan* (Harcourt, Brace and Howe, 1920); also see University of Michigan Alumni, Available at: http://alumnus.alumni.umich.edu/notable-alumni/.
10. University of California, Berkeley, Available at: www.berkeley.edu; also see Wikipedia, Available at: https://en.wikipedia.org/wiki/List_of_University_of_California,_Berkeley_alumni_in_politics_and_government.
11. University of Southern California, Available at: www.alumni.usc.edu; also see Wikipedia, Available at: https://en.wikipedia.org/wiki/List_of_University_of_Southern_California_people#Presidents_and_prime_ministers.

12. Georgetown University Alumni, Available at: www.georgetown.edu/alumni; also see Wikipedia, Available at: https://en.wikipedia.org/wiki/List_of_ Georgetown_University_alumni#Heads_of_state_and_government.
13. New York University Alumni, Available at: https://www.nyu.edu/search.html?search=alumni%20; also see Wikipedia, Available at: https://en.wikipedia.org/wiki/List_of_New_York_University_alumni.
14. *Times Higher Education World University Rankings* (2019). Available at: https://www.timeshighereducation.com/world-university-rankings/2019/world-ranking#!/page/0/length/25/sort_by/rank/sort_order/asc/cols/stats.
15. Ibid.
16. *U.S. News & World Report* (2019). Best Colleges. Available at: https://www.usnews.com/best-colleges.
17. Ibid.
18. Nian Hu, "The Culture Behind Asian Donations to U.S. Universities," *Harvard Political Review* (November 5, 2014); also see Alvin Powell, "$350 M Gift to Tackle Public Health Challenges," *The Harvard Gazette* (September 8, 2014).
19. Ibid.
20. Jason Chow, "Hong Kong Tops List of Foreign donors to U.S. Schools," *The Wall Street Journal* (September 22, 2014).
21. Ibid.
22. Shujie Leng, "Are Chinese Donations to American Universities Unpatriotic?," *Foreign Policy* (September 9, 2014).
23. Mimi Leung and Yojana Sharma, "Caltech Gift Tops Year of Generous Chinese Giving to HE," *University World News* (December 15, 2016). Available at: http://www.universityworldnews.com/article.php?story=20161214160658320&query=california+institute+of+technology.
24. Ibid.
25. Clarice Feldman, "From the Muslim World, Big Donations to American Colleges?" (May 16, 2011). Available at: https://pjmedia.com/blog/from-the-muslim-world-big-donations-to-american-colleges/.

References

Bevis, Teresa B. 2016. *Higher Education Exchange in the Twenty-First Century.* New York: Palgrave Macmillan.

Chow, Jason. 2014. Hong Kong Tops List of Foreign Donors to U.S. Schools. *The Wall Street Journal*, September 22.

Feldman, Clarice. 2011. From the Muslim World, Big Donations to American Colleges, May 16. https://pjmedia.com/blog/from-the-muslim-world-big-donations-to-american-colleges/.

Hu, Nian. 2014. The Culture Behind Donations to American Universities. *Harvard Political Review*, November 5. http://harvardpolitics.com/harvard/culture-behind-asian-donations-u-s-universities/.

Kurtz, Donn M., II 2010. Oxford and Harvard, the World's Political Universities. *Foreign Policy Journal*, May 9.

Leng, Shujie. 2016. Are Chinese Donations to American Universities Unpatriotic? *China Daily*, December 24. http://www.chinadaily.com.cn/opinion/2016-12/24/content_27758089.htm.

Leung, Mimi, and Yojana Sharma. 2016. Caltech Gift Tops Year of Generous Chinese Giving to HE. *University World News*, no. 441, December 15. http://www.universityworldnews.com.

Shaw, Wilfred Byron. 1920. *The University of Michigan*. Harcourt, Brace and Howe.

Times Higher Education World University Rankings. 2019. https://www.timeshighereducation.com/world-university-rankings/2019/worldranking#!/page/0/length/25/sort_by/rank/sort_order/asc/cols/stats.

CHAPTER 12

Approaching Midcentury

International enrollments in US colleges and universities now exceed one million, still the lion's share of globally mobile students and scholars. As a group, US institutions of higher education remain the best in the world, according to every respected ranking system. And, American colleges and universities have educated more world leaders and heads of state than any other country in history. The United States is still the place where students from around the world can find relative freedom, a venue for true research, the general acceptance of cultural diversity, a comparatively superior level of gender equity, and its legendary harbor of dreams and opportunities. Even so, with seemingly every advantage in its court, America's attraction for international students may be facing a period of decline.

Are Foreign Students Diverting from America?

Between 2015 and 2017, the number of newly admitted foreign students in the United States declined around 10 percent, according to the Institute of International Education's (IIE's) 2018 *Open Doors* report. The figures may indicate a turning point—a reversal of a general trend that has predominated for more than half a century. Overall foreign enrollments were up 1.5 percent, but that was because higher numbers of existing students are now staying in the country for Optional Practical Training (OPT), which grew 16 percent in 2017. IIE president Goodman said that new students were not saying they cannot come to the United States, but that they had other choices.

The flattening of enrollments began in 2015–2016, said Caroline Casagrande, deputy assistant secretary for academic programs at the US Department of State's Bureau of Educational and Cultural Affairs. In 2017, the number of international student visas for study in the United States was 40 percent lower than the previous year. The United States is still the top destination in the world for international students, but the number of students enrolling for the first time at American colleges in 2017 had dropped 3 percent. In 2018, numbers again declined. Meanwhile, Australia enjoyed a 13 percent increase. In Beijing, two Chinese universities entered the top 30 of the world's best universities for the first time in 2017, attracting no less than 10 percent of all international students.[1]

Other countries have been vying for increasing enrollments. In 2013, Germany's government announced plans to increase its number of international students to 350,000 by 2020, a goal it reached in 2016. Canada hopes to attract 450,000 by 2022, and it has taken recent steps to give foreign students an easier path to citizenship. And although it has no official policy, the United Kingdom hosted a record half-million foreign students in 2015–2016.[2]

Multiple factors have contributed to slowing enrollments in the United States, including the escalating cost of US higher education, student visa delays or denials, and an environment that is increasingly marked by rhetoric that can make life uncomfortable for immigrants. The current political climate, from the Trump administration's travel bans on several predominantly Muslim countries to the recent news that the president considered barring all Chinese students, for some has had the effect of posting a "Not Welcome" sign.

For decades, American universities have served as the top destinations for the world's most talented students, and the benefits of its welcoming education system have bolstered the country's economy in countless ways. According to NAFSA, international students contributed approximately $37 billion to the US economy in 2017, creating more than 450,000 jobs. In 2018, IIE reported that the figure had risen to more than $40 billion. But the most valuable contribution, according to both sources, may be the intellectual capital international students have brought with them. Traditionally, many foreign graduates have gone on to make important societal, economic, and technical contributions. Recent examples include Tesla and SpaceX CEO Elon Musk, Google CEO Sundar Pichai, architect I. M. Pei, and journalist Fareed Zakaria.[3]

Peter McPherson, president of the Association of Public and Land-Grant Universities, said the slowing growth should be concerning for educators and policymakers alike. The rhetoric of the Trump administration, which favors closer scrutiny of visa applications, has made it more difficult for foreign students to remain in the United States after graduation. Government officials promote these actions as necessary for national security, but in many cases American colleges have been casualties. As colleges lose students, the tuition revenue is negatively impacted, said the University of Central Missouri's interim provost, where their international population declined from 1500 to 944. They had to make some budgetary decisions. International students pay twice the $6445 tuition of Missouri residents, and the lost revenue amounted to $14 million. They were forced to cut computer programs, where many foreign students were enrolled.

As the revenue stream diminishes, the financial outlook may be sufficiently dire to weigh down the bond ratings for some schools, making it more difficult to borrow money, according to Moody's Investors Service. In 2018, Moody's changed its credit outlook for higher education from "stable" to "negative."[4]

The Present and Coming "Youth Bulge"

Some predict the youth demographic to be as high as 100 million by 2035. For educators, this means that many more young people will need to be educated for a changing world. It also means that, when they graduate, they need to find work. At present there is a growing divide between numbers of graduates and occupational opportunities. On one hand, if instruction can be upgraded to a point where these millions of young people become educated sufficiently to deal with the tasks at home, there could be an upswing of youthful and productive human energy that can accomplish sweeping change, a rising tide of growth. On the other hand, if the education and occupational disconnection remained unchecked, the new generation could be rendered underemployed or unproductive, and in terms of the support systems of certain countries, burdensome.

Henrik Urdal of the Harvard Kennedy School contends that a "youth bulge" makes young men more strife-prone.[5] According to his findings, when 15–24-year-old males make up more than 35 percent of a given population, a demographic common in developing countries, the risk of conflict was 150 percent higher than with a rich-country age profile.

In a country with a youth bulge, as the young adults enter the working age, the country's dependency ratio—the ration of the nonworking age population to the working age population—will decline. If the increase in the number of working age individuals can be fully employed in productive activities, other things being equal, the level of average income per capita should increase as a result. The youth bulge could be a demographic dividend. But if a large cohort of young people cannot find employment and earn sufficient income, the youth bulge can become a demographic detriment. A large cohort of unemployed or underemployed youth can become a potential source of social and political instability. One basic measure of a country's success in turning the youth bulge into a demographic dividend is the youth unemployment rate. Some of the data is worrisome. Typically, the prevailing youth unemployment rates are about twice the rate of the general workforce. The situation in the Middle East and North Africa (MENA) is especially troubling, as youth unemployment is on the order of at least 20 percent.[6]

The youth unemployment issue was in the news at the time of the Arab Spring. Many youths protesting in the streets had relatively high education levels. A World Bank report found that for oil-producing countries in the Middle East and North Africa, government sector employment is oversized relative to other countries in the region. Oil exporters have a high growth sector, oil production, that is not labor intensive. The number of jobs created in the last decade was considerably less than the number needed to address key challenges, such as high youth unemployment and low labor force participation rates, among women especially. The new leaders in the MENA region are aware of the urgent need to address youth unemployment and many are working to resolve the issue.

Some countries are better-positioned to do so. In India, by 2020 the average age will be 29, making it the world's youngest country with 64 percent of its population in the working age group. This demographic offers India and its growing economy an edge that economists believe could add a significant 2 percent to its GDP growth rate. India is currently enjoying a demographic dividend—it has a higher labor force than the population dependent upon it. For now, it seems a recipe for blissful complacency, but looking ahead, by the latter half of this century India will have an increasingly aging population, and the country so far lacks a social security net sufficient for its needs. The field of health care is where India must make strides. Malnutrition rates among India's children remain almost five times higher than China's, and twice those in Sub-Saharan

Africa, in part because of the country's low government expenditures on public health, in 2015 just 1.2 percent of the GDP. An estimated 700,000 underqualified or unqualified doctors practice in India and less than 15 percent of Indian families have healthcare insurance. It is critical that educational emphasis be put on the medical field, and India must also work with hospitals and other organizations to ensure that jobs are available for the graduates. On the positive side, India's health care is positioned to grow at an unprecedented rate, due to its growing university system.[7]

Some East Asian countries have been able to turn the youth bulge into a demographic dividend. China, since initiating economics in the late 1970s, has so far been able to generate millions of new jobs while also relocating young workers from lower productivity agricultural activities to higher productivity manufacturing, without experiencing high unemployment among the youthful labor force.

Development strategies designed to facilitate change and create job opportunities for youth were outlined in the New Structural Economics (NSE), a book published by the World Bank in 2012 and still relevant today. The NSE highlighted that a county's economic structure is indigenous to its endowment structure. Governments must play facilitating roles in the process of change, structured according to clearly defined principles and in turn, universities must work with governments in determining how to best educate workforces designed for the future.[8]

Optional Practical Training and the Migration of Intellectual Capital

As outlined in previous chapters, Optional Practical Training (OPT) is a mechanism by which the United States can compete with other countries for top talent. OPT was developed to allow F-1 visa holders to gain practical work experience after graduating from a US college or university. Only foreign students enrolled full-time at US institutions are eligible for OPT.

OPT is less well known than the H-1B visa program, the nation's largest temporary employment visa program, which provides opportunities for US companies to hire skilled foreign workers. Yet in recent years, OPT approvals have outnumbered initial H-1B visa approvals. OPT's eligible population has been rising, as international student enrollments have increased. Between 2004 and 2016, an estimated 1.5 million of America's foreign graduates obtained authorization to remain and work in the

United States through the federal government's OPT program. According to Pew Research Center's analysis of US Immigration and Customs Enforcement (ICE), data received through a Freedom of Information Act request revealed that around 53 percent specialized in science, technology, engineering, and mathematics (STEM) fields. Increasing numbers of foreign STEM graduates enrolled with OPT after executive actions in 2008 and 2016 doubled, and then later tripled (to 36 months), the maximum length of employment. Since the first employment extension in 2008, the number of international STEM graduates participating in Optional Practical Training has grown by 400 percent.[9]

In 2007 and 2013, in addition to proposals designed to increase the number of H-1B visas was legislation to add 55,000 green cards exclusively for foreign student graduates with STEM degrees. However, the proposals were not passed by Congress. With no legislation on the H-1B visa program, the residency limit for OPT was extended an additional 24 months for those with STEM degrees. In both 2008 and 2016, under the Bush and Obama administrations, residency limits were lengthened, with the intention of preventing a so-called brain drain if students were unable to obtain H-1B visas. So-called cap-gap extensions were also established by the federal government, which could add to the time a graduate was able to stay once his or her work authorization expired. These allowed graduates to continue residing in the United States if they were in the process of attempting to change status to an H-1B visa. Only those with pending or approved H-1B visa petitions were granted cap-gap extensions, valid until October 1, the beginning of the federal government's fiscal year.

These developments have made the OPT program a more popular pathway for students on F-1 visas. Foreign graduates are now given multiple opportunities to adjust their status to the H-1B visa program, which they can potentially use to obtain a green card. H-1B visas for private companies are given to employers on a first-come, first-served basis, with applications accepted each year starting in April. Employers classified as higher education, nonprofits or governmental research institutions are exempted from the cap through the American Competitiveness in the twenty-first Century Act of 2000. Participants without STEM degrees have two opportunities to find employers to sponsor them under the H-1B visa program—one during the year of graduation and the other during their one-year OPT period. OPT participants with STEM degrees could have four opportunities to find sponsorship for an H-1B visa because of the additional 24 months they receive.[10]

Between 2004 and 2016, most foreign students obtaining authorization to remain and work in the United States after graduation were from Asia, especially India, China, and South Korea. Asian foreign graduates accounted for 74 percent of all OPT approvals during this period. Graduates from India made up the largest share of those authorized to work under the OPT program during this period, with 441,400, or 30 percent of the total. The majority had STEM degrees. As far as location, major metro areas in the United States tend to attract large numbers and they also keep a significant share as OPT enrollees. Smaller schools often see local foreign graduates relocate as part of OPT employment.[11]

Apart from escalating OPT has been a different trend of intellectual migration in the United States. Rising numbers of international students are now occupying the limited number of seats in the country's top schools, causing some to worry that foreign matriculants may be "crowding out" Americans from its oldest bastions of higher learning. Escalating numbers of foreign student applicants have intensified the competition for entry into the top private colleges and universities in the United States as students angle for one of the prized seats. Tension is especially evident, according to a 2016 article in *The Washington Post*, in the eight Ivy League schools. Data shows that their freshman classes grew slightly from 2004 to 2014 (5 percent), while the number of incoming foreign students rose 46 percent. Applications to the schools were up 88 percent. At Yale University, where just 6 percent of 30,000 applicants were accepted, the foreign share of the freshman class had grown from single digits to 11 percent. Foreign students have accounted for almost all of the growth in Yale's undergraduate enrollment as it has edged upward since 2004. By 2016 Yale was building two new residential colleges, a $500 million project, preparing to increase the size of its freshmen classes, in part to accommodate international demand. It has been the biggest expansion since Yale's undergraduate college opened its doors to women in 1969. Dean of Yale College Jonathan Holloway said that the intention was to create an incredibly diverse student body, adding that if the school wanted to train the next generation of global leaders, they should have the globe right there.[12]

International growth has fostered an increasingly cosmopolitan culture on campuses, but it also injects pressure into the admissions scramble. Dean of admissions at Georgetown University, Charles Deacon, was concerned that enrollment could be reaching an unacceptable level at some schools, potentially crowding out qualified American students. The foreign population of freshmen at Georgetown had risen from 3 percent in 2004 to 11 percent in 2014, and during that time its admission rate fell 5 points, to 17 percent. "We think it works well for us," Deacon added.[13]

Data shows the international share of freshmen doubled at Duke University, from 5 percent in 2004 to 10 percent in 2014. It also doubled at Brown University and Columbia University. At Claremont McKenna College, it quadrupled to 20 percent. Still in the single digits were Dartmouth (8 percent), Cornell (9 percent), and Stanford (8 percent). Meanwhile, admission rates plummeted, making it far more difficult for applicants to gain acceptance. Stanford turns down 19 of every 20 students seeking admission. What this means for American students is another layer of difficulty, as they compete against an escalating pool of the world's brightest students. "Sure, it's tougher," said John Latting, Emory's dean of admission, further commenting that the admission rate for international students was about half the rate for domestic students. At Claremont McKenna, vice president for admission and financial aid Jefferson Huang said that its foreign and domestic applications were accepted in almost equal proportion, adding that if they wiped out the international student population, domestic students would still have a frighteningly low admit rate.[14]

IF IT SOUNDS LIKE THEFT: AMERICA'S INTELLECTUAL PROPERTY

At age 35, Ruopeng Liu has been called China's Elon Musk. A multibillionaire, he is the man behind jet-powered surfboards and is working on sending people into space.[15] An *NBC News* report in 2018 questioned whether he was guilty of stealing intellectual property from a famous American scientist. The Federal Bureau of Investigation (FBI) knows the Chinese have a shopping list of intelligence and technology that they target, said former Assistant for Counterintelligence Frank Figliuzzi. Valuable research is allowed to walk out the door of American institutions and right into the labs of America's adversaries, he said.

Liu had come to the United States a dozen years before with the intention of studying at the lab of David Smith at Duke University, who was one of the world's experts on "metamaterials." Some believe Liu may have been on a mission from the Chinese government. Dr. Smith was famous for creating a metamaterial that functions as a sort of "invisibility cloak."

As he explained, metamaterials are "weird materials" that do not exist in nature, and in this case, the metamaterial he created makes things invisible to microwave signals. The invention was so publicized that Smith was mentioned in various late-night comedy show routines, and he was the subject of a question on Jeopardy.

Liu enrolled at Duke University in 2006, where he earned a reputation for being likeable and smart, and he worked to become Smith's protégé. In late 2007, Liu won Smith's permission to bring two of his colleagues from China into his lab for a visit, a trip fully funded, it turns out, by the Chinese government. They worked on a few projects during their several-month stay, including the invisibility cloak, but when Dr. Smith was not present, it was discovered that they took photographs of the lab's paperwork and contents and measurements of the equipment. The FBI revealed that Liu had met with Chinese officials and operatives when he was in the United States. Soon an exact replica of Smith's invisibility cloak was produced in Liu's lab in China. Liu denied any wrongdoing.

The National Broadcasting System (NBC)'s Cynthia McFadden traveled to Liu's headquarters in Shenzhen to ask him directly if he had in fact been an agent of the government when he attended Duke. During the visit, McFadden said she could not help noticing that an even more advanced version of Smith's invisibility cloak had been put on prominent display in the lobby. The FBI ended its investigation, citing insufficient evidence, but years later an email sent to one of Liu's classmates was revealed, making apparent his intent to profit from Smith's research. Had the email surfaced before his graduation, Liu would not have been granted a degree from Duke. They did not wish to revoke it, however.[16]

A May 2018 article in *The Chronicle of Higher Education* reported opposition to the US State Department's move to limit the length of student visas for some Chinese students. Two higher education associations, the American Council on Education (ACE) and the Association of Public and Land-Grant Universities, released statements against the move. The planned directive meant that the time allotted in the United States would be reduced for some Chinese, applied on an individual basis, an attempt by the White House to combat the alleged theft of American intellectual property by China. Both the Council and the Association urged the Trump administration to instead work with the higher education community to formulate policies that could protect intellectual property without limiting foreign students' contributions to the United States, especially in the STEM fields.

While apparently aimed at Chinese students in certain STEM fields, said Ted Mitchell, president of ACE, the new policy would have a chilling effect on the country's ability to attract international students. Around 80 percent of Chinese doctoral holders stay in the United States and work after they earn their degrees. There are more Chinese engineers working on artificial intelligence at US technology companies than in all of China. In economic terms, Chinese students spend at least $12 billion each year on tuition and living expenses, money that supports many jobs in and around university communities.[17]

Only a tiny fraction of students from China have ever been officially charged with illegal activity involving the theft of America's intellectual property. One could argue, however, that it only takes a few ruthless students to cause far-reaching damage.

Facing Extinction? The Fulbright Program

In 2018, the Trump administration submitted a budget that would cut funding for the Fulbright Program by 71 percent in the 2019 fiscal year. A cut of 47 percent had been proposed the year before, but had been averted, and the program retained funding at the $240 million level. Now, the threat was even greater, and on their website, the Fulbright Program posted an urgent call to action. The organization was asking thousands of Fulbright supporters and constituents to contact Congress, to help avert what could be a devastating blow to the 71-year-old exchange program. As of the writing of this book, the legislation was undecided.[18]

The Fulbright Program has provided opportunities for more than 380,000 participants to exchange ideas and contribute solutions to shared international concerns, since its inception in 1946. More than 1900 US students and early career professionals in more than 100 fields are awarded Fulbright US Student Program grants each year to study, do research, or teach English overseas. More than 800 American scholars, artists, and professionals teach or do research through the Fulbright US Scholar Program annually.

A recent issue for the Fulbright Program, apart from funding, has been its diversity. In the past few years, the program has sought more diverse pools of scholars and students, according to a 2016 article in *The Chronicle of Higher Education*. It told the story of an associate professor of chemistry and biochemistry at Spelman College, an African American, who won a Fulbright scholarship to study in Antigua. But when she attended a mixer before her departure, she did not find a fellow Fulbright scholar who looked like her, or who could relate to her concerns. Spelman had long hoped to be included in the ranks of scholars who had earned prestigious Fulbright research awards, and her experience brought attention to the situation. Despite the US Bureau of Educational and Cultural Affairs' efforts, the program has had a reputation for being overwhelmingly white.

While the State Department characterizes the Fulbright Program as "elite but not elitist," underrepresented students and academics still seem to perceive the programs as designed for others, not necessarily for them. In the past decade, the State Department has been successful in increasing participation among black and other minorities in its scholar and student programs. In the 2016 student program, the number of black grantees rose from 33 in 2005–2006 (less than 3 percent) to 99 in 2015–2016 (5.2 percent). But black and Latino students remained underrepresented, compared with white participants (63 percent). The Fulbright Scholar program reflected similar comparisons. About 66 percent of the 768 award winners in 2016 were white.[19]

As early as the 1990s, the State Department has focused on increasing diversity and has encouraged applications from women, gay, and lesbian candidates, and people with disabilities. There have since been significant increases in applicants, to more than 10,000, with advances in all racial and ethnic categories. The department has been exploring new ways to disseminate Fulbright information to a broader audience, through social media and other types of outreach. International education experts agree however that nothing is as effective as potential applicants talking one-on-one with "Fulbrighters"—those with whom they can identify.

Currently, there is a wide selection of Fulbright opportunities for American undergraduates studying abroad, including the Fulbright-Fogarty Fellowships in Public Health, the Congress-Bundestag Vocational Youth Exchange, Fulbright Travel-Only Grants, Fulbright English Teaching Assistant Program, the Fulbright US Student Program, and the Fulbright-mtvU Fellowship. Other study-abroad opportunities sponsored by the bureau include the Benjamin A. Gilman International Scholarship Program, the Stevens Initiative, and the Critical Language Scholarship Program.[20]

Naysayers Be Silent: The Threat of Political Correctness

In 1915, John Dewey, famous for his work in China and at Columbia's Teachers College, issued the Declaration of Principles of Academic Freedom and Tenure, in league with the American Association of University Professors (AAUP). It defined academic freedom as a two-way street—the students' freedom to learn and faculty's freedom to teach. According to the AAUP statement, it was not the professors' business to provide students with ready-made conclusions. It was their duty to train them to think for themselves, and to provide access to ideas and materials needed in order to think intelligently. For generations, it was a fairly uniform agreement among academics that nothing was more central to scholarship than the robust exchange of ideas.[21]

Nonetheless, in recent decades, the concept of academic freedom has been under attack, largely from within, and in its place has been a regime that has increasingly put sensitivities and civility first, and free speech last. Political correctness is the idea that certain parts of life and thought should adhere to only one view, requiring no need to search for truth, because some group had already determined it. Students and faculty members have recently been punished for expressing what some viewed as offensive ideas, almost always involving race, gender, or sexual orientation. Today, students or faculty members believed to have deviated from the reigning orthodoxy, instead of being listened to, can find themselves berated, sentenced to sensitivity training, or removed. Some contend that this trend has resulted in the weakening of the core curriculum, and the waning of academic disciplines and perspectives.

Other consequences involve the curriculum. In the past, faculty and administrators defined what was most important for students to know. Students had choices, but they began with a mostly prescribed liberal arts curriculum leading to a major. This is not so now. Today, a major such as English is not necessarily a body of important works, genres, and writers, but oftentimes a jumble of courses reflecting the embrace of diversity. Shakespeare, Chaucer, Mark Twain, and Jane Austen are no longer studied in many schools, as they have been replaced by non-canonical traditions, a focus on under-represented cultures, and ethnic or non-Western literature.

This trend relates to global education exchange in a couple of ways. As mentioned in earlier chapters, the path of American university education appears to be heading in the opposite direction from those in some less-developed countries. China, for example, is working to adopt the principles of liberal education and freedom of expression and research that have been the hallmark of US higher education. As China and other nations work to open doors to unencumbered learning, America's passageways to free expression are narrowing. As migration patterns have already shown, more internationally mobile students are choosing China and other countries, drawn to their advertised openness to learning—a quality that in the past was largely reserved for US institutions. In fact, just last year the Chinese government took covert steps to further inhibit open access to information, contrary to their university recruitment brochures, but it is likely most international student applicants are unaware of such policy or personnel shifts.

The magic of an open exchange of ideas, historically characteristic of American campuses, may be disappearing. As the United States loses ground in the admission of new foreign students, it is an issue deserving of scrutiny. Choosing a campus speaker used to be about listening to a distinguished person who had perhaps taken a controversial stance. Today, on the politically correct campus, students and faculty are less interested in hearing a challenging perspective than they are in achieving freedom from unpalatable speech. What could be disdainful to a few must now be avoided by all, regardless of the topic's importance or relevance. Former Secretary of State Condoleezza Rice had to bow out of a Rutgers speaking engagement after a few students protested loudly that she was a war criminal.[22] Human rights activist Ayaan Hirsi Ali rescinded an invitation from Brandeis University to speak and receive an honorary degree after student protests. The first female head of the International Monetary Fund, Christine Lagarde, was invited to address Smith's graduating class, only to send her regrets as students protested her alleged support of imperialist and patriarchal systems.[23] On some American campuses, a small group of closed-minded students is all that is needed to cut off discussion on the grounds that their view is the only view. What happened to the right of Americans to peacefully voice their opinions without fear? If one is offended by a speech, one can exercise the right to leave, rather than denying the rest of the audience their right to listen.

A recent study called "Hidden Tribes: A Study of America's Polarized Landscape" was conducted by a research initiative named More in Common. Surveying about 8000 respondents, the study found that 80 percent believed that the current level of political correctness is a serious problem in America.[24]

Education Exchange and Online Degrees: Caveat Emptor

Today, internationally mobile students can travel to the United States to earn a university degree from a wide variety of colleges and universities and attend classes in stately brick-and-mortar buildings on manicured college grounds, in picturesque towns or bustling cities. Getting there will entail a lengthy and complicated process—obtaining an I-20, visiting an embassy, securing a visa, leaving family behind, boarding a plane for a long and expensive flight, finding a place to live, navigating the campus and community (often without the benefit of a car), and then adjusting to the surrounding environment, which can unveil a Pandora's Box of issues. Or, they can earn an American university degree from the comfort of home.

Education via computer provides opportunities for international students, but this instructional method has some drawbacks. Time zones can be a factor, if there are specific times to log in or if there are interactive components. Students have found themselves attending online sessions at 2:00 in the morning. International acceptance of online degrees can also be an issue. While online education has become accepted in the United States, that is not always the case in other countries.

In addition to earning degrees from home, taking online courses can be helpful for international students who hope to study in the United States. Remedial core subjects such as English and mathematics can be taken prior to coming to America, or students can prepare for Test of English as a Foreign Language (TOEFL) or English as a Second Language (ESL) training. Another advantage of online courses for international students is the availability of 24-hour tech support, and access to assistance with writing, especially if English is not their first language.

The growth of online education in general has not been without challenges. Since its inception, this alternative mechanism for instruction has been criticized for a lack of quality control and the scarcity of top-quality online teachers. Some have argued that distance learning deprives students of the benefits of a traditional classroom, or that Internet connections are unreliable. But the benefits regarding access are undeniable, alongside the reduction of cost. Its appeal has escalated among international students and scholars.

While escalating numbers of exceptional online programs are increasingly available from legitimate institutions, an ongoing problem has been the existence of programs that are not accredited, not applicable to actual employment, or outright scams. Some are in the business of targeting international students. A case in point was recounted in a 2015 article in *The Chronicle of Higher Education* and reprinted in *Al Fanar Media*, that reported the "world's largest university" was scamming students, according to official investigations. A global network of fraudulent online universities was found to be using high-pressure tactics and fake scholarships to extract money from students, who ended up with worthless diplomas that graduate schools and potential employers would not accept.[25]

There were commonalities across these "pretend" universities, said George Gollin of the University of Illinois at Urbana-Champaign, who was in the business of uncovering and exposing such enterprises. The universities typically claimed to be based in the United States, and they have actively solicited students, offering generous scholarships as the bait. But the bait had a hook. Because the scholarships could not cover everything, students were required to pay the balance upfront. A second commonality was the claim of accreditation. Accreditation, a common and accepted practice in the United States, audits the quality of higher education institutions to ensure students receive the proper standard of instruction. A few of these agencies provide accreditation in the Middle East as well. But some of the academics that were listed as working for the accreditation organization in the fraudulent network said they had no idea they were named as consultants, until contacted by a reporter for an interview.[26]

To test the information, a reporter placed a call to the contact number provided by the Middle East Office of Academic Regulation and Examination, which was answered by an operator identifying himself as a staffer in an institution called MUST University. When the institution would not return the journalist's phone calls, other reporters posing as prospective Arab and Western students approached them. They were offered financial aid in less than 15 minutes. Many complaints were lodged against the MUST University program, including one student who enrolled over the phone for a bachelor's degree in computer science. He was quickly offered a discount—$7500 rather than the usual $14,400. His course consisted of automated tests, he never spoke to any of the advertised staff, and he was able to complete the degree in eight months, rather than the typical four years. The degree turned out to have little or no value, although MUST University had mailed him a diploma, after they charged his account $500 for its production.[27]

International students should be especially vigilant in their selection of an online graduate degree, remembering that their academic transcripts and credentials will need to be translated into English for review. They should determine whether their already-completed undergraduate degree will be accepted by US-based online graduate programs. How that translates varies depending on the country, and the differences can be confusing. Many online graduate programs offered through US schools ask for a degree that is comparable to a four-year American bachelor's degree. And, if online students plan to work in their home country after completing the program, they should determine in advance whether US online degrees are regarded favorably by the prospective employers. Does the degree itself mention that the program was earned online? International students considering online graduate programs should know whether there is an in-person or clinical requirement outside of their country. Some universities' online graduate programs require students to come to campus or another designated location to complete degree requirements.

In 2018, *U.S. News & World Report* published a report that included a list of accredited American universities offering online degrees. The top five were Ohio State University in Columbus, Embry-Riddle Aeronautical University, Temple University, Arizona State University, and Utah State University, in that order.[28]

While anyone can fall prey to an online degree scam, international students can be particularly vulnerable, says Karen Pederson, chief knowledge officer for the Online Learning Consortium. There are several signs that an online program might not be legitimate. First, does the accreditation status seem murky? For international students looking at US programs, a good place to start is to determine if the institution is accredited, advised Tom Willard, spokesman for the Council for Higher Education Accreditation. Second, does the name seem prestigious and vaguely familiar? Sometimes programs take a renowned name and modify it a bit. If one comes across a name like Harvard Technological University, one should investigate further. Some sites also fabricate faculty names and credentials. Next, does earning the degree seem too fast and easy? Is there any evidence of student services? Is there considerable pressure to enroll? Is there a requirement to pay a large amount of money upfront? And, is an address hard to pinpoint? Some fraudulent operations have been successfully shut down, but others emerge to take their place. They are adept at avoiding detection. Diploma mills are everywhere, until you try to find them.[29]

A Recent and Critical Shift in Distance Learning

Ambient Insight (now Mataari) recently revealed that a critical shift in online learning is underway. Its 90-page report, "The 2016–2021 Worldwide Self-Paced eLearning Market: Global eLearning Market in Steep Decline," revealed that the worldwide five-year compound annual growth rate for self-paced eLearning is distinctly negative at −6.4 percent, and that global revenues for self-paced courseware are dropping. Growth rates were negative in every region except Africa where it was flat at 0.9 percent. The steepest declines were in Asia and Latin America, at −11.7 percent and −10.8 percent, respectively. In Asia, China was the greatest inhibitor. In contrast, demand for digital English language learning was positive, at 3.8 percent. Product substitution was named as the major inhibitor in the Middle East, with consumers opting for Mobile Learning products over self-paced courseware (Learning Management Systems or LMSs) such as Blackboard.[30]

Low-cost learning technologies with highly effective knowledge transfer and learning methods are now on the market. A range of studies can now quantify the effectiveness of the knowledge transfer process measured in terms of performance improvement and observable behavior modification. Mastery methods used in self-paced eLearning products are almost all text-based exams and assessments. While these are adequate for demonstrating the retention of information, they are less effective when measuring skills.

While LMSs have evolved over time, commented George Kroner of the University of Maryland, they generally have the same capabilities they had in the 1990s. At the same time, a wave of innovation has been happening in other technologies. Since 2016, learning technology has concentrated in four learning product types: Simulation-based Learning, Game-based Learning, Cognitive Learning, and Mobile Learning. Now, highly advanced, efficient knowledge transfer products are flooding the market.

The 2016–2021 worldwide growth rates for the four types (in the United States) are 17.0 percent, 22.4 percent, 11.0 percent, and 7.5 percent, respectively. Conversely, the 2016–2021 global five-year compound annual growth rates for Self-paced eLearning, Digital Reference-ware, and Collaboration-based Learning are −6.4 percent, −3.0 percent, and −5.3 percent, respectively. According to Ambient Insight's report, consumers overwhelmingly prefer mobile learning over eLearning. A fundamental problem causing the decline in LMS revenues are that the platforms are typically incompatible with new learning technology products. Some of these new products mitigate the need for courseware altogether. An example is DAQRI's Smart Helmet, which is a hardhat with a visor that displays procedural data over objects, such as machinery or construction sites.[31]

In higher education, entrenched eLearning suppliers are working fast to diversify their portfolios with products that are in higher demand than eLearning. Pearson Publishing and Houghton Mifflin Harcourt both announced that they were building content for Google's Cardboard and Daydream platforms. Blackboard, the market leader in LMS products in the higher education segments across the world, has been aggressively diversifying into non-instructional products. This happens as customers consider different options. In 2016, the State of New Mexico, for example, announced they were replacing the statewide use of Blackboard with D2L's Brightspace. The global market for digital English language learning is booming, however. The market reached $2.8 billion in 2015, and the worldwide five-year compound annual growth rate will surge to $3.8 billion by 2020, according to Ambient Insight.[32]

How does this affect international education exchange? The advance of new instructional technologies may have the effect of keeping even more foreign students home. Universities may find themselves hosting more international students online, but fewer on campus. Reigning wisdom about how distance education is used in colleges and universities will need to be frequently reassessed, as new products emerge. With new government-imposed oversights on the quality of remote education and increasing demands for evidence that alternative learning is fully effective in both knowledge transfer and learning transfer, scrutiny will only intensify. Measuring student performance within new technologies—gaming environments, for example—will predictably present challenges. The once-distinct dividing lines between traditional classrooms and instructional venues of the future are increasingly gray.

FOREIGN PROPAGANDA AND ACADEMIC FREEDOM

In March 2018, two bills introduced in Congress aimed to increase transparency requirements for foreign media outlets and governments vying for influence in the United States—a new attempt by American legislators to respond to foreign influence-peddling in America. The Countering Propaganda Act of 2018 would require government-controlled foreign media outlets with US operations to file semiannual disclosures to the

Federal Communications Commission and to include conspicuous announcements informing America consumers of the foreign government funding the content. The bill proposed to amend the 1934 Communications Act by requiring foreign outlets to disclose their ownership and government ties.[33]

The second measure is more closely tied to international student exchange. Called the Foreign Influence Transparency Act of 2018, it takes aim at organizations such as the Confucius Institutes, the Chinese government-funded cultural outposts that donate money and instruction to American schools. Proposed by Representative Joe Wilson, Republican from South Carolina, the new legislation requires the Confucius Institutes and other entities that actively promote the political agenda of foreign governments to register as foreign agents. In addition, universities would be required to disclose all donations from foreign sources of $50,000 or more. As discussed in the previous chapter, many US institutions of higher education have been the recipients of large foreign donations, some of which have been questioned as to their underlying intentions. At the time of the proposed acts, universities were only required to disclose donations to the Department of Education that were at least $250,000. Most donations from Confucius Institutes had fallen below the reporting requirements.

According to a 2018 article in *The Chronicle of Higher Education*, these relationships between more than 100 American colleges and China drew a rebuke from the American Association of University Professors. A 2017 report by the National Association of Scholars said 103 Confucius Institutes were then operating on American campuses, with the Chinese government typically contributing $150,000 for start-up costs, then $100,000 annually thereafter. The growing rivalry between the United States and China, both economic and geopolitical, will likely continue the scrutiny of Confucius Institutes. This alone distinguishes them from other cultural programs, such as France's Alliance Francaise or Germany's Goethe-Institut.[34]

New attention to the Confucius Institutes can also be traced to Senator Marco Rubio of Florida, who in early 2018 sent letters urging five Florida colleges to cut their ties with these China-sponsored centers. Christopher Wray, director of the Federal Bureau of Investigation, said the FBI shared Rubio's concerns about the institutes, which he described as one of many tools China can take advantage of. More broadly, said Wray, the open research and development environment of academe is being exploited by Chinese operatives and affiliates to influence American society. The

Confucius Institutes, and education exchange programs in general, sometimes provide countries such as China with convenient avenues for inside influence in the guise of intercultural learning. "It is something we are watching warily," Wray said, a comment that drew consternation from some students at Georgetown University, who accused him of "xenophobia, fearmongering and discrimination."[35]

All of this is happening as the Chinese government takes significantly more control over its own universities, according to Times Higher Education.[36] Scholars have warned that the state of academic freedom in China is getting worse, after the president of Peking University was ousted and replaced by Hao Ping, a professor and former Communist Party chief. Earlier in 2018, Christopher Balding, a US academic and critic of the Chinese government, lost his post as an associate professor at Peking University. Balding subsequently left the country citing fears for his safety, saying that there had been increasing party control over China's universities. In his opinion, academic freedom is on the retreat in China, adding that the idea that the party is not preeminent in the management of a university is just false.

The implications of this for American higher education exchange are multi-fold. Since the turn of the millennium, US colleges and universities have invested in Sino-American university collaborations, and have established institutions across China, with the promise to its students that such a degree would carry the same value as one earned solely in the United States. With escalating limits on information in China, how is that claim possible? In turn, Americans considering study abroad in China should consider carefully if they will sacrifice their full capacity for research in a Chinese university, and if they will be receiving knowledge and direction that is unfettered and accurate rather than politically induced.

Exchange Enrollments and Projections

In the 2017–2018 academic year, the number of international students in the United States surpassed one million for the third consecutive year, with a total of 1,094,792, a 1.5 percent increase over the previous year. (The total number of college students in the United States was 19,831,000.) According to the *Open Doors* report, released in November 2018 by the US Department of State's Bureau of Educational and Cultural Affairs and the Institute of International Education, foreign students contributed an estimated $42.4 billion to the US economy, figures supplied

Table 12.1 Chinese students in the United States and Americans studying in China 2010–2018

	# Chinese students in the United States	% change from previous year	# American students in China
2017–2018	363,341	3.6	NA
2016–2017	350,755	6.8	11,910
2015–2016	328,547	8.1	11,688
2014–2015	304,040	10.8	12,790
2013–2014	274,439	16.5	13,763
2012–2013	235,597	21.4	14,413
2011–2012	194,029	21.3	14,887
2010–2011	157,558	23.5	14,596

Source: IIE *Open Doors* annual reports 2010–2018

by the US Department of Commerce. To add perspective, in 1949 the United States was hosting 25,464 foreign students, with a total national college enrollment of 2,403,400.[37] By region, in 2018 Asia sent the most students to the United States, with a total of 758,076. Within that total China sent 363,341; India, 196,271; South Korea, 54,555; Vietnam, 24,325; Taiwan, 22,454; and Japan 18,753. China has remained the top sender of students to America for the past decade, although enrollment growth is slowing. American study abroad in China, robust in the early years of the millennium, has also slowed. Table 12.1 displays the progression of both inbound and outbound Sino-American exchange, for the years from 2010 to 2018.[38]

In 2018, Europe was the second largest regional sender, with 92,655 students in American colleges and universities. The United Kingdom sent the most (11,460) followed by Turkey (10,520), Germany (10,042), and France (8802). The Middle East and North Africa region sent 91,375 students to the United States, most from Saudi Arabia (44,432). Iran was the second largest Middle East sender, with 12,783, followed by Kuwait with 10,190. Table 12.2 displays 2018 enrollments compared to the previous year.[39]

Latin America and the Caribbean together sent 79,920 students in 2018. Sub-Saharan Africa sent a total of 39,479; South America sent 44,629; North America (Canada) sent 25,909; Mexico and Central America totaled 24,002, most from Mexico; and Oceania's combined enrollments were 7372 (Australia sent 4908 and New Zealand sent 1785).

Table 12.2 Foreign student enrollments: MENA region (2016–2017 and 2017–2018)

Country	2016–2017	2017–2018	% change
Algeria	192	212	10.4
Egypt	3715	3701	−0.4
Libya	1311	1064	−18.8
Morocco	1634	1563	−4.3
Tunisia	692	728	5.2
Bahrain	475	451	−5.1
Iran	12,643	12,783	1.1
Iraq	1698	1438	−15.3
Israel	2393	2327	−2.8
Jordan	2312	2420	4.7
Kuwait	9825	10,190	3.7
Lebanon	1556	1633	4.9
Oman	2876	3097	7.7
Palestinian Territories	423	480	13.5
Qatar	1420	1127	−20.6
Saudi Arabia	52,611	44,432	−15.5
Syria	827	726	−12.2
UAE	2753	2486	−9.7
Yemen	658	517	−21.4

Source: IIE *Open Doors*, 2018

As for fields of study, most international students in 2018 were in engineering programs (232,710), followed by business and management (196,054). Looking at academic level, most were enrolled as undergraduates (442,746). A total of 382,953 were studying at the graduate level and 203,462 were in Optional Practical Training. Leading institutions were New York University, with a foreign student population of 17,552. The University of Southern California was second with 16,075, followed by Northeastern University (14,905), Columbia (14,615), Arizona State University (13,459), the University of Illinois (13,445), and the University of California at Los Angeles (12,017).[40]

The numbers of foreign students increased, but new student enrollments fell by 6.6 percent in 2017–2018, continuing a slowing trend that began in 2015. The overall enrollment gains were mostly due to increased participation in OPT programs, which grew by 15.8 percent. Among enrolled students, drops were seen primarily at the graduate and non-degree levels. This trend is expected to continue in the foreseeable future.

American study-abroad numbers increased 2.3 percent in 2017–2018 to 332,727. By region, most US students were studying in Europe (181,145), primarily in the United Kingdom (39,851), Italy (35,366), Spain (31,230), France, (16,462), and Germany (11,492). In Asia, 38,621 Americans were enrolled, most in China (11,910) and Japan (7531). In Mexico and Central America 22,618 Americans were enrolled, along with 17,827 in South America. A total of 14,639 American students were studying in Oceania, mostly in Australia (10,400) and New Zealand (3777). The Middle East and North Africa region had attracted 6901 students from the United States in 2018, and Sub-Saharan Africa was host to 13,433.[41]

Oracles and Prognostications

In 1913, Thomas Edison predicted that books would soon be obsolete, because educators would teach every branch of human knowledge with the motion picture. Books survived, even though they are now migrating to digital platforms, and motion pictures have had comparatively little influence on education.

Over the past century, every new technology has been heralded as a revolution in higher education. In the 1930s it was the radio, and in the 1960s it was television. The need for skilled lecturers would be reduced, many believed, as the world's leading experts could be beamed into classrooms. In the late 1990s, some claimed that teaching would soon take place via mobile phones. Students and lecturers communicating by voicemail seems quaint today, but as one looks back at past predictions, they were almost always wrong. For decades, seers have claimed that personal computers, Internet-connected whiteboards, massive open online courses, computer games, and social networks would transform higher education, as learning becomes more automated, faster, and cheaper. While all of these technologies have found places in universities, nothing significant has changed. Lectures remain ubiquitous, humans still grade most examinations, and costs keep going up.

Whatever the instructional method, academic fields of study will necessarily evolve, asserts the Georgia Tech Commission on Creating the Next in Education. Space exploration, virtual reality, artificial intelligence, sustainability, quantum computing—these are the fields students now see themselves working in over the next two decades. Unlike established branches of learning such as computer science, engineering, or business, these disciplines barely exist today, yet they could emerge as drivers of the world's economy by 2040.[42]

As midcentury approaches, a number of respected organizations have offered data and opinions on the state and future of higher education and education exchange. Discussed here are those offered by Times Higher Education, *The Chronicle of Higher Education*, the Association of Governing Boards, the Institute of International Education, and Pew Research.

Times Higher Education recently asked several distinguished academics how they imagine higher education will look in 2030. The answers were disparate. One contributor suggested that the rise of artificial intelligence will consign the university to history by 2030, but others believed technology will continue to have minimal impact. Some said that by 2030 there will be no students to teach, as professional jobs for which we currently prepare students will be done by intelligent machines. Other respondents believed the pedagogic pendulum will swing back toward the lecture as the importance of an analytical mind becomes appreciated once more.[43]

Drawing upon insights from their reporters, editors, and readers, *The Chronicle of Higher Education* identified several trends that are expected to continue to affect the academic environment. According to their report, "The American Campus Under Siege," colleges have faced growing scrutiny in recent years, from legislators, the public, and parents concerned about value, and the 2016 presidential election led to fresh attacks on colleges for being elitists and out of touch. American colleges and universities are perhaps the last bastion of liberalism, suggested the *Chronicle*'s report, and in the future higher education will need to learn how to weather even more attacks from far-right groups. According to the report, there is an escalating trend of student influence on American campuses, and they are using their voices to demand "trigger warnings," and power over hiring, among other things, a movement oddly reminiscent of the student nations at the University of Bologna in medieval times. The article further suggests that studying in the United States may be losing some of its appeal in the minds of foreign students, indicated by the slowing of new international student enrollments.[44]

Third, peer review is in flux. Long considered the gold standard of scientific reliability, the Internet era has led to a proliferation of open-access journals that have weakened the notion of peer review. Scientific leaders will need to agree on a new approach that encourages transparent scientific sharing, while reserving the highest-quality peer review for when it is most needed. The *Chronicle* article also points out that higher education in the United States has entered a period of deregulation, as the current administration's Education Department has announced plans to abolish or revise key Obama-era programs. Some college leaders say the constant reinterpretations have been confusing, while others welcome less regulation.[45]

In their 14th paper summarizing federal and state public policy issues, released in the wake of the 2016 election, the Association of Governing Boards of Universities and Colleges (AGB) warned that the reverberations of new policies will be felt for years to come. AGB identified several top issues, including a changing landscape in federal education policy, increased accountability and deregulation in American colleges, enhanced scrutiny about accreditation, tax issues, and campus climate.[46]

The Institute of International Education predicts that competition for international students from countries such as Canada and Australia will continue to be robust, as their recruitment efforts over the past years are reaping positive results. In 2017, Canada saw an 11 percent increase in their number of international students (192,000) and their goal is to host 450,000 by 2022. Australia had about 480,000 international students enrolled in higher education in 2017, a 15 percent increase of the previous year. These increases happened as the United States witnessed a disappointing 3 percent overall growth in foreign student enrollments, and a decline in new admits.[47] Possible visa issues could further inhibit international enrollments in the United States. An executive order was recently leaked to the press suggesting the current administration's desire to eliminate or severely restrict J-1 programs that have a work component.

Regarding national demographics, according to the US Census Bureau millennials are now projected to overtake baby boomers as America's largest generation. Millennials, defined as ages 20–35, numbered 71 million in 2016, and boomers, aged 52–70, numbered 74 million. Millennials are expected to outnumber boomers in 2019, while Generation X (ages 36–51 in 2016) is projected to surpass boomers in 2028. This is partly due to an ongoing influx of young immigrants to America, which have expanded the ranks of millennials, according to the Pew Research Center.[48] These trends combined with the global "youth bulge" will serve to reshape the make-up of both national and international student populations with respect to age, academic expectations, and occupational aspirations.

Looking at public opinion on American higher education, the Pew Research Center released its American Trends Panel report, taken from a sample of 4587 US adults. According to the report, 61 percent believed that the higher education system in the United States today is going in the wrong direction. Most (84 percent) attributed this to escalating tuition costs, while about half felt the demise was at least partly due to professors bringing their own political and social views into the classroom. Fifty-four percent believed colleges were too concerned about protecting students from views they find offensive, and 65 percent felt that students were not getting the skills needed for the marketplace. When asked which issue should be more important on college campuses these days, 87 percent of the respondents said that allowing people to speak their minds freely, even if some find the views offensive, was their top choice.[49]

As midcentury approaches, a number of issues and trends can be identified, with varying levels of importance:

- Demographic shifts
- Availability of occupational opportunities for future graduates
- Growing constraints on academic freedom and open discourse
- Influences and intentions of foreign donations
- Potential losses of American intellectual property
- Status of visa issuance, immigration policy, and border security
- Rising costs of university degrees
- Increasing federal and state scrutiny
- Funding insecurity for exchange programs
- Economic impact of foreign enrollments
- Quality and academic efficiency of American university branch campuses
- Escalation of American university partnerships with foreign universities
- Ongoing global competition for international students
- New distance learning technologies and instructional methods

While some may think these issues are new, if one looks at the history of education exchange, many of these same concerns were being dealt with in antiquity. A period in Hellenistic Greece, for example, sacrificed some of the political and ethical functions it had served in Classical Greece, as academic freedom and open discourse became increasingly ceremonial and literary. The content of a speech became less important than the style in which it was composed. Teaching could be perilous then too, if one provided instruction on unpopular topics. The philosopher Socrates was executed by his fellow Athenians for corrupting the young with his teaching. Damon, who tutored a young Pericles, was banished from Athens for ten years, according to the Greek biographer Plutarch, accused of teaching his pupil about politics, a subject that local citizens believed to be dangerous meddling in the affairs of the city. This period of less-open discourse did not encourage a sweep of original thought or creative new works, but its features served to preserve Greek thought and literature, well into the Middle Ages of Europe.[50]

Neither is intellectual property theft a new issue for American universities and foreign students. In the 1870s, when China sent its first dispatch of students to the United States, the Qing court's long-term goal was to acquire America's scientific and military secrets. It was, and still is, China's plan. American universities have always needed to be vigilant in their oversight of scientific laboratories and other sensitive venues, when dealing with students from China or elsewhere. Recent and continuing losses indicate that better strategies are long overdue.

Nor are restrictive immigration policies that target specific nationality groups new in the United States. One of the Trump administration's stated goals is to limit immigration from certain Muslim regions and restrict foreign student access to sensitive educational and scientific materials, by imposing bans on specific countries. This is reminiscent of America's very first immigration law, the Chinese Exclusion Act, which was implemented in 1882 and directly targeted China. Threats to academic freedom and open discourse are not new either, as they reflect the red-scare days of McCarthy, and the rousting out of Communist sympathizers from American universities. Of all the issues on the list, however, losses of academic freedom and open scholarly discourse may be the most troubling, as these practices are at the core of American scholarship and have been fundamental to America's academic rise.

If the halo over American universities loses its luster, it is not difficult to forecast that their attraction for the world's brightest international students may fade as well. America's colleges and universities are now charged with making difficult choices. Uncomfortable questions will need to be honestly addressed in terms of the future. Is a continuous buildup of international students in America's colleges and universities still in everyone's best interest? In practical terms, in light of the massive industry and many salaries now dependent upon the enterprise, finding an audience receptive to considering anything to the contrary may be a challenge.

A New Golden Age?

Some speak nostalgically of a golden age of American higher education, a time in the 1950s and 1960s, when states held down tuition costs as they invested in building new colleges. Foreign students were arriving in ever-greater numbers, fresh-faced and eager to learn, and posed no real or imagined threat, and the United States was the best educational place to be. Popular opinion seems to hold that this golden age is now in decline. Some claim this view is, to some degree, media driven.

According to a 2019 article in *The Chronicle of Higher Education* titled "Is This Higher Education's Golden Age?" popular opinion does not do justice to the realized visions of the present. Evidence suggests that the golden age of research may be happening right now. But consider the recent headlines. Articles in *The Atlantic* have included "The Pillaging of America's State Universities" and "The Broken Promise of Higher Education." Published in *The New York Review of Books* was "Our Universities: The Outrageous Reality" and "The Hi-Tech Mess of Higher Education." *The Chronicle of Higher Education* has contributed articles such as "An Era of Neglect," "Higher Education is Drowning in BS," and "The Slow Death of the University." According to Steven Brint, professor of sociology and public policy and director of the Colleges and Universities 2000 program at the University of California at Riverside, the positive indicators may in fact outweigh all the negative publicity.[51]

The puzzling feature of all the negativity, according to Brint, is how little relation it bears to reality, as the statistical evidence does not support such a gloomy perspective. Statistical evidence suggests that American universities have never been stronger or more prominent in public life. At major research universities, between 1980 and 2010, research expenditures grew by more than ten times in inflation-adjusted dollars, while high-quality publications catalogues in the Web of Science tripled. Few sectors have been as important to the emerging knowledge economy as universities. Federal research and development funding, around $30 billion in 2017, has been largely responsible for the growth of research during this period. About $65 billion was provided in the form of Pell Grants, work-study funds and tax benefits, in addition to billions of dollars in available loans. Funding for international education exchange programs, until very recently, has continued to gain support.

Critics of higher education have logically assumed that as tuition becomes more expensive, demand for degrees will suffer. The opposite has been true, as even during times of recession undergraduate enrollments in

American colleges have risen. Around 20 million students now attend higher education institutions in the United States, representing a population almost 100 times larger than a century ago, and far outpacing population growth. Looking at research, the top 200 institutions produced the preponderance, and the remarkable fact is the steady and impressive growth in research output across virtually all of the leading providers.[52]

The idea of a crisis in public universities, even during the depths of the Great Recession, was exaggerated. Both the press and the professors predicted that the sky would fall, and that faculty salaries would drop. Many institutions did experience tight budgets, but in fact faculty salaries increased a little between 2008 and 2013, as did average staff size and the asset value of endowments. The article concluded, after looking at the evidence, that "beyond the din of the latest protests about sexual violence on campus or controversial speakers causing an uproar," some positive trends are leaving American universities stronger and even more influential as midcentury approaches.

Others agree that things may not be as bad as the media tends to suggest. In December 23, 2018, Fareed Zakaria interviewed Steven Pinker, a professor of psychology at Harvard, and Niall Ferguson, senior fellow at Stanford's Hoover Institution. Both had recently written books that addressed future trends. Pinker conceded that it was the nature of journalism to emphasize the negative. If something explodes or if a building collapses, that's news, but if the global extreme poverty rate declines by a few percentage points, that rarely makes headlines. In spite of news, if one looks just at the data, said Pinker, the world is now the most peaceful, prosperous, and progressive, with greater rights for more people, than ever in history. Improvements have not happened inexorably, year after year, but the overall trend over the decades is for every measure of human well-being to improve.[53]

Ferguson agreed that the world at the end of 2018 was generally better for most people than it was a century earlier. There have been enormous improvements in medical care, and in most economic measures. Inequality has actually gone down globally, he added, in part because of the extraordinary economic miracle in the world's most populous country, China. Not likely a coincidence, its meteoric rise began when Deng Xiaoping reopened its doors to higher education exchange with the United States in 1979.[54] Few would call it presumptuous to conclude that some measure of China's remarkable advances has been a result of 40 years of knowledge-sharing with the United States. While wars have not been avoided, some of the lofty aspirations of the pioneers of American education exchange have indeed been advanced.

"When Adam walked with Eve in the Garden of Eden, he was overheard to say (presumably by the angel just arrived with the flaming sword), 'You must understand, my dear, that we are living through a period of transition.'"[55] Historian Rudolph drew upon the allegory to allude to a time in American history after World War II, when the United States was on the cusp of rising to unprecedented heights, as it assumed a particular appropriateness for the history of higher education. America's college movement was over, but another was awaiting definition and recognition, and the new era was destined to be spectacular. America would deploy its ideals and its scholarship around the world. As midcentury rises, higher education exchange in the United States may be nearing another transition. Thoughtful actions taken now by policymakers and practitioners, keeping at heart the extraordinary and high-minded foundations upon which America has risen to educational prominence, will determine whether *meiguo*, the beautiful country, will preserve its place as the world's epicenter of scholarship.

Notes

1. Benjamin Wermund, "Enrollment of New Foreign Students at U.S. Colleges Slows Again in Trump Era," *Politico* (November 13, 2018). Available at: https://www.politico.com/story/2018/11/13/colleges-foreign-students-trump-985259. Accessed December 2, 2008.
2. Ibid.
3. Paul Laudicina, "Why Foreign Students Diverting from America is a Problem," *Forbes* (October 29, 2018). Available at: https://www.forbes.com/sites/paullaudicina/2018/10/29/why-foreign-students-diverting-from-america-is-a-problem/#6701a8c5f5e4.
4. Stephanie Saul, "As Flow of Foreign Students Wanes, U.S. Universities Feel the Sting," *The New York Times* (January 2, 2018). Available at: https://www.nytimes.com/2018/01/02/us/international-enrollment-drop.html.
5. Siddharth Chatterjee, "India's Youth—A Blessing or a Curse," *Huffington Post* (February 29, 2016). Available at: www.huffingtonpost.com/siddharth-chatterjee-/indias-youth-a-blessing-o_b_9288120.html.
6. Justin Yifu Lin, "Youth Bulge: A Demographic Dividend or a Demographic Bomb in Developing Countries," *The World Bank* (January 5, 2012). Available at: http://blogs.worldbank.org/developmenttalk/youth-bulge-a-demographic-dividend-or-a-demographic-bomb-in-developing-countries.
7. Ibid.

8. Justin Yifu Lin, *New Structural Economics, A Framework for Rethinking Development and Policy* (Washington, DC: The World Bank, 2012).
9. Neil G. Ruiz and Abby Budiman, "Number of Foreign College Students Staying and Working in the U.S. After Graduation Surges," *Pew Research Center* (May 10, 2018). Available at: http://assets.pewresearch.org/wp-content/uploads/sites/2/2018/05/10110621/Pew-Research-Center_Foreign-Student-Graduate-Workers-on-OPT_2018.05.10.pdf.
10. Ibid.
11. Ibid.
12. Nick Anderson, "Surge in Foreign Students May Be Crowding Americans Out of Elite Colleges," *The Washington Post* (December 21, 2016). Available at: https://www.washingtonpost.com/local/education/surge-in-foreign-students-might-be-crowding-americans-out-of-elite-colleges/2016/12/21/78d4b65c-b59d-11e6-a677-b608fbb3aaf6_story.html?notedirect=on&utm_term=3230ab8cb5cd.
13. Ibid.
14. Ibid.
15. Cynthia McFadden, Aliza Nadi, and Courtney McGee, "Education or Espionage? A Chinese Student Takes His Homework Home to China," *NBC News* (July 24, 2018). Available at: https://www.nbcnews.com/news/china/education-or-espionage-chinese-student-takes-his-homework-home-china-n893881.
16. Ibid.
17. Fernanda Zamudio-Suarez, "Higher-Ed Groups Warn Against Visa Restrictions for Chinese Students," *The Chronicle of Higher Education* (May 30, 2018).
18. Fulbright Association, "Stand Up for Fulbright." Available at: https://fulbright.org/stand-for-fulbright-2018/
19. Courtney Kueppers, "Fulbright Seeks More Diverse Pool of Scholars and Students," *The Chronicle of Higher Education* (February 22, 2016). Available at: https://www.chronicle.com/article/Fulbright-Seeks-More-Diverse/235379. Accessed December 3, 2018.
20. U.S. Bureau of Educational and Cultural Affairs, Exchange Programs. Available at: https://exchanges.state.gov/us/search/solr?f%5B0%5D=bundle%3Aexchange_program&f%5B1%5D=im_field_program_participant_typ%3A64&from_redirect=1.
21. John K. Wilson, "AAUP's 1915 Declaration of Principles: Conservative and Radical, Visionary and Myopic," *AAUP Journal of Academic Freedom*. Available at: https://www.aaup.org/sites/default/files/Wilson_1.pdf.
22. Emma Fitzsimmons, "Condoleezza Rice Backs Out of Rutgers Speech after Student Protests," *The New York Times* (May 4, 2014).

23. Richard Perez Pena, "After Protests, IMF Chief Withdraws as Smith College's Commencement Speaker," *The New York Times* (May 14, 2014).
24. "Hidden Tribes: A Study in America's Polarized Landscape," *More in Common* (October 2018). Available at: https://www.moreincommon.com/hidden-tribes.
25. Benjamin Plackett, "World's Largest University Is Scamming Students, Investigation Reveals," *Al Fanar Media* (February 24, 2015).
26. Ibid.
27. Ibid.
28. *U.S. News & World Report*, Online College Rankings (2018). Available at: https://www.usnews.com/education/online-education/rankings.
29. Devon Haynie, "7 Warning Signs an Online Degree is a Scam," *U.S. News & World Report* (June 9, 2015). Available at: https://www.usnews.com/education/online-education/articles/2015/06/09/7-warning-signs-an-online-degree-is-a-scam. Accessed November 30, 2018.
30. "2016–2021 Worldwide, Self-paced, e-Learning Market," *Ambient Insight*. Available at http://www.ambientinsight.com/Resources/Documents/AmbientInsight_The%202016-2021_Worldwide_Self-paced%20eLearning_Market.pdf.
31. Ibid.
32. Ibid.
33. Bethany Allen-Ebrahimian, Elias Groll and Robbie Gramer, "New House Bills Take Aim at Foreign Propaganda" (March 20, 2018).
34. Dan Bauman, "Amid Fear of Foreign Influence, Colleges' Confucius Institutes Face Renewed Skepticism," *The Chronicle of Higher Education* (February 28, 2018).
35. Ibid.
36. "Alarm as Peking Head Replaced with Communist Party Secretary," *Times Higher Education* (November 14, 2014). Available at: http://www.timeshighereducation.com/news/alarm-peking-head-replaced-communist-party-secretary.
37. *Open Doors*, Annual Report (Institute of International Education, 2019).
38. Ibid.
39. Ibid.
40. Ibid.
41. Ibid.
42. Gordana Goudie, "Lifetime Learning Becomes the Focus," George Tech University (May 24, 2018). Available at: https://pe.gatech.edu/blog/creating-the-next-report.
43. Times Higher Education, "Future Perfect: What Will Universities Look like in 2030?" (December 24, 2015). Available at: https://www.timeshighereducation.com/features/what-will-universities-look-like-in-2030-future-perfect.

44. Steve Kolowich, "The American Campus Under Siege," *The Chronicle of Higher Education* (March 4, 2018).
45. Ibid.
46. Association of Governing Boards, Top Strategic Issues for Boards 2018–2019. Available at: https://www.agb.org/store/top-strategic-issues-for-boards-2018-2019.
47. *Open Doors* (Institute of International Education, 2017–2018).
48. Richard Fry, "Millennials Projected to Overtake Baby Boomers as America's Largest Generation," *Pew Research Center* (March 1, 2018). Available at: http://www.pewforum.org/2016/12/13/hindu-educational-attainment/. Accessed December 14, 2018.
49. Pew Research Center, American Trends Panel (2018). Available at: http://www.pewresearch.org/topics/american-trends-panel/.
50. "Education and Rhetoric, Greek," Erenow, Ancient Greece and Rome, an Encyclopedia for Students. Available at: https://erenow.net/ancient/ancient-greece-and-rome-an-encyclopedia-for-students-4-volume-set/148.php.
51. Steven Brint, "Is this Higher Education's Golden Age?," *The Chronicle of Higher Education* (January 2019). Available at: https://www.chronicle.com/interactives/golden-age?cid=FEATUREDNAV.
52. Ibid.
53. Fareed Zakaria GPS, *CNN* (December 23, 2018). Available at: http://edition.cnn.com/TRANSCRIPTS/1812/23/fzgps.01.html.
54. Ibid.
55. Frederick Rudolph, *The American College and University* (University of Georgia Press, 1963): 483.

References

Allen-Ebrahimian, Bethany, Elias Groll, and Robbie Gramer. 2018. New House Bills Take Aim at Foreign Propaganda. *Foreign Policy*, March 20. https://foreignpolicy.com/2018/03/20/new-house-bill-takes-aim-at-foreign-propaganda-russia-today-foreign-agent-manafort-fara/.

Anderson, Nick. 2016. Surge in Foreign Students May Be Crowding Americans Out of Elite Colleges. *The Washington Post*, December 21.

Brint, Steven. 2019. Is this Higher Education's Golden Age? *The Chronicle of Higher Education*, January.

Chatterjee, Siddharth. 2016. India's Youth—A Blessing or a Curse. *Huffington Post*, February 29.

Fitzsimmons, Emma. 2014. Condoleezza Rice Backs Out of Rutgers Speech after Student Protests. *The New York Times*, May 4.

Fry, Richard. 2018. Millennials Projected to Overtake Baby Boomers as America's Largest Generation. *Pew Research Center*, March 1.

Haynie, Devon. 2015. 7 Warning Signs an Online Degree is a Scam. *U.S. News & World Report*, June 9.

Kolowich, Steve. 2018. The American Campus Under Siege. *The Chronicle of Higher Education*, March 4.

Kueppers, Courtney. 2016. Fulbright Seeks More Diverse Pool of Scholars and Students. *The Chronicle of Higher Education*, February 22.

Laudicina, Paul. 2018. Why Foreign Students Diverting from America is a Problem. *Forbes*, October 29.

Lin, Justin Yifu. 2012a. Youth Bulge: A Demographic Dividend or a Demographic Bomb in Developing Countries. *The World Bank*, January 5.

———. 2012b. *New Structural Economics: A Framework for Rethinking Development and Policy*. Washington, DC: The World Bank.

Lindsey, Ursula. 2010. Online Program Connects Students across Cultural and National Borders. *The Chronicle of Higher Education*, December 4.

McFadden, Cynthia, Aliza Nadj, and Courtney McGee. 2018. Education or Espionage? A Chinese Student Takes His Homework Home to China. *NBC News*, July 24.

Plackett, Benjamin. 2015. World's Largest University is Scamming Students, Investigation Reveals. *Al Fanar Media*, February 24.

Rudolph, Frederick. 1963. *The American College and University*. University of Georgia Press.

Ruiz, Neil G., and Abby Budiman. 2018. Number of Foreign College Students Staying and Working in the U.S. after Graduation Surges. *Pew Research Center*, May 10.

Saul, Stephanie. 2018. As Flow of Foreign Students Wanes, U.S. Universities Feel the Sting. *The New York Times*, January 2.

Times Higher Education. 2014. Alarm as Peking Head Replaced with Communist Party Secretary, November 14. http://www.timeshighereducation.com/news/alarm-peking-head-replaced-communist-party-secretary.

Wermund, Benjamin. 2018. Enrollment of New Foreign Students at U.S. Colleges Slows again in Trump Era. *Politico*, November 13. www.politico.com/story/2018/11/13/colleges-foreign-students-trump-985259.

Zamudio-Suarez, Fernanda. 2018. Higher-Ed Groups Warn against Visa Restrictions for Chinese Students. *The Chronicle of Higher Education*, May 30.

Index

A

Academic freedom, 37, 126, 135, 222, 233, 236, 306, 312–314, 320, 321
Accreditation, 112, 237, 246, 247, 309, 310, 319
Admissions, vii, 20, 38, 42, 57, 58, 63, 76, 88, 94, 112, 116, 117, 125, 152–154, 175, 186, 192, 195, 206, 207, 209, 210, 220, 222, 228, 247, 249, 253, 301, 302, 307
African Airlift, 163
Al Azhar University, 35
America-Mideast Educational and Training Services, Inc (AMIDEAST), 145–147, 174–176, 210, 245, 252, 255–257
American Journal of Science and Arts, The, 60, 61
AMIDEAST, *see* America-Mideast Educational and Training Services, Inc

B

Beasley, Delilah, 119
Bolivar, Fernando, 72, 272
Bolivar, Simon, 69, 72, 272
Borjas, George, 210, 211
Boxer Indemnity scholarships, 122, 126, 127, 142, 216
Boxer Rebellion, 91, 103, 104, 117, 123, 141
Buddhism/Buddhist, 8, 9, 11, 12, 14–16, 119
Buisson, Ferdinand Eduard, 71
Burlingame, Anson, 79–82
Byzantine Empire, 4, 29, 30

C

C-9 League, 220
Carter, James E., 171, 172
China
 100,000 Strong Initiative, 228
 culture, 8, 88, 128, 179, 218, 227, 228, 235
 education, 129, 180, 183, 219
 migrant children, 224–226

China (*cont.*)
  one-child policy, 223, 224
  ten-year plan, 226–227
Chinese Educational Mission
    (CEM), 83–92, 123, 125,
    127, 130, 183, 216
Chinese Exclusion Act, 93, 94, 321
Cold War, 138, 156–159, 208, 259
Colonial colleges (American), 56–58,
    274, 286
Committee on Friendly Relations
    Among Foreign Students, the,
    103, 109, 113–115, 118, 136,
    150, 159
Committee on Scholarly
    Communication with the People's
    Republic of China (CSCPRC),
    179, 180, 182
Competing countries and international
    students, 251, 319
Confucius/Confucianism, 7–9, 11, 235
Confucius Institutes, 226, 235–239,
    313, 314
Constantine, 28
Constantinople, 19, 29, 30
Cosmopolitan Clubs, 110–112, 114, 117

D

Demographics, 61, 105, 223, 253,
    297–299, 319, 320
Deng Xiaoping, 11, 179, 181–182,
    215, 216, 220, 323
Dewey, John, 123, 127, 129, 306
Distance learning, 185, 202, 308,
    311–312, 320
Duggan, Stephen, 120, 121, 135,
    147, 148

E

Edmonds, Harry, 118–120
English as a Second Language (ESL),
    203, 216, 308

F

Female literacy, 10, 11
Fidler, Isaac, 70
Foreign student evaluations, 152
Fulbright Program, 140–143, 164,
    210, 267, 304–305
Fulbright, William J., 140–143, 157,
    163, 164, 305

G

Garcia Menocal, Mario, 73, 272, 279
Germany
  gymnasium, 71
  influence on American
    education, 71
Golden Age, 6, 124, 322–324
Goodman, Allan E., 190, 223,
    228, 295
Grand tour, 50–51
Greek/Greece
  academies, 18
  foreign students, 18
Guilds, 38, 40–45
Gurukula system, 13, 14

H

Hamilton, Thomas, 70
Hanjour, Hani, 202, 203
Harvard University, 160, 249, 253,
    254, 274–275, 286–288
Hausknecht, Emil, 71
Hong Kong, vi, 77, 123, 182–183,
    229, 231, 289–291
Hu Shi, 10, 127, 128

I

Illegal Immigration Reform and
    Immigrant Responsibility Act
    (IIRIRA), 191–193, 204
Immigration policies, 69, 93–95, 105,
    204, 320, 321

INDEX

India
  early universities, 15, 16
  enrollments in U.S., 215
  Gurukula system, 13
Institute of International Education (IIE), 115, 120–122, 135, 141, 147–149, 152, 159, 164, 209, 210, 229, 295, 314, 318, 319
International Houses, 103, 118–120
Iran
  enrollments, 162, 173, 245
  Hostage Crisis, 171
  universities, 173
Iraq, vi, 2, 3, 151, 173, 176, 256–259, 262, 273
Islam/Islamic, vi, 4–7, 16, 35, 178, 191, 202, 203, 255, 264, 265

J

Japan
  early universities, 71
  enrollments in U.S., 95
  first students in America, 95–97
Jefferson, Thomas, 61, 63, 72, 173, 285

K

Karaouine, University of, 35
Kennedy-Lugar YES program, 261

L

Land-grant colleges, 64, 209
Li Hongzhang, 78, 88, 89
Literacy, 5, 10, 11, 105
Literati, 9, 10

M

Mao Zedong, 153, 179, 220
McCarran Act, 156–159

McCarthy Era, 157
Medieval universities, 9, 15, 36, 38, 41, 43, 45, 48–50, 219
Mesoamerica, 21–26
Mesopotamia, vi, 2, 3
Michigan, University of, 97, 108, 109, 111, 137, 160, 177, 221, 232, 249, 279–280
Middle East studies, 177–178
Miranda, Francisco de, 72, 272
Mohammed, Khalid Sheikh, 201, 202
Morrill Land Act of 1862, 64
Muhammad, the Prophet, 4, 5
Museum at Alexandria, 20, 21

N

NAFSA, *see* National Association of Foreign Student Advisers
National Association of Foreign Student Advisers (NAFSA), 146, 149–150, 153, 175, 176, 195, 205, 209, 210, 296
Nations, *see* Guilds
Neesima, Joseph Hardy, 95, 96
Nixon, Richard, 148, 163, 180

O

Optional Practical Training (OPT), 20, 188, 295, 299–302, 316
Organization of the Petroleum Exporting Countries (OPEC), 171–173
Ottoman Empire, 5, 29
Oxford University, 71, 160

P

Pensionados, 106–108
Phoenicia, 2
Protestant Reformation, 30

Q
Qing dynasty, 76, 87, 90, 125, 130

R
Al Rashid, Harun, 6, 16
Rockefeller, John D., Jr., 97, 103, 118–122, 129
Roman Empire, 19, 20, 28, 29, 36
Roosevelt, Theodore, 90, 103, 120, 125
Root, Elihu, 120
Russell, Bertrand, 8, 129

S
Sadler, Michael E., 71
Saudi Arabia
  education, 144, 178, 245, 246, 257, 258, 265
  enrollments, 144, 171, 245, 251, 257
  exchange programs, vii
  King Abdullah Scholarships, 258
Seelye, Julius H., 95, 96
Silliman, Benjamin, 59, 60
Smith-Mundt Act, 142
Student and Exchange Visitor Information System (SEVIS), 20, 194, 204–209
Studium generale, 39, 40

T
Taiwan, 153, 180, 182, 183, 229, 236, 279, 290, 315
Teachers College, Columbia University, 122, 149, 225, 306
Thomasites, 106
Trump, Donald, 239, 297, 303, 304, 321
Tsinghua University, 125, 129, 218, 221, 223, 234

U
UNESCO, *see* United Nations Educational, Scientific and Cultural Organization
United Nations Educational, Scientific and Cultural Organization (UNESCO), 139–140, 148, 177, 196, 226, 245
University rankings, 287

V
Vedas, 14, 15

W
Wang, Y.T., 130

X
Xu Jiyu, 80

Y
Yale Report, 61, 62, 75
Yale University, 60, 74, 231, 275–276, 301
Young Men's Christian Association (YMCA), 110, 113, 114, 118, 126
Young Women's Christian Association (YWCA), 103, 110, 114
Yung Wing, 73–76, 78, 82, 83, 85, 87, 130, 276

Z
Zeng Guofan, 78